D1748570

NILE GREEN & NUSHIN ARBABZADAH
(*Editors*)

Afghanistan in Ink

Literature between Diaspora and Nation

HURST & COMPANY, LONDON

First published in the United Kingdom in 2013 by
C. Hurst & Co. (Publishers) Ltd.,
41 Great Russell Street, London, WC1B 3PL
© Nile Green and Nushin Arbabzadah, 2013
All rights reserved.
Printed in India by Imprint Digital

The right of Nile Green and Nushin Arbabzadah to be identified as the editors of this publication is asserted by them in accordance with the Copyright, Designs and Patents Act, 1988.

A Cataloguing-in-Publication data record for this book is available from the British Library.

ISBN: 978-1-84904-204-8

This book is printed using paper from registered sustainable and managed sources.

www.hurstpublishers.com

Dedicated to the Memory of
Mohammed Nasser Arbabzadah

CONTENTS

List of Illustrations ix
Note on the Authors xi
Preface and Acknowledgements xv

1. Introduction: Afghan Literature between Diaspora and Nation
   Nile Green 1
2. Modernizing, Nationalizing, Internationalizing: How Mahmud Tarzi's Hybrid Identity Transformed Afghan Literature
   Nushin Arbabzadah 31
3. The Afghan Afterlife of Phileas Fogg: Space and Time in the Literature of Afghan Travel
   Nile Green 67
4. Demarcating Pashto: Cross-border Pashto Literature and the Afghan State, 1880–1930
   Thomas Wide 91
5. Ambiguities of Orality and Literacy, Territory and Border Crossings: Public Activism and Pashto Literature in Afghanistan, 1930–2010
   James Caron 113
6. The Poetry and Prose of Pazhwak: A Critical Look at Traditional Afghanistan
   Chaled Malekyar 141
7. Mastering the Ego Monster: *Azhdaha-ye Khodi* as an Allegory of History
   Wali Ahmadi 163
8. Lyric Realism: Poetic Reflections of Refugee Life in Iran
   Zuzanna Olszewska 185
9. Afghanistan and the Persian Epic *Shahnama*: Historical Agency and the Epic Imagination in Afghan and Afghan-American Literature
   Shafiq Shamel 209

CONTENTS

10. Gnomics: Proverbs, Aphorisms, Metaphors, Key Words and Epithets in Afghan Discourses of War and Instability
   Margaret A. Mills   229

Notes   253
Index   289

LIST OF ILLUSTRATIONS

Fig. 1.	Publishing the *Jihad*: Mujahidin Printing Press	7
Fig. 2.	Literary Officialdom: Kabul Literary Society (Anjuman-e Adabi), 1933	14
Fig. 3.	The Literary State: Afghan Boy Reads a School Textbook	23
Fig. 4.	Urdu in Afghanistan: Muhammad Iqbal on Sale in Kabul	26
Fig. 5.	Female Participants: Princess Khariyya Reads Egyptian Newspaper in Kabul	34
Fig. 6.	Afghan News, International Style: Mahmud Tarzi discusses his Newspaper	44
Fig. 7.	The Founding Father's Father: Ghulam Muhammad Tarzi	60
Fig. 8.	*Da Hind Safar*: A Pashto Travelogue to India	75
Fig. 9.	The Aeronautical Afghan: King Amanullah in Berlin, 1928	87
Fig. 10.	Without Proper Type: Early Pashto Printing in *Siraj al-Akhbar*	100
Fig. 11.	Journalist and Diplomat, Poet and Minister: 'Abd al-Hadi Dawi	101
Fig. 12.	*Pata Khazana*: Pashto Poetry as Antiquity and Nationalism	125
Fig. 13.	The Poet as Diplomat: Pazhwak at the United Nations	144
Fig. 14.	Official Outlets: Baihaqi Government Bookshop, Kabul	152
Fig. 15.	The Philosopher-Poet in Pakistan: Majruh in Peshawar, 1987	166
Fig. 16.	Literary Exiles: Zahra Hosseinzadeh and Hossein Heidar-beigi Hold Meeting at Dorr-e Dari Office, Mashhad	189
Fig. 17.	A Slow Day at the Dorr-e Dari Office, with Poet Ali Jafari	195
Fig. 18.	Amanollah Mirzai Walks through Back Alleys of Mashhad towards Dorr-e Dari Office	202

LIST OF ILLUSTRATIONS

Fig. 19. The Circulation of Texts: Booksellers in Kabul, 2011   218
Fig. 20. Literary Beginnings & Ends? Muhammad Ghulami's *Jang-nama* ("Book of War")   243

NOTE ON THE AUTHORS

Wali Ahmadi was born in Kabul and received his PhD in Comparative Literature from UCLA. He is currently Associate Professor of Persian Literature at UC Berkeley. He is the author of *Modern Persian Literature in Afghanistan: Anomalous Visions of History and Form* (Routledge, 2008) and the editor of *Converging Zones: Persian Literary Tradition and the Writing of History* (2011). He is the founding editor of *Naqd va Arman: An Afghan Journal of the Humanities and Social Sciences* (1995–2003).

Nushin Arbabzadah was raised in Afghanistan. She holds graduate degrees in Germanic and Romance Literatures from Hamburg University and in Middle Eastern History from Cambridge University. She worked for The British Council and the BBC as an editor before becoming a Research Scholar at the UCLA Center for the Study of Women. She has edited *No Ordinary Life: Being Young in the Worlds of Islam* (2004) and *From Outside In: Refugees in British Society* (2007); co-edited Sadiq Hidayat's short-story collection, *Three Drops of Blood* (2009); and translated from the Persian Houshang Assadie's memoir, *Letters to my Torturer* (2010). Her most recent book, *The Afghan Rumor Bazaar: Secret Subcultures, Hidden Worlds and the Everyday Life of the Absurd* (Hurst, 2012), is on contemporary Afghan society and politics.

James Caron is a lecturer in Islamicate South Asia at SOAS, University of London. He received his PhD from the University of Pennsylvania in 2009. He has held academic appointments at Rutgers University-Newark and the University of Pennsylvania. He teaches social and cultural history of Afghanistan, Pakistan, and Islamicate South Asia; and South Asian, Central

NOTE ON THE AUTHORS

Asian, and Indian Ocean history more broadly. His primary research is centred on eastern Afghanistan and Punjab from the 1500s to the present.

Nile Green is Professor of South Asian History at UCLA and founding chair of the UCLA Program on Central Asia. His research focuses on the history and literature of the Muslim communities of India, Pakistan, Afghanistan, Iran and the Indian Ocean. His books include *Indian Sufism since the Seventeenth Century* (Routledge, 2006); *Religion, Language and Power* (edited with Mary Searle-Chatterjee, Routledge, 2008); *Islam and the Army in Colonial India* (Cambridge University Press, 2009); *Bombay Islam: The Religious Economy of the West Indian Ocean* (Cambridge University Press, 2011, winner of the Albert Hourani Book Award); *Sufism: A Global History* (Wiley-Blackwell, 2012); and *Making Space: Sufis and Settlers in Early Modern India* (Oxford University Press, 2012).

Chaled Malekyar is an Afghan literary historian based in Germany. He was born in Kabul to an Afghan father and a German mother. After migrating to Germany in December 1978, he studied for his Abitur at a German school before university studies in Orientalism, Politics and History at the University of Cologne, the University of Chicago and Kuwait University. He holds a PhD in Orientalism from the University of Cologne where he is Associate Lecturer, with his main teaching topics comprising Afghanistan, Arabic and Persian handwriting. His publications include the book, *Das Bild Afghanistans im 20. Jahrhundert: Das Werk Des Schriftstellers und Diplomaten Ostad Abdol Rahman Pazwak (1919–95)* (Berlin, 2008).

Margaret A. Mills has taught Folklore and Central Asian/Persian Studies at the University of Pennsylvania and currently at Ohio State University, where she is a Professor in the Department of Near Eastern Languages and Cultures. Her book, *Rhetorics and Politics in Afghan Traditional Storytelling*, won the 1993 Chicago Folklore Prize for best academic work in folklore. Her previous dissertation research in Afghanistan in the 1970s initiated an extensive collection of Afghan (Dari-Persian) oral narrative recordings now housed at the US Library of Congress. She continues to conduct field research on oral history and oral narrative performance in Afghanistan and Tajikistan.

Zuzanna Olszewska is a Junior Research Fellow in Oriental Studies at St. John's College, Oxford University. She studied at Harvard College and Oxford University, where she completed her doctorate in Social Anthropol-

NOTE ON THE AUTHORS

ogy on "Poetry and its Social Contexts among Afghan Refugees in Iran". She is the author of numerous articles on Afghan refugees in Iran and translations of Dari-Persian poetry into English.

Shafiq Shamel is Assistant Professor of German, Persian-Dari, and Persian-Farsi at the Defense Language Institute Foreign Language Center, Monterey, California. After completing his doctoral studies in German Studies at Stanford, Shamel taught as a lecturer in the departments of Comparative Literature and German Studies at Stanford University. His publications on Afghanistan and the Middle East include "Epic Poetry and *The Kite Runner*: Paradigms of Cultural Identity in Afghan Society," *Telos* 138 (2007) and "Forgotten Futures: History, Memoir, Afghanistan", *The Middle East Institute Publication Viewpoints* 6 (2009).

Thomas Wide holds a Faculty Studentship at the Oriental Institute, Oxford University, where he is completing a DPhil on Afghan intellectual history. He has travelled and researched widely in Afghanistan.

PREFACE AND ACKNOWLEDGEMENTS

Afghanistan in Ink presents the first multi-authored survey of the literature written by Afghans, both at home and abroad, in the course of the twentieth century. Aimed at historians, anthropologists and political scientists as much as scholars of literature, the purpose of the book is to use literary texts as source materials on both the workings and the self-reflections of Afghan society. This is important because in spite of the huge growth of commentary on Afghanistan since the fall of the Taliban, studies continue to rely on an astonishingly small number of source materials, of which an even smaller proportion were written by and for Afghans themselves. If it is an unusual agenda for a literary study, the aim here is therefore to use texts in an empirical manner as intellectual, artistic and political responses to concrete life conditions. The implication here of positioning Afghans as informants on and critics of their own society leads us to the second aim of *Afghanistan in Ink* of recognizing the agency of Afghans themselves in the multiple traumatic transformations of their modern history. For if through British imperialism or Cold War strategism, the world certainly did creep upon (and create) Afghanistan's borders in modern times, then through their own importing of multiple conflicting ideologies from different corners of the world Afghans themselves brought the world to their doors. This internationalism in turn brings us to the third aim of *Afghanistan in Ink*, which is to excavate an alternative history of modern Afghanistan in which the nation's fragility is seen to be directly linked to the sheer range of its cross-border connectivity. Overturning characterizations of a country remote from world events, the following chapters show how in terms of literature—and so of ideology and politics—Afghanistan has since the first years of the

PREFACE AND ACKNOWLEDGEMENTS

twentieth century been closely connected to the multiple sites of the ever-expanding networks of diasporic Afghans. Like the peoples of Afghanistan, both Afghan literature and the Afghan nation state have been formed through exchange with transnational flows of ideas, persons and resources.[1]

The following pages draw on literary texts in Dari-Persian and Pashto as an artistic database of transnational interactions. If all this is to suggest a rather blunt and instrumentalist approach to literature, then it should be added that none of the contributors are blind to the aesthetic dimensions of their chosen texts. We hope that this sensitivity to source materials shines through their analyses. But as a volume of studies written by historians and anthropologists as well as literary scholars, in its attention to the transnational flows and internal faultlines that have shaped Afghan society, culture and politics, *Afghanistan in Ink* unapologetically promotes contextual analysis. This is literature served for social scientists.

In spite of the comprehensive agenda which we initially set ourselves, it has not been possible to portray the full linguistic range of Afghans' literary output. While due attention has been paid to both of the dominant written languages of Pashto and Dari-Persian (including many instances of Persian texts written by Pashtuns), it has not been possible to include studies of the much smaller number of modern texts written by Afghans in such minority languages as Hazaragi, Uzbek and Pashai. In this we have been at the mercy of existing expertise, which is scarce enough on Afghan Pashto and Dari-Persian, let alone on writings in the minority languages. As editors, we made several attempts to commission chapters on these languages but were ultimately unsuccessful. Rather than commission unanalytical studies by amateur commentators, we chose instead to focus on the professional expertise on Pashto and Dari-Persian, while also bringing into focus Afghans' increasing adoption of such non-Afghan languages as English and French. If *Afghanistan in Ink* is not in this sense comprehensive, its weight of attention to Dari-Persian and Pashto works does fairly reflect the literary balance of power in which, through their interactions with the state, the writers of these languages have dominated the political no less than artistic spheres of Afghan life. From the early 1900s onwards, the role of the command over such western languages as French and English can also be fitted into this same pattern, as seen in the links between foreign language expertise, literary production and government service in the following chapters.

Afghanistan in Ink had its origins in the conference "Afghanistan in Ink: Literatures of Nation, War, and Exile" organized by Nushin Arbabzadah

PREFACE AND ACKNOWLEDGEMENTS

and held at UCLA in January 2010. For both the funding and organizational assistance of the original 'Afghanistan in Ink' conference we are extremely grateful to the G.E. von Grunebaum Center for Near Eastern Studies at UCLA. We would like to extend our especial gratitude to the Director of the Center, Susan Slyomovics, for generous support, to Megan Rancier and Amy Bruinooge for organizational assistance and to Kevin Matthews for publicity. The conference was in turn linked to the series of seminars and conferences on Afghanistan organized by the UCLA Program on Central Asia, chaired by Nile Green. In literary terms, the highlights of this seminar series were talks by the Afghan-American writer, Mir Tamim Ansary, and the Afghan-French writer, Atiq Rahimi. We are deeply grateful for both writers for enriching our appreciation of the global reach of Afghan intellectuals. On behalf of the UCLA Program on Central Asia, we would like to thank the UCLA Asia Institute, in particular Elizabeth Leicester, Nick Menzies, Bin Wong, as well as Program committee members Nancy Levine and Sanjay Subrahmanyam for support of other Program events that provided the intellectual context for the "Afghanistan in Ink" conference. Thanks to Aamir Mufti for acting as panel discussant.

For help in tracking down texts we are grateful to: the Young Research Library at UCLA; the Afghanistan National Archives (Archif-e Milli) in Kabul; the Afghanistan Digital Library at New York University; the British Library; the Forschungsstelle zur historischen Reisekultur in Eutin; and the various booksellers we encountered in Afghanistan who keep the country's literary culture alive. Nile Green would also like to thank the American Institute for Afghanistan Studies for the award of the John F. Richards Fellowship which allowed research in Kabul and Germany. For suggestions and advice on a variety of practical and academic matters, we are grateful to: Mir Tamim Ansary, Farhad Azad, Ingeborg Baldauf, Thomas Barfield, Saddik Barmak, Robert Crews, David B. Edwards, Karl-Heinz Golzio, Shah Mahmoud Hanifi, David Hirsch, Nikki Keddie, Nadia Maiwandi, Magnus Marsden, Robert D. McChesney, Reza Mohammadi, Alessandro Monsutti, Sakhi Muneer, Fariba Nawa, Stefano Pellò, Homira Qaderi, Atiq Rahimi, Mir Hekmatullah Sadat, May Schinasi and Khalid Ziai. Final thanks to Michael Dwyer at Hurst and Co. for manifold encouragements.

We are grateful to the following persons and organizations for permission to print the following illustrations: the Afghanistan Digital Library for figure 11; David B. Edwards and the Khalilullah Enayat Seraj Collection, Williams Afghan Media Project, courtesy of the Afghan Media Resource

PREFACE AND ACKNOWLEDGEMENTS

Center, for figures 1, 3, 5, 6, 10; Nahid Majrooh for figure 15; Zuzanna Olszewska for figures 16, 17, 18; Farhad Pazhwak for figure 13; Shaista Wahab and the Arthur Paul Afghanistan Collection at the University of Nebraska, Omaha Library for figure 2; and Khalid Ziai for figure 7. Figures 4, 8, 9, 12, 14, 19, 20 draw on photographs taken by the editors and books in the editors' private collection.

Note that we have used the spelling 'Paxto' to transliterate the letter *shin/khin* when referring to titles of books and organizations and in quotations from literary works, while maintaining the standard English usage of 'Pashto' for all other sentences.

Nile Green & Nushin Arbabzadah   Los Angeles, October 2012

1

INTRODUCTION

AFGHAN LITERATURE BETWEEN DIASPORA AND NATION

Nile Green

The Dilemma of an "Afghan" Literature

In 2010, the Afghan Ministry of Education published a series of new textbooks for students taking compulsory classes in Dari-Persian literature in the new high schools being funded through international aid.[1] In the message from the education minister included at the beginning of each copy, the aim of the textbooks was outlined as being to educate a new generation in the values of individualism, Islam and national unity "for the purpose of achieving the supreme goals of the nation".[2] Like the curriculum and schools to which they were related, the textbooks formed part of a larger project of national reconstruction: their express aim was to bring literature to the service of nation-building. In itself, there was little uniquely Afghan about such an agenda, for language and literature have helped lay the basis for nationalisms and nation-building in numerous other contexts.[3] What was specific to Afghanistan was the extraordinary difficulty of framing a literature that was clearly "national" in its remit, a dilemma seen repeatedly in the school books' contents. For while a small number of self-consciously "Afghan" writers, such as the nationalist Dari-Persian poet Khalilullah Khalili (1907–87), did appear in the textbooks, far more common were "classical" poets who belonged to a pre-national Persian literary culture that stretched from Istanbul to Delhi. This literary transnationalism was not limited in the textbooks to the likes of North Indian poets such as Amir Khusrow (d.1325) and Bedil (d.1720), and rubbing shoulders with these premodern Muslim poets were seventeenth century French fables by Jean de la Fontaine, an account of industrial progress from Victorian Britain and a translated excerpt from the United Nations Declaration of Human Rights. Nor was such transnationalism limited to the textbooks' contents. It was writ through their very existence by the funding of their publication by international aid donors and the location of their printing in distant Indonesia.

In drawing on so wide a flow of literary traffic in their attempt to forge a new citizenry that was both Muslim and modern, loyal to both the nation state and the international community of nations, the textbooks echoed a dilemma that reverberated to the foundation of the Afghan nation in the late nineteenth century.[4] That dilemma was one of containing and channelling towards national ends a literary culture that has at every step outreached the spatial and ideological confines of the Afghan nation state. Phrased differently, it was a dilemma of the slippage between a geographically immobile state and the mobile (and often diasporic) writers who at different moments have alternatively aided or undermined the state-building efforts of Afghan governments over the past century.[5] For if Afghanistan is often considered to be a country until recently cut off from the wider world—a country whose problems were born from too little exposure to "modern" ideas developed in other regions of the globe—then the essays in *Afghanistan in Ink* reveal how since the early twentieth century, literary travellers, exiles and diasporas have used their writings to import to Afghanistan a bewildering and ultimately competing array of ideologies sourced from every corner of the planet. Whether formed by liberal modernism or civic patriotism, by communist or Islamist internationalism, the ideologically varied literatures that Afghans have produced in the twentieth century have been integral to the attempts, erstwhile successes and outright failures to build a nation state in Afghanistan, whether envisioned as a liberal or absolute monarchy, a socialist republic, an emirate or (that most transnational of all political hybrids) an Islamic republic.

Afghanistan in Ink aims to unravel the complex and obscure history of these many literary movements, with "movements" conceived here in both the figurative sense of associations of writers and the more literal sense of imported literary traffic.[6] The story of the many literary movements traced in this book therefore points to the dilemma of a fragile emergent state challenged by the smuggling of ideologies through its borders in the saddlebags of literature. It also points to the obverse dilemma of writers who, when not rewarded for loyal service to the government of the day, have been killed, imprisoned or exiled for their disloyalty. Whether through textbooks designed to educate an expanding population or exile novels on the human impact of war, in the modern era Afghan literature has never been far from the project of nation-building, albeit viewed in different texts as an ascendant or failed project.[7] Yet through the exile of Afghan writers, the importing of non-Afghan genres or the production of Afghan books beyond the borders of the nation, this close and frequently estranged relationship between literature and nation has often been one of physical distance. What emerges from this volume's focus on literature is an altogether less familiar Afghanistan whose tragedies have resulted less from the medieval parochialism of its citizenry than from the relentless internationalism of their search for a state and society that could be presented as both modern and loyal to the fractious cultural traditions that have been marshalled to create a collective Afghan identity.

A Nation Undefinitively Redefined

For many Afghans, the founder of Afghanistan was Ahmad Shah Durrani (1722–73) who, from the fragmenting dominions of the last great Central Asian conqueror Nadir Shah Afshar (1688–1747), built a short-lived Afghan empire centred on Qandahar that stretched deep into what is now Pakistan. That Ahmad Shah considered it proper that regions such as Punjab should be governed from Qandahar by Afghans is less surprising than it may appear. For Ahmad Shah himself appears to have been born in Multan in the Punjabi heartlands of modern Pakistan, where he was raised as part of a centuries-old diaspora of Afghans who migrated to the subcontinent in search of trade and employment.[8] Far from being a native son-of-the-soil, the symbolic founder of the nation regarded by the nationalists of the twentieth century as the *Baba-ye Afghanistan* or "Father of Afghanistan" emerged from a pre-national era of widely-dispersed Afghan diaspora communities. As Ahmad Shah's short-lived empire began to collapse, in 1776 his successor, Timur Shah (himself born in Mashhad in what is now Iran), relocated the capital from Qandahar to Kabul, where his mausoleum still stands today. What was ruled from this first "Afghan" capital was not a nation state in the modern sense and in this eighteenth-century period "Afghan" still denoted members of the Pashtun (or Pakhtun or Pathan) tribes to whom Ahmad Shah and his twentieth-century successors all belonged.

In the course of the nineteenth century, the actual territorial unit governed by these Pashtun Afghan dynasts was reshaped and reduced several times as British rule crept over the adjoining territories to the south and east, Russia expanded across the steppes to the north and Iran seized territories to the west.[9] The geographic space which now constitutes Afghanistan emerged as a result of a series of alliances and wars with its surrounding powers, its boundaries formalized through the commissions that culminated in the 1893 drawing of the Durand Line which marked the eastern border of Afghanistan.[10] The name "Afghanistan" itself does not seem to have been regularly used among the inhabitants of the territories ruled from Kabul to designate the entire territorial unit until as late as the 1860s and 70s, when it appeared in the pioneering newspaper *Shams al-Nahar* and historical works such as the *Tarikh-e Sultani*.[11] While acquiring the name of "Afghanistan" in place of earlier designations, such as "Khurasan", the nation state that emerged in this period was far more heterogeneous than was implied by the meaning of its new name: "land of the Afghans". Since the term *Afghan* was synonymous with *Pashtun* well into the twentieth century and for many inhabitants of the territory has kept this meaning until the present day, the premise of a "land of the Afghans" (that is, an 'Afghanistan') presented a host of problems.[12] While the ruling class were almost exclusively members of prominent Pashtun lineages, the territory over which they ruled was inhabited by a variety of ethnic groups, many with their own distinct languages and literary traditions. Moreover, large populations of "Afghan" Pashtuns lived on the other side of the Durand Line in British India (and, from 1947, in Pakistan). While, in geographic terms, the nation state of Afghanistan had taken clear shape by the reign of 'Abd al-Rahman Khan (r. 1880–1901), at the turn of the twentieth century it remained unclear in cultural and political terms which people were referred to by "Afghan" and which of them the state should serve.

A note of caution is in order at this point, for it would be simplistic to overstate the role of ethnicity in the shaping of the Afghan nation; 'Abd al-Rahman Khan won his moniker of "Iron Amir" through his willingness to execute Pashtun enemies as much as to suppress the non-Pashtun peoples of Hazarajat and Kafiristan.[13] In presenting himself through the Islamic political model of an *amir* ("commander") rather than as a king or sultan, 'Abd al-Rahman Khan made religion a central feature of the state and its rulers' legitimacy.[14] Created and curtailed as a buffer between two empires, and after two wars with the armies of British India, increasing ideological importance was lent to the notion that the purpose of the Afghan state was the defence of the land, its people and their religion from outside imperial aggression. Already apparent in the reign of 'Abd al-Rahman Khan, these themes recurred during the reigns of Habibullah Khan (r. 1901–19) and Amanullah Khan (r. 1919–29), when an agenda of building a modern and independent nation gathered steam through state-building initiatives that ranged from the founding of new schools to establishing the transnational infrastructure of roads, overseas embassies and newspapers.[15]

Yet while the agenda of Habibullah and particularly Amanullah was to secure the independence of Afghanistan as a viable and governable polity, both rulers drew many of their modernizing ideas from their own and their advisors' travels to India and Europe. Before entering the inner circles of the state in 1905, the key nation-building Afghan ideologue of the early twentieth century, Mahmud Tarzi (1865–1933), spent twenty-three years as an exile in the Ottoman Empire.[16] On being overthrown in 1929, King Amanullah was himself exiled to Italy, from where he watched as Nadir Khan, the former general of his armies, seized the reins of power and named himself king. Born and raised in India as the son of exiled notables and more at ease in Urdu than in the Pashto spoken by his kinsmen, Nadir Khan (or Nadir Shah as he modelled himself after his Iranian contemporary, Reza Shah) likewise reflected the transnational character of nation-building in Afghanistan. The following decades saw the promotion of a more familiarly nationalistic model of identity in the 1940s and 1950s, with the term "Afghan" being used in new ways to designate all citizens of the state regardless of ethnicity. During the reigns of Nadir Shah and his family successors between 1929 and 1978, the nation-building venture achieved its greatest successes. At the ideological level this was seen through the creation of cultural and political institutions aimed at promoting national consciousness. At the practical level it was seen through the successful channelling of the outside resources of the Soviet Union and United States for infrastructural and military development.[17] Once again, transnational resources were crucial to the building of the nation.

If the mid-century high point of Afghan nationalism and political stability was thus reached through a balancing of domestic and transnational factors, then the undoing of that balance in the series of wars unleashed by the Soviet invasion of 1979 was no less transnational in character. The Afghan socialist governments that the Soviets protected during their decade-long occupation were made up of members of the two wings, Khalq ("The Masses") and Parcham ("The Flag"), of the socialist People's Democratic Party of Afghanistan (PDPA). Many of their members had previously studied in the Soviet Union and, like the modernizing Mahmud Tarzi earlier in the century, imported new (in this case Marxist-Leninist) ideologies of nationhood. In the Democratic Republic of Afghanistan that the communists established, the purpose of the state was now seen as being to serve its poorest citizens. If attachments to ethnicity or even religion stood in the way of such "progress" (*taraqqi*), then it was the duty of the state to encourage or even enforce the renouncing of traditional values. As we will see below literature again formed one of the crucial cultural weapons in the struggle for and against communism in Afghanistan, just as it had in the nation-building projects earlier in the century.

Inheriting the binary logic of the Cold War, it is easy to see the forces behind the uprisings against the Afghan socialist government and its Soviet supporters as a mirror image of the transnationalism of the PDPA and the Soviet Union. Yet while the United States became a major funder of the anti-Soviet *jihad*, the Islamist transnationalism of the various *mujahidin* groups led in many different directions, whether to Pakistan, Iran, Saudi Arabia, Egypt, or even to Muslims in Europe. Like their Afghan communist contemporaries in the army, who had studied in the Soviet Union, future jihadists, such as Sibghatullah Mujaddidi, were undertaking Islamic studies in such countries as Egypt as early as the 1960s. There they became exposed to the new political Islam of the Muslim Brotherhood and of radicals like Sayyid Qutb (1906–66), whose own anti-western ideology had crystallized after a two year study period in the United States.[18] Whether conceiving the nation as the agent of progress or as the protector of religion, the ideologies at war in Afghanistan during the 1980s and 90s were of global as much as local provenance. The members of the Taliban movement which seized power in 1996 were more likely to have studied in the makeshift refugee madrasas of Pakistan than the more hallowed institutions of New York's Columbia University and Cairo's al-Azhar seminary, which had respectively educated the communist president, Hafizullah Amin, and the *jihad* leader, Burhan al-Din Rabbani. But in drawing on theologies that had gradually moved northwards from the great Indian madrasa at Deoband, the Taliban's

INTRODUCTION

Fig. 1: Publishing the *Jihad*: *Mujahidin* Printing Press.

vision of Afghanistan as an Islamic emirate was a similar fusion of local realities with transnational ideologies.

To emphasize such transnational patterns is not to downplay the role and agency of Afghans in the many endeavours of state-making that characterized their twentieth century. The revolutionary internationalists of the Kremlin or al-Qaida were certainly players and sometimes manipulators in these developments. But Afghans were themselves the most active importers and adaptors of the variously nationalist, communist or Islamist ideologies employed to articulate a form of statehood capable of dealing with the geographical constraints and the ethnic multiplicity that was their legacy from the shrunken empire of Ahmad Shah Abdali. What becomes clear from this emphasis on the transnational is that the dilemma of Afghanistan has not so much been one of the parochial intransigence of a region frozen in its traditionalism as one of a region exposed to so escalating a flow of ideologies across its borders as to weaken every attempt at state formation. The recent "import" of liberal democracy is only the most recent stage in this process. The dilemma of modern Afghanistan has been that of balancing a young and weak state with a culturally diverse and progressively globalizing population. By the beginning of the twenty-first century, this long trajectory of transnationalism had reached new levels as the sheer number of refugees from the *jihad* and Taliban rendered Afghanistan the country with the highest proportion of its population living outside its borders in the world. If, in the early 1900s, the flow of ideas into Afghanistan was carried by exiles in British India, the Ottoman Empire, and Tsarist Central Asia, the exiles who returned after 2001 were as likely to have lived in Scandinavia as Saudi Arabia. In an attempt to balance so many political visions, the new constitution of 2004 declared Afghanistan an "Islamic Republic", governed by a democratically-elected president but maintained by an alliance of unprecedented international scope.

The Literature of Nationalism and Transnationalism

How, then, was literature—even language—configured in these multiple and fraught projects of defining and giving cultural meaning to a nation state that, in substantial part, had come into existence through external pressures beyond borders drawn by foreign imperialists? In the previous section we saw the state's eye perspective on the dilemma of Afghan transnationalism. But there were also literary dimensions to the unstable chemistry of a static weak state and a mobile diverse population. The tensions between a literature of statehood and a literature of diaspora were already present in the reign of 'Abd al-Rahman Khan, whose state-making legacy laid the foundations for the cultural nationalist ventures of the twentieth century. 'Abd al-Rahman Khan's own autobiography, *Pandnama-ye Dunya va Din* ("Book of Worldly and Religious Guidance"), was itself a transnational text seeking a national agenda. Its second volume was written in English by his Indian secretary, Sultan Muhammad, before being published in London in 1900, translated into Persian by an Afghan resident of the Iranian city of Mashhad, and then published in Persian under the new title of *Taj al-Tavarikh* ("The Crown of Histories") in Mashhad and Bombay rather than Kabul.[19]

As we will see in the following chapters, such transnational literary circuits were a common feature of many subsequent Afghan writings. While 'Abd al-Rahman Khan had been happy to rely on Persian for his autobiographical guidance to his subjects, in the decades after his death in 1901 Afghanistan's modernizers saw problems with Persian and all other linguistic options in their attempt to reach a "national" audience. Regional or ethnic languages such as Pashai and Uzbek were known to too few members of the general population, to almost none of the ruling classes and were in any case too linguistically different to the languages spoken by other Afghans to be effectively taught as national lingua franca.[20] In effect, this left early twentieth-century Afghan nation-builders with either Persian or Pashto as the sole options for the creation of a national language and its accompanying literature, even if by the 1930s intellectuals such as Ya'qub Hasan Khan were drawing on European linguistic scholarship to write nationalistic accounts of Bactrian, Soghdian, Herati, Persian, Pashto, Ghalcha "and other groups of Afghan languages" (*digar zaban-ha-ye dasta-ye Afghani*).[21] Yet the pragmatic realities of literacy were much more limited. While the ruling dynasty and the upper echelons of the army and bureaucracy were ethnic Pashtuns, many of them only wrote (and in some cases only spoke) Persian and not Pashto. Even Habibullah Khan (r. 1901–19), the first modernizing ruler of the early twentieth century, knew Persian, Urdu and even Uzbek, but apparently had only a poor grasp of his ancestral Pashto.[22]

For unlike Pashto, Persian had for centuries functioned throughout Central and South Asia as a supra-ethnic language of government and high culture. By the 1900s, the Persian republic of letters that had once stretched from the Bosphorus to the Bay of Bengal had been undermined by the rise of vernaculars such as Urdu and Turkish and colonial languages such as Russian and English.[23] Uzbek, meanwhile, was from the 1920s being better supported by the Soviets than by the Afghans and its literary expression within Afghanistan would remain almost exclusively oral and folkloric.[24] But Persian maintained its older role in Afghanistan as the cosmopolitan lingua franca of the court, the bureaucracy and the educated among any ethnic group. While significant literary works in Pashto had begun to emerge as early as the mid-sixteenth century, poets had been producing masterpieces in Persian more than five hundred years earlier. Even for ethnically Pashtun nation-builders such as Mahmud Tarzi or Amanullah Khan, as late as the 1920s it remained clear that Pashto lacked the prestige no less than the social reach of Persian. Consequently, whether in terms of education in the newly established schools or publishing in the new genres they imported, the *rawshan-fikr* or "enlightened" intellectuals who aligned themselves with the modernizing regimes of the early twentieth century overwhelmingly invested in Persian. It became the dominant language of the Afghan state and the literature that would edify and celebrate its people.

Yet such linguistic pragmatism was not without its contradictions and herein lay the dilemmas of establishing a national language for the emergent nation state of Afghanistan. Ironically for a state-building project, the continued expertise of many Indian Muslims in Persian meant that a significant proportion of the teachers in the new Afghan schools of the period were Indian migrants rather than Afghans. Even though many classical Persian poets spent part of their lives in the territory that later became Afghanistan, including such key figures as Ferdowsi (d.1020), Sana'i (d.1131), Rumi (d.1273) and Jami (d.1492), the problem with Persian was that much of its literary history had not only happened elsewhere in the past but continued to be produced elsewhere in the present. For from the 1920s, the new nationalist government of Iran was increasingly laying claim to Persian as its own national language, celebrating the style of "Iranian" rather than "Indian" Persian poets, elevating the *Shahnama* of Ferdowsi into a narrowly Iranian "national" epic, naming the university founded in 1949 in Mashhad after Ferdowsi and physically laying national claim to the memory of such poets through the construction of new concrete monuments on their tombs.[25] Even in the case of Persian texts that explicitly celebrated the Afghans, such as the series of seventeenth- and eighteenth-century Persian histories of the heroic acts of Pashtun "Afghan" lineages, the problem was that these were written among the early-modern Afghan diaspora in India rather than in Afghanistan itself.[26] As late as the 1940s, Afghan intellectuals seeking to reclaim the literary heritage of Pashto for their own nation were forced to search in the bookshops and libraries of India for their "own" Pashto texts, as seen in an article (itself in Persian) from the magazine of the Afghan Historical Society (Anjuman-e Tarikh-e Afghanistan) that detailed a series of important Pashto poetry manuscripts available only in the library of Islamiyya College in Peshawar.[27] The infrastructure of literary memory was better elsewhere. The infrastructural problems of claiming Persian for the nation were no less acute, for Persian printing and book production remained far more developed in India and Iran than in Afghanistan well into the twentieth century.[28]

The Afghan response to this dilemma of claiming a language and literature already substantially "owned" by others took several decades to formalize. But its strategies—which like all nationalizing agendas had both institutional and imaginative dimensions—are clear enough in outline. First, there was the government's investment in founding Afghanistan's first printing presses, which issued not only the first Afghan newspapers and journals but also the literary works of intellectuals attached to the state. While the first press and newspaper, *Shams al-Nahar* ("Morning Sun"), had been founded in 1873 after the Afghan ruler Shir ʿAli returned from India where such newspapers already flourished, it ceased publication after only four years in 1877. Moreover, aside from the newspaper, only eleven books are known to have been printed in Afghanistan before 1901, most of them addressing religious and administrative issues rather than comprising literary texts.[29] Although ʿAbd al-Rahman Khan re-introduced printing to Afghanistan after the demise of *Shams al-Nahar* in 1877, printing was fraught with the paradoxical pressures of state control on the one hand and reliance on imported technology on the other. Many of the texts published on the new press consisted of ʿAbd al-Rahman Khan's own writings, while the press and its master printer, Munshi ʿAbd al-Razzaq of Delhi, had to be imported from India. In an echo of the dilemma we have seen in the previous sections, the making of a national literature depended again on transnational resources.

The development of Afghan printing, and literature alongside it, made much greater progress during the reign of Habibullah Khan from 1901 to 1919. Largely through the activities of Mahmud Tarzi and his collaborators, the major Persian newspaper, *Siraj al-Akhbar*, was founded in 1911, along with the official governmental Dar al-Saltana Press and the private (if nonetheless royal) ʿInayat Press, which issued the earliest literary translations, travelogues and poetry anthologies to be published in Afghanistan.[30] While newspapers are not often classified as literature, *Siraj al-Akhbar* played an enormously important role in the formation of a modern, national literature for Afghanistan. This was seen through its cultivation of a simplified Persian prose style suitable for the reading public rather than the courtly connoisseur; through its formal *adabiyat* ("literature") section and through its ideological promotion of the Afghan *millat* ("nation") as a literary subject.[31] Presented in Tarzi's many editorials in *Siraj al-Akhbar*, as well as in the numerous poems on technological subjects published in its pages, was what Wali Ahmadi has described as an ideology of "scientism".[32] While this is correct, it is also important to link Tarzi's manifestos of literary and national renewal through technology and science to the agendas of the European Futurists of the same period. In doing so, we are able to latch onto the distinct temporal horizon of Tarzi and his Young Afghans, a horizon that not only connects them to their contemporaries elsewhere on the planet, but also to the future they sought to create in their local setting. In 1909, only two years before Tarzi seized the editorial reins of *Siraj al-Akhbar* to use literature and publicity to create a new technologized future for his country, the celebrated Futurist manifesto of Filippo Tommaso Marinetti (1876–1944) appeared on the front page of the French newspaper, *Le Figaro*.[33] Like Tarzi and his fellow Young Afghans, Marinetti and the other Futurist writers were obsessed with the machinery of travel, a theme that by the 1930s was to resurface in Afghan literary celebrations of Marinetti's streamline motor cars.[34] Connecting technology and literature to national revival, Tarzi and Marinetti were also both committed to aggressively nationalistic politics.

If there is no evidence for direct links between Marinetti's Futurism and Tarzi's future-gazing ideology of "progress" (*taraqqi*), then their parallels are still important pointers to the global contemporaneity of Afghan artistic agendas in the early twentieth century. If Tarzi was not directly linked with Marinetti, then *Siraj al-Akhbar* and other nationalistic Afghan publishing ventures of the 1910s and 1920s had transnational contacts a plenty. Tarzi had himself spent more than twenty years exiled to the Ottoman Empire, where he read Turkish newspapers and imported European books; Kabul's printing machines (and several of their printers) were imported from India, Turkey and, by the 1920s, Germany; and many of the earliest texts printed on them were translations of the French novels of Jules Verne and Xavier de Montépin, albeit taken from the Turkish translations of Ahmad Ihsan Tokgöz.[35] If the literary resources employed were in this way multiply transnational, then between 1910 and 1930 the Afghan state nonetheless made rapid and substantial progress in establishing the venues and infrastructure for a national literature.

The second response to this dilemma of claiming a language and its literature for the nation was the attempt to "nationalize" Persian by calling it "Dari", a decision that closely echoed developments in Iran and Turkey in the 1920s and 30s.[36] In Persian itself, the language is usually known as Farsi (or sometimes Parsi) after the region of Fars, where many of the language's classical poets spent their lives. But, celebrated with new monuments above the tombs of these poets, by the 1920s the region of Fars lay at the imaginative no less than geographical heart of the Iranian nation state. In response, Afghan literary nationalists promoted the idea that Afghans spoke not "Farsi" but "Dari", a reinvented older term referring to the language spoken around the *dar* or "gateway" to the court. Although it would not be fully cemented in the constitution until much later, the notion that Afghans spoke a distinct language called Dari was already being promoted in the 1910s in the writings of Mahmud Tarzi, who described Dari as a distinct language which was a combination of Farsi and Arabic.[37] In the generation or two after Tarzi, the nationalistic investment in Dari gained greater cultural momentum through the writings of other Afghan literary scholars and historians. The proposition that Afghans speak a different language to Iranians is not in itself unreasonable: Afghan Persian is, in practice, more different from Iranian Persian than is often realized and these differences were exacerbated by the distinct literary trajectories pursued by Iranian and Afghan writers in the twentieth century. But the impulses behind the renaming of Afghan Persian as Dari were more nationalistic than linguistic: Afghanistan needed its own language for its own people.

This simple act of renaming was in turn buttressed by the promotion of a national Afghan school of literary criticism and linguistics. Governmental scholars such as the historian, diplomat and founder of the Vatan ("Homeland") party, Mir Ghulam Muhammad Ghubar (1897–1978), began to write histories of "Dari" literature, the forerunners of the school textbook cited at the opening of this chapter. Such works sought to draw a direct (though often far from clear) lineage between the premodern poets of Iran and India and the self-consciously Afghan writers of the twentieth century, in some cases pushing back both "Afghan" literature and the Afghan nation state into distant antiquity.[38] Special attention was given to the emergence of a "national" tradition of Afghan Dari-Persian poets in the period of the nation's "birth" in the mid-eighteenth-century reign of Ahmad Shah Abdali, the *Baba-ye Afghanistan* who, from the 1930s, became the subject of patriotic historical biographies.[39] In partial reaction to the modern Iranian denigration of the metaphysical Persian poetry of the "Indian School" (*sabk-e hindi*) in favour of the simpler "Iranian" style of medieval Shiraz, Afghan literary historians vehemently championed such Indian Persian poets as Bedil (d.1720). From 1947, as the new nation states of India and Pakistan officially "disowned" Persian, with neither state listing it as a national language in their constitutions, Afghan literary scholars increasingly claimed the "Indian school" as part of their own lineage, creating a celebratory school of "Bedil studies" (*Bedil-shinasi*) in the process. Other itinerant poets of the premodern Persian republic of letters were also claimed for the nation. The poet known in the West as "Rumi", in reflection of the Anatolia (in Persian *Rum* or "Rome-Byzantium") in which he spent his adult life, was now instead referred to as "Balkhi" in deference to the northern Afghan city of Balkh in which he was supposedly born.[40]

The third response to this dilemma of claiming Persian and its literature for Afghanistan was for the state and its aligned intelligentsia to create literary and cultural institutions for the study of a past "Afghan" literature and for the production of a new national literature. The new wave of literary criticism described in the previous paragraphs was itself a product of these institutions and the journals they published. In this, the study of language, literature, archaeology and history became closely intertwined.[41] Founded in 1922 as one of the showpieces of the new governmental suburb of Kabul established by Amanullah Khan, the National Museum of Afghanistan gathered the history of the Bactrian Greeks and Gandharan Buddhists into an antique lineage for the nation state just a decade before the Kabul Literary Society (Anjuman-e Adabi-ye Kabul) was established in 1931 by Amanullah's successor, Nadir Shah (r. 1929–33). Yet the very creation of this institution aimed at the nationalizing of Afghan literature was itself a transnational event. Its founder, Nadir Shah, was inspired by the model of the Académie française as observed during his years as ambassador to France. Similarly, an early description of the library of the Kabul Literary Society in 1936 described it as predominantly containing books in English.[42] Yet such transnational literary traffic was still imported in service of the nation. As

هیئت دفتر انجمن ادبی کابل
Le bureau du Cercle Littéraire de Kaboul

Fig: 2. Literary Officialdom: Kabul Literary Society (Anjuman-e Adabi), c.1933.

INTRODUCTION

poets associated with the Literary Society, such as 'Abdullah Qari (d.1944) and Sufi 'Abd al-Haqq Bitab (d.1969), wrote verse in celebration of Afghanistan's independence and progress, the position of poet laureate (*malik al-shu'ara*) was revived and linked to the Literary Society. Tying literature to the state, the founding secretary of the Kabul Literary Society was also the chief royal secretary and his successor was a close relative of the king.[43]

The Literary State

The primary official aim of the Kabul Literary Society was to promote the study of "Dari" literature, though the subtitle of its journal, *Kabul*, as *'Ilmi, Adabi, Ijtima'e, Tarikhi* ("Scientific, Literary, Social, Historical"), points to the way in which literature was linked to a larger modernizing intellectual and social agenda. The secondary aim of the Literary Society was to standardize Dari-Persian usage in the manner of the language academies of Europe and so further promote the notion of Afghan Dari as a national language distinct from Iranian Farsi. If the agenda was nationalistic, then once again the cultural resources on which the Literary Society drew were transnational. During the 1930s and 40s, one of its other major activities was to oversee the translation into Dari-Persian of the writings of a diverse body of writers, ranging from Lord Byron and the Lebanese-American author Khalil Gibran to the Indian Nobel laureate, Rabindranath Tagore.[44] Over the following decades, other state-sponsored institutions were established to further promote a national tradition of literature. In 1942 the Afghan Historical Society (Anjuman-e Tarikh-e Afghanistan) was founded under the direction of the nationalist historian 'Abd al-Hayy Habibi (1910–84), who also served as dean of Kabul University's Faculty of Letters when it was established in 1944.[45] In the next few years, its magazine, *Aryana*, published articles of literary advice, such as the 1946 essay "*Fan-e Roman Navisi* (The Art of Novel-Writing)", itself an anonymous translation from the French.[46] Other imported genres also flourished. The following year of 1947 saw the inauguration of the Kabul Municipal Theatre by the city's mayor, Ghulam Muhammad Farhad, though the first theatrical performances in Kabul had taken place twenty years earlier when King Amanullah invited a touring company to perform. Its cosmopolitan players comprised two German Jews, a New Yorker, an Italian, a girl from the East End of London and two children born in Latin America and Paris.[47] As the *Daily Mail* correspondent Roland Wild glibly phrased the theatrical importing at the time, "the grease paint was coming to the wilds".[48]

Nation and transnation existed in a precarious balance and each of the new cultural and literary institutions promoted nationalist writings and performances along with the translated works of foreign scholars and playwrights. That literature continued to induce transnational influence can be seen in statistics from Kabul University where, in 1958, eight out of twenty-four (that is, one in three) of the university's literature professors were foreign, a proportion that was even higher than among professors of medicine.[49] It was not only from the West and Russia that literary influences were flowing in these years and the 1960s saw a burst of translations into both Persian and Pashto of the Urdu writing of the poet and ideological founder of Pakistan, Muhammad Iqbal (1877–1938).[50] Literature was seen as nation-building knowledge. Statistics from the period point to the increasing social importance of literature among the growing educated class: by 1963 literature was Kabul University's second most popular degree subject after medicine, with twice as many students studying literature than economics, social sciences and technical subjects.[51]

If these efforts to create a national school of literature attempted to nationalize the transregional language of Persian, then the dilemma of claiming a language and literature claimed by others across the border similarly shaped the evolution of Pashto literature in Afghanistan. As in the case of Persian, most of the major early literary works in Pashto, such as the writings of Khushhal Khan Khattak (1613–90) and 'Abd al-Rahman Baba (1650–1715) were written in what was, by the twentieth century, the geography of British India and, subsequently, Pakistan. These older texts emerged as part of the Pashtun-Afghan interaction with the Mughal Empire which had also led to the writing in India of the first histories of the Afghans in Persian.[52] The position of Pashto was also similar to that of Persian with regard to the actual production of the earliest Pashto books and journals. This first occurred among Christian missionaries and long-settled Afghan diaspora communities in such Indian cities as Calcutta and Delhi, before, from around 1950, the Pakistani city of Peshawar emerged as the main centre of Pashto printing (as it remains to this day).[53] Within Afghanistan itself, Pashto first began to be printed from around 1914, when the occasional Pashto poem began to appear in Tarzi's newspaper, *Siraj al-Akhbar*, albeit lacking type for the special letters used for writing Pashto.[54] In 1916, a grammar of Pashto and a translation of a Persian guide to the Qur'an were published by the government functionary, Salih Muhammad, who overcame the lack of Pashto type through the use of lithographic printing (itself introduced from India).⁵⁵ However, aside from such pedagogical works and the occasional bilingual text in Persian and Pashto, it was not until the 1930s that Pashto printing emerged in any sustained fashion in Afghanistan.

As in the case of Persian, governmental figures played the leading role in the programme to nationalize Pashto. As early as 1913, Mahmud Tarzi had written an article in his newspaper, *Siraj al-Akhbar*, in which he loftily claimed that Pashto was the ancestral language of all Indo-European languages. He presented Pashto as having been kept pristine and pure in its mountain strongholds and as the *Ursprache* of the refined literary languages of Europe.⁵⁶ Despite the fact that his own publishing endeavours were entirely directed towards Persian, elsewhere Tarzi even went as far as to explicitly refer to Pashto as the "language of the community and nation" (*zaban-e qawmi va milli*), so prefiguring the language policies of the 1930s.⁵⁷ Such notions were already implicit in the descriptive terminology of Afghan languages around 1900, in that the Pashto language was widely referred to as "Afghani". In pace with the nation-building venture at large, Tarzi's nationalistic reframing of Pashto gathered momentum in the following decades.

One of the most important figures among the second generation of Pashto supporters was Muhammad Na'im Khan, the minister of education between 1938 and 1946. In 1936, he inaugurated the formal policy of promoting Pashto as Afghanistan's national language, leading to the commission and publication of Pashto textbooks to be used even by non-Pashto speakers.⁵⁸ The new place for Pashto in the national capital was signalled by the foundation in 1937 of the Paxto Tolana (Pashto Academy), charged with the mission of acting as national arbiter of literary and linguistic standards. Echoing the foundation of the Anjuman-e Adabi-ye Kabul (Kabul Literary Society) in 1931, the following year saw the establishment in Qandahar of Da Paxto Adabi Anjuman (Pashto Literary Society) for the promotion of Pashto literature, which served as the forerunner of the more nationally-focused Paxto Tolana in Kabul. The leading figure behind the foundation of the Pashto Literary Society in Qandahar was Muhammad Gul Mohmand (1885–1964) and through his and the Society's efforts, the 1930s saw the establishment of Afghanistan's earliest Pashto journals, *Paxto* and *Da Mu'alim Paxto* ("The Teacher's Pashto"). The foundation of the Paxto Tolana in 1937 also coincided with the publication of Gul Muhammad Muhmand's dictionary of Pashto by Muhammad Na'im Khan's Education Ministry.⁵⁹ Through the work of such figures as the scholar-journalist Salih Muhammad, the larger linguistic policy behind the creation of the dictionary saw attempts to reform the Pashto alphabet, to better distinguish "Afghan" from "Pakistani" Pashto and to standardize Pashto grammar.⁶⁰ The establishment of the Pashto Academy not only reflected the earlier attempts to nationalize "Dari" Persian in Afghanistan. It also echoed the inception of the Turkish Linguistic Society in 1932 with its aim of creating a purified national Turkish language, and the establishment in 1935 of the Iranian Academy, with its own nationalistic agenda of standardizing and purifying "Farsi" Persian.⁶¹ Across the border in Soviet Central Asia, the same period also saw "Tajik" Persian undergo alphabetical transformation in the pursuit of a national consciousness along the cultural road towards socialism.⁶²

As we have already seen, while they were themselves ethnically Pashtun, the modernizing Afghan intellectuals of the 1910s and 20s were generally more literate in Persian than in Pashto. For the latter was a language which before the deliberate "Pashtunizing" agenda of the 1930s had not developed the prose genres or even vocabulary to deal with the new technological and ideological concerns of the intelligentsia. As a result, the attempt to nationalize and modernize Pashto took place only after several decades of heavy state investment in Persian. Since no amount of rebranding of Persian as "Dari" could hide the fact that Persian was also the national language of Iran, from the 1930s some Afghan nationalists began to promote the idea of Pashto as the true and unique language of the Afghans and thence the proper national language of Afghanistan. Even so, the responses to the dilemmas of Pashto were broadly similar to those directed towards Persian. Ironically, in these same years that a case was being made for Pashto as the "authentic" language of the Afghans, Pashto literature was enjoying a rich period of development among Pashtuns living across the Durand Line in British India. The earliest Pashto newspapers had already been established there several decades earlier and the flourishing Pashto literary scene in the northern reaches of British India had seen poets such as Amir Hamza Shinwari (1907–94) adapt the Persian and Urdu genre of the lyrical *ghazal* for Pashto. Meanwhile, small-town Pashtun patrons adopted the Urdu poetic performance of the *musha'ira* ("poetry gathering") for the promotion of their own literary heritage. From the 1930s, these developments were imported in turn across the border to Afghanistan. Still, the cultural traffic was certainly not one way and, in 1955, Pashto-speakers in what was by then Pakistan founded their own Pashto Academy in Peshawar to rival the older Paxto Tolana of Kabul.

INTRODUCTION

This state investment in Pashto was conceived of as being at once a programme of national and of literary uplift. This was a twinned undertaking signalled by the foundation in 1942 of the Theatre of Learning (Puhani Nandari) in Kabul, though many of the actual plays performed consisted of translations from the works of Egyptian and even American dramatists. Since the literary heritage of Persian was clearly far older than that of Pashto, research by state-sponsored scholars attempted to develop the history of Pashto in ways that echoed the national histories of "Dari" literature we have seen earlier. The most significant development on this front came in 1944 when the historian 'Abd al-Hayy Habibi claimed to have discovered a manuscript of an eighteenth-century Pashto anthology entitled *Pata Khazana* ("Hidden Treasure"). His purported discovery contained the biographies and verses of Pashto poets going back as far as the eighth century, so pushing back the history of Pashto literature to a period considerably earlier than that of Persian.[63] While this is not the place to reprise the debate on the text's widely-questioned authenticity, it was certainly felicitous timing for the *Pata Khazana* to be discovered by a nationalist historian who, in the years surrounding his publication of the *Pata Khazana*, had served as president of the Pashto Academy and as the first head of Kabul University's Faculty of Letters. Moreover, once again linking literature to the organizational arenas of politics, a few years later the text's discoverer became a prominent member of the Pashto nationalist party, Wishzalmayan ("Awakened Youth") after its foundation in 1947.[64]

Whether the origins of the verses collected in the *Pata Khazana* lay in the eighth or the twentieth century, what is more important here is the way in which state-sponsored members of the intelligentsia sought to claim, reshape and promote Pashto as a prestigious literary language for their young nation. One of the first published anthologies of Pashto narrative poetry, for example, was the 1939 *Milli Hindara* ("Mirror of the Nation") edited by Muhammad Gul Nuri.[65] Such policies continued in the following decades. In an ongoing counterpoint to the linguistic strategies of nationalizing Persian, the 1950s saw the publication of an official Pashto-Dari dictionary entitled simply as *Afghan Qamus* ("Afghan Dictionary"). It was part of a word-coining venture that not only sought to ensure that Pashto had the vocabulary required to deal with the modern world, but also signalled the language's newly-achieved status as the twinned national equivalent of Dari-Persian.[66] Other Pashto dictionaries followed. As had already happened with Dari-Persian, the 1950s and 60s saw the writing of literary histories of Pashto, with *tazkira* anthologies of Pashto being published on state-owned presses that prevented the expression of social criticism. Such prominent nationalists as 'Abd al-Hayy Habibi and 'Abd al-Ra'uf Benawa (1913–84) again played a leading role.[67] The result of these literary efforts was that Persian and Pashto became enshrined as the twin languages of state in Afghanistan, with the 1964 constitution recognizing them both as official languages, whereas the first constitution of Afghanistan in 1923 had made no provisions for language at all. It was also the 1964 constitution which finally cemented the designation of Afghan Persian as "Dari", a move designed to placate Pashtun nationalists opposed to the "foreignness" of Farsi, that is, the language of the Fars province of Iran.[68]

The educational expansion of the 1960s led to important new developments. While 1965 saw an important step forward in literary freedom of expression through the passing of laws recognizing the freedom of the press, in practice the state remained a powerful arbiter of literary matters. The exposure of a new generation of left-wing Afghan intellectuals to Soviet models of literature in the 1960s and 70s encouraged the emergence of a school of social realism, led by such Pashto writers as Asadullah Habib (1942–), Sulayman Layeq (1930–) and Nur Muhammad Taraki (1917–79).[69] Given the violence and wars that emerged out of the Afghan and Soviet socialists' agenda, the role played by literature in the spread of leftist ideas in Afghanistan is often forgotten. Not only were the leading leftist intellectuals, such as Taraki, fiction writers, but the day-job of Ghulam Dastagir Panjshiri, one of the other founders of the leftist study groups that emerged into political parties, was a literature teacher at Kabul's Teachers' College.[70] When the socialist PDPA split into two rival organizations, Khalq ("Masses") and Parcham ("The Flag"), the new parties were named after their journals.[71] Once again, transnational flows were as important for leftist literature as its predecessors. Asadullah Habib, for example, was notable not only for writing in 1965 the first major Afghan social-realist novel, *Sepidandam* ("The White Figure"), and such gritty dramas as *Khashm-e Khalq* ("The People's Wrath"), but also for translating Russian, European and American novels and short stories into Dari-Persian.[72] As the ideology and purpose of the Afghan state was again redefined after the socialist coup of 1978, several such writers found themselves in positions of power, with Layeq becoming the minister of television and radio, Habib the president of the Writer's Union of Afghanistan and vice-chancellor of Kabul University, and Taraki the president of Afghanistan. New state-sponsored literary associations were established to encourage writers to produce works in harmony with socialist ideological orthodoxy. In the wake of the 1978 Saur Revolution, all of Afghanistan's publishing houses were nationalized and Bayhaqi, the official publisher of the Ministry of Education, came to play an increasingly important role in the mediation of literature and other reading materials to the public. The state also took further steps to control literary and cultural affairs; in 1979, the Pashto Academy and the Afghan Historical Society become incorporated into the new Academy of Sciences of Afghanistan established on the Soviet model.

Another important development of the socialist period was the promotion in 1980 of Baluchi, Uzbek, Pashai and Nuristani to the status of official languages. In turn, 1983 saw the publication of the first dictionary of Hazaragi, defined as the dialect of Dari-Persian spoken by the long-marginalized Hazara ethnic community.[73] The ruling People's Democratic Party of Afghanistan also supported the foundation of Hazara literary and cultural journals such as *Gharjistan* (1987). However, the most important of the new literary societies was the Afghan Writers Union. Between its foundation in 1980 and its collapse during the post-Soviet civil war in 1992, it was responsible for publishing some two thousand literary works which ranged from short poems to lengthy novels on social-realist themes.[74] While the Taliban regime which came to power in 1996 is not known to have established any formal literary societies, it did sponsor the production and distribution of Pashto poetry that celebrated its warriors, albeit through audio cassette as much as printed text. As with the historical concerns of the regimes that preceded the Taliban in twentieth-century Afghanistan, the Taliban were also concerned through the literature they sponsored to link themselves to a much older tradition of holy warriors, whom Taliban poets assured their listeners had always defended Afghanistan from foreign imperialists and infidels. Once again, in the 1990s literature was called upon to articulate the shifting purposes of the nation, this time as the defender of Islam.

From Nation to Diaspora (and Back)

If the previous pages have emphasized the centrality of the state in the shaping of a modern literature for Afghanistan, then this should not foster illusions of literary stability, whether in an ideological or geographical sense. We have already seen how the ideology of the Afghan state was redefined several times over in the course of the twentieth century. One result of this was that even writers who at certain points of their careers served in influential official positions, such as Mahmud Tarzi or ʿAbd al-Hayy Habibi, at later points in their careers found themselves exiled to regions often far distant from Afghanistan, from where they continued to publish their work. The instability of the nation they were attempting to fix and define was in this way responsible for the geographical instability of both writers and the literature they produced. Ever since its emergence in the early 1900s, modern Afghan literature has been perpetually shaped by this cross-border shuttling between homeland and exile, nation and diaspora. Having traced the role of the nation state in the shaping of modern Afghan literature, we must now therefore turn to the role of diaspora in the production of many of the most important works written by Afghans in the twentieth century.

In the Afghan ruler ʿAbd al-Rahman Khan's late nineteenth-century autobiographical *Pandnama-ye Dunya va Din*, we have already seen how the nation-building projects of Afghanistan's governors drew on a wide range of transnational literary resources. Even at the very birth of printed literary production in Afghanistan in the reign of Shir ʿAli (r. 1863–79), the state press had apparently published a Persian translation of an Urdu version of Daniel Defoe's *Robinson Crusoe*, so creating a multi-layered transnational text that would be echoed in the Persian translations of Turkish versions of Jules Verne's novels that were published in Kabul in the 1910s.[75] With their technophilic celebrations of submarines and aeroplanes, the imported novels of Jules Verne, which their translator Mahmud Tarzi had first encountered during his exile in the Ottoman Empire, point to the way modernists such as Tarzi conceived of literature as a means of importing the modernity enjoyed in other regions of the world. Between 1911 and 1919, Tarzi included regular discussions of literary topics in his pioneering newspaper, *Siraj al-Akhbar*, in which he was critical of traditional Afghan literary forms, viewing them as vehicles for superstition and obstacles to the modern thinking required for national progress.[76] As part of this project of national renewal, the novel itself was a deliberately imported genre, self-consciously adapted for disseminating new ideas among the wider population by Afghan intellectuals exposed to the wider world. As exposure to the novel occurred among the Afghan diaspora in the Ottoman Empire, India and Egypt, even the French and English terms for the genre were adapted into Dari-Persian as *ruman* and *navul*.[77] As exiled and diasporic Afghans returned to their homeland during the developmental decades of the early twentieth century, and as cross-border trade brought in books from the far richer publishing economies of colonial India, Iran and Turkey, bookshops were set up in Kabul to sell French, Turkish and Urdu novels and educational books.[78]

If imported European texts by Defoe, Verne and de Montépin represented the first novels to be published in Afghanistan, then cross-border literary exchanges also shaped the first novels to be written by Afghans themselves. The first novel published in Afghanistan that was actually written by an Afghan was *Jihad-e Akbar* ("The Greatest Jihad"), which appeared in serial form in the journal *Ma'rif-e Ma'arif* between 1919 and 1921. In a pointer to the nationalist concerns we have seen surrounding the birth of modern Afghan literature, *Jihad-e Akbar* was set during the First Anglo-Afghan War and recounted the heroic deeds of the Pashtun warrior,

Fig: 3. The Literary State: Afghan Boy Reads a School Textbook.

Muhammad Akbar Khan. Yet while the novel was printed in Afghanistan, its author, Mawlavi Muhammad Husayn Punjabi, had been born and raised in the Indian city of Jalandhar as a member of the Afghan diaspora that had been settling Punjab since the middle ages.[79] He effectively imported the genre of the novel from India, where it had already spread through the vernacular languages during the past half century. Like many other Muslims from India, Mawlavi Muhammad had moved to Kabul to work in one of the new schools founded as part of King Habibullah's modernization programme. In a fitting echo of the links we have seen between literature and nation-building, in addition to his novel Mawlavi Muhammad also wrote over a dozen school textbooks for the young Afghans in his charge.

Nor was this Afghan from Indian Punjab the only literary importer from the Afghan diaspora in this period. *Tasvir-e 'Ibrat ya Bibi Khor Jan* ("The Warning Picture or Bibi Khor Jan"), the second novel to be written in Dari-Persian by an Afghan, was both written and published among the Afghan diaspora in India.[80] The book's author, Muhammad 'Abd al-Qadir Effendi, was the son of the exiled Afghan ruler Muhammad Ayub Khan (r.1879–80). According to the autobiography he appended to English language history of Afghanistan that he wrote in his by-then Pakistani exile, Effendi was born in Baghdad in the Ottoman Empire before being raised and educated in India, where he was to spend his entire life.[81] Although in his autobiography Effendi referred to himself as the "Afghan refugee", he was in fact one of the privileged pensioned elite of British India, where he was frequently a guest of Indian princes and senior colonial officers.[82] It was therefore in the Indian city of Madras rather than in Afghanistan that his Dari-Persian novel was published in 1922. The novel, *Tasvir-e 'Ibrat ya Bibi Khor Jan*, took as its topic the story of an upper class Afghan woman (the Bibi Khor Jan of the subtitle), to argue why superstitions and traditions were in need of reform if Afghanistan was to be modernized. Given the scornful account of the "disgusting rites" and "superstitions" that surrounded his own upbringing among Afghan women, these were clearly subjects about which Effendi felt strongly, voicing his criticisms through the idioms of reform shared with educated Indian Muslims of his exiled milieu.[83]

Whether Effendi's *Tasvir-e 'Ibrat* or Mawlavi Muhammad Husayn's *Jihad-e Akbar*, in terms of their themes—war and women, nationalism and reform—these two pioneering Afghan novels were far from unique. This was especially true with regard to the Indian context from which both novels emerged. The previous decades had similarly seen the first novels written in Indian languages, novels which (whether in Marathi, Bengali or Urdu) presaged the themes of the first Afghan novels. This is particularly striking with regard to the Urdu novel, the pioneering examples of which—*Mir'at al-'Arus* ("Bride's Mirror", published 1869) of Nazir Ahmad (1836–1912) and *Fasana-e Azad* ("Tale of Azad", published 1878–9) of Ratan Nath Sarshar (1846–1902)—were respectively dedicated to the themes of women's life and its reform and a heroic Muslim warrior fighting in the Crimean and Anglo-Afghan Wars (albeit on the British side).[84] It is unclear whether the Afghan novelists, Mawlavi Muhammad Husayn Punjabi and Muhammad 'Abd al-Qadir Effendi, actually read these two Urdu novels. But given the huge impact of these Urdu novelists among the North Indian Muslim intelligentsia among whom the novel-writing Afghan exiles lived, it is hard to imagine the latter being unaware of Ratan Nath Sarshar and Nazir Ahmad's work.

Whether voiced in the Indian Urdu or the Afghan Persian novel, this sense of a new reformist conscience being imported in the guise of literature through Afghan links with the wider world was also seen in the third early Afghan novel, *Nada-ye Talaba-ye Ma'arif ya Huquq-e Millat* ("Voice of the Knowledge Seekers, or the Rights of the Nation"). Its author was Muhyi al-Din Anis, who was born and raised in Egypt of Afghan parentage before he 'returned' to Afghanistan in 1921 to associate himself with the modernizing enterprises of King Amanullah.[85] A novel of ideas, *Nada-ye Talaba ye Ma'arif* used dialogues between the four students who were its main characters to explore new ideas about national independence, citizen's rights, and modern education. However, perhaps the most striking example of the global literary reach of the Afghan diaspora was a novel written among the Afghan merchant community in Latin America by Murtaza Ahmad Muhammadzai, who blended the romantic tale of a love affair with a celebration of political freedom. In a pointer to the linguistic transactions that were no less a part of this literary traffic, Murtaza Ahmad wrote the original version of his novel in English before it was translated into Persian and serialized in 1927 in one of the early Afghan newspapers, under the title *Jashn-e Istiqlal dar Boliviya* ("Independence Celebrations in Bolivia").[86] In the first half of the twentieth century, these cross-border movements of books and writers also saw the entry of non-Afghan writers to Afghanistan. This included such major Indian figures as the great Urdu and Persian poet Muhammad Iqbal (1877–1938), who visited Kabul in 1933 and addressed two major Persian works to the modernizing Afghan rulers of the period, celebrating them as champions of Muslim independence against a godless European imperialism.⁸⁷ Several of Iqbal's major poems, such as *Asrar-e Khodi* ("Secrets of the Self"), were also translated into Pashto by Samandar Khan Samandar (1901–90).⁸⁸

If all this points to the flow of literary traffic into Afghanistan, then we must also recognize that the enforced or voluntary mobility of Afghans also exported literary traffic across its borders to the wider world. During his second period of exile, Mahmud Tarzi continued his writing career in Istanbul, where he had already published a volume of his poetry in 1923, a westerly counterpart to the sole edition of his father's poems printed in the Indian (now Pakistani) city of Karachi in 1892.⁸⁹ After Mahmud Tarzi died in Istanbul in 1933, his Oxford-educated son, 'Abd al-Vahhab, maintained the family's links with the Turkish intelligentsia and, reinvigorating the old transnational roots of Persian, co-authored a Persian grammar book for Turkish students.⁹⁰ Nor were the Tarzis by any means the last Afghan writers to be exiled. For as we have already noted, the proximity of literary intellectuals to the state placed them in a precarious balance between

Fig. 4: Urdu in Afghanistan: Muhammad Iqbal on Sale in Kabul.

patronage and persecution: Tarzi's grammar-writing son would subsequently return to Afghanistan to become director of the state-run Afghan Tourist Organization.[91] Among other important literary exiles in this period were the diplomat and poet, 'Abd al-Rahman Pazhwak (1919–95), and the official historian, 'Abd al-Hayy Habibi, whom we have already seen "discovering" the manuscript of the Pashto literary anthology, *Pata Khazana*. After falling from favour for critiques of the government, Habibi fled to Pakistan in 1951, where he founded the republican journal *Azad Afghanistan* ("Free Afghanistan"). From across the border, *Azad Afghanistan* published poems and stories dedicated to the constitutional reform of the Afghan state, a theme then taken up by several major poets in the later 1950s.[92]

In the pattern we have now seen repeatedly, the mobility and exile of Afghan intellectuals such as Pazhwak and Habibi enabled a diverse and destabilizing flow of ideologies in the guise of literature across the nation's frontiers. Republicans and pro-modernist reformists represented only two bands of the spectrum. Between the 1960s and 1980s, exiled Afghan Islamists affiliated with the Hezb-e Eslami ("Islamic Party") and its many factions smuggled in their writings from Pakistan. These Islamist texts came in genres that ranged from theological-political tracts to more literary works of jihadist resistance poetry. They were distributed in formats that ranged from handwritten copybooks to low-tech mimeographs and audio cassettes.[93] Like the first Afghan printing presses of the late nineteenth century which were imported across the border from India, in physical terms this Islamist literature was produced through the importing of such technologies as cheap Japanese cassette recorders and American mimeograph printers. The model was no less transnational than the technology. For the jihadist counterblasts to the Soviet invasion were Islamist heirs of the hand-reproduced Russian *samizdat* ("self-published") booklets and *magnitizdat* ("magnetic tape") recordings that had spread literary dissent through the Soviet Union since the 1960s.[94] Yet there was an important and destabilizing difference between Afghanistan's two periods of importing the technology of literature. From the first Afghan presses of the late nineteenth century until at least the 1950s, printing machines were largely confined to government-approved circles, while the newer and cheaper literary technologies available by the 1960s were accessible to a wider range of (in many case anti-state) litterateurs.

However, it was by no means only Islamist groups who contributed to the exile literature of resistance during the struggle against the Soviets and the Afghan communist government in the 1980s. Exiled major poets such as Khalilullah Khalili (1907–87) wrote stirring poems of nationalistic resistance, while the former diplomat Pazhwak turned his skills as a poet to writing anti-Soviet *shab-namas* or "night letters" which were smuggled into the country under the cover of darkness.[95] Other exiles established literary circles and formal societies to articulate ideological alternatives to both the Islamist *jihad* organizations and the official communist Afghan Writers Union in Kabul. These exiled literary societies ranged from the Writers Union of Free Afghanistan, founded in Peshawar in 1985 by the former Kabul University professor, Rasul Amin (1939–2009), to the Informed Writers' Circle founded in the same period by Afghan refugees in Delhi, who published the journal *Gah-nama* ("Calendar").[96]

From the 1980s and 90s, Afghanistan's refugee diaspora led to the creation of new Afghan communities in cities as far apart as Paris, San Francisco, Hamburg, London, Sydney and Stockholm. While Afghans were already travelling as far as Europe and Australia in the early 1900s, what was distinctive about the late twentieth-century diaspora was the sheer number and social variety of Afghans living in exile. As exiled writers began to establish themselves in Europe and the United States, other literary groups emerged, such as the Afghanistan Cultural Association established in the late 1990s in the Swedish city of Skärholmen, which published the Persian journal *Ariana-ye Birun Marzi* ("Ariana Beyond the Border").[97] Forming the little-known literary background to the celebrated novels of Khaled Hosseini, a whole series of English and Persian Afghan magazines were established in San Francisco from the mid-1980s onwards. Among this Afghan diaspora in the United States, *The Kite Runner* was by no means the first Afghan novel to be published in America. Twenty years before its publication, the exiled former poet laureate, Khalilullah Khalili, had published in New Jersey his Dari-Persian novel *'Ayyari az Khurasan* ("The Bandit Hero of Khurasan"), a fictionalized account of the tumultuous reign of the Tajik Afghan rebel Habibullah Kalakani in 1929.[98]

However, by no means all of Afghanistan's exiled and diasporic writers were concerned with political topics. From the 1980s onwards, many poems concerning such perennial Persian and Pashto literary themes as existential anguish and unrequited love were written by Afghan refugees in Iran and Pakistan.[99] In 2004, the exiled female writer Homayra Qadiri won a major literary award in Iran for a short story from her collection *Gushvara-ye Anis* ("Anis's Earring"). While she is said to have written the stories in secret during the years of Taliban rule, Qadiri published the story collection in Tehran.[100] Afghanistan's early twentieth century literary connections with Turkey have also recently been revived through the Afghan-Turkish literary journal, *Rah-e Nayestan* ("Road to the Reedbed"), which specializes in contemporary Afghan poetry. Founded by Mas'ud Khalili, the journal is published from the Afghan embassy in the Turkish capital, Ankara.[101]

In literary terms, what was new with the younger generation from the 1990s was the decision to adopt the languages of diaspora for writing rather than the Pashto and Dari-Persian languages of state which had, until this point, been Afghans' most important literary media. The best example of this transition is the work of 'Atiq Rahimi (1962–) who, despite residing in France, wrote his early novels such as *Khakestar va Khak* ("Earth and Ashes") in Dari-Persian before deciding to write his later novel *Pierre de Patience* ("The Patience Stone") directly in French. Even so, diaspora literature has continued to be produced in Pashto and Persian. Moreover, the experience of diaspora has led to literary no less than linguistic innovations within Afghan languages, whether through Hazara Afghans informally writing in what they claimed as a distinct "Hazaragi" language or through Afghan men and increasingly women breaking traditional taboos on privacy by writing autobiographical memoirs. Taking shape in American-style English formats, Iranian-style Persian formats and Islamist-style Arabic formats, the tremendous growth of the memoir points to the globalization of Afghan literature that accompanied the repeated collapses of the Afghan state between the 1980s and 2001. Important examples of this autobiographical literature include Muhammad Hasan Sharq's Dari-Persian *Karbaspush-ha-ye Berahna Pa* ("The Wool-Wearing Bare-Foots", 1994), Mir Tamim Ansary's English *West of Kabul, East of New York* (2003) and Mullah 'Abd al-Salam Za'if's Pashto *Da Gwantanamu Andzwar* ("Picture of Guantanamo", 2006).[102] In other cases, a truly transnational memorial literature has emerged through multilingual and multi-author enterprises. One example is the memoir of Sidiqa Mas'ud, the non-literate wife of the resistance leader, Ahmad Shah Mas'ud (1953–2001), which was dictated to an Afghan NGO director and French journalist, translated into French and published in Paris before then being translated back into Persian and published in Tehran.[103] Other female autobiographies include Shabibi Shah's poignant *Where do I Belong?*, written in Britain, and *Opium Nation*, written by the California-based Afghan journalist, Fariba Nawa.[104]

But it is of course the novel that has brought Afghan literature to a truly global audience, whether through the internationally-acclaimed and award-winning work of the Afghan-French writer, 'Atiq Rahimi, or of the best-selling Afghan-American writer, Khaled Hosseini. Even though these authors have chosen to write in languages with no relationship to the Afghan state, the state has remained a force in controlling the distribution of their writing: while such diasporic writers have had their novels published in Persian in Iran, they have found a limited readership in Afghanistan itself.[105] Literary flows have their limits, then, and not every work of Afghan literature is capable of crossing the borders of the nation.

2

MODERNIZING, NATIONALIZING, INTERNATIONALIZING

HOW MAHMUD TARZI'S HYBRID IDENTITY TRANSFORMED AFGHAN LITERATURE

Nushin Arbabzadah

Introduction

This chapter analyzes the connections between the life and work of Mahmud Tarzi (1865–1933) to explore how, in the early twentieth century, the basic paradox of modern Afghan literature as a literature that is simultaneously national and transnational came into being. A polymath whose career combined international diplomacy with literature, translation and journalism, Tarzi was the founding figure of modern Afghan literature because he was central in transforming it by linking his literary modernization project to the reformist Afghan state of the early twentieth century.[1] To do so, he gained access to the Kabul court through a combination of genealogical, professional and marital connections. In the absence of established state-run cultural institutions in the early twentieth century, it was only natural that personal inclination as much as state policies shaped literature and literary tastes. For this reason, this chapter explores the role played by Tarzi's own hybrid identity and his international literary tastes in transforming—at once modernizing and internationalizing—Afghan literature. An early twentieth century example of a hybrid identity, Tarzi's complex cultural identity drew on the international influences of French, Turkish, and Arabic literary, journalistic and scientific writings. This was, moreover, a taste in literature shaped by direct life experiences when Tarzi lived in Damascus, in the multi-ethnic and cosmopolitan cultural realms of the Ottoman Empire, a cultural sphere from which the isolated kingdom of Afghanistan was disconnected during the 1880s and 90s.

Mahmud Tarzi was the youngest son of Ghulam Muhammad Tarzi (1830–1900), an exiled nephew of the Afghan ruler Dost Muhammad Khan (r. 1826–63). As such, he was part of the ruling dynasty by virtue of his birth, with a genealogical link to the state that was itself inherently family- and clan-based. After his father's death, in 1903 Tarzi took advantage of an amnesty extended to the elite Afghan families who had been exiled during the reign of 'Abd al-Rahman (r. 1880–1901), returning from Damascus to Kabul. After running a translation bureau for several years in Kabul—itself a pointer to the transnational flow of words if not necessarily literature—in 1911 Tarzi began editing and printing the first regularly published Afghan newspaper, *Siraj al-Akhbar Afghaniya* ("Torch of Afghan News"). It was a professional venture for which he had the support of King Habibullah (r. 1901–19), with whom he carried on an unsteady alliance whose failure would ultimately bring the newspaper's closure in 1918. A blend of court chronicle, literary journal and political periodical, *Siraj al-Akhbar* allowed Tarzi to link his literary modernization project to the Afghan state whose resources substantially funded it. Having gained influence at the court in Kabul, Tarzi succeeded in turning his own personal vision of literature into state policy through his tutelage of the country's future political leadership by way of the Princes 'Inayatullah and Amanullah. These relationships were solidified through the marriage of Tarzi's daughters, Soraya and Khayria, to Prince Amanullah and Prince 'Inayatullah respectively. In 1919, this marital relationship with the Afghan state reached its climax with the accession to the throne of his son-in-law, Amanullah (r.1919–29), who appointed Tarzi as his foreign minister. Through Tarzi's institution-building efforts by way of setting up printing presses and publishing *Siraj al-Akhbar*, Afghan literature was at once both nationalized and internationalized. In this way, the history of modern Afghan literature can be said to have begun with Tarzi's launch of his newspaper in 1911.

MODERNIZING, NATIONALIZING, INTERNATIONALIZING

Siraj al-Akhbar was the key instrument for the propagation of Tarzi's ambitious literary modernization project. Printed between 1911 and 1919, this first regularly-published Afghan newspaper contained a section called *adabiyat* devoted to the discussion of literature. As the newspaper's editor-in-chief, Tarzi not only wrote the bulk of its editorials and news articles, but also chose the contents of its *adabiyat* or "literature" section. In order to explore the model of literature that Tarzi promoted in what was the most widely distributed Afghan publication of its day, this chapter focuses closely on the contents of this literature section. As we see below, this *adabiyat* section served as a platform for the modernization of Afghan literature. We have already noted that his personal taste in literature was shaped in Ottoman exile and in order to trace the links between Tarzi's literary ideas and life experiences, the chapter also turns to the diary of Tarzi's travels which he wrote in the late 1880s, during his years of exile, and published after his return to Kabul. It was the expulsion of his family from Afghanistan that allowed him to become fluent in both Turkish and Arabic, giving him access to European novels in Turkish translation and the Arabic newspapers of Cairo that were sold in Istanbul's bookshops. Exposed to European literary trends via Turkish translations and Arabic journalism, Tarzi already had a broad and international taste in literature as a young man.

In this way, we will see how international experience was crucial to the development of a national literature for Afghanistan through such transnational carriers of culture as Tarzi the traveller and the books he imported on his return to Kabul. Tarzi's multilingualism impressed and influenced his contemporaries and newspaper colleagues such as the poet 'Abd al-Rahman Kabrit who, under Tarzi's influence, learned Urdu, Turkish, English and Arabic.[2] This internationalism was reflected in the European literary styles that Tarzi offered to *Siraj al-Akhbar*'s Afghan and international readers, pleasing its modernist supporters and antagonizing its traditionalist critics. The fact that in the first issue of *Siraj al-Akhbar*, Tarzi chose to print in Persian translation a serialized version of Xavier de Montépin's popular French novel, *Les Viveurs de Paris* (1852), demonstrated from the outset his dedication to the European genre of the novel. Under pressure to accommodate the tastes of both traditionalist and modernist readers in Kabul, this serialized novel appeared alongside classical *ghazal* poetry in Dari-Persian, Iranian-Persian, Pashto and Urdu. The combination of very different literary norms and tastes was bound to create conflict, a tension that marked Tarzi's personal, political and literary life until his death in exile in Istanbul.

But the *adabiyat* column was more than just a space to be filled with an eclectic repertoire of oriental and occidental poetry; Tarzi also used the column as a space to expound his views of literature and linguistics, printing extended essays and theoretical writings in which he laid out his critique of traditional Afghan literature and his thoughts about the politics of language in the multi-ethnic state of Afghanistan. Given the sheer size and thematic scope of his productivity, which included an extensive body of literary, political, pedagogic and journalistic writings as well as translations of four French novels, this chapter's initial statement that Tarzi single-handedly modernized Afghan literature is scarcely an exaggeration. He became the founding figure of modern Afghan literature not only through his own remarkable productivity but also through creating a new and revolutionary school of literature whose adherents later became known as the *mutajaddid* or 'innovators' of the Habibi period (1901–19).

Fig. 5: Female Participants: Princess Khariyya Reads Egyptian Newspaper in Kabul.

MODERNIZING, NATIONALIZING, INTERNATIONALIZING

His legacy as an editor, journalist, translator, publisher and advocate of modern political poetry continues today.[3] Nearly a century after *Siraj al-Akhbar*, contemporary Afghan newspapers still use the layout that Tarzi first introduced to Afghanistan in 1911.[4] Moreover, his legacy as a composer of political poetry lived on through subsequent generations of poets, reaching a climax with the young leftist circle of political activist poets who came of age in the 1960s and 70s.[5] His pioneering career trajectory as translator, literatus, newspaper editor, diplomat and foreign minister was the first instance of the merging of literature with modern international statesmanship, solidifying the relationship between Afghan literature and nation-building. These steps were later followed by such figures as 'Abd al-Rahman Pazhwak, whose career is analyzed in Chaled Malekyar's chapter in this volume.

This chapter aims to explore the impact of Tarzi's life on his literary tastes and his views on the meaning and purpose of literature. These personal inclinations and convictions later influenced the direction taken by modern Afghan literature, as a result of Tarzi's efforts to institutionalize his views through exploiting his ties to the state. Evidence revealing the profound way his life story informed, influenced and inspired his literary, journalistic and political ideas can be found in his own writings, sometimes with striking parallels. Judging by works such as *Siraj al-Akhbar* and the travel diary of the journey he undertook with his father in 1887, his life and work were inseparable, which is why understanding the story of his life is crucial to unlocking the meaning of his work. There are two aspects to Tarzi's life that are particularly relevant for our understanding of his work. The first aspect is his literary and political genealogy, which, as we have already mentioned, placed him firmly at the heart of the Afghan political elite. His father, Sardar Ghulam Muhammad (1830–1900), was a nephew of the Afghan ruler Dost Muhammad (r. 1826–63). But even though he was connected to the state through such blood ties, he found himself and his family exiled from Afghanistan in 1881, a year after Amir 'Abd al-Rahman (r. 1880–1901) came to power.[6] The reason for the exile is explained in Tarzi's travel diary as being the result of Ghulam Muhammad's political rivalry with 'Abd al-Rahman, which was expressed through his opposition to the ruler's reconciliatory policy towards the British government in India.[7] Judging by Tarzi's diary, by 1887, when Ghulam Muhammad was an aging exile preparing for his death by taking a trip to Mecca, he regarded his opposition to 'Abd al-Rahman as a mistake and thought that by contesting the ruler's legitimacy he had brought his banishment from Afghanistan upon himself. At the time of his exile, Mahmud Tarzi was sixteen years old. His family first moved to Karachi, in British India, where Ghulam Muhammad published his poetry collection and married Mahmud to an Afghan woman who then died prematurely. His family spent two years in Karachi before continuing their journey of exile from British-ruled India to the independent Muslim state of the Ottoman Empire. The Ottoman ruler granted asylum to Tarzi's father, allocating the family to Damascus, the remote eastern province which was the final destination for political exiles of the Muslim world.[8] His father was given the status of the Ottoman ruler's special guest and received a regular monthly stipend of forty Ottoman liras from Istanbul.[9]

Tarzi's dislocation from the Indo-Persian cultural realm of Afghanistan and India was to have a profound impact on his intellectual, literary and political development, directly affecting his future work as a newspaper editor and later, diplomat. Arriving in Damascus at the age of eighteen, he underwent a successful cultural assimilation process, assuming the personality of a worldly Ottoman gentleman. The fact that he was fluent in Arabic and Turkish and socially at ease in the cosmopolitan cities of Istanbul and Alexandria alike meant that he could pass as a born and bred Ottoman gentleman without raising suspicion or doubt.[10] This quality made him the perfect travel companion for his father whose traditional Afghan Muslim looks, as we know from the travel diary, drew curiosity from fellow passengers and suspicion from Ottoman security officials. Insight into just how successfully he had assimilated into the Ottoman culture and way of life can be gained through examples from the travel diary. It is explained openly in the diary that, during the trip, Tarzi deliberately concealed his "Afghanness" from his fellow boat passengers, presenting himself as his father's employee and interpreter instead. Tarzi wrote in his diary that hiding his Afghan identity gave him freedom, because being an employee rather than son created distance between him and his father so that the son's actions were not seen as reflecting on his father's reputation. Whether this concealing was for social, political or bureaucratic expediency, the pertinent point here is not only that he kept his Afghanness secret but that he succeeded in doing so in a credible manner. If his fellow European and Ottoman passengers found nothing suspicious about Tarzi's public personality of an Ottoman gentleman raised in Istanbul, his fellow Afghans were equally, if not more, convinced of his Ottomanness. So for example, upon meeting in the port town of Jaffna a group of recent arrivals from Afghanistan, Tarzi deliberately addressed them in Pashto. But the men failed to respond to him because they thought he was a foreign gentleman. When he explained to them in Pashto that he was Afghan just like them, they responded bluntly: "We had no idea that this sort of curious Afghans even existed".[11] Tarzi thus was a nineteenth-century example of a cultural hybrid, drawing for his identity on both the Afghan and Ottoman cultural worlds. Afghan by blood, native languages and early life but Ottoman by choice, adult socialization and education, it was his hybrid identity that informed his taste in literature, later propagated via *Siraj al-Akhbar* to a wider circle of Afghan readers. The modernization of Afghan literature was, in this way, also an accidental side-effect of the Afghan ruler 'Abd al-Rahman's policy of exile as a form of punishment for unruly relatives.

Tarzi's hybrid identity shaped and informed his work for the rest of his life. A nineteenth-century prototype of an intercultural communicator, he began his professional life informally, by acting as his father's personal interpreter on trips to various parts of the Ottoman Empire. Upon returning to Afghanistan in 1903, his subsequent career was as a translator, editor, writer, journalist and, finally, a diplomat and minister of foreign affairs. In all these roles, whether translating French novels, writing essays on the politics of language or working as a diplomat, he acted as an intercultural bridge-builder, linking Afghanistan to the wider world. As such, Tarzi's biography has much in common with the life stories of contemporary Afghan writers like Khalid Hosseini and Atiq Rahimi who are also cultural hybrids acting as bridge-builders, linking Afghanistan to a global audience of readers.

Tarzi acquired his taste in literature, which he later promoted through *Siraj al-Akhbar* and his translated novels, in the cosmopolitan cultural realm of the Ottoman Empire. His favourite bookshop was located in Istanbul, a city he visited, sometimes with the specific purpose of purchasing books. In his travel diary he wrote about the bookshop's location and stock:

We left the large, covered market through the gate and entered the narrow bazaar of book-binders, book-sellers and engravers. In these bookshops one can find scientific and technical books as well as novels and old and new publications. The books are cheaper here and there are more of them. In my previous travels I purchased many books in these book shops.[12]

In his travel diary Tarzi described the lively debates he had about literature, music, politics and poetry with his fellow boat passengers and Ottoman friends he knew in Istanbul.[13] It becomes clear from such description that debating, for example, eastern versus western literature was part of his routine conversation repertoire in talks with strangers as well as with his father. Such debates were later conceptualized in political commentaries published in *Siraj al-Akhbar*. We also know from his travel diary that even though it was his father's political activism that had caused the family's banishment from Afghanistan, in exile it was poetry that his father turned to for solace. By then his father had a much more conciliatory approach to the Afghan ruler of the time, 'Abd al-Rahman, who had exiled him. Throughout the journey recorded in the travel diary, his father crafted new *ghazal* poems in Persian which Tarzi transcribed in his diary entries. The ex-tempore poems were sometimes given as parting gifts to friends and acquaintances father and son met during their trip. From such entries it becomes clear that Tarzi's intellectual and emotional link to classical Persian poetry and literature was through his close father-son relationship more than through having spent the first sixteen years of his life in Afghanistan. The most touching display of his appreciation of his father's poetry was his decision to adopt his father's literary pen-name, Tarzi, instead of using the family's prestigious tribal title of Muhammadzai *Sardar* ("lord"). After all, Tarzi was not the name that the family was known as in Damascus. We know through the telegraphs he dispatched on his trip to his family in Damascus that in their Arab hometown they were known as the household of the Afghan Sardar, and not as the Tarzi family. In a way, Tarzi's modernization of literature began with a personal gesture with the choice of his name which he shortened to a simple Mahmud Tarzi, altogether abandoning the tribal and political connotations that would have come with his using of the full aristocratic title.

Summing up his life and work, we can say with confidence that the two major literary influences in his life were his father's role as an Afghan poet and his own immersion in the cosmopolitan culture of the Ottoman Empire in the late nineteenth century which exposed him to the craft of modern newspaper writing as much as the popular science fiction and socially critical French novels that he later translated into Dari-Persian and spread in Afghanistan.[14] Such cultural influences were turned into conceptual essays, poetry, articles and translated novels that he produced in Afghanistan upon his return from the Ottoman exile in 1903. The propagation of Tarzi's literary modernization project took also the shape of inspiring and encouraging Prince 'Inayatullah to set up a private printing press, the 'Inayat Press which, as Nile Green discusses in the next chapter, published Tarzi's translations of Jules Verne's novels as well as his travel diary. It was through such merging of literature and state that Tarzi succeeded in institutionalizing and nationalizing literature in Afghanistan. But since his personal tastes in culture and literature were international, through his editorial control of what was at the time the only Afghan newspaper in existence, modern Afghan literature became exposed to international influences.

In practical terms, Tarzi's modernization of literature was made through three distinct innovations. Firstly, at the basic level of writing, he prioritized the functionality of plain language as a tool of communication over the convoluted eloquent prose of court bureaucrats that was the standard style until his period. Secondly, he introduced Afghan readers to the hitherto unfamiliar genre of the European novel by publishing Dari-Persian translations of science fiction and of what he regarded as socially-critical French novels. Thirdly, he modernized Afghan poetry by breaking away from traditional concerns with love, nature and metaphysics to instead write poems about politics, military affairs and the technological advancements of the period. Such radical innovations amounted to a redefinition of the term literature itself, requiring a new theoretical framework to justify and explain it. It is to this new framework that we now turn.

A Theoretical Framework for a New Afghan Literature

Tarzi's views on literature are scattered throughout *Siraj al-Akhbar*, appearing in conceptual essays, critical pieces and responses to readers' letters. In his theoretical writings about literature, we encounter three recurrent themes. First, that literature represents an innate human need for creativity that is a response to the world human beings encounter around them. Second, that the outward forms of this creativity are always subject to change and, as such, are mirror images of larger social developments. Hence, the more advanced a society, the more complex its literature. Third, that literature must be relevant to the demands of the time.

This latter point needs further elaboration because Tarzi's views on the demands of his time were specific to his Afghan context. We know from the writings published in *Siraj al-Akhbar* that his views about the demands of his time mostly failed to resonate with Afghans, finding more outspoken approval by readers who resided outside of Afghanistan. Readers abroad knew the world that Tarzi referred to from first-hand experience of living in technologically advanced societies that were either already colonized or were, like the Ottoman Empire that Tarzi had left, under the threat of war with European states of superior military capacity. By contrast to this shared understanding of international politics, there was a clear gap of knowledge that separated Tarzi from many of his Afghan peers who, unlike him, had not experienced what it was like to live in the much more developed Ottoman Empire. As we have already pointed out, his literary, cultural and political vision for Afghanistan was shaped far away from the country he was trying to reform. We know from the travel diary he wrote in Ottoman exile that he became acutely aware of the dynamics of international politics shaped by a Europe that was technologically and militarily on the rise and by an Ottoman Empire that was in decline and under threat. It is possible that it was his awareness of the decline of this last bastion of Muslim power that triggered his return to Afghanistan in 1903. We certainly have evidence in his travel diary that his conversations with Christian missionaries forced him to think critically about the place of Islam in the twentieth century and to debate issues such as *hijab* and polygamy with Christian critics of Islam. We also know from his diary that he met fellow travellers who took an interest in Afghanistan. On one occasion, a conversation with the Russian captain of the boat on which he was travelling shook Tarzi to the core, leading to a sleepless night in which he experienced an identity crisis.[15] During the conversation, the Russian had told Tarzi bluntly that Afghanistan was not an independent state but was ruled indirectly by British India. The following morning, Tarzi found solace in his father's reassuring words that he knew 'Abd al-Rahman personally and could vouch for the fact that the Amir would have never signed the kind of treaty that would allow the British government to control Afghan policies. His father's reassurance that Afghanistan was indeed an independent state put an end to Tarzi's worries and the trip resumed as normal. But in the anecdote, we have clear evidence that Tarzi's understanding of the demands of the time was shaped through encounters with critics of Afghanistan and Islam. The fact that such criticism was expressed at a time when the Ottoman Empire was itself in decline further convinced Tarzi of the urgency of Muslim reform.

Living in exile far from the protective isolation of Afghanistan, through such painful affronts to his identity as a Muslim and an Afghan, Tarzi became firmly convinced that the demands of the time required Afghans to awaken to the reality of their nation's underdevelopment. Like other radicals of the period, he believed that it was the purpose of literature to jolt his countrymen into action and propel them towards rapid modernization. The propagation of literature that triggered action rather than contemplation and concerned itself with the aesthetically unpleasant themes of politics and technology rather than beauty and spirituality amounted to a total abandonment of traditional Afghan literature. But this was exactly what Tarzi achieved in the pages of *Siraj al-Akhbar*. Despite his rootedness in Afghan literature by blood and domestic upbringing as the son of a traditional poet and courtier, he thought that traditional literature was not only irrelevant but also dangerous, as it encouraged readers to daydream and so escape reality to a realm of fantasy inhabited by demons and fairies. Tarzi's goal was to wean Afghans away from the *afsana* ('fairy tales') and self-indulgent poetry of custom by introducing them to a literature that was intellectually more demanding through its dealings with political and social concerns. Such a radical new approach to literature required both a new theoretical conception and an endorsement by members of the Afghan cultural establishment. For this, Tarzi found his chief helper in court bureaucrat and cleric Mawlavi 'Abd al-Ra'uf (1851–1915), a reformist cleric who is credited with first suggesting the idea of *Siraj al-Akhbar* to King Habibullah.[16]

In 1911, 'Abd al-Ra'uf's groundbreaking essay on the meaning of literature appeared in the first issue of *Siraj al-Akhbar*. To understand 'Abd al-Ra'uf's importance as an endorser of Tarzi's ideas, we need to turn to his intellectual background.[17] His education was rooted in the traditional Islamic system which involved many years of study with a reputed master, leading to mastery of the Arabic and Persian languages, their theology and their literature. This traditional education is evident in the style of 'Abd al-Ra'uf's writing, from the vocabulary he used to the poets he referred to in support of his arguments. Structurally, the essay provided a chronological overview of the shifting definitions of the term *adabiyat* ("literature") in the history of Persian writing. Starting with the etymology of the term *adabiyat* (from the Arabic verb *adaba*, which meant "knowing the limit of all things"), the essay explained that the word initially referred to Arabic philology and to the language of the Quran in particular. It then explained that, despite being rooted in Islamic theology and taught in traditional madrasa schools, the scope of *adabiyat* had widened over time to include the rules that governed the crafting of classical Persian prose and poetry alike.

This display of mastery of traditional literature served to endorse two radical new arguments. Firstly, that the definition of literature had always been subject to change in the course of history and secondly, that its interpretation was ultimately open to each individual. To illustrate the validity of these arguments, 'Abd al-Ra'uf quoted classical Persian poets such as Hafiz and Sa'di to show that each poet offered a different interpretation of *adabiyat*. Having thus established that change and flexibility had always existed in even the most canonical definitions of Persian literature, 'Abd al-Ra'uf then explained that the contemporary definition of the term was now being formulated by a new class of professionals, namely the *ruznamachi negaran* or "newspaper writers" of Egypt and the Ottoman Empire. By contrast to the traditional definition of literature, the new definition that appeared in the first issue of *Siraj al-Akhbar* encompassed everything that engaged the intellect, from theology and philosophy to the scientific writings of contemporary European scholars. Having so widened the scope of *adabiyat*, 'Abd al-Ra'uf then defined literature as the totality of collective human knowledge. This was a radical proposition implying that literature had an international as much as national remit. In this new definition of literature, 'Abd al-Ra'uf discarded geographic, disciplinary and linguistic boundaries, allowing for everything that constitutes knowledge to be regarded as literature. Not only internationalizing, his definition of literature was also individualizing, as seen in his declaration that "everyone has their own understanding and definition of literature".[18] Such statements by a traditionally-educated member of the *'ulama* gave Tarzi a much needed intellectual framework for his choices of literature printed in *Siraj al-Akhbar* and, in turn, licence to publish essays on scientific innovations in Europe, poems about coal lumps or zincography, and translations of French novels and German verse. All of these were unfamiliar and hitherto unknown in Afghanistan.

The new theoretical conception of Afghan literature was, in this way, formulated through a radically universalist approach. Its core assumption was that literature was not delimited by geographic, linguistic or even disciplinary boundaries and so could be equally appreciated by an Afghan in Kabul and a Frenchman in Paris. Drawing inspiration from European novels as much as Middle Eastern journalism, Tarzi opened Afghan literature to international influences in order to encourage Afghan readers to engage with transnational trends in the cause of their own national progress. Here again we see the paradox of modern Afghan literature as a literature that is simultaneously national and international, a paradox first seen in the pages of *Siraj al-Akhbar* in the early twentieth century.

MODERNIZING, NATIONALIZING, INTERNATIONALIZING

Exactly how Afghan readers received the new literature published in *Siraj al-Akhbar* can be deduced from readers' letters that were published in the newspaper and responses to them in Tarzi's own editorials and essays. His preference for European literature must have been already known before the newspaper was even launched, because in its first issue he responded pre-emptively to concerns that the newspaper might not publish any literature produced in *sharq*, "the East". Clearly Tarzi already felt the need to reassure potential readers that the newspaper's provision of literature would be balanced:

We are free in our uses of the world of literature and so we will bring to the fore and discuss both Eastern and Western literatures, by which we mean contents that are the result of the imagination of Asian poets and literati and the fantasies of European poets and literati.[19]

In spite of this reassurance, Tarzi's preference for European literature was already evident in the choice of the first poem and prose published in *Siraj al-Akhbar*, both of which were of European origin. The first poem published in the newspaper was a Persian translation of a German love poem, though Tarzi gave no indication of either the poet's name or the poem's title, simply referring to it as "a Persian translation of a poem by a German of delicate sensitivity". The poem was, however, strikingly light-hearted, playfully describing how men of different occupations might use the language specific to their profession to declare their love to the women they desire.

> If he were the captain of a ship, he would say:
> "When faced with all kinds of storms and disasters,
> It is in your gentle embrace,
> That I find, shoulder to shoulder, the shore of happiness".
> If he were a vendor of wine, he would say:
> "Just how long will you refuse to fill my cup of life,
> So that it spills over and you become mine".[20]

The poem was in fact a neat illustration of 'Abd al-Ra'uf's argument that literature was universal and not tied to specific cultures. After all, Persian poetry had numerous parallel examples of this type of love poetry in which the German poet skilfully played with words, showing his mastery of language while musing on the theme of love. We can assume that the choice of the poem was quite deliberate, since it focused on the familiar theme and genre of the love lyric. At the same time, we can surmise that the poem also resonated with Tarzi personally because in his travel diary we encounter numerous anecdotes of him flirting with the beautiful young women he met on board the ships that carried him between Syria and Istanbul.[21] Tarzi recorded how these women commented on the poetic turns of phrase he skilfully used in his love conquests. Once again, the personal and professional were intertwined in his literary life.

In the first issue of *Siraj al-Akhbar*, the German poem was followed by entertaining anecdotes about such European political giants as the French revolutionary and orator, Comte de Mirabeau (1749–91); Napoleon Bonaparte (1769–1821); and the British prime minister, Lord Palmerston (1784–1865), who famously termed the Ottoman Empire "the sick man of Europe". The anecdotes were light-hearted examples of European wit that dealt with such universal themes as beauty, vanity and the quest for fame.

Fig. 6: Afghan News, International Style: Mahmud Tarzi discusses his Newspaper.

Like the German poem, these transnational literary imports were nineteenth-century European equivalents to the Persian *nuqta*, a popular genre of witty anecdote. In this way, Tarzi in all likelihood chose both the poem and the anecdotes because their themes and format were already familiar to Afghans, offering a gentle introduction to a foreign literature that might otherwise have been rejected outright for being incomprehensible and strange.

Despite this easy introduction to European literature, we have evidence in *Siraj al-Akhbar* that Afghans did indeed find the newspaper's contents hard to follow. This was not only because of its unfamiliar contents, but also because it was published in typographical print rather than the flowing calligraphic hands they were used to.[22] It is hard to verify whether such complaints were an excuse for not wanting to engage with the newspaper or whether they reflected real concerns, though it would be true to say that any of the printed Persian texts that Afghans would have accessed from India or Iran would have been printed in calligraphic lithography rather than in sharper (and often smaller) typography. Whatever the fact of the matter, Tarzi was dismissive of the complaints, because he expected his readers to make an effort in their reading. One of the letters published in *Siraj al-Akhbar* was a response to such complaints of the newspaper's incomprehensibility:

What can be done if people see words printed in a new fashion and assume that what they see is English or Arabic and hence become so frightened that they fail to muster the courage to read in their own Farsi language? People just have to make sure that their eyes become used to typography, so that reading in typographical print becomes normal to them.[23]

The fact that this letter from a reader was signed with only initials rather than a full name suggests that it was in fact written by Tarzi himself, who used its anonymity to openly criticize his readers without the risk of antagonizing them.

As already mentioned, Tarzi's key criticism of traditional Afghan literature was that it encouraged readers to fantasize and daydream rather than to think. He thought that modern literature, by contrast, demanded discipline and intellectual effort as it dealt with the problems of the real world. He included science fiction in this category of intellectually demanding literature, because even though the genre was fantastical, it was nonetheless useful in explaining science and technology through the accessible form of a story. Given that people's literary tastes do not change overnight, it seems reasonable to suggest that, contrary to his hopes, it was the strange and wondrous subjects of his translated science fiction novels that attracted Afghan readers more than their edifying explanations of technology. After all, the stories that featured in such novels had little in common with life in Afghanistan of the 1910s and were, therefore, a kind of fantasy for Afghans.

We can assume that as their translator and promoter, Tarzi was himself an admirer of such science fiction novels. Though he rationalized his taste for European literature in a theory that such literature responded to the demands of the time, his critics had their own interpretation of what made him admire European literature. Their interpretation, which can be deduced from Tarzi's own reactions to their comments, was that he preferred European literature and modern poetry because he was ignorant of the classics of Persian literature. The fact that he had spent nearly two decades of his life faraway from Afghanistan in the Ottoman Empire supported this criticism. His preference for European literature was in itself beyond dispute, given that he translated four French novels and facilitated their publishing in Afghanistan through the 'Inayat Press in Kabul. As for preferring modern poetry, in *Siraj al-Akhbar* he rarely printed poems with traditional themes. But if, in his critics' view, ignorance of traditional Afghan literature was the reason why he openly attacked Afghan literature and praised European alternatives, the reasons that Tarzi himself gave for his choices were political and ideological. His political vision for Afghanistan had been shaped through his embracing of the Pan-Islamism that in the last years of his exile had become part of Ottoman state policy. This ideology advocated the embrace of European scientific, technological and literary inventions but strictly within the confines of an Islamic code of morality and identity.[24] Tarzi's pursuit of this ideology created animosity with his opponents, who tried to stop the publication of *Siraj al-Akhbar*. These high stakes suggest the seriousness with which he regarded his mission to reject traditional literature as obsolete and dangerous.

Tarzi was quick to respond to this criticism of being enamoured with European literature and unlearned in Afghan literature in two ways. One element of his response was to draw on his own family's literary pedigree as evidence of his rootedness in Dari-Persian culture. In an obituary of his father, Sardar Muhammad Khan Tarzi, he wrote that his father was a distinguished poet who had mastered every genre of classical Persian poetry from the *ghazal* to the *qasida* and *masnavi*. More importantly, he credited his father with having created a new *tarz* or "style" of poetry, an innovation of such significance that it became his father's (and in turn his own) *takhal-*

lus or "pen-name" as Tarzi. Portraying himself as the son of a man who was both a literary traditionalist and incipient modernizer, Tarzi wrote in the obituary of Sardar Muhammad Khan that,

This humble scribe, who is the youngest son [of Sardar Muhammad Khan], heard him say with his own tongue that he had chosen that penname because he had taken on a new style of poetry.[25]

The article then expanded on the family's wider involvement in the literary and publishing world, from Tarzi's calligrapher brother transcribing his father's poems to his cousin facilitating their printing in Karachi. Elsewhere in *Siraj al-Akhbar*, Tarzi wrote about himself that "this unassuming scribe is a poet by nature and prides himself of being born to a poet and counts himself among those who respect and appreciate poetry".[26] It was as a gesture of respect and appreciation of this literary pedigree that in his own writings he adopted his father's poetic pen-name in preference to his aristocratic family name.

The other major element of Tarzi's response to the linked accusations of his "foreignness" and ignorance of classical poetry was to insist that he was a patriotic Afghan whose love of his country had made him return to Kabul from Damascus. To further these credentials, he regularly published his own patriotic poems dedicated to Afghanistan in *Siraj al-Akhbar*. In a preface to one such poem, *For the Love of the Homeland*, he explained that some of his contemporaries thought he was insane to voluntarily return from Damascus to Kabul, given the sharp contrast between Afghanistan's poverty and underdevelopment and the Ottoman Empire's wealth and technological advances. In the poem, in which the homeland is the beloved and Tarzi the lover, he wrote at length about the pain of exile that motivated him to return to Afghanistan, so linking the new poetry to the love of the nation, even as that love was expressed through the pain of international exile and travel:

> The wounds of departure and separation from you,
> Burned for many years your lover's heart and soul.[27]

In the travel diary that he wrote when he was twenty-six years old, Tarzi drew a picture of himself as a young man who was intellectually, linguistically and culturally at ease in the cosmopolitan cities of Istanbul and Alexandria. But at the same time, when he wrote in the diary about his inner emotional life, he described himself as a sensitive young man who had strong emotional attachment with Afghanistan, a country from which he had been exiled as a teenager. We can presume that these two sides of Tarzi's personality were equally real, but that in exile he kept his Afghan self private. Alternatively, it is quite possible that Tarzi felt more Afghan over time and that his identification with Afghanistan intensified with his father's death in 1901. What is certainly clear from his work is that nationalistic patriotism was a recurrent theme in the articles and poems he published in *Siraj al-Akhbar*. In the context of the debates over his Afghanness, they served as evidence for his love for and his rootedness in Afghanistan despite the many years he had spent abroad.

A Simplified Persian Prose

Through his state-sanctioned organ of *Siraj al-Akhbar*, Tarzi's attempt to modernize Afghan literature included the introduction of a new way of writing prose. Prioritizing the functionality of language as a tool of communication over the aesthetic considerations of eloquence and style, his approach was consistent with his political agenda of Afghan nationalism, because mass participation in the nationalist ideology he promoted in the newspaper was key to its success. By simplifying the newspaper's prose style, he aimed to reach as many readers as possible with his writings. It was with this aim in mind that he wrote his *Siraj al-Akhbar* pieces, crafting a deliberately easy-to-follow style. This simplified style of writing was one of the chief components of his literary modernization project. He purposely avoided the traditional writing style used by contemporary court bureaucrats and literati, a style characterized by deliberately complicated prose filled with metaphors, allusions and Arabic terminology that could only be understood by the highly educated. Produced and received by the same small circle of bureaucrats and literati, the purpose of such traditional prose was to show off the author as an *érudit*, with the result that it was never able to reach a wide circle of readers.

To understand the full implications of the new purpose Tarzi lent to prose as a means of mass communication, we should bear in mind that, during his lifetime in Afghanistan, the number of literate Afghans was exceedingly small and that illiteracy was common among both ordinary Afghans and members of the ruling elite. Writing was the monopoly of two small groups of professionals, the first being the clergy class, whose education allowed them to work as scribes, teachers, lawyers, court chroniclers and literati, and the second being the returnee former exiles who had received an education in either British India or the Ottoman Empire (and perhaps Czarist Central Asia). The fact that members of the ruling dynasty were themselves often illiterate might appear extraordinary, but as Tarzi himself pointed out in an essay, Afghanistan's ruling class had historically relied on martial rather than intellectual skills to acquire and rule over their territories.

Since the Afghan people were mostly preoccupied with wars and military conquests, they had little time for matters of administration that required writing skills. If anything, they regarded the writer's occupation as below their social standing and even looked down on the men of writing, as evidenced by such phrases as, "He's just a little writer" or "He's just a little mullah".[28]

In Tarzi's time, the ability to read and write was only just beginning to be regarded as a valuable skill in Afghanistan, a new recognition that saw the launch of the first state schools. An avid supporter of mass literacy and public education, Tarzi printed lengthy essays about the necessity and merits of mass education. To further encourage King Habibullah's education drive, in the 1910s Tarzi even resorted to writing panegyric poems on the subject, lavishing praise on the king every time he opened a school or showed interest in facilitating the education of his people.

Here and elsewhere, Tarzi wrote easy-to-follow poems and prose that drew on the familiar vocabulary of everyday spoken language, a simplified style of writing that was consistent with his politics of mass Afghan nationalism. If the court literati and bureaucrats wrote for the benefit of an exclusive club of appreciative peers, Tarzi tried to write for everyone. This even included housewives and children, as illustrated by his pieces about child care in his *Siraj al-Atfal*, a children's newspaper that was also read by adults and of which Tarzi was also the editor. To illustrate the extent to which his style differed from his contemporaries, we can turn to a comparison of passages from articles on literature by Tarzi and Mawlavi ʿAbd al-Raʾuf, who we saw earlier writing about the shifting meanings of the term *adabiyat* ("literature"). According to Tarzi,

Telling tales and listening to stories is a natural instinct of mankind. From the early days of childhood, one's ears get used to hearing stories, so much so that most people can't fall asleep unless they first listen to a story.[29]

By contrast, Mawlavi ʿAbd al-Raʾuf asked in more convoluted terms,

What is literature? This concise question resembles a mulberry seed that triggers the growth of a tall and able-bodied tree. Furthermore, it is like the iris of the eye, at once containing the earth and sky… And it can also be said that the majority of the world's knowledgeable people understand the term *adab* and the term *adabiyat* to mean the 'etiquette' of personal conduct at royal gatherings and other occasions, as well as the etiquette of living with those superior to oneself and co-existing with those subordinate to oneself. For some, it is expressed as "such and such is a *mu'adab* ('polite person') and knows *adab* ('etiquette')".[30]

The simplicity of Tarzi's vocabulary and sentences stood in sharp contrast to the convoluted eloquence of 'Abd al-Ra'uf's writing, even though the latter passage is taken from an essay that endorsed Tarzi's approach to literature. Yet Tarzi's simplification of prose writing was anything but straightforward. While he simplified vocabulary and shortened sentences, he also introduced a new layer of complexity by making heavy use of Persian adaptations of English and French terminology. In his columns and commentaries, readers thus encountered unfamiliar and sometimes difficult to pronounce loanwords such as "gymnastics", "zincography", "rail", "motor", "novel" or its French rendition, "*roman*". Yet if such foreign borrowings point to the international dimensions of his project, then Tarzi's writings in *Siraj al-Akhbar* also point to his expressly national concerns by way of his keen interest in the domestic politics of language. This can be seen most clearly in the two essays he dedicated to the key paradox of Afghan language politics: the fact that even though the ruling dynasty was ethnically Pashtun, the official language of the state and administration was Persian.

Tarzi explained that the roots of this linguistic paradox were to be found at the time of the Afghan state's inception. In an essay entitled *Language and its Importance*, he wrote:

> The official language (*zaban-e rasmi dawlati*) of the sacred state of Afghanistan is Persian, while its national language (*zaban-e milli*) is Afghani [i.e. Pashto]. Persian became the official language of our state because prior to the establishment of the sacred state of Afghanistan, and prior to our becoming independent and gaining our national sovereignty, the pure soil of our sacred homeland was part of the Iranian realm… When His Majesty Ghazi Ahmad Shah Baba [r.1747–72] succeeded in establishing the Afghan sultanate, matters relating to administration and bureaucracy (including the writing and reading aloud of the state decrees that were the fundaments of government) were conducted in the Persian language and carried out by Persian-speaking people of Iranian descent who were the leftovers of the previous Iranian rulers. The Afghani [i.e. Pashto] language had not been reformed to a sufficient extent as to allow it to be used for the purposes of government administration… Equally, the books that were available on science and literature were either in Persian or Arabic, leaving Afghani [i.e. Pashto] deprived of all these developments.[31]

MODERNIZING, NATIONALIZING, INTERNATIONALIZING

Having in this way explained the historical origins of Afghanistan's political linguistic paradox, Tarzi then elaborated on the complex present reality of Afghanistan as a multilingual and multi-ethnic nation. He pointed out that "the people who have Persian as their mother-tongue are an essential part of our nation", adding that even though, from the Sadozai to the Muhammadzai, the Afghan ruling dynasties were ethnically Pashtun, they too were Persian speakers.[32] Such considerations led him to conclude that "no one can demand that Pashto replace Persian as the state language of Afghanistan".[33]

In his analysis of Afghanistan's linguistic paradox, Tarzi also argued that Persian had the added transnational advantage of being understood outside of Afghanistan in Iran, India, Central Asia and even the Ottoman realms. He had gained this insight through his own life experience, by meeting Ottoman officials who were fluent in Persian. In his travel diary, we have evidence that while Persian was his chosen written language, Pashto was the language of intimacy that he used when speaking with his father, particularly when they did not want to be understood by others. Even as late as in 1891, it was still possible to meet Ottoman officials who were fluent in Persian.[34] In the multilingual cities of the Ottoman Empire, where the educated norm was a command of the key languages of Asia and Europe (including Turkish, Arabic, Persian and French), Pashto was just about the only Islamic language not understood outside the Afghan exile community. Tarzi was therefore aware at a personal no less than political level that the balance of linguistic power was heavily in favour of Persian, and in his essay he pointed out that Persian was the eastern equivalent of French as a lingua franca of international diplomacy.[35] In this way, Tarzi gained his awareness of the political importance of Persian both inside and outside Afghanistan.

Yet despite his support for Persian, his 1915 essay then took a surprising turn, laying out a new set of arguments, this time in support of Pashto. Linking literature to language and the state, his arguments were rooted in the ideology of Afghan nationalism:

We are called the nation of Afghans and our country is called Afghanistan and we possess plenty of morals and habits that are particular only to us. We also possess a language called Afghani [i.e. Pashto] that is particular to us. We must protect our language as though it were our soul. We must make serious efforts to reform and develop it. To learn this language of the homeland is the duty of all of the different peoples who make up the Afghan nation, not only those who speak the language as their mother tongue. In our schools, the most important subject of study should be the teaching of this [Pashto] language. Its teaching should be given greater importance than English, Urdu, Turkish and even Persian.[36]

As throughout his literary career, Tarzi then called on the resources of the state by way of the Afghan High Council of Education, demanding that they prepare school textbooks in Pashto. Linking Pashto to modernization in the same way he had with the loanwords he introduced to Dari-Persian, he asked the council to ensure the incorporation of words describing new scientific and technological inventions by creating Pashto translations of European terms. But despite this passionate defence of Pashto, the contents of *Siraj al-Akhbar* remained almost exclusively in Dari-Persian.

There was arguably a practical—and again, transnational—dimension to this. We have seen that Tarzi was aware of Persian's importance as a lingua franca through which his newspaper could reach not only Afghan readers, but also readers in India, Iran, Central Asia and the Ottoman Empire. We also have evidence in *Siraj al-Akhbar* that the readers who responded to its contents mostly resided abroad and their letters show that many of them understood Persian but could not write in it. This broader readership was the key political consideration that made Tarzi publish *Siraj al-Akhbar* almost exclusively in Persian. That the newspaper was popular (perhaps even more popular) outside than inside Afghanistan is seen in the fact that both the Russian and the British Indian governments at times attempted to ban the newspaper, regarding its politics as dangerous to their interests. As expressed in editorials, poems and articles that were profoundly anti-colonialist, the newspaper's political line, after all, was to call for Muslim independence and, at times, for a collective Muslim struggle against the Russian and British attempts at colonizing Muslim territory. In particular, the publication of photographs and pieces exposing Muslim maltreatment at the hands of Europeans triggered bans in India and Russia. But such antagonism was not only restricted to the European powers who were concerned about the newspaper's impact on the Muslims under their rule. *Siraj al-Akhbar* had its fair share of enemies in court circles at home in Afghanistan. Although nominally an independent state, King Habibullah's court received subsidies from the British Indian government for limiting foreign influence and representation in Afghanistan to the British. In return for these subsidies, the king ensured that no other European power (the Russian Empire in particular) had outposts and influence in Afghanistan. Given its anti-British stance, *Siraj al-Akhbar* thus risked antagonizing the British Indian government, even to the point of cutting off their subsidies to the court or launching a military invasion, especially in the fraught years of the First World War. Given the risks involved, it was natural that the pro-British camp in the Afghan court was hostile to the newspaper. We get a sense of the sheer intensity of this animosity from an editorial that launched the first issue of *Siraj al-Akhbar* in the new style of typographic print. In this editorial, Tarzi alluded to his critics as:

> those who have no love for their country and no pride in their homeland. That is because such individuals never accept anything that is created in the homeland and only think about their own personal interests. And so of course they will not accept the homeland's newspaper and will reject it. They even think that this newspaper is harmful and useless and hope that it would vanish altogether.[37]

The personal interests that Tarzi mentioned were a veiled reference to the British subsidies which, after all, ensured the survival of the court in Kabul. By printing anti-British articles, he jeopardized the source of income of those courtiers who did not share his political views which is why they tried to sabotage the newspaper. The newspaper's survival ultimately owed itself to Amir Habibullah's support. Recognizing the newspaper's dependence on royal backing, in the above quoted editorial Tarzi showered the king with praise and then printed a piece thoroughly detailing the newspaper's services to the king in its first year of publication. The services included printing reports about the king's modernization projects, which *Siraj al-Akhbar* meticulously followed, and documenting every single modernization project with words and pictures, from dams to bridges, new schools and vaccination drives. Judging by the detailed listing of the newspaper's columns that reflected positively on King Habibullah, it becomes evident that the threat to the newspaper was real and Tarzi's desire to maintain the king's support correspondingly intense.

As we have outlined earlier, the animosity with which the newspaper was received by some Afghan court circles had little to do with Tarzi's simplification of language, his support for Pashto or his taste for European literature. It was his anti-British politics which alarmed the group of '*ulama* and courtiers who supported Habibullah's pro-British policies for which the court in Kabul was paid with subsidies. Since the king's support was crucial to the newspaper's survival, his politics also threatened the survival of his own newspaper, undermining his own literary modernization efforts. The result of this conflict of interest between his nationalist politics and his dependence on royal protection was inconsistency in his style of writing. This inconsistency is illustrated in the first issue of the second year of the newspaper's publication, where to praise the king, Tarzi resorted to the convoluted style of eulogy associated with traditional court bureaucrats rather than writing in his own simple style of prose:

> Under the shadow of his majesty, who is adorned with the pearls of knowledge, known as the Torch of the Nation and the Faith, the Sovereign King of the supreme and independent state of Afghanistan, amir son of an amir son of an amir, King Habibullah (may Allah sustain his kingdom until the end of the world!), the typographical printing press of the Kingdom of Afghanistan has succeeded in printing this respected newspaper (the first issue of the second year) in that supreme printing press in a beautiful, glorious and delicately decorated manner.[38]

This brief resumption of the traditional style of eulogy paradoxically served to celebrate the introduction to Afghanistan of the newest technology of typographic print. That the celebration of the most advanced printing technology to Afghanistan had to be expressed in the most old-fashioned style revealed the delicate situation in which Tarzi found himself. The short eulogy contained the core dilemma that he faced as an editor: the fact that in order to succeed in his modernization campaign through his newspaper he relied on royal backing and the added factor that to sustain the support, he sometimes had to compromise, abandoning his own style of writing to print eulogies of a style that he detested because the style represented everything that in his view was wrong about traditional Afghan writing.

Nonetheless, even though such effusive eulogies were sometimes printed in *Siraj al-Akhbar*, the newspaper's overall language remained remarkably simple, particularly if judged against the standards of his time. Overall, through *Siraj al-Akhbar*, Tarzi succeeded in single-handedly modernizing prose writing in Afghanistan. The newspapers that followed *Siraj al-Akhbar* from the 1930s onwards, from *Anis* to *Etefaq-e Islam*, were all written in the prose style first introduced by Tarzi in 1911.

The Introduction of the Novel

Tarzi was a vigorous advocate and importer to Afghanistan of the European genre of the novel. In his view, the novel was the literary genre best-suited to respond to the moral and intellectual demands of the time, demands that required the awakening of Afghans to the reality of their underdevelopment in an age of rapid European technological advancement. Tarzi believed it was the purpose of literature to jolt Afghans into action to respond to this reality. To understand the contrast of their underdevelopment with Europe's advancements, Afghans needed to become aware of life outside of their isolated kingdom. But given that gaining a first-hand experience of life in Europe was impossible for a great majority of Afghans, he thought the novel could replace the physical journey to Europe by taking readers on an imaginary tour of Europe. In terms of usefulness for moral and general edification, he singled out two types of novels. Firstly, he advocated science fiction novels which he termed "technical novels". Tarzi thought that despite their fantastical content, science fiction books were useful because they familiarized readers with science and technology. Secondly, he advocated the genre of socially critical novels which dealt with poverty, unemployment, crime and political conflict in Europe.[39] Under his influence, Afghan poets such as 'Abd al-Hadi Dawi (1896–1983) started the trend of writing socially critical poetry though, like Tarzi himself, Dawi would later join forces with the state and serve as a diplomat and minister.

If the purpose of science fiction was to inform readers about technology and science, the socially critical novels fulfilled the aim of providing readers with a political education. A supporter of modernist Islam, Tarzi wanted Afghan readers to believe that unless progress was accompanied by an Islamic code of morality, its consequence would be the kind of economic inequality and social deprivation that had triggered the French revolution in Europe. The socially critical novel, then, served to underline his own modernist Pan-Islamist ideology. In the introductory piece to his translation of Xavier de Montépin's popular French novel, *Les Viveurs de Paris*, he unambiguously explained his thoughts about the political purpose of reading this novel. He said that the aim of serializing the translated novel was to "introduce our readers to the contemporary forms of storytelling (*afsana-goyi*) and to inform our readers about the strange and wondrous conditions of developed European countries and the bloody crimes and oppressions that occur there, so that readers become aware what kind of terror is dressed up in the guise of civilization".[40]

The quotation above illustrates Tarzi's approach to literature as a tool of political awakening as much as a means of entertainment and education. Ironically and perhaps unbeknownst to Tarzi, Xavier de Montépin was famous in his own homeland of France as the author of popular but frivolous stories of little literary merit. Hence, the publication in 1856 of de Montépin's particularly controversial novel, *Les Filles de Platre* ("Platre's Daughters"), led to a scandal for which de Montépin was sentenced to three months of imprisonment. But arriving in Afghanistan via Turkish and then

Dari-Persian translation, and after a time-lag of around six decades, the work of the controversial French author of frivolous stories was introduced to Afghan readers as an illustration of the moralizing power of the European novel. More crucially, the paragraph quoted above shows that Tarzi did not allow readers the freedom to interpret de Montépin for themselves. Instead he provided readers with an interpretative guide, directing them on what lessons to draw from reading the novel. His political use of literature is illustrated in this introduction.

Tarzi's views on the novel also appeared in essays, readers' letters and advertisements throughout *Siraj al-Akhbar*'s publication years. He was aware that the novel was an unfamiliar genre in Afghanistan and that its foreignness could discourage readers from engaging with it. In the first issue of *Siraj al-Akhbar*, he wrote a short instructional article entitled 'About the Novel' to introduce his readers to the genre, clarifying the novel's purpose and merits. His key two arguments both appear in this introduction: firstly, that literature represents a universal human urge for creativity, and secondly, that the outward form of this creativity changes over time. To emphasize literature's universality, he deliberately used the Persian term *afsana* or "fairy tale" interchangeably with the borrowed English term "novel" and its French equivalent, "*roman*".

In recent times, just as everything else has undergone change and transformation, stories have also taken on such a new shape that they do not at all resemble our own old and antiquated fairy tales. These fairy tales of our time are called "*romans*" in France and the Ottoman Realms while in England and India, they are known as "novels". In our time, novels are considered the most important works of written literature.[41]

Tarzi clearly admired the European literature and his promotion of the novel went beyond serializing a French novel in his newspaper. He succeeded in encouraging King Habibullah's son, Prince 'Inayatullah, to set up a private printing press, through which he subsequently printed his translations of three Jules Verne novels as well as his own literary works. Judging by pieces published in *Siraj al-Akhbar*, Tarzi had an optimistic view of the future of publishing in Afghanistan and believed that many more printing presses would be set up following Prince 'Inayatullah's example. The novels published by 'Inayat Press were regularly advertised in *Siraj al-Akhbar* and their content summed up Tarzi's views on the novel. An advertisement in the newspaper for Jules Verne's *Around the World in Eighty Days*, for example, read:

What a useful and sweet read, especially given the journey's length and width. Those who wish to go on this same journey just have to pay the small sum of two rupees to re-live the journey of the traveller, Phileas Fogg… The book is not only a novel but also teaches geography and geographical mathematics in the guise of an imagined story.[42]

In Tarzi's view, it was this combining of entertainment and useful information that made the novel the genre best suited for the demands of the century. But if Tarzi exalted the European novel, his views on traditional Afghan literature revealed contempt for the home-grown. He believed that the novel's equivalents in Afghan literature—for example, the popular *Arabian Nights* tales, or the equally famous classical Persian tale, *Pari-ye Surkh* ("The Crimson Fairy")—had not only become irrelevant and outdated but also were dangerous and damaging to the morality of readers. In a letter published in *Siraj al-Akhbar* entitled "How to Read a Novel", we encounter the following strong condemnation of traditional Afghan literature:

The novels of the old literature are based on nonsensical beliefs that have been proven wrong. Far from serving a positive purpose, they are completely damaging to the morality of readers.[43]

Even though this categorical rejection of traditional storytelling is presented in the guise of a reader's letter, in all likelihood the letter's author was in fact Tarzi himself. There are three reasons that underline the plausibility of this hypothesis. Firstly, the readers' letters published in *Siraj al-Akhbar* were almost exclusively by individuals who lived outside of Afghanistan, often either Afghans in exile or non-Afghans. Such letters allowed people in faraway places to communicate with the newspaper despite geographical distance. Secondly, we have evidence in *Siraj al-Akhbar* that the newspaper's small circle of Afghan readers tended to talk to him in person rather than send him letters. This was made possible because the editor and his readers were all part of the same circle of educated elite courtiers that met regularly, particularly during state ceremonies. Thirdly, the letter's content clearly reflected Tarzi's own taste and take on literature. Writing disguised as an anonymous reader enabled him to openly publicize his rejection of traditional Afghan literature without the risk of upsetting his more traditional readers.

The letter also provides insight into how Afghan readers reacted to the novel. For example, we can deduce from the letter that Afghan readers had difficulty understanding the concept, structure and content of novels because all three were alien to them. The novel's narrative structure was completely different from the structure of traditional fairy tales. Structurally, the fairy tales were divided into self-contained sections, enabling readers to open a book at any random chapter and still make sense of the story. The novel's structure, by contrast, was linear and this meant that to make sense of the story, readers had to read the novel from the start to the end. Only through concentrated page by page reading of the novel was it possible to make sense of the novel's plot, its protagonists and the moral of the story, which would be revealed as the novel progressed. The letter described what happened when Afghans unfamiliar with the genre tried to read a novel: "They open chapter five of the book, and after reading one or two lines, suddenly their eyes are overcome by tiredness because instead of finding the start of a new story, they are in fact finding themselves in the middle of the story".[44]

By contrast to the novel, in traditional storytelling the theme and the plot were explained at the beginning of each self-contained chapter, informing readers about what to expect in the story. The concept, the structure and the idea of the novel and traditional fairy tales were radically different from what Afghan readers were familiar with in their own literature. We also gather from the letter that Afghan readers grappled too with the unfamiliar French names that appeared in novels translated by Tarzi:

In addition, they see some strange and peculiar names that they had never heard before. Hence they are left confused and think, "What sort of story is this? It's difficult to comprehend because it's not clear where it starts and where it ends". Saying this, they put the book back in its place. It's not their fault because since childhood, they have learned reading by familiarizing their eyes with stories told in the antiquated style.[45]

In Tarzi's view, reading was a matter of habit and he believed that people had the capacity to abandon old reading habits and acquire new ones instead. Dismissing complaints about the difficulty of reading novels, he soldiered on, continuing the serialization of the French novel he had chosen for *Siraj al-Akhbar* and regularly advertising the science fiction books of Jules Verne that he had translated into Dari-Persian.

The Call for a New Poetry

We have already established that Tarzi took pride in his family's literary pedigree to the extent that he chose to adopt his father's poetic pen-name,

Tarzi, instead of using his family's tribal name. We also mentioned that his father had chosen this pen-name to claim credit for creating a new "style" or *tarz* of poetry. Tarzi's adoption of his father's pen-name was therefore symbolic, publically representing his identification with new and innovative poetry. In practical terms, his innovative approach to poetry amounted to writing and publishing poems about the new themes of global politics and scientific and technological discoveries and innovations. The inclusion of such scientific and current affairs themes in the repertoires of poetry was consistent with his view that literature had to be relevant to the demands of the time.

Tarzi explained his theory of poetry in various pieces published in *Siraj al-Akhbar*. We can deduce from the content of such articles that his critics assumed that he did not understand and hence appreciate classical Persian poetry, and it was this lack of appreciation that led him to prefer modern poetry to its classical Persian counterpart. He was aware of this perception and responded to it by establishing that he was rooted in classical Persian poetry by flesh and blood as much as by education. He clearly felt pressured to publically acknowledge his appreciation of classical poetry:

In our beloved nation there have existed and still exist plenty of accomplished poets. We praise the ones of the past and greet them from the bottom of our hearts and we pray for those who are still with us.[46]

The quotation is part of a column in which Tarzi proudly announced that he had managed to persuade a notable poet of his time, 'Abd al-'Ali Khan Mostaghni of Wardak (d.1933), to stray from the traditional pleasant themes of love and beauty to instead craft a poem about gymnastics. Mostaghni belonged to a group of poets influenced by Tarzi's idea of a new school of poetry. Known as the *shu'ara ye-mutajaddid* ("innovative poets"), members of this group not only experimented with new themes but also wrote poetry in their local dialects, including the Hazaragi dialect of central Afghanistan.[47] In spite of his public acknowledgement of his respect for classical poetry in this statement, the poems published in *Siraj al-Akhbar* revealed an exclusive taste for the new themes of the early twentieth century. The only traditional poem that appeared in *Siraj al-Akhbar* was one by his own father, Sardar Ghulam Muhammad Tarzi, published as part of his father's obituary. From the fourth year of the newspaper's publication in 1914, Tarzi also began occasionally to print poems in Pashto and we have evidence that the neglect of Pashto beforehand was linked to a lack of

Fig. 7: The Founding Father's Father: Ghulam Muhammad Tarzi.

appropriate technology. For in a poem entitled *Ghazal-e Afghani Mafz-e Huruf-e Afghani* ("A Pashto Poem without Pashto Letters"), it was suggested that the absence of Pashto was due to the lack of Pashto type for the printing press.[48] Even Pashto verse was, in this way, connected to the modern subject matter of printing machines.

To understand Tarzi's approach to the modernizing of poetry, it is crucial to bear in mind that his push for poetic innovation was limited to the thematic content of poems and did not touch such technical aspects as rhyming structure. The new themes of science, technology and global affairs that he introduced into the repertoire of Afghan poetry were all conveyed through established poetry formats, chiefly the classical genre of the *ghazal*. Again reflecting the paradox of a transnational literature of nationalism, we have evidence in *Siraj al-Akhbar* that the new technological and political themes had greater appeal to readers outside of Afghanistan, because it was they rather than Afghan poets who sent their Persian (and sometimes Urdu and Pashto) poems for publication in *Siraj al-Akhbar*.[49] We can assume that Afghan poets' reluctance to embrace political poetry in particular had to do with their unwillingness to antagonize King Habibullah, whose patronage was after all crucial to the financial survival of the literati.[50] Several literati executions and exiles in this period were also major disincentives.[51] Such political considerations aside, the rejection of the new themes suggested by Tarzi also had to do with the coarseness of the borrowed vocabulary that was attached to the new themes of politics and particularly technology. For, even though he was a nationalist and a skilled translator, for reasons that are unclear Tarzi chose not to translate the vocabulary of science and technology into Dari-Persian or even create Dari-Persian neologisms, but instead simply adopted foreign loanwords according to their English or French pronunciation. The wholesale adoption of such new words meant that not only did his new literary vocabulary sound strange and unfamiliar, but also that in belonging to a foreign phonological system the loanwords' syllabic structure was incompatible with the rules of Persian phonology and prosody. Most crucially, the new terminology lacked "balance" and rhyme with Persian and this, in turn, was seen as a crucial technical impediment to the widespread adoption of new themes outside of the pages of *Siraj al-Akhbar*.

Even so, Tarzi's promotion of a modern poetry based on international themes and loanwords was more than a private and self-indulgent project that no other Afghans shared. In a preface that introduced Mostaghni's poem about gymnastics, we learn that he was regularly in touch with the leading Afghan poets of the age and spent a considerable amount of time discussing with them his ideas about poetry. As a critic as well as publisher of the new poetry, in the pages of *Siraj al-Akhbar* Tarzi not only outlined a formal definition of poetry, but also expounded his views on the typical personality of the poet and on old versus new poetry. According to his definition, a poet is a person who is sensitive to the sounds, colours and shapes that he perceives around him—to the singing of birds, the colour of flowers, the sound of water flowing in a stream—and in response translates such impressions into poetry.[52] Perhaps more characteristically, elsewhere in *Siraj al-Akhbar*, he turned to metaphors of factory products and marketplaces to describe the process of the production and consumption of poetry:

The powerhouse of the imagination is the factory in which poetry is constructed. The foreman (imagination) uses the power of the machine (thinking). After twisting and turning it a thousand times, and after adorning and beautifying it, he churns out poems, throwing them into the jewellery markets of speech, one by one, in different shapes and colours.[53]

Such a mechanical view of poetry shows that Tarzi believed that literature was as much a product of craftsmanship as inspiration. He believed that poetry was comparable to other cultural (or even mechanical) products that were similarly the fruits of human creativity and craftsmanship. This was why he (in line with 'Abd al-Ra'uf) believed that poetry was not static but developed over time, becoming more refined with the passing of decades and centuries. This was a notably positivist and progressivist model of literature that reflected his wider concerns for national progress and for literature as its vanguard. Furthermore, he argued that since poetry was the poet's creative response to his environment, it was only natural that in the twentieth century the poet's repertoire should include such new subject matters as newspapers and coal, hot-air balloons and motor cars, which were, after all, part of the environment of the modern poet. But in spite of its logic, his argument failed to convince his critics in whose perception the new vocabulary of science and technology was too coarse and crude to merit inclusion in the repertoire of Persian poetry. His critics argued that, with its coarse sounds and crude syllabic structure, the new terminology could not fit the defining rhyme structures of Persian poetry. While Tarzi acknowledged this criticism, he believed that if the poets made sufficient effort, they would learn to craft poems that remained true to traditional formats but celebrated new themes and used new loanwords. When he succeeded in persuading Mostaghni, a famous poet of his time, to write a poem about gymnastics, he triumphantly published the poem in *Siraj al-Akhbar*, bestowing lavish praise on it by describing it as "a *ghazal* that is as sweet as honey".

But if Tarzi hoped that such praise and publication would encourage other poets to write about cars and railways, his hopes were largely in vain. Resistance to the new themes persisted, compelling him to write an article summing up his debates with his peers about the merits of new versus old poetry. The tone of the debate was fair and friendly, allowing both sides to express their views through the personification of Old and New Poetry:

Old Poetry: It is very curious that nothing of the poetry's delicacy and elegance can be found in you, New Poetry. With such coarse and crude words as "education" (*tahsil*) or "literacy" (*ma'arif*), or "gone and passed away" (*begozasht va raft*), or "homeland" (*vatan*), or "the merits of good manners" (*fayz-e khulq-e husn*), and worse of all "lumps of coal" (*zughal-e sang*), you have blackened your face and your very being. You are not only beyond recognition, but a dark stain on the pure robe of poetry.[54]

If this representation of their views is anything to judge by, it seems that Tarzi's critics refused to even recognize the poems he wrote as poetry. They took particular offence at his poem about coal, a coarse and dark material that was after all the opposite of the trees and flowers that were the recurrent themes of traditional poems. In the course of the debate, New Poetry defended itself against the accusations of the established Old Poetry, arguing that literature had no choice but to give in to the demands of the time. To this, Old Poetry responded again:

Old Poetry: What has time to do with this? A poem is always a poem: its subject matter is always the beauty of the beloved, love and caring. Time can never force you to pollute your pure ink, mixing it with the blackness of coal.

To this, New Poetry responded:

New Poetry: I am not talking about your time. I am talking about my time. This is a time and age in which everything has undergone utter and complete transformation and change (*taghirat va tabadulat*).[55]

Continuing to speak in the persona of New Poetry, Tarzi then argued that in their own time, no one had originally appreciated the traditional metaphors and themes of love poetry when poets first compared the elegant tallness of the beloved to a cypress tree or her lips to a rosebud about to blossom. What becomes clear in this rather rarefied literary debate is that Tarzi's perception of his time was shaped by an acute sense of change that he had experienced through spending the crucial years of his life exiled in the much more developed Ottoman Empire. His Afghan interlocutors, by contrast, had been spared this experience, with the result that their world remained limited to Afghanistan, where in the 1910s change was beginning only slowly and gradually. He felt that his experience of the world beyond Afghanistan's borders was a burden that he could not escape and voiced this through the persona of New Poetry:

New Poetry: You should be grateful a thousand times that unlike my unfortunate self, you have never put even a step into this age… where because of its usefulness, a book about coal mines is regarded as better and holier than a book that contains hundreds and thousands of verses about beauty, the kind of book that we [Afghans] unfortunates write.[56]

Tarzi ended the debate by making Old Poetry see the world through the eyes of New Poetry, acknowledging that because in the modern world practical usefulness was to be given priority over beauty, writers had no choice but to adopt new themes in their poetry. Having seen the world anew through the eyes of New Poetry, Old Poetry felt compassion for New Poetry and the dialogue ended with the hope that the Afghan people would open their eyes to Tarzi's wisdom and learn to distinguish truth from falsehood.

Conclusions

The previous pages have argued that, in the early twentieth century, the modernization of Afghan literature was chiefly the single-handed project of Mahmud Tarzi and, of course, the assistants who helped publish his newspaper. Not only was Tarzi the first person to successfully introduce modern journalism and newspaper-printing to Afghanistan, he also widened the repertoire of Afghan poetry by introducing such new twentieth-century themes as international politics and technological innovations. Connecting Afghan readers with literary developments far beyond their national borders, he also familiarized Afghan readers with the hitherto unknown European genre of the novel. His involvement in this ambitious modernization project went beyond editorial and literary questions. He encouraged the royal princes, 'Inayatullah and Amanullah, to become involved in the printing business, efforts which saw Prince 'Inayatullah set up the first privately-owned printing press in Afghanistan. It was on this press that Tarzi's translations of Jules Verne's French novels were printed, a moment that marked the first ever publications of novels on Afghan soil. For his part, Prince Amanullah attended the printing sessions of *Siraj al-Akhbar* and, after becoming Tarzi's son-in-law and then the ruler of Afghanistan in 1919, launched his own newspaper, *Aman-e Afghan*, as a successor to Tarzi's prototype. Whether through newspapers, imported or domestic novels, or political and "progressive" poetry, Mahmud Tarzi was to cast a long shadow over subsequent Afghan literature in the twentieth century.

It was also a shadow in the darker sense of foreshadowing the links between literature and state that were to both strangle and sustain Afghan writers for most of the twentieth century. If in the form of music and poetry culture had always been linked to the Afghan court in the form of entertainment, then through Tarzi's efforts the Afghan state became a major player in cultural life through the rendering of literature as ideology. Yet if such an analysis is to emphasize the role of the state, then this chapter has also sought to show that the individual and private life of Tarzi played a shaping role in the evolution of his ideas. His life experiences—his years in the Ottoman Empire especially—were deeply intertwined with his writings in *Siraj al-Akhbar* in the years after his return to Afghanistan. In this sense, in life as in art, he prefigured later developments in Afghanistan, for like other Afghan writers in his wake, Tarzi presents an example of a hybrid Afghan identity—in his case, a writer whose cultural tastes were shaped by the cosmopolitan environment of the Ottoman Empire. The paradox of modern Afghan literature as a literature that is simultaneously national and international was the result of the cosmopolitan tastes in culture that Tarzi as an individual writer introduced to Afghanistan through his professional and familial alliances with the Afghan state. In such ways, the transformation of his thoughts from private idea to public ideology required his alliance with a state whose collapse in 1929 would once again propel him into Turkish exile. This second time, it was an exile from which he was never to return. In 1933, Tarzi died in Istanbul, with his last poetic works on the tragedy of a second exile being published there under the anthologized title of *Zhulida* ("Dishevelled").[57] For all his efforts to forge a national literature that was both dedicated to and produced in Afghanistan, Tarzi's last literary efforts were both written and printed abroad.

Yet in terms of the sheer volume of writing and the diversity of themes and writing styles, no other Afghan writer has succeeded in matching Tarzi's productivity. Written during the crucial decades that saw the attempt to forge a modern state and society in Afghanistan, his body of work includes journalism; poetry and literary prose; school textbooks and historical essays; political and diplomatic writings; and translations of a pioneering series of novels. Given his productivity and impact, his contributions to Afghan literature are comparable to Johann Wolfgang von Goethe's services to German literature. It is no exaggeration to claim that Mahmud Tarzi was the founding figure of modern Afghan literature.

3

THE AFGHAN AFTERLIFE OF PHILEAS FOGG

SPACE AND TIME IN THE LITERATURE OF AFGHAN TRAVEL

Nile Green

Introduction

Among all of the forms of literature related to Afghanistan, the genre that is most revealing of Afghan interaction with the surrounding world is travel writing. For Afghanistan has a particularly close relationship with this genre, with few regions of the planet so thoroughly registered in the consciousness of the wider world through the literature of travel and exploration. While many regions of the globe first entered the European imagination through the travel writings produced in the European ages of "discovery" and colonization, Afghanistan is arguably unique in the continuity of this tradition from the nineteenth century through to the present day. While modernization has seen other regions of the world either fade out of the canon of travel or undergo literary reinventions in pace with their modernization, Afghanistan has not only maintained its attraction as a literary destination but also preserved the image formed in the imperial travelogues of the nineteenth century as a space of mountain emptiness and wild tribesmen.¹ From the pioneering writings of Sir Alexander 'Bokhara' Burnes in the 1830s through the sporty boundary marches of C.E. Yate in the 1880s to Eric Newby's jocular *Short Walk in the Hindu Kush* in the 1950s and Rory Stewart's less innocent walk through post-Taliban Afghanistan, a self-conscious tradition of British travel writing has formed from Afghanistan a kind of Central Asian Scotland whose wilder highlands provided a primitive literary space in whose emptiness it was possible to explore the limits of the British self.² Tinged with the romanticism and danger that from its renaissance origins through its nineteenth-century heyday have been such potent literary ingredients in the European travelogue, such representations of Afghan "wildness" were not unique to British writers and were similarly created by travellers from other regions of Europe.³

While in English it is Scottish writers such as Burnes and Stewart who have been among the most noted celebrants of the Afghan highlands, in mainland Europe it has been the Swiss who have been the most notable travel writers on Afghanistan. With its potent heritage of literary romanticism and political trauma, the Swiss literary sphere offers a particularly acute example of the creation from Afghanistan of a space of anti-modernity. In the journalistic German travel pieces written in the late 1930s by the avant-garde Swiss heroin addict, Annemarie Schwarzenbach (1908–42), and the retrospective memoir written by her fellow Swiss companion, Ella Maillart (1903–97), in Indian exile from the war in Europe, Afghanistan appeared as a kind of counter-space to the industrialized cities of a Europe on the brink of self-destruction.⁴ In the decades after World War II, touched by the romanticism of his former studies of Sanskrit, the young Swiss adventurer Nicolas Bouvier (1929–98) made a detour from his journey to India to drive through Afghanistan in 1953. The detour would become the subject of his pre-hippy classic, *L'Usage du Monde* ("The Way of the World").⁵ The dramatic accounts of pristine mountaineering written in German by Bouvier's compatriot, the celebrated climber Max Eiselin, reprised the theme of upland emptiness, as though seeking to relive abroad the solitary mountain walks of Jean-Jacques Rousseau in an era of mass tourism in Switzerland's Alps.⁶ With their own heritage of Indophile and alpine romanticism, German writers also contributed to this discourse of Afghan anti-modernity. These included the journalist and admiring acquaintance of Rabindranath Tagore and Mahatma Gandhi, Hans Queling (1903–84), whose account of his Afghan travels in the late 1930s similarly dwelt on wild open spaces and their tribal inhabitants.⁷

THE AFGHAN AFTERLIFE OF PHILEAS FOGG

This brings us to the second major characteristic of travel writing on Afghanistan. For whether in European or Asian travelogues, alongside the tropes of Afghan wildness, remoteness and emptiness, Afghanistan has been represented as a place unchanged since remote times, a conjured "medievalism" that continues to echo through popular representations today.[8] Distant and unchanged; innocent and preindustrial; empty and unspoiled: these twin sets of characteristics that resound through so much of the literature of Afghan travel play on a particular notion of time and space in which Afghanistan was configured as the most remote spot of the inhabited earth and thereby the least touched by modern history. While the evocation of "nostalgia" for an imagined past has also characterized European travel writing on other regions, the case of Afghanistan has seen an extreme version of this tendency through its repeated presentation as the most remote and unchanged space on earth, a place to escape modernity.[9]

The implicit use in such writings of spatial travel to move through, even out-manoeuvre, the passing of time becomes more apparent when we turn to another set of European travel writings. Written more typically by scholars than professional travellers or politicians, these travelogues were expressly concerned with Afghanistan as a space of history, a place where past time could be observed in the present day. Like the tropes of spatial wilderness, these concerns with the visible past in both its material and human forms had already been voiced in the nineteenth-century travelogues that were so formative of the European discourse of Afghan travel. They appeared in the writings of such travellers as Charles Masson (1800–53) and Joseph Pierre Ferrier (*fl*. 1839–48) in particular.[10]

As the professionalization of these historical interests into the formal disciplines of archaeology and ethnography coincided with the opening up of Afghanistan to European visitors from the 1920s, there began a series of academic voyages that sought to emulate in Afghanistan the headline-grabbing Central Asian archaeological journeys of Sir Aurel Stein (1862–1943) and Sven Hedin (1865–1952). The most important early group of such history-seekers comprised the members of the Délégation Archéologique Française en Afghanistan, particularly Alfred Foucher (1865–1952), Joseph Hackin (1896–1941) and Jules Barthoux (1881–1965) who, in the years between 1923 and the outbreak of World War II, travelled extensively in Afghanistan in search of archaeological sites.[11] The many publications that emerged from Foucher and Hackin's excavations were not travel literature in any conventional sense. But in their primary concern with unearthing the archaeological legacy of the Greeks in Afghanistan, the Délégation's excavation reports from the 1920s and 30s echo the travel writings of the period in the Eurocentric orientation, concerned as they were with the quest for a European historical self that lay hidden in the earth of Central Asia.[12]

These historical concerns were similarly voiced by the most celebrated British literary traveller in Afghanistan, Robert Byron (1905–41). His classic, *The Road to Oxiana*, was accompanied by a series of scholarly pieces on the architecture of the Timurids based on inspections made during his journey of 1934.[13] In the eyes of educated Europeans in the post-war years, Afghanistan continued to offer travellers a gateway into past time. In 1960, travelling from Peshawar to Kabul "on board Her Britannic Majesty's lorry", the British historian Arnold Toynbee (1889–1975) conceived of his drive as one through the Arachosian Corridor and the Paropanisadae, the lands of ancient Greeks and Persians.[14] "Musing on the terrace at Istâlif", he wrote in tones reminiscent of the famous lines of Byron, "I thought of Alexander crossing the Hindu Kush… I thought of Demetrius, the later Greek king of Bactria, crossing the same mountain-wall from north to south".[15] A decade later, while Toynbeean notions of the continuity of "European civilization" were being rejected by a new generation of travellers to the east, for remaining Hellenophiles such as the Oxford classicist Peter Levi (1931–2000), Afghanistan remained primarily the site of a lost European past. In the account of his 1970 journey in the wake of the French excavations of the Bactrian Greek settlements, Levi presented a poeticized vision of a lost eastern Greece in which the ways of antiquity were kept alive in the customs of unchanged country people.[16] Nor was this representation of Afghanistan as a space in which time had moved more slowly unique to European travellers. For, writing after the defeat of Japan in World War II, the Japanese ethnographer Tadao Umesao (1920–2010), represented Afghanistan as a living museum where one could discover an alternative imperial past based on the Mongols, whose descendants he claimed to find in the remoteness of Afghanistan.[17] With its obscure mountain settlements described in ethnographic genres of professionalized travel writing from the 1960s, and represented in the exotic images of the French photographers Roland and Sabrina Michaud, Afghanistan was presented in the records of European travel as the land that time forgot.[18]

Powered as they were by desires and motivations produced by the political and social upheavals in Europe, these representations of Afghanistan need not be critiqued for their epistemological failure to accurately reproduce an external "reality". After all, many of these writings were first and foremost literary texts which like so many examples of travel writing used the outside and foreign world as a mirror of inner and more domestic concerns.[19] While the romanticization of the distant and primitive may be specific to European travel writing, the writing of foreign places in the ink of domestic aspirations is perhaps common to travel writings in all languages. This becomes clear when we turn to some examples of Indian travel accounts of Afghanistan. For from the early 1900s, Afghanistan also afforded a space of escape and projection for Indian travellers, albeit involving distinct imaginaries of space and time from European images of the antique and distant. This was partly seen through the recounting of the sheer spatial proximity of Afghanistan to India recorded in Urdu accounts of Afghanistan written in the first half of the twentieth century.

In the writings of Indian Muslims in particular, not only was Kabul described as easily reached by a train journey to Peshawar and a car drive through the Khyber Pass, it was also represented as a place that was culturally and linguistically adjacent to India. By the same token, the writings of several Indian travellers formulated an alternative modelling of Afghan time in which the country was represented as a space through which to enter not the distant past but the more proximate future, whether a future of communist progress or Muslim self-rule. This shifting of the temporal gaze can first be seen in memoirs written of the stay in Kabul between 1915 and 1922 by such Indian revolutionaries as the communist Raja Mahendrapratapa (1886–1979) and 'Ubaydullah Sindhi (1872–1944). In their writings, Afghanistan was presented as an imperial counter-space in contradistinction to the British Empire, a place into which a new era of historical time could be imported from Russia and from there carried across the border into India.[20] At the same time as the international comrades of the "Indo-Turko-German mission" conceived of their own revolutionary Afghanistan, residing in Kabul from 1921 to 1923, the Polish communist journalist, Larisa Reišner (1895–1926), envisioned the message of Lenin spilling across the border from Soviet Central Asia. She painted in her news reports on "education in the harem" and the opening of Kabul's first modern hospital a feudalistic Afghanistan on the brink of progress into the new age of the proletarian.[21]

For Indian Muslim intellectuals who travelled there in the decades leading up to the foundation of Pakistan in 1947, Afghanistan held the futuristic promise of becoming an independent Islamic utopia based on a union of Muslim morality and modern technology (if only, that was, Afghans would follow Indian advice and put the good of other Muslims before themselves). One example is the Urdu account of the road trip made in autumn of 1933 by the leading Indo-Muslim men of letters, Sir Muhammad Iqbal (1877–1938), Sir Ross Mas'ud (1889–1937) and Sayyid Sulayman Nadwi (1884–1953).[22] For in between its celebrations of the modern schools, shops, hotels, airstrip and hospitals of Afghanistan, Nadwi's *Sayr-e Afghanistan* ("Afghan Journey") created for its readers an image of a country of both moral innocence and political hope. It was a land whose women dressed like the family of the Prophet in the Arabia of scripture but whose forward-marching men expressed stirringly Pan-Islamist sentiments.[23] For these Muslim Indian travellers no less than their Hellenophile European contemporaries, Afghanistan offered access to the past no less than the future. Yet this was not a history populated by eastern sons of Alexander, but one in which the heroes of a past age of Islamic greatness offered guidance at the dawn of a new Muslim renaissance. In the months after his journey, Muhammad Iqbal was inspired by its memory to compose in Persian his late masterpiece, *Musafir* ("The Traveller"). In this travelogue in verse, Afghanistan was represented as a vast holy burial ground for the mighty Muslim dead, from the conqueror of India, Mahmud Ghaznavi (r. 997–1030) and the court poet Hakim Sana'i (d. 1131), to the founder of the Mughal Empire, Babur (r. 1504–31) and the late Afghan ruler Amanullah Khan (r. 1919–29), to whom Iqbal had previously addressed his didactic poem *Payam-e Mashriq* ("The Message of the East").[24] Disappointed with the secularization of Turkey and Iran, and seeing Muslims in India, Africa and Malaya under British rule, for Iqbal Afghanistan possessed a unique opportunity to drive the Muslims of the world into a brave new era. In the imagination of Iqbal as both traveller and poet, Afghanistan occupied a distinct continuum of space and time in which, unbroken by the interruptions of colonial rule, the grandeur of the distant Muslim past was channelled directly to the future through the reforming Afghan rulers in whom Iqbal placed hope. When within weeks of Iqbal's departure from Kabul in 1933, the Afghan king Nadir Shah was murdered. Iqbal dedicated his poetic travelogue to his nineteen-year-old successor, Zahir Shah (r. 1933–73).

Between these two sets of travelogues, European and Indian, we have seen Afghanistan presented through two radically different paradigms alternatively positing an Afghanistan of proximity or distance, futurism or historicism. What is striking about the increasing number of European travelogues that appeared from the early twentieth century is the paradox that underlay their celebration of this space of counter-modernity. For whether in the case of Robert Byron or Annemarie Schwarzenbach, the very access to Afghanistan of these aesthetes and anti-moderns was predicated on automobile technology and the road building projects of the modernizing rulers of Turkey and Iran, that from the 1920s, connected Afghanistan to Europe.[25] While buried beneath the celebrations of ancient buildings and tribal customs, and avoided as much as possible in the sub-genre of the "walking tour", this technological enabling slipped into the portrayals of a Central Asian land that time forgot. Yet whether by steamship and train, by automobile and aeroplane, it was these very technologies of movement that rendered possible the great explosion of travel writing on Afghanistan from the early twentieth century. The distant space in the lost heart of Asia described by so many European travellers was the paradoxical offspring of its very accessibility. Driving up to Kabul from Peshawar on the best road in the entire country, for the increasing number of Indians who visited Afghanistan from the 1910s, their own perceptions of proximity and futurism were technological creations of the modernizing policies of the Afghan rulers Habibullah Khan (r. 1901–19) and Amanullah Khan (1919–29).[26] Shaped as they were by radically different social environments from the European anti-modernists, and often entering Afghanistan in search of employment or political support, the Indian travellers were far more conscious of these technological developments and appreciative of the Afghan and, in some cases, British policies that had put them in place. Driving to Kabul in the 1930s, even an Indian Pan-Islamist like Sulayman Nadwi could marvel at the sight of the Khyber Pass Railway and describe it with no compunctions as the "most wondrous miracle" (*hayrat-angiz karamat*) of British engineering.[27]

Whether they expressed it or not, the increasing body of travel literature on Afghanistan produced by Asians and Europeans alike from the early twentieth century was therefore a product of the country's closer integration into the shrinking world of the twentieth century. The global interconnections of Afghanistan that made such integration possible were the result of the employment of engineers and technicians brought from Japan, Europe and America to work on Afghanistan's infrastructure in the 1920s and 30s. But despite such exceptions as the posthumous compilation of letters written in the 1910s by A.C. Jewett (1870–1926), the American engineer employed to construct Afghanistan's first electrical power plant, few of these mobile dispensers of modernity composed travelogues, leaving the country's description to the anti-modernists and aesthetes.[28] With the spread of aviation technology to Afghanistan from the 1920s, by 1939 the German journalist Hans Queling could even travel to Afghanistan by aeroplane, but still chose to focus his writing on the unblemished and timeless mountains.[29] Despite the spread of the modern infrastructure of travel within Afghanistan, in such travelogues as Jason Elliot's *An Unexpected Light* and Rory Stewart's *Places in Between*, for Europeans at the end of the twentieth century the primeval that remained the favoured literary mode of locomotion.[30]

Afghan Travellers and the Quest for Modernity

If the previous pages have traced the creation in European and Indian travel writings of a variant set of representations of Afghanistan, it is now time to turn to literature that concerns Afghans as travellers themselves. For the political and technological opening up of Afghanistan that we have seen as underlying the increasing number of travel writings devoted to Afghanistan also underwrote travels by Afghans themselves and the writings that accompanied these journeys. One set of such travel accounts concerns Afghan journeys within Afghanistan, the most important early example being Burhan al-Din Khan Kushkaki's Dari-Persian account of the journey in 1922 of the Afghan general Nadir Khan (later the ruler Nadir Shah) to the mountainous regions of Qataghan and Badakhshan. Scarcely a straightforward domestic itinerary, it was a journey to a region that had only recently been incorporated into the nation, represented as a strange and distant land for the denizens of Kabul.[31] This literature of internal travel also includes more recent Dari-Persian texts which provide accounts, mainly descriptive and historical, of specific regions of Afghanistan.[32] From the 1930s, for example, the development of Pashto prose writing fuelled the growth of a travel literature in Pashto that was in large part devoted to journeys to Saudi Arabia, India or the Soviet Union.[33] As in the other Afghan travelogues discussed below, these works often celebrated travel as the ultimate modernist act. For example, the 1955 Pashto travelogue *Da Hind Safar* ("Indian Journey", actually comprising a tour to the Gulf States as well) of Sidiqullah Rixtin (1919–98) was replete with accounts of the motor cars, trains and by then even aeroplanes that made the journey possible.[34] Here was consider-

Fig. 8: *Da Hind Safar*: A Pashto Travelogue to India.

able contrast to the emphasis on anti-mechanical journeys by foot that were found in European travelogues even at the end of the twentieth century.

Yet it is the period of the modernizing opening of Afghanistan in the first third of the twentieth century that offers the most interesting accounts of Afghan travellers. This is not least in terms of the contrast that these Afghan accounts of the outside world offer to European travellers' representations of a disconnected "land that time forgot". Such evocations of the title of Edgar Rice Burroughs' 1918 account of a lost land overlooked by history are surprisingly apt in this context. For in the early 1900s, the new Afghan literary concern with travel expressed itself not in the prosaic itineraries of Afghan shepherds and merchants, but in the translation of the most fantastical of all European travel narratives by way of the novels of Jules Verne

(1828–1905). While in the English-speaking world, Verne's novels have usually been regarded as juvenile fiction (partly as a result of their poor translation into English), in France as well as many of the regions into whose languages the *Voyages Extraordinaires* series of novels was translated, Verne was regarded as a serious scientific thinker and impresario of technological progress.[35]

By 1900, for example, Verne's novels were held in high esteem by the modernizers of the late Ottoman Empire, who regarded Verne's heroic technological travellers as models in planning their own journeys.[36] It was through these Ottoman literary middlemen that the novels of Verne made their way to Afghanistan by way of the translations of the Afghan modernist Mahmud Tarzi (1865–1933) who, as Nushin Arbabzadah's chapter has discussed, spent his formative years exiled in Ottoman Damascus in the 1880s and 90s. Working from the Turkish versions of the Ottoman publisher and publicist Ahmad Ihsan Tokgöz (1868–1942), between 1912 and 1914 Mahmud Tarzi published four Dari-Persian translations of Verne's novels, which became the first novels to be published in Afghanistan.[37] Tarzi had previously translated the novels in his capacity as chief of the state translation bureau, where according to a later source the Verne project was his "primary task" due to the fact that his patron King Habibullah Khan was "an avid Verne fan".[38] Be that as it may, as we will see below, there were certainly many correspondences between the narrativization of Habibullah's own travels and those of Verne's heroes. Here was the beginning of the Afghan afterlife of Phileas Fogg.

In the prologue to his translation of Verne's *Robur-le-Conquérant* that he re-titled *Siyahat dar Javv-e Hava* ("Voyage into the Atmosphere"), Tarzi offered a programmatic rationale for these translations. He argued that in contrast to the superstitious popular works imported from India, such the *Qissa-ye Chahar Darvish* ("Tale of Four Dervishes"), or the complicated classical Persian poetry of Ferdowsi and Nizami, Verne's writings offered Afghan readers a vital glimpse of the new "age of progress" (*zaman-e taraqqi*).[39] Tarzi also used his newspaper, *Siraj al-Akhbar*, to issue advertisements for his translation of Verne's *Around the World in Eighty Days*, describing the book as "not only a novel but a book on the art of geography and mathematical geography narrated in the form of a tale" that "also teaches science".[40] Tarzi regarded Verne as something of a prophet of industrial progress, describing in an essay in *Siraj al-Akhbar* how Verne had correctly predicted such technological advances as the wireless telegraph.[41]

THE AFGHAN AFTERLIFE OF PHILEAS FOGG

As a traveller in his own right who, during his years of exile, had already witnessed much of the outside world, Tarzi's choice of works with which to bring both the novel and the writing of travel into the new Afghan printed literature is telling. For among all European literature and all of Verne's fifty-four novels, Tarzi selected Verne's travel tales in which, from the Pacific steamships and Pan-American railroads that carried Phileas Fogg around the world and the balloon flight and telegraphy of the visitors in *Mysterious Island* to the propeller-powered flying machines of *Robur the Conqueror* and the submarine, *Nautilus*, that ferried Captain Nemo twenty thousand leagues under the sea, the experience of technology was celebrated as the defining characteristic of modern travel. This strategic use for modernizing purposes of what we would now classify as science "fiction" was by no means unique to Afghanistan and the same period as Tarzi's translations saw a flurry of science fiction translations into Chinese. As China's own modernists sought the literary keys to national progress during the birth years of the Republic in China. No fewer than eighty works of science fiction were published in Chinese between 1904 and 1918, the peak years of Tarzi's literary activities in Afghanistan.[42]

In Kabul in 1915, Tarzi published his own Persian account of his earlier exilic travels around the Mediterranean. Echoing the fantastical travel writings of Jules Verne, its title referenced a journey through Europe, Asia and Africa in twenty-nine rather than eighty days.[43] Here was another stage of the Afghan afterlife of Phileas Fogg. Yet, in his own travelogue no less than his translations from Verne's *Voyages Extraordinaires*, Tarzi did not echo the romantic concerns of British and Swiss travellers to Afghanistan. Instead, he voiced the technological vision of travel writing represented in late Ottoman Turkey by Verne's earlier translator, Ahmad Ihsan Tokgöz, and in Europe by the aeronautical enthusiasms of Tarzi's Italian contemporary, Gabriele D'Annunzio (1863–1938).[44] Yet by the time Tarzi translated Verne into Persian, the original French novels were already forty years old, and almost everything that Verne had futuristically imagined in them had now come to pass. The missing stretch of the trans-Indian rail that almost defeated Phileas Fogg had long been completed; the wondrous submarine of Captain Nemo was being mass produced in the shipyards of Germany; and within five years of Tarzi's translation of *L'Île mystérieuse*, the aeroplanes that had surpassed the hot air balloon with which the railway engineer Cyrus Smith had fictionally flown over the Pacific would be raining bombs over Afghan conscripts in the Third Anglo-Afghan War of 1919. But the places in which Verne's futuristic machines had been manufactured were elsewhere; and so for modernisers like the statesman Tarzi and the ruler Habibullah these past achievements of other places would have to be brought to Afghanistan through the transformative act of travel. While European travellers in Afghanistan sought entry to a living past, in the royal journeys of the Afghan rulers, Habibullah Khan and his son Amanullah Khan, was an alternative vision of travel through which India and Europe were viewed as spaces in which to access a living future which the traveller could carry back to Afghanistan.

This use of travel as a means of propulsion into the "futurism" of the modern elsewhere characterized two of the most important Afghan travelogues ever written. Configuring the travel narrative as a celebration of technological modernity, these are the two texts which recount the journeys of Habibullah Khan to India in 1907 and of Amanullah Khan to Europe in 1927–8. As documents recounting the travels of the two rulers most associated with the modernization policy that opened and connected Afghanistan to the wider world, the travelogues are important historical documents in their own right, not least in testifying to the intellectual and material baggage that the two modernizers brought back from their journeys. In terms of assessing the Afghan side of the closer interaction with the wider world that made possible so many outsider accounts of Afghanistan, they are also important records of a distinctly Afghan conception of travel. Here the passage through space brought access not to unsullied nature and remote peoples but to the technological futurism of factories, railways and, ultimately, the submarines imagined in Tarzi and Verne's *Bist Hazar Farsakh Siyahat dar Zir-e Bahr* ("Twenty Thousand 'Farsakhs' under the Sea").

For all their importance, the accounts of Habibullah Khan and Amanullah Khan's travels have been entirely neglected in the scholarship.[45] In large part, this appears to be due to the language in which they were written, namely Urdu. While Urdu is not usually considered an "Afghan" language, the long history of cross-border Afghan interactions with the North Indian (and, after 1947, Pakistani) heartlands of Urdu have meant that large numbers of Afghans have been exposed to the language. In recent times, the use of Urdu has become increasingly common in Afghanistan itself through the combined effects of refugee migration and exposure to Indian and Pakistani television and film. Prior to the establishment of Persian (and later Pashto) publishing in Afghanistan from the 1910s, the emergence of Urdu as the main language of South Asian Muslim intellectuals, and the vast expansion of Urdu newspaper and book publishing that accompanied it, saw Urdu reach across the border into Afghanistan. The exile to India of various Afghan notables (particularly the Sardar elites expelled by 'Abd al-Rahman but invited back by Habibullah Khan after 1901) meant that by the early 1900s many Afghan elites were literate in Urdu, including Habibullah Khan himself.[46] In addition, the employment by the Afghan government of Urdu-speaking Indian Muslims as secretaries and later as teachers and technicians put in place literary and linguistic middlemen who further enabled the cross-border passage of Urdu. This literary traffic was by no means one way and the far greater development of publishing in India meant that many Afghan Persian texts were sent to such North Indian (now Pakistani) towns as Lahore to be printed. This was a process which, from the middle of the twentieth century, would be mirrored in the publication of many Afghan Pashto texts in the Pakistani city of Peshawar. It is against this background of cross-border literary traffic that we should place the Urdu travelogues of Habibullah Khan and Amanullah Khan, both of which were published in India.[47] In the case of *al-Habib*, the account of Habibullah Khan's travels, its publication occurred almost a decade prior to the establishment of the first printing press in Afghanistan itself. Published on lithographic presses that emerged from the industrialization of printing in nineteenth-century Europe, the very existence of these travelogues points to the engagement of Afghan literature with the wider industrial world. Neither of the travelogues was written by the Afghan rulers themselves and, though this could hardly be expected, the identities of their writers remain obscure. In the case of the Habibullah Khan travelogue, the author Khaksar Nadir 'Ali is known to have written several other travel-related texts in Urdu, one of them being *Mir'at al-'Arab* ("The Arab Mirror"), a guide to the practicalities of making the *hajj* to Mecca, and the other being *Vaqa'at-e Hijaz* ("Happenings in the Hijaz"), an account of developments in Arabia in 1905 and of the pilgrimage there of the female ruler of the princely state of Bhopal.[48] The author of the Amanullah Khan travelogue, Mawlana Zahid al-Qadiri, was a member of the Royal Asiatic Society of Great Britain, though other than this and his apparent presence on Amanullah's tour, nothing more is known of his identity. Despite the biographical obscurity of their authors, it is the texts themselves that are most important, constituting as they do literary documents of travel out of Afghanistan that contrast sharply with the literary record of travel into Afghanistan. It is to their contents that we now turn to trace the fulfillment of Verne and Tarzi's vision of technologized travel in the description of two royal journeys into Europe's spatially distant futurity.

Royal Progress: The Indian Travels of Habibullah Khan

Khaksar Nadir 'Ali's *al-Habib*, the travelogue of Habibullah Khan, was written in response to the official visit of the Afghan ruler to British India in 1907. In some respects, the Urdu text mirrored G.F. Abbott's *Through India with the Prince*, which recounted each stage of the tour of the Prince of Wales a year earlier.[49] Yet the journey of the Afghan king captured the imagination of far more readers in the region and was accompanied by such other Urdu texts as *Zikr-e Shah-e Islam* ("Commemoration of the King of Islam"), which combined a biography of the king with a description of his mountainous kingdom.[50] Within the larger political context of the 'Great Game', Habibullah Khan's visit was the culmination of the improvement of relations between British India and Afghanistan that followed the death of the isolationist "Iron Amir", 'Abd al-Rahman Khan, in 1901.[51] As a result of these improved relations, Habibullah Khan was granted the royal title of "His Majesty" by the imperial government in Calcutta, an important diplomatic signal of the growing recognition of Afghanistan as a sovereign nation. In a kind of counter-narrative to Abbott's account of the Prince of Wales, *al-Habib* portrayed the Afghan king being greeted by military salutes and representatives of the Raj throughout the journey. The travelogue dwelt with especial detail on the journey's diplomatic centre point, by way of Habibullah Khan's official reception at Agra by the commander-in-chief of the imperial forces in India, Lord Kitchener, and the Viceroy, Lord Minto, in a series of ceremonies that lasted an entire week.[52] However, Habibullah Khan made use of the official invitation to make a much more extensive tour of India, every stage of which Khaksar Nadir 'Ali described in detail in *al-Habib*. Lasting a total of sixty-four days, Habibullah Khan's visit took in the towns of Jamrud, Peshawar, Nowshera, Sirhind, Agra, Kanpur, Jabalpur, Gwalior, Delhi, Panipat, Ajmer, Calcutta, Bombay, Poona, Karachi and Lahore, before returning to Kabul via Peshawar.

What is immediately striking about this vast and rapid itinerary is the fact that it was only made possible by the existence of India's extensive rail and steamship network, of which the text described Habibullah Khan making full and enthusiastic use. Indeed, one of the key sequences of the travelogue described Habibullah Khan stepping onto a train for the first time in his life just beyond the Khyber Pass at Jamrud.[53] Given that one of the key sequences of the fictional global journey of Verne's Phileas Fogg as translated by Habibullah Khan's closest advisor, Mahmud Tarzi, involved the crossing of India by train, in Habibullah Khan's own Indian rail journeys there was a vivid sense of life imitating art. Given that in Verne's novel, the incomplete state of the Indian rail system saw Phileas Fogg forced to abandon the train for an expensively-purchased elephant, in making the same crossing between Calcutta and Bombay in a single train journey, Habibullah even succeeded in outdoing Verne's fictional hero. While we should not make too much of these parallels—Tarzi's translation of Verne's novel would not be published until several years after Habibullah Khan's own journey—there nonetheless remains a strident parallelism in the mutual stress placed on trains and steamships in both novel and travelogue. For *al-Habib* voiced a celebration of the virtues of steam travel that was hardly matched by Verne himself. This was seen in terms of the standard of the carriages on which Habibullah Khan travelled, the times of each train's arrival, the precise details of the train routes on which he travelled, the exact number of hours and minutes that each journey comprised, the persons present on the platforms or, indeed, the perpetual recurrence of the loan-words *esteshan* ('station') and *plitfarm* ("platform") as the spatial locators of an itinerant Afghan king for whom India was more a sequence of locomotive sheds than a land of ancient wonders.[54] Nor were trains the only transportational novelty that India offered to Habibullah Khan. For in Calcutta he bought a fast boat intended for river hunting and in the company of an alarmed Duke of Manchester drove it at breakneck speed along the river where it was docked.[55] On reaching Bombay a few days later, he made a tour of the great harbour known as Apollo Bunder, where he was not only greeted by a royal salute from the cannons of a warship docked in the harbor but, aboard another warship, was invited to press an electric button and fire one of the ship's cannons himself.[56] This was the first time that the king had ever seen let alone travelled on the sea and within days of the harbor trip he sailed out of Bombay for Karachi aboard the Steamship Dufferin on the next leg of his journey.[57]

Al-Habib is not only important for marking the entry of Afghans into the age of steam travel. It also marked the introduction of Afghans to the newer technology of the automobile. For in his enthusiasm for all things mechanical, Habibullah Khan took the opportunity in Calcutta and Lahore to drive in a motor car.[58] While automobile technology was still poorly developed in 1907—even the author of *al-Habib* had to admit that the car only drove very slowly out of Lahore—it was this newer and privatized form of transportation that most captured the imagination.[59] During the tour of India, the King was presented with two motor cars as a gift from the Government of India. His subsequent enthusiasm for the new form of transport became sufficiently well-known to reach the ears of the American journalist, Edward Alexander Powell (1879–1958) who, in an article on the subsequent Afghan rail-building scheme, picturesquely described Habibullah "roaring up and down the narrow mountain roads in a great red motor-car which stampeded the camel caravans".[60] Powell was himself no stranger to the opening of the region to motorized transport. A few years after Habibullah Khan's own journey Powell crossed Iran by car, an achievement which, unlike the more romantically-inclined European travel writers, he proudly advertised in the title of his account of the journey.[61] Between Edward Powell and Khaksar Nadir 'Ali, we glimpse the experiences which led to Habibullah Khan's subsequent policy of building modern roads in Afghanistan, the policy that in reaching its fruition a few decades later would ultimately allow the European aesthetes and romantics to write their own accounts of that "disconnected" country. Capturing as *al-Habib* did not only the first moment of Afghan exposure to railways and motor cars, but also the moment in which through the royal nature of that exposure, personal experience was turned into public policy, the Urdu travelogue marks a crucial moment in both the poetics and practicalities of Afghan travel in which technology served as both the means and the end of the royal journey. If so many Europeans regarded their travels to Afghanistan as a route into past time, then for Habibullah Khan the journey to India offered a road into a living future that he envisaged for his own homeland.

If much was made in *al-Habib* of Habibullah Khan's exposure to technological modernity, then in the other great theme of the text, the author moved his royal subject from the passive to the active mode by rendering Habibullah not merely an observer but a purchaser. It would not be too flippant to characterize the journey described in *al-Habib* as a sixty-four day shopping trip. Here was certainly an elevated degree of extravagance: as his American engineer, A.C. Jewitt, put the matter a few years later, "The Amir [King] had a fine time. Special trains and escorts waited while he made purchases in stores, talked to the pretty shop girls, and made them presents".[62] The contrast between the celebration of such consumerism in the Afghan Urdu narrative and the asceticism of the literature of European travel in Afghanistan is striking. But the larger point is that, as for African rulers on the fringes of empire in the same period, to become a consumer of industrialized products was to become a participant in modernity. The mere act of spending money was a ritual of "purchasing power" that *al-Habib* celebrated on page after page.[63]

For at almost every juncture of his journey, Habibullah Khan was described in the act of purchasing: in the repeated visits to buy such domestic goods as children's clothes, furs and bed sheets in Calcutta's Mina Bazaar; in the more masculine treats on display at the Army & Navy Store where he bought three motor boats; in the Dallaji furniture factory in Bombay from where he shipped furniture to Kabul; in the jewellers where he shopped in Lahore.[64] Elsewhere in the text, he was described as visiting factories, from where he made larger scale or infrastructural purchases, making an order for an iron bridge from the Calcutta firm of Messrs Brown & Co., for example, or perusing the products on display at the cannon and other armaments factories of the city.[65] On other occasions, Habibullah toured places whose names represented an industrializing Asia that was hidden in the travel accounts of European writers: the Ganesh Flour Mills, the Jumna Cotton Mills, the Hindu Biscuit Company.[66] On his return to Afghanistan, Habibullah attempted to recreate what he had seen in India, establishing a cotton mill in Kabul, building iron bridges through a contractor from Calcutta, laying roads for motor vehicles and making plans for a railway. He even dressed the officers of his army in the smart second-hand uniforms of Indian railway inspectors.[67] It was this vision of Habibullah Khan's journey as a movement into a future that could be purchased and transported across the border that was captured on the pages of Khaksar Nadir 'Ali's *al-Habib*.

Twenty Thousand Leagues under the Solent: The European Travels of Amanullah Khan

In 1919, Habibullah Khan was killed and succeeded as ruler of Afghanistan by his son, Amanullah Khan. The second account of Afghan travels to which we will turn is that of Amanullah Khan's tour of Europe with his wife, Queen Soraya, between December 1927 and May 1928. An even more enthusiastic modernizer than his father, Habibullah Khan regarded this official tour of the capital cities of Europe as the zenith of a strategy that had seen him gain independent control of Afghanistan's foreign policy after the Third Anglo-Afghan War of 1919.[68] However, what concerns us here is the journey as it was articulated in Zahid al-Qadiri's travelogue as a literary document. Like the account of his father's travels, that of Amanullah Khan's voyage was also written in Urdu and published in Delhi through India's more developed publishing industry. In the text, the author Zahid al-Qadiri recounted the king's five month journey through India, Yemen, Egypt, Italy, Switzerland, France, Germany, Belgium, England, Poland, Russia, Turkey and Iran. In reflection of what we have already seen in the account of Habibullah Khan's travels, what is immediately striking about every section of the tour is the emphasis placed on the king's usage of the most modern forms of transportation. In contrast to the fetishism of camel-riding and mountain walking in European accounts of Afghanistan, this account of Afghan travellers featured only high speed and mechanized forms of travel. As a self-proclaimed quest for the technological knowledge of Europe, in Zahid al-Qadiri's narrative the actual journeys were themselves as important as their destinations and the forms of transport were treated with as much detail as the places that the king visited. As in the earlier *al-Habib*, railway journeys played an important role in the text, though these were not only the Indian rail crossings of Habibullah Khan but a more international itinerary. It was not only the trains with their "special" and "royal" carriages that the text dwelt on, for to an even greater degree than *al-Habib*, the travelogue of Amanullah Khan described one railway station after another. In the account of the Egyptian leg of the tour, Zahid al-Qadiri devoted more space to his description of the Cairo Junction railway station than to any other building in the city. Beautifully constructed, and gorgeously decorated for the royal visit, the station was pictured filled with eager crowds of commoners and a formal party of dignitaries, while the Egyptian King Fu'ad awaited his Afghan counterpart at the station in a specially designed "royal compartment".[69] Here, as elsewhere in the text, the train station served as the proper environment in which the forward-looking ruler should be described.

Even when the text presented the king outside of such mechanical settings, he was rarely to be seen outside spaces of "progress". Even in the account of Cairo, the king was presented touring the Engineering College, the High Court and Lawyers' Association, the parliament building, and even appearing vicariously in Egyptian newspapers of the kind only introduced to Afghanistan fifteen years earlier.[70] A new kind of traveller quite distinct from the romantic European tourists of the period described earlier, in Zahid al-Qadiri's telling of the king's progress through Egypt he studiously avoided presenting Amanullah Khan beside the pyramids of antiquity. In Europe too, Amanullah Khan was shown again and again on his characteristic stage of the railway platform. In Paris, the entire station was decorated for his arrival, with a red velvet carpet laid out to meet his carriage and the vast space of the platforms filled with greeters in place of commuters. When the king stepped down from the train, a French military band played the new Afghan national anthem as he was escorted to his rooms in the luxurious railway hotel.[71] The station again formed the primary space in which the king was pictured in Brussels, where the Belgian king and queen awaited his train and a guard of honour announced his arrival with a fanfare.[72] His entry to the imperial capital of the country on which he had declared war in the first months of his reign was likewise framed in this railway setting, with all of the gates to London's Victoria station decked out with gorgeous arrangements of flowers.[73] A few days later, he made his first excursion beyond the capital cities of Europe to inspect the Great Western Railway's Swindon Works. It was a visit deemed of such propaganda value for his reformist policies that it was recorded in a black and white film intended to be shown in the first cinema in Kabul.[74] Ironically, in its section on the Berlin leg of the tour, the Urdu travelogue gave no account of the most enduring of Amanullah Khan's station visits. There the king made his first inspection of an underground railway, after which his enthusiasm for the newly-designed A-II U-bahn train led to its being named after him in Berlin slang as the *Amanullah-Wagen*.[75] This omission notwithstanding, in the narrative itinerary provided by Zahid al-Qadiri, the Europe of Amanullah Khan was conceived as a mechanized geography of interconnecting railway stations. In contrast to the Afghan mountains beloved of European travellers, such stations formed the ideal overseas environment for a king whose locomotive enthusiasms had five years earlier seen the laying from his palace of Afghanistan's first short rail track.[76]

While trains and stations were certainly prominent in the travelogue, its presentation of travel as the acme of a mechanical modernity was by no means limited to them. While in the earlier Urdu travelogue, the motor car was only glimpsed on the horizon of what was still essentially an age of railway travel, the travelogue of Amanullah Khan actually opened with a journey from Kabul to Qandahar in a "princely red motor car" along one of the roads built after Habibullah Khan's tour of India.[77] While the king first entered cities through their railway stations, whether in Quetta or

Bombay, London or Rome, after his arrival in each of these cities Zahid al-Qadiri was careful to describe the king being driven in motor cars that were alternatively "beautiful" or "royal".[78] At the very end of his journey, it was by car that he was driven into Afghanistan through northern Iran. He was making the same road journey that Robert Byron would follow five years later in the Afghan quest for medieval architecture described in *The Road to Oxiana*.[79]

If trains and cars featured in the story of his land travels, then Amanullah Khan was also presented aboard such ocean-going vessels as the *SS Manila* and the luxury P&O liner *SS Rajputana*, which was greeted at Aden by a fly-by of a dozen aeroplanes.[80] It was from this point in the travelogue that Amanullah Khan began to outreach the transportational accomplishments of the earlier travelogue and truly live out the *voyages fantastiques* recounted in Tarzi's translations of Jules Verne. Having inspected one airport after another, in London he finally left the earth behind to fly over London in a mail plane. Sifting through the postbags with his princely prerogative, he found a postcard inscribed with Persian verses.[81] In Berlin, the Junkers Company presented him with an aeroplane of his own, "very beautiful and expensive, able to seat ten passengers in great comfort", as Zahid al-Qadiri described it.[82] Nor did the king's initiation into the future of travel stop there. In Bournemouth, he inspected armour-plated vehicles with impenetrable skins.[83] And then, as though living out the adventures of Captain Nemo translated by Tarzi a decade earlier in Kabul, in the distant port of Southampton Amanullah Khan was taken aboard a submarine. On the commander's word it sank in an instant beneath the waves of the Solent, outmanoeuvred a warship and "in the most strange event of all" fired a weapon called a *tarpidaw* that despite weighing a tonne and a half could silently destroy a target a thousand yards away.[84] In such repeated sequences throughout the text, travel was in itself celebrated as the quintessential experience of modernity. In the writings of European travellers of the period such as Hans Queling and Robert Byron, aeroplanes and motor cars were merely a means to escape the modernity of Europe for an Afghanistan they imagined untouched by the twentieth century. But in the literary imagination that enclosed the journey of Amanullah Khan, such vehicles represented a sufficient purpose for travel in their own right.

If in Zahid al-Qadiri's travelogue the act of moving between places was primarily presented in mechanical terms, then this mechanization of spatial movement was paired with a consistent vision of time. For from the very

Fig. 9: The Aeronautical Afghan: King Amanullah in Berlin, 1928.

moment at which Amanullah Khan set off on his journey, the timing of his movements was recorded in precise detail. As with Verne's perpetual recourse to Passepartout's pocket watch in structuring the narrative of *Around the World in Eighty Days*, Zahid al-Qadiri marked every moment of his own hero's journey with no less precision. Boarding the steamship *Manila* in Karachi at 3.30pm on 12 December, Amanullah Khan arrived in Bombay at 4.30pm on 14 December; and so on through every stage of his five-month journey.[85] If Verne relied on Passepartout's pocket watch, then there is reason to suspect that for the precision of his narrative, Zahid al-Qadiri relied on telegraphic news reports. For the 'Reuters representative' and translated excerpts from the newspapers of the various countries that the king visited slipped repeatedly into Zahid al-Qadiri's Urdu prose. As we have already seen in Nushin Arbabzadah's chapter, the telegraph and similar technologies had already been presented by Mahmud Tarzi as fitting topics for poetry, let alone prose. If Zahid al-Qadiri's account of the king's travels had relied on such telegraphic assistance, then it would be a fitting narrative ordering of Amanullah Khan's journey on a template of telegraphic time. For no less than the European anti-moderns who tried to reverse time through their travels to Afghanistan, in the speeches Zahid al-Qadiri recorded him making on his counter-journey westwards, Amanullah Khan was similarly concerned with time. But it was not to seek the past or revel in the splendours of a lost antiquity that the king set out to travel. For, as he announced in the speech on the eve of his departure, it was towards the distinct and forward-looking time of *taraqqi*, "progress", that he was travelling. It was to a forward shifting of time that had already been made in the Europe to which he set off.[86] In a signal that this future time would be carried back to Kabul itself, the space in which he made his speech was Maydan-e Taraqqi, "Progress Square".[87] As though signalling a symbolic transmission of the time-machine of progress from an atheistic Marxist to a Muslim king, in the final section of the travelogue, Zahid al-Qadiri described Amanullah Khan reading the opening verse of the Quran before the tomb of Lenin in Moscow.[88] And from there he drove east into the future in his fine motor car.

Conclusions

As a form of inherently cross-border literature, the travel writings surveyed in this chapter show how central movement and transnationalism have been in the relationship between Afghanistan and literature. Whether in the many travel accounts written by European travellers into Afghanistan, or the Urdu works describing the voyages of Habibullah and Amanullah outside Afghanistan, the writing of travel conceived as movement in space and time has been central to the literary mediation of Afghanistan's encounter with the world. However different the perceptions we have seen in these travel writings of Afghan connections (or lack thereof) to this wider world, in processual terms the European and Asian texts were symbiotic. For both sets of travelogues developed as responses to the same circumstances of the easing of travel both out of and into Afghanistan through the development of the travel infrastructure of neighbouring Iran and India no less than Afghanistan itself.

THE AFGHAN AFTERLIFE OF PHILEAS FOGG

Yet if travel was an action, and its writing a narrativization of those actions, it was also an idea that could be elaborated in fictional and imaginative terms. The starkly differing representations of Afghanistan that we have seen in this chapter suggest that no clear boundary can be drawn between the "factual" and the "fictional" in this literature of Afghan travel. For on the pages of these travel accounts, the same space on the map could be imagined as impossibly remote or as a mere motor ride from its neighbours, as a museum of the living past or as a cradle of a new Muslim era. This interweaving of desires, of the fictional and factual, of the imagined and the enacted journey, was present at the very birth of modern literature in Afghanistan. It was present through the state-sponsored translating, printing and teaching programme of the former exile Mahmud Tarzi, in which the *voyages extraordinaires* of Jules Verne played so important a part. Whether through such French novels translated through Turkish, through the Dari-Persian account of Tarzi's own travels, or through the Urdu descriptions of King Habibullah and Amanullah's journeys, the writing of travel occupied centre stage during the years in which a printed prose literature first developed in Afghanistan.

This web of overlapping languages was in turn constitutive of the literature itself. Here the fact that the royal travelogues were written in Urdu, a language more usually associated with northern India (and later Pakistan), shows how increasing Afghan interaction with the wider world was not only reflected on the pages of a coherent "Afghan" literature composed in a discrete "national" language. It also shaped the linguistic medium of that literature itself in a period in which Afghan elites were greatly exposed to the more developed literary sphere across their eastern borders in India. Rendering neologisms as it did from countless English loanwords, the Urdu in which these texts were composed was itself reconfigured by the sociolinguistic shuttling of the age. The process is glimpsed nowhere better than in the repeated printing in modified Arabic letters of the borrowed English title of *Hiz Majisti* in these "Urdu" accounts of the kings of Kabul. In the same years, Mahmud Tarzi was himself criticized for introducing such imported loanwords into the poems he published in his newspaper. Through such *Wanderworten* or "wandering words", travel reshaped the linguistic medium no less than the message of this modernizing Afghan literature.

As the literary expression of the opening of Afghanistan through the industrialized travel of train and steamship, motor car and aeroplane, travel writing has constituted a two-way literature of interdependent movements into and out of Afghanistan. Yet for all their connection as the literary offspring of mechanized travel, the European and Asian travelogues articulated the meaning of travel in radically different terms, presenting travel through space as a movement either forward or backward in time. Unlike the European travelogues that formed factualized versions of Edgar Rice Burroughs' disconnected "land that time forgot", the literature produced from the Afghan side of these movements articulated a highly distinct (and oppositional) location of Afghanistan in terms of both the time and space in which the land and its peoples existed. Unlike the romantics and aesthetes, the art historians and archaeologists, responsible for so large a proportion of the European literature of Afghan travel, the accounts of the royal travellers Habibullah Khan and Amanullah Khan did not conjure an Afghanistan that was disconnected from the world in the lost heart of Asia. Their Afghanistan was not a country impossible to reach except through camel or on foot; it was not a land preserved in the frozen time of the medieval. Instead, through their triumphant celebrations of planes, trains and automobiles, Afghan travellers envisaged a very different Afghanistan. At the heart of their Kabal stood a spatial marker of an era unrecognized by the travelling savants of Europe. It was from that place of the new time, Maydan-e Taraqqi or "Progress Square" that, in December 1927, King Amanullah Khan had begun his journey to the future.

4

DEMARCATING PASHTO

CROSS-BORDER PASHTO LITERATURE AND THE AFGHAN STATE, 1880–1930

Thomas Wide

Introduction: Pashto and Power

The aim of this chapter is to offer a broad survey of Pashto literature, both written and unwritten, as it stood at the dawn of the twentieth century, and to chart its unsteady transition into print during the first three decades of that century. It concerns itself primarily with Pashto poetry, since this was by far the dominant form of literature produced during the period. The term "literature" is used in a broad sense to include oral as well as written sources; as shall be seen, oral Pashto poetry has often proved a far more effective means of transmission, circulation, and intervention than the written word. At the centre of the story of Pashto literature's development is the relation of Pashto literature to political power. After tracing the emergence of written Pashto literature in productive tension with the rise and fall of the Persianate Mughal Empire, the chapter focuses on the polyphonic oral "resistance" poetry stemming from internal fragmentation and new imperial encounters in the nineteenth century. Finally, the chapter addresses the fractious relationship between Pashto literature and the Afghan state in the refashioning of Pashto as the "national" (*milli*) language of Afghanistan during the first half of the twentieth century.

Although the chapter is concerned primarily with Pashto literary production inside Afghanistan, any such survey cannot ignore the flow of writers, texts, forms, and ideas, between Pashtuns on either side of the Afghanistan-Pakistan border. Prior to the demarcation of that border in 1893, Pashto literature travelled as widely and freely as did long-distance Pashtun traders and the Afghan diaspora in India. Even after the formation of Afghanistan as a firmly bounded nation state, such cross-border flows have continued to play a central, at times problematic, role in the development of Pashto literature in Afghanistan.

Pashto into Ink

The emergence of Pashto written literature is inseparably connected to South Asian imperialism. The first Pashto texts did not emerge until the sixteenth century, during a period of intense contact between an Afghan diaspora seeking economic and political opportunities in India, and a rapidly expanding Mughal empire. This large-scale migration led to encounters with different forms of socio-political organization, religious and philosophical thought, and modes of literary expression current at the time in cosmopolitan India. These encounters played a fundamental role in the shaping of a self-consciously Afghan identity and historical consciousness, as well as the evolution of a Pashto written literature.[1] A cornerstone of this cosmopolitan Mughal world was the Persian language. Persian was the language of the state bureaucracy, official history, canonical texts, as well as a *lingua franca* for communication with other states. The great antiquity and prestige of Persian literature, and its well-established connection to state power throughout Central and South Asia, afforded the language a hegemonic quality in written literary production. It is thus no surprise that the 'classical' Pashto written literature that emerged was heavily influenced by Persian models.[2] Persian poetic genres—the *ghazal*, *ruba'i*, *qasida*—were all imported wholesale into Pashto, as were many of the images, tropes, and vocabulary of the Persian classical tradition. Persian models were also adapted, such as the frequently extended *charbayta*, and the specifically Pashto *ghazal*, which has a different rhyme scheme from its Persian model.[3]

The influence of Persian models, however, did not extend to the socio-political role of Pashto written poetry. Indeed, the encounter with Mughal rule, and frequent Afghan resistance to it, led Pashto written poetry to develop to some extent in opposition to Persianate state power. This is clear from the very first extant Pashto text, Bayazid Ansari's (c.1521–72) *Khair al-Bayan*. The text was written in four languages as a manifesto for the Rowshaniyya movement (c.1560–1640), a predominantly Pashtun popular Sufi movement which arose in opposition to the elite Sufism of previous centuries, and to encroaching Mughal imperial power in Pashtun areas.[4] Ansari was not himself a Pashtun; the decision to write in Pashto reflects a conscious use of vernacular languages as both a political challenge to forms of elite Sufism of the past, and as an expedient means of attracting followers. So too with the work of Khushhal Khan Khattak (1613–89), one of the most highly regarded of all Pashto poets to this day. Khushhal Khan frequently adopted Persian poetic models and themes, translated Persian idioms into Pashto, used Persian vocabulary, at the same time as he incited "the Pashtuns" to overcome their factional divisions and unite to overthrow Mughal rule. The burgeoning sense of a Pashtun identity, forged in opposition to the Mughal Empire, found some of its earliest expressions in his work:

> The whole of the deeds of the Pattans are better than those of the Mughals;
> But they have no unity amongst them, and a great pity it is
> The fame of Bahlol, and of Sher Shah too, resoundeth in my ears-
> Afghan Emperors of India, who swayed its scepter effectively and well.
> For six or seven generations, did they govern so wisely,
> That all their people were filled with admiration of them.
> Either those Afghans were different, or these have greatly changed;
> Or otherwise, at present, such is the Almighty's decree.
> If the Afghans shall acquire the gift of concord and unity,
> Old Khushhal shall, a second time, grow young therefrom.[5]

In the poem, Khattak posits a unified concept of "the Pashtuns" at the same time as he laments its disunity. The desire to create such a Pashtun ecumene trumping tribal affiliation, geographic situation, and regional dialect is mirrored in Khattak's use of different regional dialects in his own poetry, creating a Pashto that drew its unity from its incorporation of difference.[6] As was to be repeated in the early twentieth century, although this time in the context of modern nation state consciousness, this unification of the language was a political project accompanying a burgeoning pride in a unified Afghan identity and its language:

> In Persian, thou must know, such strains will not be heard,
> As those that Khushhal, Khattak, reciteth, in the Pus'hto tongue.[7]

This is not to deny that Pashto could be put to the service of the Persianate state. Pashto, like any language, was just as capable of reinforcing imperial ideologies and orthodoxies as of resisting them.[8] However, the emergence of Pashto written literature during a period in which upper-register Persian had a political and cultural hegemony, did lead to classical Pashto literature frequently being used to formulate a burgeoning Pashtun ethno-nationalism, and to reinforce normative ideals of independence and resistance to outside powers. These historically contingent formulations, enshrined in the works of the classical period of the seventeenth and eighteenth century, were to prove an important influence on later poets in new contexts of modern imperialism and the rise of the nation state.

The Other Pashto Literature: Popular Poetry in the Nineteenth Century

Despite the development of a written Pashto literature during the sixteenth to nineteenth centuries, Pashto literary production and circulation at the end of the nineteenth century remained an overwhelmingly oral activity. This unwritten literature—frequently known as "people's literature" (*walesi adab, gharnai adab*) in Pashto—drew on a common cultural stock of Persian, Arabic, and Urdu stories in the region. And yet, at the same time, the idiosyncrasies of the Pashto language and metre ensured that forms unique to the Pashto tradition developed and flourished:[9] the Pashto narrative ballad (*charbayta*), the Pashto wedding song (*shadi*), dance (*atan*), and two-line poems (*landay, tappa, gharay*) as well as a vast compendium of proverbs (*matal*)).[10] At the same time as developing in their own right, these forms also proved a continual source of inspiration for the authors of Pashto written literature, as they still do today.

Fortunately, a sample of this oral literature was collected by the nineteenth-century orientalist James Darmesteter during a research trip to Peshawar in the 1880s. His collection offers an invaluable snapshot of Pashto popular literature in the late nineteenth century: its role in commemorating great events, providing articulations of Pashtun ethical values, and inciting popular protest and resistance. At the same time, this oral literature presents a world caught between national consciousness and nation state: although there is a sense in the poetry of shared Pashtun values and a Pashtun "homeland", however vaguely articulated, resistance to outside powers is nevertheless mostly framed in religious, not nationalist, terms. Clearly this reflects the various resistance movements themselves, which drew much of their power and unity from Islamic symbols and liberation theology.[11] More than this, however, the lack of nationalist sentiment reflects the fragmentation of the Afghan Durrani Empire, and the bitter infighting amongst the Barakzai sardars for control of what remained of it. In the division of Pashtun lands between the British Empire and a newly formed British-backed Afghan nation state, there was no single ruling power or movement that could claim to speak on behalf of the Pashtuns as a coherent community. The popular poetry of the time reflects this fragmentation and disunity: a plurality of competing voices, only sporadically unified by the universalist symbols of Islam in opposition to an external threat.

Poetry and Patronage Along the North West Frontier

The popular poetry of the nineteenth century was composed and sung primarily by professional poets known as *dums*. The setting for such poems was the village *hujra* ("guest-house") where villagers and travellers would congregate to gather news and hear songs. *Dums* would be invited to play, paid for their services, and frequently asked to compose songs on particular themes. Contests were often held at poetic gatherings (*musha'ira*) where poets would vie with one another by quoting and improvising two-line poems (*misra*) in order to win the patronage of local notables. *Dums* had an apprenticeship system through which songs would be transmitted from *ustad* ("teacher") to *shagird* ("student"), and songs could travel fast and far, following the thousands of long-distance traders (*powindas*) moving between Afghanistan and India.[12] Darmesteter described the *dums* as "the journalists of the Afghans", and certainly these poems frequently record and comment on historical events: the wars with the Sikhs, particularly the religiously-inspired campaign of Sayyid Ahmad Barelvi (1786–1831), the internal feuding of the Barakzai, and the Ambela Campaign of 1863.[13] More than a mere record of events, however, this poetry was frequently an active intervention designed to incite resistance.[14] The following poem is a *misra'* in reference to the battle of Buner of 1863, in which the British launched a punitive expedition against the religiously-inspired Sahib of Swat:

O *Ghazis*, hold on to your ramparts, the cannon-balls of the Firangis rain down by the bushel

The Lord's mercy upon Babaji (the Sahib of Swat), for he has driven the Firangis back to Calcutta

O Babaji, would that you had a son who could extend his lands to Calcutta!
Flee, O Firangis, if you wish to save yourselves; the Sahib rides and the Akuzais follow him.
The Whites [the British] lie in the ravines, with their yellow belts, their heads dishevelled.[15]

While poems such as these suggest a composition during or soon after the battle itself, the continuing popularity of these songs decades later attests to their perceived cultural value: oral poems, unlike written literature, are never preserved by accident. Even if some of these songs were later compositions, it is still instructive that these previous battles were the popular subject of songs. For in this way, Pashto popular literature was able to preserve a memory of resistance to outside rule, which would serve as justification and encouragement for later resistance. Such was the case with the Second Anglo-Afghan War (1878–80), which produced a new slew of resistance ballads, stylistically and thematically modelled on earlier nineteenth-century poems. These poems substituted the British for the Sikhs and encouraged Islamic resistance, at the same time as they reinforced normative Pashtun values of honour (*nang*), courage (*ghayrat*), and valour (*tora*). The greatest vitriol was saved for traitors, who are usually described as motivated by greed, as with the accounts of Khavvas Khan, Malik of the Afridis, who sided with the British:

> Havas let himself be bought; he is not ashamed of his bad renown.
> Before the Lord his forehead is black.
> He told Kamnari [i.e. Louis Cavagnari, the British representative at Kabul]: "I shall serve thee loyally".
> Havas is a traitor; he nourishes treason's self in his veins.
> Great is the glory of the Ghazis. Glory to the Ghazis![16]

Women also played an important role in the reinforcing of Pashtun normative ideals through poetic production; a lullaby still circulated by women in the North West Frontier Province in the 1880s tells the purportedly true story of a Yusufzai Pashtun girl kidnapped by a Sikh, and taken to Lahore where she is forced to marry him and have his child. When she notices her brothers come to rescue her, she resourcefully sings a lullaby to her child, which informs her brothers how to rescue her:

> Come not, ye robbers. Come not by the lower side:
> Come by the upper side, sweet and low…
> There is a bear [i.e. her Sikh husband] asleep, come quickly therefore.
> If he becomes aware of you, there will be no salvation in your distress.
> The infidel is a drunkard, he does not perceive the noise.[17]

The role of women in popular poetic production is also central to the most famous of Pashto folk traditions, the *landay*. This is a two-line poem, which expresses a single idea (patriotism, love, grief, etc.) usually linked to a strong visual image, similar in this way to a haiku.[18] Like short-hand forms of the *charbaytas* and *ghazals* of the *dums*, these *landays* often preserve a folk memory of an event, reinforce societal ideals of valour and honour, and are frequently designed to incite action. Such is the famous *landay* supposedly composed by the Afghan heroine Malalai to rouse the Afghan troops during the Battle of Maiwand in 1879:

> "If you do not fall a martyr in Maiwand
> by God you will be praised with dishonour".[19]

These examples should not, however, give the impression that Pashto popular poetry of the late nineteenth century constituted a coherent expression of "Pashtun" anti-colonial resistance. The nature of poetic patronage and the ever-changing relationship of Pashtun khans to Sikh and British rule meant that the poetry of the period provides a plurality of competing voices and judgments. Indeed, Pashto poetry could be used to defend colonialism, translating British colonial ideals of benevolent rule into a religio-ethnic idiom of justice, equality, and honour:

> The Sahibs have the same law both for the weak and for the strong.
> They practice to perfection justice (*'adl*) and equity (*insaf*),
> And make no difference in a lawsuit between the strong and the weak.[20]

Moreover, the popular poetry circulating orally between Afghanistan and India could be as critical of the Afghan ruling powers as of outside powers. Yaqub Khan (1849–1923), the Amir at the time of the Second Anglo-Afghan War, is described as "turning his back to Islam" and fleeing to India where "he forgot his native place".[21] 'Abd al-Rahman (r.1880–1901), the Afghan Amir backed by the British after 1880, is also frequently attacked for his financial greed and brutality:

> Since Amir 'Abd al-Rahman sits on the throne at Kabul,
> Man has lost his faith in man.[22]

It is said that when 'Abd al-Rahman heard these lines, while riding through the bazaar at Jalalabad, he dismounted from his elephant, found the poet, and apologized before him.[23] Even if apocryphal, the story highlights the power that people granted to oral popular poetry, which was to remain a remarkably diverse and potent form of social expression and public intervention into the twentieth century.

Printing Pashto

The dividing up of Pashtun populations between rival powers in the nineteenth century, crystallizing in the Durand Line agreement of 1893, which demarcated the border of Afghanistan and British India, was to have a profound effect on the development of Pashto literature in the two countries over the next few decades. On the Afghan side of the border, 'Abd al-Rahman attempted to seal off his country from external influence, while using British subsidies to build up a powerful centralized state centred in Kabul.[24] Although this state could not silence the popular poetry of dissent emanating from its rural borders, Afghanistan's enforced isolation did ensure that Pashto literature in Afghanistan was shut off from new technologies, linguistic research, and cultural forms, which were to be creatively adapted by Pashtuns there in order to forge potent new mediums, genres and publics for Pashto literature. At the centre of these developments was the introduction of the printing press into British India, which was seen by the British Empire as an integral part of its complementary project of 'development' and control. It is perhaps no surprise that the first book in Pashto off the press was a translation of the New Testament, published in Serampore, in 1818.[25] Unfortunately, the book was poorly translated, urging Pashtuns "Do not be just to others, lest they be not just to you", a rather un-Christian adaptation of the verse, "Judge not, that ye be not judged". Indeed, the weakness of the work—one Pashto-speaking colonial officer describing it as "the most ridiculous thing I have ever met with"—was testament to the colonial knowledge gap about Pashto in the early nineteenth century.[26] This was to change as a slew of Pashto grammars, dictionaries, primers, and linguistic studies were to be produced from the 1850s onwards, following the annexation of the NWFP border region by the British East India Company in 1849. Pashtuns themselves were to play an important role in this process; from the 1830s Pashto speakers were employed to teach colonial officers, and several of these teachers went on to produce textbooks, collections of stories, and grammatical and lexicographical works.[27] On the popular level, the new technology of inexpensive mass print also led to new ways of circulating previously oral stories, and adaptations of popular poetry for a new medium. Although always extremely fluid categories, the distinction between "written" and "oral" literature became even further muddied as originally "oral" poetry was increasingly preserved in print and widely distributed by, and for, a burgeoning literate public. Of particular importance in this regard was the rise of "chapbook" printing, a chapbook being a small, mass-produced booklet of poetry of the kind which became a very popular form of book all across India from the mid-nineteenth century.[28] In contrast to classical Pashto poetry, and even the narrative *charbaytas* of the *dums*, chapbook narrative poetry was freer of lengthy descriptive passages, and coloured by a lower register and simpler vocabulary, which suited its mass-produced and mass-consumed form.[29]

However, all these developments in British India seemed to have had remarkably little impact on Afghanistan. 'Abd al-Rahman's neglect of educational development had led to blanket illiteracy outside a tightly-knit elite bureaucratic class, thus ensuring that any audience for printed material, even "popular" printed material such as chapbooks, would be negligible. Moreover, 'Abd al-Rahman had little or no facility with the Pashto language, and certainly had no interest in encouraging Pashto literary production.[30] 'Abd al-Rahman may have been ethnically Pashtun, but his rule relied on a Persianate administration and on British financial and political backing. It is thus fitting that his autobiography, "The Life of 'Abd al-Rahman, Amir of Afghanistan", was composed in Dari-Persian, translated into English, and then published by the great patron of nineteenth-century colonial literature, John Murray, in London.[31]

The Rise of the Intellectual at Court

In 1914, a Pashto poem by an Afghan school-teacher, Salih Muhammad Qandahari (born 1891), was printed in the Afghan newspaper, *Siraj al-Akhbar*. It began:

> What an interesting time this is/which has fastened upon the Afghan! Everywhere is progress/what a wonderful thing it is![32]

Unfortunately for the readers of the newspaper, the printing press did not have Pashto letters, so the poem had to be printed using Persian letters instead. Nevertheless, its significance outweighs its odd appearance, for it was the first Pashto poem ever printed and published inside Afghanistan. Over the next two decades, the Pashto language, for so long treated as subordinate to Persian as a language of cosmopolitan ideologies and statecraft, was re-imagined as a language, in many ways the language, of the new "modern Afghanistan". This vision of modernity was created by a small group of urban elite intellectuals, who attempted to unite the Pashto lan-

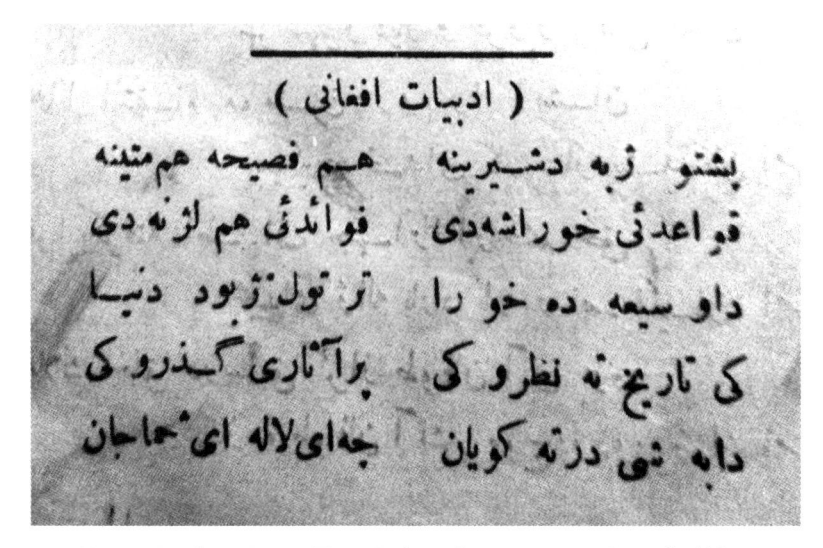

Fig. 10: Without Proper Type: Early Pashto Printing in *Siraj al-Akhbar*.

guage with "modern" ideals of constitutionalism, educational reform, and nation state consciousness Although this attempt was to remain in many ways incomplete, it was during these three decades that the intellectual groundwork and inspiration was laid for the powerful state-sponsored project of "Pashtunization", which took place under Nadir Shah in the 1930s and beyond.

Although Afghanistan's 'modern' moment is traditionally located in the period of Amir Habibullah (r. 1901–19), it is necessary to look to 'Abd al-Rahman's reign if we are to understand the roots of these changes: it was the authoritarian, coercive, isolationist state of 'Abd al-Rahman which was to create the conditions for a new class of intellectuals to arise who would drive reform in the twentieth century. For a centralizing state needs a bureaucracy, and a bureaucracy needs educated managers to run it. 'Abd al-Rahman's reliance on such managers led to a shift in political power, away from traditional land ownership, and into the hands of that tightly-knit group of men at the centre. Along with the political power that was newly invested in state management, these men were also able to take advantage of trade privileges in an increasingly centralized economy, and of land grants provided by the Amir as a reward and surety for their continued support. In this changed political climate, the old aristocratic families, particularly those from the

DEMARCATING PASHTO

Pashtun centre of Qandahar, were quick to move to recover their traditional influence. The young well-educated scions of these lineages now moved to Kabul and reinvented themselves as court-intellectuals.[33]

These intellectuals were to become even more prominent after the death of 'Abd al-Rahman in 1901 and the accession of his son Habibullah. Habibullah was a very different man from the Iron Amir—young, fanciful and, in relative terms, progressive. Superficially, Habibullah liked the look of modernity, particularly the pleasures it brought: photography, telephones, golf. He also made some early reformist concessions to illustrate his distance from his father, one of these being the return of a number of prominent Afghan families exiled by his father.[34] Mirroring the "homegrown" aristocratic elite scholars at court, these returning exiles also took

Fig. 11: Journalist and Diplomat, Poet and Minister: 'Abd al-Hadi Dawi.

jobs in the state administration or the newly-founded state educational institutions, creating a powerful group of individuals in Kabul with close links to both the state and traditional rural political and economic power structures. It is striking how many of these men were ethnically Pashtun; the majority of the leaders of the Constitutional Movement were not only Pashtuns, but Qandahari Pashtuns;[35] the returned exiles Mahmud Tarzi (1865–1933) and Muhyi al-Din Afghan (1862–1922) were both from prominent Qandahari Pashtun families; the journalists 'Abd al-Hadi Dawi (1894–1922) and 'Abd al-Rahman Lodin (d. 1930) were both native Pashto speakers from Pashtun families, although ones that had settled in Kabul prior to their birth; the religious scholars Mawlavi 'Abd al-Wasi' Qandahari (c.1873–1929), Mawlavi 'Abd al-Ra'uf Qandahari (1850–1915), and the educationalist Salih Muhammad Qandahari, were from one of the most prestigious aristocratic Pashtun lineages in Qandahar.[36] While not constituting a Pashtun "bloc" *per se*, and frequently having Persian not Pashto as their first language, their great influence in state and educational administration and policy-making over the following two decades, goes some way to explaining the increasing focus placed on Pashto language reform, education, literary societies, journalism, and poetry during the period.

Ambiguous Praise: Pashto Printed Poetry, 1901–19

In 1917, Salih Muhammad Qandahari wrote a short poem in *Siraj al-Akhbar*:

> Qandahar, Mazar, Herat, even Badakhshan are my own
> Give thanks for this garden of ours, and for our Gardener.[37]

Although a seemingly simple sentiment, these two lines capture the ambiguous relation of Pashto literature to state power during Habibullah's reign. On the one hand, the poem gives thanks to Habibullah ("our gardener") and offers a proud articulation of nationalist sentiment. At the same time, however, the lines express a subtle challenge to the absolute power of the Afghan monarch, Habibullah: in describing him as "our gardener", Salih Muhammad inverts the traditional representation of power relations by which the Afghan people are the possession of the Afghan monarch; here, the monarch is the possession of the people. The poem also offers one of the first articulations of a new Afghan nation state consciousness in printed Pashto. The four places mentioned represent the territorial scope of the Afghan nation state (Qandahar in the south, Mazar-e Sharif in the north, Herat in the west, Badakshan in the north-east), whose boundaries had recently been affirmed by Habibullah.[38] In aligning himself with all those living inside Afghanistan's nation state borders, regardless of ethnicity, Salih Muhammad was translating a cosmopolitan ideal of Afghan citizenship, a continual refrain of Persian writings in *Siraj al-Akhbar* into Pashto.

More than mere translation work, however, the use of Pashto to express such sentiments represents the attempt during this period to "deprovincialize" the Pashto language itself,[39] i.e. to illustrate its compatibility with the "modern", multi-ethnic, twentieth-century Afghan nationalism, thus far only espoused in Persian. This project had a number of elements. The first, as seen above, was by writing "cosmopolitan" poetry in Pashto as a means to legitimize it as a language of the modern Afghanistan. Another bilingual Pashtun poet, 'Abd al-'Ali Mustaghni (1878–1934), put it thus:

> I am Mustaghni/my name is 'Abd al-'Ali
> I am a Pashtun/no other *qawm* is important to me
> My Farsi poetry is famous throughout the world
> And my poetry (*shi'r*) in Pashto is no mere sloganeering (*shu'ar*).[40]

With his word-play on *shi'r* ("poetry") versus *shu'ar* ("sloganeering"), Mustaghni rejects the Persianate bias against Pashto, suggesting that Pashto is the equal of Persian as a vehicle of poetic expression, not merely of political protest or resistance. Conversely, he also suggests that a pride in Pashtun identity is perfectly compatible with writing in Persian. 'Abd al-Hadi Dawi, another Pashtun journalist and later editor of *Siraj al-Akhbar*, illustrates the opposite tendency, in which he inserts Persian and originally Arabic words into a Pashto poem titled "Afghan Literature" (*Adabiyat-e Afghani*):

> The Pashto language is sweet (*shirin*)
> It is both eloquent (*fasih*) and strong (*matin*).[41]

This legitimizing of Pashto as a suitable vehicle for modernity is a continual refrain in the work of Muhyi al-Din Afghan. In the poem below, Afghan develops Salih Muhammad's image of the *vatan* ("homeland") as garden:

> My heart is full of love for the homeland (*vatan*)
> My homeland is as precious to me as my own body
> Every flower of my homeland is dear to me
> Dearer than Kashmir, Paris, London.[42]

Here, a common expression of love for the homeland is coupled with a new conception of equal citizenship, where "every flower of the homeland" is to be equally respected. Moreover, Afghan's "modern" Pashto poetry draws on older Pashto cultural stock: in the final line, Afghan references a well-known Pashto *matal* ("proverb"), which runs: "Everybody's homeland is a Kashmir to them", adapting traditional Pashtun forms to a newly-minted universalist sentiment. This use of the folk tradition also illustrates a nascent interest amongst intellectuals in the Pashto folk and classical heritage. Afghan was a pioneer in this regard, collecting together 104 Pashto proverbs and publishing them in *Siraj al-Akbar*.[43] At the same time, with Tarzi professing his ignorance of Pashto literature, it was Afghan who took charge of writing about Pashto literature, producing biographical sketches of historical Pashtun poets, such as Khushhal Khan Khattak.[44] Poets glorified these classical poets in their own Pashto verse, suggesting that a figure like Khushal Khan Khattak was quite the equal of Persian poets such as Bedil (d.1720) or Qa'ani (1808–54).[45] At the same time, these poets self-consciously referenced traditional Pashto poetic tropes, such as the lips and beauty spot (*khat aw khal*) of the beloved, as being equal or superior to those of the Persian tradition.[46] In this "rediscovery" of Pashto tradition, these modern nationalist intellectuals were self-consciously attempting to create a pride in a shared past. Tarzi himself joined in this project. In one essay in Persian, he uses contemporary nineteenth-century philological and ethnographic theories to link Pashto to the ancient "Aryan peoples", stressing the language's antiquity and prestige.[47] He also consistently used the older term "*Afghani*" to describe the language instead of "Pashto". In this way, "Afghans"—the term now being used to signify any citizen inside the territory of the Afghan nation state regardless of ethnicity, rather than a purely ethnic marker for Pashtuns as it had signified in the past—could all be closely associated with an ancient shared civilization. In this way, the past could be revived and revitalized to serve the present. As Muhyi al-Din Afghan wrote in another Pashto poem:

> If we were well-educated about our past
> We would also be well-prepared for production, and for conflict.[48]

Muhyi al-Din Afghan's focus on the role of education in Afghanistan's transition to modernity was extended to widespread concerns amongst intellectuals about Pashto language education itself. This is perhaps unsurprising considering how many of the intellectuals were themselves educationalists of one sort or another. For Afghan, a Pashto teacher at Habibiyya College and later head of the teacher-training college in Kabul, Pashto language education complemented the development of Pashto poetry writing in the project of raising Pashto up to the status of Persian and for the development of a cosmopolitan national consciousness. Salih Muhammad Qandahari, too, combined his Pashto poetry with the development of Pashto language education, writing the first printed Persian-Pashto grammar in Afghanistan, in 1916, while deputy-director of elementary education in the country.[49] This writing of grammars and textbooks was another way to deprovincialize Pashto, since it required creating a standard Pashto, which would be studied and understood by all.

A corollary to this forging of a new nation that was "modern" and "Afghan" was a fierce hostility to Britain and a call for complete independence from British control. Pashto poetry played an important role in this, as poets re-oriented traditional Pashto poetic idioms of resistance into the new context of the nation state. Such was a famous poem by Salih Muhammad Qandahari, published in 1917:

Look at the Earth!/Oh, look, my brother!
The whole world is in uproar/blackened and angry
The world is beset with a great din/which covers Europe and Asia
Everywhere is engaged in war/cloaked in red blood
God has appointed the Germans/and set them against the Russians and British
The British are filled with fear/sorrowful and sad
Look at the bravery of the Turks/the Byzantines and the Ottomans
God has granted us a great opportunity/He has created the right moment
Those that are fighting with the infidels/and those that are cloaked in red blood
Thank them and may they increase in number/may all the infidels be destroyed.[50]

This poem was to achieve widespread popularity on both sides of the Durand Line. Anti-British sentiment was high in the Pashtun areas of British India at the time, influenced by the Khalifat movement (1919–24) which called on British Indian Muslims to rise up and support their Muslim co-religionists in the Ottoman Empire. Indeed, such was the poem's impact in the North West Frontier Province that the British complained vehemently to *Siraj al-Akhbar* about the tone of the piece.[51] The fact that a poem could incite such concern in the British illustrates the easy flow of poetry across the Durand Line. It is also testament to the transformation of poetry, through memorization and oral transmission, from an elite print setting into widespread popular discourse.[52] However, something that would have been lost on the Pashtuns of British India was the implicit critique of Habibullah contained in the poem's anti-British sentiment. For Habibullah had refused to side with the Ottomans in the First World War, or seek independence from British influence, as the Afghan nationalists wished. Indeed, a poem of very similar sentiment, written in Dari-Persian by 'Abd al-Hadi Dawi, incited the wrath of Habibullah, who threatened him with retribution. It is said that Salih Muhammad escaped Habibullah's displeasure because Habibullah could not read Pashto: a telling example of the ambiguous relation of Pashto to state power during the first two decades of the twentieth century, and of Pashto's enduring value as a means of criticizing—and evading—the state.[53]

Pashto inside the State, 1919–29

The 1920s saw a shift in the role of Pashto literature from being a vehicle of reformist Afghan nationalism with an ambiguous relation to state power, to being a full-blown articulator of state ideology. The primary catalyst of this change was the accession to the throne of Amanullah (r. 1919–29) after the assassination of Habibullah in 1919. Amanullah was heavily influenced by the intellectuals of *Siraj al-Akhbar*, seeing social and political reform as the key to Afghanistan's survival, with the state as the driving force of that reform. The intellectuals, in turn, were impressed by Amanullah's desire for reform, and flattered by his espousal of their own ideas, to the extent that they were happy to take up posts in the state apparatus and for their cultural activities to be increasingly state-sponsored and state-endorsed. A case in point is Mahmud Tarzi. Previously a journalist, Tarzi walked a fine line between pleasing his royal patron and offering thinly-veiled critiques of the Afghan monarchy, and in 1919 he became the foreign minister responsible for the post-war negotiations with the British. So too with 'Abd al-Wasi' Qandahari, a key figure in the constitutional movement, who under Amanullah wrote the legal code for his reign, and became one of the central authorities for many of the controversial edicts passed during the period. Amanullah's focus on developing education in Afghanistan ensured that prominent Pashtun educationalists such as Salih Muhammad Qandahari, and the young teacher and folklorist Ghulam Jilani Jalali (1896–1980), were endorsed by the state in their development of Pashto textbooks and linguistic studies.[54]

In this new political climate, Pashto print literature thus increasingly served to reinforce, not undermine, state power and ideology. Such was the role of the first Pashto newspaper, the *Ittihad-e Mashriqi* ("Eastern Unity"), founded soon after Amanullah's accession in 1919. Its purpose, as its name suggests, was to stress the mutual goodwill between notables in the east of Afghanistan and the state, and contained Pashto prose pieces that defended the legitimacy of the monarch, and of the rural notables themselves. Whereas 'Abd al-Rahman had used brute force and substantial payments to "subdue" rival power bases in Afghanistan, Amanullah used Pashto and played up his Pashtun heritage, as a means of ensuring the support of powerful provincial groups.[55] Amanullah also supported and promoted a variety of new Pashto societies and institutions which, though not founded as state organizations *per se*, were to become official state bodies in the 1930s. Much of the focus of these Pashto activities centred on Qandahar, which points not only to the political influence of Qandahari intellectuals in the new regime, but also to the growth of a mercantile class in Qandahar during the 1920s, which had benefitted from the decline in long-distance nomadic trade in Afghanistan and the increasing integration of Afghan trade with British India. With links to elite Pashtun lineages at court, these middle-class merchants played an important role both in funding public education in Qandahar, and creating an audience for such state-endorsed Pashto literary production.[56]

In 1922, Da Paxto Maraka ("Pashto Committee") was formed in Qandahar under the leadership of the ever-present 'Abd al-Wasi' Qandahari in order to promote Pashto literature.[57] In 1932, this was to become the state-run Paxto Adabi Anjuman ("Pashto Literary Society"). Alongside this committee, a literary magazine, *Tulu'-e Afghan*, under the editorship of Salih Muhammad Qandahari, was also formed in Qandahar. *Tulu'-e Afghan* would run to forty-four issues during the 1920s and had nationwide distribution, so becoming a driving force for a renewed interest in Pashto lexicography and dialectology, as well as literature.[58] This lexicographical focus combined with Salih Muhammad's earlier production of textbooks and grammars to help solidify a "standard" "Afghan Pashto", if only for the written word. From this burgeoning Qandahari literary and scholarly world were to come many of the key Pashto writers and state intellectuals of the 1930s and 1940s. A Pashto poem by 'Abd al-Wasi' Qandahari, written in 1925, captures well the new socio-political context these state intellectuals found themselves operating in, and the new use of Pashto literature for legitimating state structures and ideology. As we have seen, 'Abd al-Wasi' was both a legislator and litterateur. His poetry offers an attempt to justify the controversial legal codes he had helped formulate, by appealing to the ideals of individual sovereignty, rationality and the rule of law:

Lack of conscience has disgraced the whole universe/
Every man has exchanged conscience for impulse
Impulses of various sorts were born/And became the guide for the world
And discord arose in our path/Disputes and disagreement filled the environment
In order to heal this contradiction of impulses, friend/
Laws of justice came circulating down
Defending against natural impulses, look!/
Conscience fosters unity in all directions.[59]

In this justification of the state legal system, 'Abd al-Wasi' also reveals the tension in elite intellectuals' writing about the "Afghan people", and particularly Pashtuns, during this period. For at the same time as 'Abd al-Wasi' stresses the importance of the individual autonomous subject, there is a concurrent impulse to objectify non-elites, especially rural Pashtun groups, as backward and provincial in opposition to his utopian universalist vision. This is illustrated in the middle section of the poem, where he imagines an anarchical vision of Pashtun rural life, beset by disunity and self-interest, and laments:

Those who don't want guidance can't be guided/
Hungry, blind, wretched, needy, powerless
Cooperation is gone from the *qabila* (tribe), and the *qawm* (tribe/people/nation)/
We may have long beards but we act like boys.[60]

This image of the people as "child-like" reflects the mix of pessimism and optimism that colours elite intellectual views of rural life of the time. In this view, the rural people, identified preeminently with rural Pashtuns, were characterized as backward and provincial, and yet nevertheless the raw material from which could be created the new Afghan nation. The poem thus perpetuates and solidifies older elite conceptions of the "provincial" Pashtun at the same time as it attempts to overcome them with an optimistic vision of personal agency and participation in the modern state.

Between Pashtun *and* Pakhtun: *Cross-Border Connections in the 1920s*

These developments in Pashto cultural activity coincided with a period of increased, at times problematic, contact with Pashtuns in British India.[61] The Third Anglo-Afghan War (1919) had greatly relied on the support of

Pashtuns in the Tribal Areas along the border with British India, both sides of the Durand Line united in anti-British efforts.[62] These connections could be seen in the magazine *Ittihad-e Mashriqi*, which had printed Pashtun nationalist poems from across the border, using these poems to further legitimate Amanullah's anti-British pro-independence stance. The Hijrat ("migration") movement (c. 1920–21), in which many Indian Muslims left British India in protest against its war with the Ottoman Empire, had also led to thousands of Pashtuns moving across the border into Afghanistan. Amongst them was 'Abd al-Ghaffar Khan (1890–1988), the "Frontier Gandhi" and founder of the Khudai Khidmatgar ("Servants of God") movement, which promoted Pashtun ethno-nationalism as part of a resistance movement against the British. Ghaffar Khan met Amanullah in Kabul in 1920 and encouraged him to take an interest in Pashto:

"What a pity it is that you, who know so many languages, do not know Pashto, though it is your mother tongue and your national language!" The king agreed with me and soon he began to learn Pashto.[63]

The 1920s saw a reflorescence of Pashto language and literature in the NWFP. As part of his attempts to instill a unified Pashtun conscience amongst groups living in the NWFP, Ghaffar Khan pushed for Pashto language education in schools where the British had previously had a general policy of solely Urdu instruction. To further this end, in 1921 Ghaffar Khan founded an association for overseeing Pashto-medium education, the Anjuman-e Islah al-Afaghina (Society for the Reformation of Afghans). The Anjuman helped create new publics for Pashto written and oral literature in its quest for mass support: teams of students and teachers visited different villages, sang nationalist songs, and delivered speeches in mosques and *hujras* ("guest-houses"), the traditional location for oral poetic performance.[64]

The Anjuman-e Islah al-Afaghina also held annual meetings, which grew in numbers year on year until 1927 when 80,000 people are said to have attended.[65] These became important rallying points for anti-British sentiment, and stages for poetry recitals, declamation contests, and dramas. As discussed further in James Caron's chapter, in the later years *musha'ira* "poetry contests" took place, but in a new form. Rather than competing for local patronage between professional poets, as in the nineteenth century, these *musha'iras* were transformed into a vehicle for social and political comment, concerned with issues such as the unity of the Pashtuns, the savagery of the British and the importance of education. Two starting lines give a flavour of such occasions:

> If you have any idea for the liberty of your country…

and

> Young men had always gone out to fight the battle of freedom…[66]

It was also at one of these annual events that the first play in Pashto, *Drai Yatiman* ("Three Orphans") written by 'Abd al-Akbar Khan Akbar, was performed by students of Azad High School. As with increasing numbers of plays that were to follow, it was concerned with a landlord's unjust treatment of the poor, and the hypocrisy of certain government-backed *'ulama*.[67] Lamenting that "the Pakhtuns… had no love for their own language", Ghaffar Khan also oversaw the first issue of a Pashto literary journal, *Paxtun*, in May 1928.[68] The title page carried lines, said to be written by Ghaffar Khan's son Ghani Khan (1914–96), which couples the Islamic vocabulary of nineteenth century resistance poetry to an awareness of a unified supra-tribal body of people, "the Pashtuns":

> If I a slave, lie buried in a grave, under a resplendent tomb-stone,
> Respect it not, spit on it.
> When I die, and not lie bathed in martyr's blood,
> None should his tongue pollute, offering prayers for me.
> O mother, with what face will you wail for me,
> If I am not torn to pieces by British guns?
> Either I turn this wretched land of mine into a Garden of Eden
> Or I wipe out the lanes and homes of Pakhtuns![69]

This vision of Pashtun unity transcended nation state boundaries to include all Pashtuns, regardless of whether they were living in British India or Afghanistan or indeed anywhere: the journal's biggest audience turned out to be in America, where many Pashtuns had recently settled, and it was American Pashtun communities who also gave the most financial assistance to the journal.[70] From the Indian side, there was much overt support for Amanullah's reform project, and Afghanistan was idealized by many Pashtuns in British India as a model for what they should try to achieve. A Pashtun female poet named Nagina used Amanullah's progressive policies towards women as ammunition with which to berate Pashtuns in India's treatment of women:

O Pakhtun, when you demand your freedom, why do you deny it to women?
If you want us to do national work, then dispel our darkness with education…

… A satanic ordinance is imposed on us.
It is a sin to sympathise with us, for only yesterday,
King Amanullah Khan was declared a kafir for championing our cause![71]

However, this cross-border support for Amanullah could not disguise the tensions between the Afghan state's vision of a territorially bounded multi-ethnic Afghan nationalism and Ghaffar Khan's borderless Pashtun ethno-nationalism. Ghaffar Khan himself captured this tension in the opening editorial of *Paxtun*, in which he emphasized his solidarity with his "Afghan brethren", at the same time as he criticized them:

The Paxtuns, including those in Afghanistan, form one nation… we are disappointed with our Afghan brethren. It is a Paxtun nation by language, traditions and custom, but their state language is Persian. We fervently hope that they will give serious thought to it.[72]

As has been seen, serious thought was given to the development of Pashto language and literature in Afghanistan. But during the 1920s at least, it was not part of a larger "Pashtunization" programme. Rather, the development of Pashto was seen by elite Afghan intellectuals more as a tool in a larger project of creating a cosmopolitan multilingual multi-ethnic nationalism, where Pashto would have the same status as Dari-Persian, not replace it. At the same time, the Afghan intellectuals who drove developments in Pashto-written literature and language reform during the 1920s could not have been more different from the rural, mass mobilizations of the Pashtuns in British India. The Afghan intellectuals were frequently from elite lineage families who had been co-opted into state management; their intellectual activities constituted state policy, not resistance to it. Their roles as administrators, teachers, and jurists meant that they now had such a stake in the state that Pashto print production was largely designed to reinforce their cosmopolitan state-endorsed ideologies and legitimize the Afghan monarchy and its system of elite patronage. These tensions within alternative visions of Pashtun nationalism, and the role of Pashto within those visions, did not stop a flow of poems and texts between Afghanistan and the North West Frontier Province of British India. The journal *Paxtun* itself was popular and widely distributed in Afghanistan, and Tendulkar's biography of 'Abd al-Ghaffar Khan tantalizingly mentions an Afghan version, *Paxtun Jagh*, which ran for nine issues before the overthrow of Amanullah's regime in 1929.[73] But the type of social critique of unequal power relations found in the Pashto poetry and plays of the Anjuman-e Islah al-Afaghina was more of a threat than an ally to Amanullah's regime, and was thus treated with ambivalence by Afghan intellectuals keen to make Pashto serve not subvert the state that they had helped to create.

Conclusions

The aim of this chapter has been to chart the ambiguous relationship between the Pashto language and political power in Afghanistan up to 1930. At the centre of the story has been a paradox: while political power in Afghanistan has frequently been identified with "Pashtun" rule, Pashto itself has almost always been subordinate to other politically dominant languages at court. However, as this chapter has suggested, Pashto has actually drawn much of its activist power from this marginalized, subordinate status. This is particularly true of its oral traditions, in which idioms of resistance have developed in relation to imperial and colonial expansionism. The Pashto language has been represented, and frequently represented itself, as a difficult language for the state to "learn"; its unique orthography, perception as a "difficult" language for non-native speakers and the face-to-face nature of popular oral transmission, have all proved an effective means of evading control. Indeed, it was not until the 1910s, through a concerted effort of state-backed reformist intellectuals, that Pashto was imagined as a language of the "modern" Afghan nation state. Even here, however, the project remained incomplete: in escaping its status as subordinate to Dari-Persian, it never escaped its status as a symbol, rather than living and breathing component, of the Afghan state.

Moreover, this project of fixing Pashto inside the Afghan state took shape at the same time as the rise of a reformist ethno-nationalist Pashto literature based in British India which knew no boundaries, either geographically or politically. Drawing more on the social activism of nineteenth-century oral poetry, this literature offered a critique of traditional power structures, both local and national, and a vision of cross-border Pashtun ethno-nationalism quite antithetical to Afghan intellectuals' vision of a bounded nation state nationalism legitimately ruled by its monarchy and political elites. These two separate strands in Pashto literature of the period, towards state rule and away from it, were to develop and interact in Afghanistan in the 1930s and 1940s, helping foster new publics and possibilities for Pashto literature. At the same time, it was these dissonances, between state and society, nation state and cross-border nationalism, which were to provide the internal dynamism which has driven Pashto literature forward, right up to the present day.

5

AMBIGUITIES OF ORALITY AND LITERACY, TERRITORY AND BORDER CROSSINGS

PUBLIC ACTIVISM AND PASHTO LITERATURE IN AFGHANISTAN, 1930–2010

James Caron

Introduction: Pashto as a Literary Periphery

In 1936, Afghanistan's prime minister, Muhammad Hashim Khan (in office, 1929–46), made a pronouncement establishing a special role for Pashto literature in the country. It was to be an icon of unique national identity, and a tool for fostering greater national unity in a state populated by several distinct communities. Explaining a new series of bureaucratic regulations, Hashim declared that Pashto would gradually become

the national language of our officials, doing away with Persian. Our legends and our poems will then be understood by everyone. We shall draw from them a pride in our culture of the past, which will unite us.[1]

But this vision would not be realized. Alongside the rich oral tradition of folk romances and resistance ballads that Hashim Khan hoped to appropriate, and a vast store of other oral material besides, Pashto had long boasted a refined written literary culture. It incorporated most intellectual currents present in neighbouring languages and developed several genres all its own. However, it did not possess the millennium of precedent that cosmopolitan registers of Persian enjoyed as a language of command, the elaborate sociolinguistic complex of letters, documentation, and edicts through which the Afghan state—like most regional states prior to colonialism—projected discourses of civilization and technologies of rule.

The real-world result, in the field of Afghan language policy, was predictable. Sayyid Qasim Rishtiya describes how certain policy-makers in Kabul became alarmed that some protagonists of Pashto—a rustic language in their view, the provincialized language only of its own speakers—wished to extend its influence beyond the realm of the symbolic, and inject it into the everyday for all Afghanistan's inhabitants, Pashtun and non-Pashtun alike. Calling a conference of major cultural stakeholders in 1946, the new prime minister, Shah Mahmud (in office 1946–53), came to be convinced that such an extension of Pashto as actually dominant would be a political liability in a country where Pashtuns formed only a plurality. It was decided that Pashto would thenceforth be promoted by the state only via the Directorate of Publications, which in practice meant the realm of fine arts literature, limited regional media, and linguistic and cultural studies—emphatically not through mandated education or widespread adaptation as a bureaucratic language.[2]

In so deciding, the government officialized a paradoxical socio-political role that Pashto occupied over the past few centuries: the heritage, simultaneously championed and disavowed, of Afghanistan's urbanized dynastic rulers who continued to rule through Persian; a vehicle for the expression of most aspects of everyday, particularly rural, life in regions that were increasingly marginalized before the monarchic Afghan state; and a language of activist critique from those margins. The twentieth century added to this formula the domain of Pashtun reformists, urbanized though often of rural origins, who came to occupy the majority of posts in official cultural and linguistic research institutions. As the century pushed on, Pashto literature came to reflect new political worlds, new imagined aspirations, possibilities not only of localized subversion of hierarchies, but of horizontal brotherhood across regions. Further, poetic literature was the primary activity through which political activists were able to carve out the public arenas that their critiques would inhabit.

AMBIGUITIES OF ORALITY

Periodization and Themes

This chapter surveys Pashto literature in socio-political context, and introduces ways that poetic literature in particular has been used as activist public speech in Afghanistan, especially from the 1930s onwards. The decade coincided with the reconsolidation of an aristocratic state under the monarch Nadir Shah, after a brief seizure of power by the commoner Habibullah Kalakani in 1929. It focuses on the social domains of Pashto literary circulation, and considers Pashto poetic literature in Afghanistan as many practitioners viewed it: as social ammunition and one of the dominant vehicles available for public intervention. Finally, it pays attention to how the creation of new publics was integral to Pashto literary activism, and how Pashto literature was a primary activity leading to the articulation of new forms of public interaction. It does this through a broadly chronological narrative, tracing the interplay over time of decentred and rooted cultural circulation, from local to national and transnational; of oral and literate cultural production; and of strategies for contesting inequalities. The section following this one explores the Pashto literature of the post 1930s period, during which urban and rural disjuncture was accentuated. Urban literary writers reflect a greater integration of Afghanistan's urban elites into an Afghan national literary public, but also into a coalescing world order of global capitalist markets and nation states, as Nile Green's chapter in this volume also illustrates. Poets adopted multiple idioms of cosmopolitanism, deploying both Persianate and Enlightenment metaphors in arguing for liberal democracy.

For rural eastern populations, however, the 1930s were different. *Tazkira* literary-biographical directories attest to how scholars from the lower rural gentry circulated through a more local, fragile grassroots cosmopolitanism spanning Persian and eastern Pashto dialects, Hindko and Urdu, with prominent examples as late as the 1930s. Still, educational networks, textually-transmitted ideas, and local yet interlocking oral public domains extending from the Hindu Kush to the Gangetic Plain rapidly became fragmented, reoriented domestically and corralled into state institutions, especially after the first third of the century. Meanwhile, folklore collections attest in blurrier detail to a constricting of geographical scope in self-expression of petty traders and labourers, while colonial sources note truncations in these economic areas too. Activist literature also became directed inward after 1930, pointing out domestic class divides obliquely even from within new monarchic state forums that ranged from print to oral performance.

Amid region-wide political-economic stresses, the period from 1945 through 1965 saw new domestic cross-class alliances between urbanizing, reformist Pashtun scholars and rural oral poets from the swelling casual agrarian labour pool. As ostensibly monarchic public forums developed, incorporating this cross-fertilization, new genres emerged, helping to create and popularize opposing self-images among Pashtun rural poor and intellectual elites alike—abstract images of mass society and egalitarian ethnic belonging that transcended local rooting and national borders. Meanwhile, governments attempted to defuse these new technologies of resistance through co-opting and segregating urban and rural public domains, especially after the mid-1960s.

In the war period of 1978 through 1992, we see an acceleration of this trend. The People's Democratic Party of Afghanistan (PDPA) implemented unprecedented levels of direct control over cultural circulation in urban centres, in contrast to earlier techniques of channelling and surveillance. The same was also somewhat true of rural resistance literatures, linked to militant factions. Yet the story is not only one of control. Rural poets supporting the war effort developed resistance genres, wedding political analysis with metaphysical and emotional rhetoric. These linked refugee and local populations in transnational publics of circulation and consumption and extended conceptual frontiers of belonging far beyond the geographical boundaries of a hollowed state, or the patronage boundaries of any one faction.

The trauma of war and dislocation has continued unabated until the present, as we see in the final section of this chapter. Yet we also find evidence that dislocation engendered a kind of cross-fertilization, as social domains were integrated with each other in new ways. New possibilities for contestation foster in literature a critical socio-political scepticism of all political structures, while activists imagine new kinds of egalitarian belonging. Can we draw some broad themes linking text and context in modern Pashto literatures? It is clear that many Pashto literary cultures in contemporary Afghanistan were not dominated by the fixity of vertical, rooted "strategic" power of what we might call Dari-Persian's "command" registers. Rather, fluid discourses of more contingent "tactical" resistance, transgression, or evasion often flourished even in cultivated Pashto literature.[3] Along with tacit recognition of rootedness in dominant identities—in bounded political territories of the state, or in social categories like lineage that were useful to monarchy—much Pashto literature evidences avoidance, transgression, disregard, or creative repurposing of those categories. Often, as this chapter particularly demonstrates, we see exploitation of ambiguity within elite media, alongside repeated appropriations of elite forums for non-elite concerns. We see constant flux between oral and literate domains, and urban and rural ones.

Orality and Literacy in Kabul and Beyond, 1930–45

The 1930s were marked by the relatively rapid articulation of new urban and rural publics; that is, imagined and diffuse social spaces that were defined, textured, stratified, and demarcated by strangers participating in specific genres of ideas. New channels of circulation for poetry infused it with new activist potentials. This was especially true for a nascent intellectual class in Kabul, Qandahar and Jalalabad, alongside the rural areas of the Eastern Provinces. In urban centres of the 1920s and 30s, in the few sources available we see an increasing awareness of Pashto literature as a public activity. Printing in Pashto flourished in Qandahar even in the 1920s, and the primarily Pashto weekly *Tuluʻ-e Afghan* ("Afghan Rising") attracted cross-regional readership during that decade. Also, a number of small literary salons among Qandahar's hybrid mercantile-intellectual classes coalesced into institutions that attracted governmental interest. Foremost seems to have been the Da Paxto Maraka (Pashto Salon), which was appropriated early in the 1930s through the offices of then interior minister of Afghanistan, Muhammad Gul Momand (1885–1964), himself an intellectual and a zealous supporter of Pashto letters. The Maraka was soon brought to Kabul and merged with the Dari-Persian Anjuman-e Adabi-ye Kabul (Kabul Literary Society), along with many of the intellectuals staffing it. It eventually morphed into the Da Paxto Tolana (Pashto Academy), an official linguistic academy, inaugurating an ambitious programme of research into Pashto linguistics and literary history.

Over the course of the 1930s and early 1940s, the publications that this body issued generally served to articulate at least an orthographically standardized Pashto. Also, early Pashto print activities articulated the territorial space of Afghanistan as nation state, as well as the privilege of the lineage that ruled it. Nationalist poetry was often based on earlier Persian models, revamped to develop Pashto into a vehicle for a national Afghan urbanity. Meanwhile, print participation in lexicographical debates tied far-flung dialect regions together in a common linguistic space that, by default, stopped at the Durand Line.[4] For readers, consuming this activity in depersonalized print served to internalize feelings of Afghan citizenship among the urban, Pashto-literate, mercantile and administrative classes of Qandahar (and, to a lesser extent, Kabul and Jalalabad too). Still, print—monopolistically controlled by the state, as it would remain throughout much of the century—was nothing like a major sphere of Pashto poetic circulation in Afghanistan. Nor was it the primary vehicle through which poetic discourses circulated over long distances. Attention to interactions of Pashto oral, literate and print culture is important.

Extensive notes by the literary historian Nasrullah Nasir to a thin poetry volume provide some of the most valuable information available on the practice of poetic exchange (*musha'ira*) in Pashto, as well as on the role of poetry in forging publics prior to print.[5] For centuries, elite literate poets engaged in written dialogic exchanges by composing new work in the over-rhyme (*qafia* and *radif*) of well-known poems—almost like leaving their signatures on a public wall, albeit one accessed mostly by cross-regional literate Pashtun elites familiar with the developing canon.

One exchange initiated by Qadir Khan Khattak (c.1652–1730) of Nowshera in contemporary Pakistan, building on a poem by his father Khushhal Khan (1613–89), stretched across the years into early twentieth-century Afghanistan. Qadir Khan's answer to Khushhal's verse changed the *qafia*, to a rhyme in /-un/. But this minor change was significant, as he used it to rhyme with "Pashtun", thereby inaugurating a public, dialogic inter-elite document that engaged identity across borders of time and administrative geographies. It has come to be known as "the historic *musha'ira*". Qadir writes:

This ghazal that I, 'Abd al-Qadir, expressed in Pashto –
I'd be lying if [I said that], other than this *khan*, another Pashtun composed its like.[6]

To this provocation, six other eighteenth-century contemporaries composed responses; and the chain continued sporadically down to 1930s Afghanistan where it was revived by Mawlavi Salih Muhammad Qandahari (1890–1960). At this time, Salih Muhammad's colleague 'Abd al-Hayy Habibi (1910–84) printed the *zamina* ("foundation couplet") in the weekly *Tulu'-e Afghan* of Qandahar, which served elite literate Pashtuns across the country, prompting cryptic yet unmistakably activist responses in the context of a largely pro-constitutionalist print public under absolute monarchy:

> Latent in the law, a red-hot poker lays next to a fragrant censer,
> If only participation in a gathering of friends could be like that.

AMBIGUITIES OF ORALITY

The following verse, by the eminent folklorist M.G. Nuri (1902–73), author of the earliest compilation of Pashto folk stories, *Milli Hindara* ("Mirror of the Nation"), has potential to be interpreted as nationalist desire as well as individual passion, when it arises in this context:

> The way that I care about you, no other Pashtun can care,
> Sorrowful in my care for you, none can be so sorrowful.[7]

The activities and tropes of at least this written *musha'ira* moved from individual braggadocio to collective activism, by virtue of the public forum they were adapted to. And at the same time, others were started in the *Tulu'-e Afghan* for similar purposes. On the other hand, the idea of *musha'ira* maintained face-to-face, contingent aspects too, articulating oral publics that were far more extensive than the written. Generally, and far more commonly, *musha'ira* referred to a gathering in which poets exchanged both composed and extemporaneous poems. Before 1920, this was common in Afghanistan and the Pashtun regions of British India primarily as an oral folk activity, through which rural professional intellectuals (poet-musician parties) would compete for exclusive rights to perform in local territories under the patronage of landed notables (*khans* or *maliks*).[8] However, in Urdu culture to the south-east, the practice had urbane precedent.

Over the 1920s and especially the 1930s, a recombination of these trends appears to have gentrified the Pashto folk *musha'ira* in British India's Peshawar Valley and its surroundings, at the same time as it popularized the practice widespread among elite amateur intellectuals. This was also an activist innovation: Ajmal Khattak (1925–2010) notes that the competitive practice of village intellectuals was gradually subsumed by the mass campaigns of the Da Khudai Khidmatgar (Servants of God) movement.[9] Like others of the time across British India, this movement—building on Gandhian ideals and tactics as well as homegrown Islamic liberation theology—pioneered the transformation of rural public interactions. Mass participation in nationalist rallies, marches, print media recited orally in Pashto, and cross-class *musha'iras* created interfaces between multiple, previously unrelated publics. At their upper register these publics interfaced with cross-regional Urdu print publics, while on the most vernacular level they encouraged private, individualized recirculation of nationalist poetry through formerly extemporaneous or anonymous genres like the two-line *tappa/landey*. Often, literate small landowners with access to both domains would serve as nodes of interaction; and it was they who formed the organizational backbone of the movement.[10]

Further, these nationalist publics interfaced with various pre-existing educational and devotional religious publics. The work of Sana Haroon focuses on the importance of activism emanating from individualized face-to-face networks of allegiance in the tribal regions, networks which also had important nodes, such as Hadda, in Afghan territory.[11] Meanwhile, self-descriptions in Afghan *tazkira* biographical-anthological sources tell us that mid-ranking, mobile rural Pashtun scholars ranging from Kabul to Delhi in the 1920s defined their relationships to others in terms of shared interaction in textual canons, as often as they defined them in terms of personal allegiances.[12] And, when serving as local teachers and small landowners, this rural scholarly gentry (as opposed to the ritual technician mullah class) adapted ideas from canonical texts into poetic Pashto compositions that spoke to local socio-political concerns, and were recirculated by other poets and musicians.

Thus, both textual and devotional understandings of social relationships informed a hybrid public domain that incorporated both personalized and depersonalized interactions. These domains were further hybrid in that the ideas they adapted to Pashto were taken up by local *musha'ira* poets and translated into the concerns of rural society beyond scholarly domains.[13] Finally, these rural publics—particularly dense and mutually-integrated in the regions between Kabul and Peshawar—were transformed over the 1930s and early 1940s. They too came to be articulated with the mobilized publics described above.

This was true even as mobility across Afghanistan's eastern regions and the border with India changed in character after 1915 and especially after 1930. For urban elites, Afghanistan was further opened to the world while, for most Pashtuns, this access drastically decreased. Some scholars continued to enjoy cross-border links with each other, though fewer than before; while traders and especially migrant labourers were far more circumscribed in both their range and their numbers. Simultaneously, scholars from the lower gentry—like the lower gentry as a whole—were increasingly edged out politically and economically by allies of monarchy from favoured lineages and families. As demands from below became locally-concentrated, and as mobile scholars of the lower gentry increasingly threw in their stake with the rural poor, it seems that activism became more domestically-concentrated as well. We take up all these processes from the period of 1930–65 in the next two sections.

AMBIGUITIES OF ORALITY

National Appropriations; Resistance through Ambiguity: 1930–45

Alongside state consolidation, the governments of Nadir Shah (r. 1929–33) and Zahir Shah (r. 1933–73) attempted to consolidate their ideological apparatus by segregating rural and urban intellectuals into bounded categories and rounding them up in quasi-official bodies like the Da Paxto Tolana (for literary and cultural studies) and the Jami'at-e 'Ulama (a circle of scholars formed by Nadir Shah to standardize a state-approved religious curriculum), or government schools and courts on the lower levels. Rural intellectuals with roots in eastern small gentry were heavily recruited into the top ranks of these bodies: in the early Paxto Tolana, Qiyam al-Din Khadim (c. 1907–79), Siddiqullah Rixtin (1919–98), Gul Pacha Ulfat (c. 1909–77) were all from Nangrahar.

Was this measure designed to reign in the disturbing possibility of British Indian-style reformist-Islamic and Pashtun-nationalist mass mobilization in eastern Afghanistan? That is, was it an attempt to prevent the articulation of these kinds of publics on monarchic soil; or, failing that, to co-opt them into state structures? If so, it was only partially successful on both counts. For scholars interacting in these realms, there was a contradiction between the solidifying claims and demands of a territorial monarchic nation state of Afghanistan, and their memory of growing up in a shared social space of ideas that knew less top-down structuring (and fewer borders). Could this lived disjuncture be one reason why, near the middle of the century, it was these scholars who eventually reshaped the content of Pashtun nationalism in Afghanistan to fit a liberalist model?

As scholars like Rixtin, Khadim and Ulfat found their way into state agencies, this disjuncture became visible in their activities. As officials in governmental cultural bodies, the state relied on them to coordinate new sorts of public events including *musha'iras* in the style of those in British India, but in service of the state and its concerns. Did the impetus for this borrowing come from the side of reformist, modernist scholars, or from royalist administrators? Anecdotal evidence suggests that people of vastly different outlooks all saw value in the practice; more than this is difficult to say.[14]

From the 1930s onward, and especially in the 1940s, the public *musha'ira* spread in Afghanistan as a new domain of discourse bringing together rural power brokers and non-elites. Poems lauded royalty, nation, and beneficent public works, among other topics.[15] Yet evidence also suggests the persistence of face-to-face politics in state *musha'iras*. Even down to the 1960s, rural oral poets received cash prizes and land grants from aristocratic patrons, a practice similar to village-scale discipline.[16] These contradictions sharpened by the 1940s for many sectors of rural society, labourers and small gentry alike, as we will see.

Disjunctures of territory and identity between elites and others are likewise visible in the weekly publication, *Ittihad-e Mashriqi* ("Eastern Unity"), the sole news publication in eastern Afghanistan and one that Ulfat and Khadim both edited at different points. This paper was originally inaugurated to mark a compact between eastern lineage, religious, and landowning notables and the monarchy during the 1919 war of independence. Along with printing that compact, the first issue described icons of honour that the monarchy bestowed upon the leaders, such as rifles with tribal genealogies engraved upon them.[17] Throughout its early years, it printed Pashto prose articles that reinforced this type of heavily unequal yet ostensibly voluntary regime of layered sovereignty, undergirded by honours and service, and monarchically-enforced access to local land and power. In other words, it was not only on the state level that monarchy rooted populations. It also served to root local populations in lower orders of territorial sovereignty (what is often, misleadingly, analyzed as "tribalism"), through political, economic, and ideological means.

At the same time, the *Ittihad-e Mashriqi* journal heavily featured in its poetry sections the Pashtun nationalist poems from British India that the rural Afghan scholarly gentry were already personally familiar with, alongside others that were composed in similar veins by Afghan scholars themselves.[18] These tended to speak out against colonialism, sometimes in contrast to the "free" kingdom of Afghanistan. Their appearance in a state print forum may seem to bolster elite ideologies of nation through the act of reading—just as Afghanistan-internal lexicographical debates over standardized language did. And there is little doubt that for some circles in the royal family and other aristocratic actors in Kabul, Pashtun nationalism and Afghan nationalism were congruent. For such circles, it seems plausible to follow up on certain arguments of Shah Mahmoud Hanifi and argue a sort of external reification as a genealogical ancestor for elite Pashtun-Afghan nationalism.[19] That is, there was an overlap for national elites, in many of the families and their retinues that had earlier spent considerable time in exile in British India, between several ideologies: earlier colonial constructions about Pashtuns; Pashtun dynastic rule over a nation state "Afghanistan"; and a proud complacency in Afghanistan's post-1919 independence.

AMBIGUITIES OF ORALITY

Yet for scholars in the lower gentry, increasingly constrained in their social possibilities by landed and lineage elites whose local power and monarchic power reinforced each other, songs from British India and, after 1947, Pakistan's North West Frontier Province's Pashtun nationalist movement, held radically different meanings. In eastern Afghanistan, these reformist songs resonated with a critique not only of colonialism's inegalitarianism, but of local power relations too. As with elite *musha'ira* practice, here too a limited development of new public forums carried some possibility of engagement with reformist-modernist ideologies to populations primarily through poetry, rather than prose.

Even oral poetry from the margins interacted with this domain. Early work by the non-literate sharecropper poet of Jalalabad, Malang Jan (c.1921–57), appeared in *Ittihad-e Mashriqi* in the mid- to late 1930s, reproduced by literate scholars who heard it spread through local word of mouth, or at some of the events they managed. Some of Malang Jan's earliest printed work was about the importance to society of education; while another famous early couplet used the metaphor of talking birds to describe an embryonic yet growing activist sense of a citizen-maintained, not state-centric, grassroots public:

> Let not this orchard of parrots be overgrown with thorns,
> For its sake this Pashtun gardener will kill himself in it.

This trend of oral and literate cross-fertilization would flourish over the coming decades in remarkable ways.

Short-Lived Alliances: Cross-Class, Urban and Rural, 1945–65

In 1949, Amir Hamza Shinwari (1907–94), the great Pashto lyric poet of the newly-formed state of Pakistan, was part of a delegation to Kabul aimed at standardizing Pashto orthography in both countries, alongside a more diffuse goal of improving relations between the two suspicious neighbours through cultural exchange. The versified travelogue that he wrote speaks of many things, but a recurrent theme is the westernized, enclave character of urban Afghanistan.[20] And if one did not access other Pashto sources, one would imagine that the now-prominent literary scholars his delegation worked with—the aforementioned Ulfat, Khadim, and Rixtin of Nangarhar; 'Abd al-Ra'uf Benawa (1914–84) from Qandahar, among others—also kept to an elite literary enclave. True, during the mid- to late 1940s, one stream of the critical nationalism that developed did come to represent an enclaved composite culture, not overly tied to the local life of regions outside the capital. It is important to sketch out its boundaries. The Second World War and its effects on the Indian economy brought catastrophic socio-economic stresses on Afghanistan, which exacerbated tensions in the royal family. Muhammad Da'ud Khan, in particular, aligned himself with oligarchic capital and especially with 'Abd al-Majid Zabuli (1896–1998), minister of national economy and founder of the state bank, in a drive for a centralized, planned economy and a Turkish-style republican state. This latter goal involved creating university-based intellectual cadres in the major cities beginning with Kabul, and encouraging underground modernist, reformist and radical circles that were already coalescing there. This was abetted by the replacement of the authoritarian Hashim Khan with his more open brother, Shah Mahmud, as prime minister in 1946, amid increasingly strident demands by the urban population of Kabul for liberal reform.

By 1948, a number of critical intellectuals were released from prison and participated in a new, intellectual-dominated seventh parliament—an assertive body, for the first time. By 1951, a law was pushed through that provided freedom of press. Activists from the Pashtun gentry of Qandahar City and rural Nangrahar, as described above, successfully participated in both arenas (Ulfat was deputy of the National Assembly), alongside a new generation educated in urban secular institutions. Among the new publications that sprang up were critical-left publications like *Angar* ("Ember"), *Vatan* ("Homeland"), and *Nada-ye Khalq* ("Voice of the People"). In this print milieu, Pashto gained ground as an intellectual vehicle for reformist and radical ideas in prose, expressing concerns similar to those in the capital's Dari-Persian press.

The Pashtunistan issue—a nationalist attachment to the freedom of Pashtun regions in the new state of Pakistan—was an exception. Many non-Pashtun intellectuals dismissed it as a stunt by Da'ud, designed to divert attention from domestic reform while encouraging exceptionalism and chauvinism. This eventually led to much ethnic self-segregation among urban activists. Whether or not this was a calculated policy on Da'ud's part to "divide and rule" while still pressuring more traditional royalist factions, it had that effect.

Still, here too, beyond the fact that cross-border society was very real for intellectuals with roots in regional Pashto scholarly cultures, it seems that a major part of liberalist Pashtun commitment to the Pashtunistan cause stemmed from the possibility that a critique of human rights in the new state of Pakistan opened up a discursive space for discussion of the same in Afghanistan. In a 1949 broadcast on official radio directed at Pakistani "Pashtunistan", organized and scripted by a combination of the older and newer intellectual classes described in the sections above, what should we make of Aminullah Zmariyalai's deployment of the following classical couplet as a title for his speech?

> Take freedom out from under the foot of monarchy,
> When one is under the command of another, he is imprisoned.

Khadim, in his contribution to the broadcast, dramatized the dialogue between a number of prisoners and their jailer, as they gradually discover their bondage. This was a reference to what Afghan intellectuals saw as a continued oppression of Pashtuns in Pakistan despite the end of British

Fig. 12: *Pata Khazana*: Pashto Poetry as Antiquity and Nationalism.

rule. Still, Khadim's liberal universalism relies on both Islamic and global discourses of human rights that were used generations earlier in anti-monarchic struggles. It critiques assertions of the existence of masculine egalitarianism in society and divine right which were a more pronounced feature of monarchic Afghan hegemony than Pakistani. And in the wake of the severe shortages of precisely food and clothing that Afghanistan suffered during the Second World War period, the following seems designed to resonate with more than a Pakistani Pashtun audience:[21]

Jailer: What do you mean, you're in pain? I don't understand; and, how do you define freedom? You're free to sleep and work whenever you feel like it; what more do you want?

Prisoner: Don't you see our condition? Look!

Jailer: Even if you're naked and starving, that's God's business. So repent, and go talk to God about it.

Prisoner: Fine, forget about food, and whether we have no wheat or lots of it. The fact is, I am a free human being and was born free; so what is the meaning of these iron bars that are all around me? Why am I not free to decide good and evil for myself? In the end, what is my sin?[22]

In the conclusion, even after the prisoners break out, they have no idea how to arrive at the "Frontiers of Prosperity". They find that they are still bound in place by "golden chains" of ideology, a charge that Khadim frequently made in relation to the rural poor of Afghanistan as well. And this was not just a complaint in elite media. Khadim intended to do something about it.

Pashtun intellectuals from older rural religious-educational networks, including Khadim himself, mark the point where elite Pashto-language literary activism intersected with rural domains. Unlike many of the non-Pashtun Kabuli critical intellectuals, these scholars had roots in intellectual cultures that had tapped into a sub-state, local cosmopolitanism, and were indirectly tied to quasi-Gandhian publics of mass mobilization. They cultivated links with critical scholars across the border, however tenuous those links were, and with them pioneered the realist Pashto short story as a way to convey the sufferings of the rural poor, especially women. Also, as part of their duties in the Paxto Tolana, the Publications Directorate, and other cultural bodies, they maintained local links with casual intellectuals from among the landless and non-literate classes in their Afghan home regions: that is, oral poets.

The life of the aforementioned landless labourer, Malang Jan (c.1921–57), can serve as a token of change among oral poets more generally. In his early work, Malang Jan (like most marginal rural poets) appears to have focused largely on didactic and romantic poems, in abstract folk genres that expressed inequality in highly stylized terms. After working with Khadim and some lower-ranking officials, though, he found a new voice. Malang Jan began developing explicit critiques of rural power which spoke directly to alienation of the rural poor, and articulated ideals of cross-regional horizontal citizenship while claiming that the dominance of locally-rooted, vertical authority is what prevented their realization. Speaking, as usual, as a microcosm for "the mass", Malang Jan protested:

> My throat has gone dry from shouting, but no one listens,
> How long will I be a sharecropper to a deaf landlord?
> I've never been free to serve the nation,
> How long will I have to be servant to each individual *khan*?

As I argue elsewhere, the transformation of the lyric or narrative folk *charbayta* genre into an analytical-argumentative "subaltern political science" genre was directly correlated to the differing scale of publics that marginal intellectuals like Malang Jan found themselves addressing in the late 1940s and early 1950s and the new allies that they found.[23]

During this period, bankrolled by Zabuli as a way to pressure the more conservative royal family, Khadim and a number of other intellectuals helped forge a grassroots social movement integrating oral poets. The Wex Zalmiyan or "Enlightened Youth" organization was an attempt to amplify demands on the state from the margins of society, and to link elite and marginal allies in reformist opinion. Official membership was small; but this was not a movement built on formal allegiance. It was, rather, a movement aimed at changing public opinion by creating a popular sense of "the public" in the first place. It depended on casual recirculation of ideas of morality by like-minded individuals, of which there were eventually many thousands.

As described by one of their activists in Nangrahar, 'Abdullah Bakhtani (1927–), the Zalmiyan organization worked back along the rural cross-regional public domains that they grew up in, deliberately transforming those domains in the process as a way to transform rural political-cultural consciousness. They worked with rural preachers and local religious officials, encouraging them to incorporate discourses of equality based on traditional religious sciences into their sermons. They also made sure that the "right" oral poets would be invited to official *musha'iras* and to semi-public events like weddings, across the Pashto region. And in those official events, they appealed to ideas of the power of "the rural mass" in full public view, as a way of protecting poets from local reprisals.[24] This performative act served to further reinforce the new social categories—mass, nation—present in new poetic works and emergent popular genres. Poems like Malang Jan's later, more critical work were one result of new possibilities and new audiences that oral poets' more elite allies opened up.

Sometimes, Zalmiyan intellectuals composed their own poems in folk genres for musicians to circulate. Other times, the voice of grassroots poets was angry enough and employed categories that furthered the goals of the Zalmiyan organization, while oral performers found an alliance with urban intellectuals useful in projecting their own concerns. There is a tension in the work of some like Malang Jan: support for the Zalmiyan's liberal nationalism coexists with an anxiety that economic developmentalism and the abstract equality of liberal citizenship might involve the namelessness of proletarianization. This sometimes emerged in interesting desires for the future, which continued to articulate rural poor concerns with individual dignity while folding those concerns into ethno-national identity:

Make each Pashtun the master of his own factory; Make all students into teachers
[…]
God, through the power of your Beloved [Prophet]; Never lower the Pashtuns' banner in the world's eyes,
Sorrow's son, in this era, am I, Malang Jan; I live in hope of progress for the Pashtuns.
I am the beggar mingling on every door in every hamlet; If only this world's bazaar didn't mix things up so![25]

The Afghan historian, Hasan Kakar, describes how other local poets picked up this sort of literature, and amateur singers reproduced it in village lodges across the countryside. In the process, critical genres transformed political discourse and participants effectively internalized the idea of a national mass.[26] But the ambivalence in their speech with liberalism provided ammunition that Da'ud Khan could use.

Once he came to power in 1953 as prime minister, Da'ud Khan pressed Malang Jan and other popular poets into service on behalf of the state: building them houses and paying them a stipend to perform on the radio, but dictating the sorts of songs they could sing and utilizing them to forge direct links between his republican monarchic state and the (recently constituted) mass.[27] In so doing, he outmanoeuvered the activism of liberalist intellectuals through the very infrastructure that they helped forge. Meanwhile the most bothersome intellectuals in the Wex Zalmiyan cadres were arrested or resigned.[28]

Elite intellectuals remained in positions of cultural authority, while the events they managed were more directly disciplined by a strong bureaucracy even after Da'ud Khan himself was forced out of power (for playing up the Pashtunistan issue to the point of international crisis). Even in Da'ud Khan's absence, though, state festivals such as the new *Da Naranj da Gulo Mela* ("Tangerine Blossom Festival") in Jalalabad, which started in the 1960s, no longer served largely as arenas for performing the individualized authority of state, as public *musha'iras* did in years past; they remained something of a poetic free speech zone not reducible to the performance of national belonging.[29] Face-to-face, top-down discipline continued to contour performance in some situations: the following song by non-literate erstwhile *Zalmiyan* poet, singer and comic Hazrat Baz (b. 1901), performed in the mid-1960s at the opening of the Nangrahar Kanal project, earned the artist ten *jeribs* of irrigated land for his intellectual tribute:

All Drunta and Samarkhel will be built up—Nice and beautiful, beautiful!
Streets everywhere; bazaars full of merchandise—Nice and beautiful, beautiful!
All these beautiful youths gathered up for service—Will produce a good result!
They will toil for a few days, for your eternal ease—And will produce a good result!
They have set aside their time as a sacred trust for your beauty—Dear Nangrahar![30]

Yet we can easily read this in two ways. Did this poem celebrate the monarchic state's beneficence in building the canal? Or did it articulate local rural labourers' ideas of something like a social contract, in evolving public forums where elites were forced to recognize a mass? Elsewhere we see examples of a sparsely-documented but rising proletarian populist poetry.[31] Indeed, some ideologies of the Zalmiyan mobilization took root even as activists were subdued. The transformed and popularized use of the word *ulas* to refer to "mass" (not "a specific administered population" as before) is a testament to this, as is the word's adaptation to a new post-Daud institutional concept: the Walasi Jirga or "lower house" of parliament.

Still, as a younger "university generation" gradually took over as the intellectual elite of Afghanistan, cultural separation between urban and rural areas became exaggerated. Struggles between liberalists, statists, and monarchists were largely confined to urban domains. There would not be that degree of urban and rural connect present in the 1940s and 1950s, either in ideology or in social domains, for many years in Afghanistan. This was particularly true after Daud again took power in 1973, and formed the heavily statist republic centred upon himself and the state networks he forged. In so doing, he sought to remove intermediary social institutions and collapse any independent public sphere into the state's channels of circulation. This project lasted all of five years.

Urban and Rural Revolutions, 1978–92

Reasons for Daud's overthrow by communist cadres in the army are too numerous to address here. But regarding cultural dimensions of this, and highlighting the disconnect alluded to above, philosopher Baha al-Din Majruh (1929–88) describes the overthrow of the state in his poetry-prose *magnum opus* blending Sufi romance, socio-political theory and historical allegory, *Ego-Monster*. Towards the end of Book One, a disembodied, vengeful, revolutionary voice emanates from nowhere and everywhere, rebuking one of three characters in the story: the Great Sovereign Champion, the Dragon-Leviathan, the embodiment of The State (as indeed Da'ud Khan saw himself). Can one read that voice, in its disembodiment, as a commentary on the recent history of the Afghan public domain itself, in both monarchic and republican Afghanistan?

In the beginning of the construction,/You were preoccupied with decorating and beautifying your citadel/You never acquainted yourself/With the deep foundations, the underground passageways/You made the uppermost story of the citadel very grand/Intending to live there/You never bestowed favor/Upon the dark corners of those hidden passageways. […]

You were only able to find two kinds/Of servants, that's it:/One was Reason; the other, Thought/They both became your advisers/And then, at your order, they took on the job/Of guarding the prison as well/In short, Reason and Thought were your faithful slaves,/The prison guards, and tyrants in their own right as well/But whenever they would advise you,/It was always mostly hypocritical, sycophantic flattery/They'd write panegyrics/And pay homage to the delusions/Of your grandeur, your power, your exaltedness. […]

Your other great sin was this:/You imprisoned the drive for freedom/You locked up, underground/The forces of ecstatic, uninhibited revolution/How tragic/That that same power to build, to construct/Is now the power of demolition/So many years have passed/With them laying there in the pitch-dark prison/Bound in chains/That they've found a new shape, a new face/They've been remade into spirits of Hell/…

AMBIGUITIES OF ORALITY

Yesterday's power of "Passion" and "Emotion"/Now refers to itself as "Spiritual Insurgency"/There used to be a certain life-instinct,/An angel, wearing a green robe/Now she's become the "Angel of Death and Terror"/And she wears a black robe.[32]

Majruh saw processes of repression transforming both ruling authority and domains of cultural resistance and avoidance too, once they finally reemerged into confrontation. Majruh initially composed parts of *Ego-Monster* in Dari-Persian, as *Azhdaha-ye Khudi*, before the Saur coup. But by the time he finished it, alongside various other versions in Pashto (*Da Zanzani Xamar*, excerpted above) and French (*Ego-Monstre*), can one decide with certainty that the insurgent periphery refers to the communist cadres, or to *mujahidin* counter-revolution? Could the State refer to Da'ud Khan's Republic, the post-1978 "communist" People's Democratic Party of Afghanistan (PDPA), or maybe even the Shah's Iran? Perhaps by this point, living in exile in Peshawar and running a non-partisan NGO while serving as teacher to Afghan and western scholars alike, Majruh intended his allegory to apply philosophically to states in general.

Inside Afghanistan, some PDPA writers wrote stirring poems on oppression and social reform; while a growing cultural-production bureaucracy mass-produced optimistic party-approved messages in print, on the stage, and over the airwaves. The following song was performed on state television, by a party of reserved young women in iconic rural Pashtun costumery, accompanied by modish young men on synthesizers. The package as a whole seems representative of prevailing Pashto literary sensibilities in the ruling party's middle ranks:

> We are an army of knowledge; we will change darkness to light;
> We will enlighten our country!
> Misery and adversity—We want it out of our country!
> The darkness of ignorance—We want it out of our country!
> Bribery and corruption—We want it out of our country!
> We will hold aloft lamps of knowledge and education;
> We will enlighten our country!
> We are an army of education—We are idealists of peace!
> For the correction of lifestyles—We are idealists of peace!
> We will fly the flag of peace up to the sky
> We will enlighten our country![33]

On the more refined end of elite socialist poetry during this period, the Parcham faction's Sulayman La'iq (1930–) dominated the official domain of Pashto letters during the 1980s, while the leader of the communist Khalq party, Nur Muhammad Taraki (1917–79), had earlier revolutionized the Pashto short story and novel. Both bodies of work spoke sensitively and eloquently of the pains of the rural masses, especially women. La'iq also pioneered and sponsored much work in a reinvigorated, sometimes sophisticated folklore studies field. Multidimensional analyses of the pain that (pre-revolutionary) common people expressed in folklore, especially in "women's genres" such as *landay*, implied the moral legitimacy of revolution while complicating the PDPA cadre's reductive brand of Marxist thought.[34] Those genres, bristling with social subversion in their original quotidian contexts, were finally explicitly recognized as such on the central stage. At the same time, the impact of this sort of folklore study remained restricted to urban domains throughout the 1980s, while those domains lost any claims to meaningful dominance. The Afghan state's exclusive claims to "nationalness" were gone; instead, a "tactical" popular culture of resistance came to adopt "strategic" scopes, aspiring to dominance—as we will see later in this section.

For now, let us remain on the subject of urban literature and note that within wartime Afghanistan, the social domains of countryside and urban centres were polarized. Vertical ties of survival through patronage in both settings outweighed other ties. In earlier periods, the history of urban Pashto literature was distinct but inseparable from Dari-Persian literature, as both overlapped in their public readership. The rise of the PDPA changed that, except in the case of official literature.

Compared with Majruh's philosophical allegory, literary scholar Zarin Anzor (1956–) paints a more empirically-oriented picture of Pashto literary culture during this period. Anzor's monograph, *Da Sawr pa Trazhedi ke Farhang, Adabiyat aw Azadi* ("The Impact of the April Tragedy on Culture, Literature, and Democracy") is, despite its polemic tone, among the most interesting works of Pashto literary history produced in the 1990s.[35] Anzor describes a process mirroring Majruh's characterization of "Reason and Thought": a tightly controlled bureaucratic-intellectual sphere came to reward party loyalty first and foremost, resulting in a series of unravelled literary threads outside it. Rather than implying cultural fragmentation, though, it is more accurate to describe a reshuffling of literary domains, and a reinvigoration of face-to-face media. New domains, interfacing between oral and written zones of circulation, can be divided into several arenas: urban authors inside Afghanistan; transnational *jihad* cassette poetry building on earlier popular traditions; expatriate cultivated poetry composed and printed in Pakistan; and overseas expatriate poetry.

AMBIGUITIES OF ORALITY

According to Anzor, non-party authors within Afghanistan were forced, for a period of several years, into private salons and social circles. Each circle developed idiosyncratic code vocabularies for discussing socio-political hardships, and expressed their discontent in semi-private *musha'iras* more than print.[36] After some years, though, this urban trend in Pashto literature gradually infiltrated official *musha'iras* too, edging out party literature in popularity. While emphasis generally focused on "literariness" in opposition to "sloganeering" (*shi'r* versus *shi'ar*), this trend was political. Poets regularly portrayed the Soviet relationship with local allies as a situation of colonialism, and used words like "stranger", "Britisher" and "Mughal" in coded language that became more transparent over time.[37] Eventually, by 1986, the government began experimenting with greater openness, in attempts to stave off at least some opposition, and allowed the formation of independent writers' unions.[38] An example of increasingly bold opposition poems is the following, printed in 1987:

What complaint of autumn, when its spring is like this?
What blame on the beloved, when the lovers' go-between is like this?
S/he ground my sorrow-filled heart into the dust,
What does a carefree one know of grief, when even the sympathetic are like this?
As the caravan of my dreams was looted, s/he laughed at it,
It's no sin of the animal-driver's, when his caravan leader is like this […]
The breath of life becomes free when force is removed from it.
One should be counted among the dead, when one's free will is like this
[They] held up the road of life, alongside thieves,
What would [their] dreams be like, when awake [they are] like this?
Its every corner, every lane is a graveyard of the wretched.
What do you expect of the wasteland, if its city is like this?
Nurturing thorns, but not even thinking to check on the flowers.
What sort of flower will result, when the gardener is like this?[39]

Also, a 1988 monograph by Asadullah Sho'ur, through the Journalists' Union, explored the obvious: oral poetry had been far more potent both in circulating information and in stoking the fire of mass mobilization than any medium employed by the state.[40] It might still have been risky to point this out directly; but the contemporary relevance of Sho'ur discussing the oral poetry of Afghans' resistance to British imperialism, and its role as political communication, could not have been lost on many readers.

This would especially be true given the volume of *jihad* poetry cassettes floating through the region's bazaars, again transforming popular genres in

Afghan Pashto poetry. David Edwards presents translated examples in an important essay on cassette songs while a notable *tazkira* by 'Awaz Siddiqi illuminates a greater range of themes present among a wide cross-section of rural Paktia's *jihad* poets.[41] In an environment where ordinary news media were constrained, themes ranged from factual reporting of events to metaphysical discussions on martyrdom, moral exile (*hijrat*), defensive gender conservatism, and other topics that resonated with the 20 per cent of Afghans—their former lives destroyed—who came to live outside Afghanistan's borders. Resistance poems were interventions in public life, transforming public opinion through persuasion as much as reflecting pre-existing opinion. More importantly, they cumulatively created a new hybrid poetic public domain, one that mediated the dislocated transnational hegemony of militant factions. This poetic public was premised on orality at the point of creation, live performance in Pakistani refugee studios. But it allowed for individualized, market-driven, mass-reproduced consumption at the point of the listener, alongside the live re-performance that drove earlier mass engagements with oral poetry. Paying to consume one poet's work among many was an agentive act that helped internalize perspectives, as much as individual re-performance did.

Yet this was no unregulated mass market of public speech. Patterns of consumption and circulation, and the hierarchical dynamics of militant commanders dictating studio patronage, often reinforced the divisions of war-era *tanzim* (militant faction) that Anzor notes regarding *jihad* poetry.[42] Divisions deepened during the late *jihad* and civil war periods, when *tanzims* began fighting each other in addition to the Afghan government, and contended for ideological control as well as material. By 1988, struggles for supremacy made Peshawar a treacherous place for critical authors not attached to *tanzims*. 'Aziz al-Rahman Ulfat (son of Gul Pacha) and Baha al-Din Majruh were among those assassinated that year.

Transnationalism: Cultural Regenerations and Activist Resurgences, 1992–2010

Notwithstanding the violence and trauma of the period, *jihad* poetry as public activism caught people's imaginations and spurred cultural change. Writing years later in Peshawar, Khost-born Pir Muhammad Karwan (1959–) dramatized the affective power of *mujahidin* (or was it Taliban?) poetry in his 2000 work "*Lag ra tam sha larawiya*" ("Wait up for me a little,

Traveller")—one poem in an oeuvre that has helped revolutionize Pashto art literature:

[…] Perhaps you've forgotten […]/When that platoon showed up/In our village; that troop of young-men/Red-lipped beautiful youths/With lion-whiskers and wild locks/And black, penetrating eyes like *gwargwaras*/ And halfway maroon like the *kirkan* [both wild fruits]/Intoxicated from their cries of the *takbir* ("Allahu Akbar!");/From drums and *atan* dancing;/Do you remember those six young-men?/ Whose clapping grew hot and fast/Who whipped their turban-tails around/Who slicked back their long hair?/When they gave off those clipped cries,/When they drew out the final syllables of their *tappas* [a folk genre],/With a single *tappa* for a martyr/They moistened the whole world's eyes!/Those ones who were all saying, "God! May you put out the eyes of death itself!"/Who, with their hashish pipe/ Turned their own eyes red and bloodshot. […]/They all lifted their eyes up at me,/ And inside them sat a city of love/Within the heart of that city/There was a caravan loaded with *tappas*/And the clothes on that crowd of strangers/Were woven out of sacrifice and lamentation./Right to its pillaged heart went/A sorrowful strain of sitars/And around this city of love/A great serpent encircled itself/Those six young-men came out,/Hunting this dragon. […][43]

Over its much longer course, this poem offers a kaleidoscopic image of the recent history of Pashto poetry's mobility across public domains during war. In it, Karwan—himself from a semi-nomadic childhood—channels much more than *mujahid* poetry. He alludes to face-to-face literary networks alongside print publication; to mobility across older socio-cultural and geographic boundaries; and to a cross-fertilization among multiple social domains that ultimately catalyzed new outlooks on society through the trauma and dislocation of war. Local transnationalism during the war in general, for Pashtuns at least, was such a feature of so many people's lives in so many profound ways that Zarin Anzor excludes Peshawar-based Afghan authors from his discussions of "expatriate authors", reserving that distinction for those who relocated to Europe or North America.

This transnationalism does not apply only to face-to-face spheres of literary activity. During this period, the Writers' Union of Free Afghanistan was formed as an umbrella in Peshawar as a non-partisan alternative to the faction-based patronage structure. The WUFA's various journals occasionally provide some of the most interesting essays on Afghan cultural history in the history of Afghan publishing. Slightly later, in 1987 or 1988, the participant-funded Danish Publishing Society was founded with a press in a Peshawar bookstore. While others later arose alongside it, this press continued as the premier literary and academic publisher in a new transnational

Afghan-Pashto print sphere, having offered 16,000 titles and opening offices in both countries by 2010.[44] Elsewhere in Karwan's poem, the press's chief editor and founder, Asadullah Danish (1965–), appears in a cameo, wielding an editorial scalpel, personifying a new influence on printed Afghan Pashto poetry: a shifting mass market, directing fashions of elite poetry away from confronting the trauma of war:

> […] One evening a friend of mine came/With my heart in his hand/I don't know whether it was of out love or of vengefulness,/But he came with a knife in his hand also/He said, this heart of yours is worth nothing/Go find a new heart from somewhere/All your raw, experimental songs-/Find them a tender heart somewhere/One nourished on love songs/Go find the kind of heart/That steals kisses from the stars/ Go find a heart that worships the sun.
>
> I said, Oh, sure! As if hearts/Can be bought four to a rupee;/As if, in the marketplace which is your two eyes/You can pick out just anyone at all to love./I'll pay in full with the cash of my sorrows/If songs are what sells on credit/I'll buy a forceful *ghazal*/If *ghazals* can be expressed with force/I'll just sacrifice this sobbing of mine/ If music and revelry is what sells […][45]

Still, there was a tension between the transnational public circulation that enabled these print publics, and desires of national territory that show up in more popular domains of poetry during the 1990s civil war period:

> Those who grew up so cherished now beg for charity in tents.
> Days of hardship… Oh Kabul! Your princes, in the streets of Peshawar
> Our Pashto honor has not remained in our turbans
> Days of hardship… Oh Kabul! Your princes, in the streets of Iran
> O Allah, the girls of our homeland working menial jobs
> Days of hardship… Oh Kabul! Your princes, in the streets of Karachi
> The soil of my homeland, sold in foreign bazaars
> Days of hardship… Oh Kabul! Your princes, in the streets of Punjab […][46]

The above is excerpted from a song composed in popular style by Shafi'ullah Babarzai (1960–), performed by 'Abdullah Muqurai on a 1990s cassette patronized by 'Ya'qub Khan' of Quetta. The song builds on earlier *jihad* poetry structures in genre and in circulation, but its themes are different. It articulates widely-felt tensions of nation and transnationalism, alongside reservations with armed factions' ties to foreign agencies. It unsettles, through more than explicit lyrics: the arrangement above reshapes a participative genre often reserved for celebratory or wartime *atan* dancing.

The tension of living in an imagined nation while existing outside it extended to elite Pashtun intellectuals living further afield—Europe and

America—who interacted with the Afghan-Pakistani Pashto print sphere mostly as individuals, through personal correspondence and submissions to regional-based periodicals.[47] They eventually began forming their own salons, in Europe and then the Persian Gulf more so than in North America. Qandahar-born, Virginia-based poet 'Abd al-Bari Jahani (1948–) stands out; his body of work begins before the 1978 coup and extends through the *mujahidin* and then Taliban periods to the present day. Since his self-publication of *Wraka Mena* ("A Missing Homeland") in 1989, his poetry has given voice to the pain of exile; to a celebration of anti-communist heroism as the expression of a basic human life-force; sorrow over Afghanistan's devastation; and, more recently, an expatriate's fear for his country amid the rise of the Taliban. Reprising an earlier poem, "Blue Sky", that praised the heroic creative vitality of anti-communist resistance, he writes more recently:

Blue sky, I never said/That fire should be heaped upon fire
That I see the flag of my honor lowered/My graveyards, insulted
Blue sky, I never asked/That I should cry at the funerals of cities
That my villages should birth a demon/That I should cry at the graveyard of youth
Blue sky, I never wanted fire/Poured down Kabul's collar
My house, visited by demons/A serpent, nurtured in my own sleeve[48]

It is a token of Pashto poetry's shifting twenty-first century domains that the above poem is far more available to contemporary audiences via streaming internet video than print. Contemporary technology is not new in making print redundant for the mass reproduction and consumption of poetry. However, it differs from older technology in people's greater ability to publish poetry electronically themselves, and opens up more audio-visual genres to more people. At the end of 2009, over half of Afghans had access to a mobile phone, at least some of which could record, distribute, and replay audio and video.[49] Percentages would be higher if cross-border and diaspora interactions in a global informal Pashto mediascape are considered.

Recording of and interacting in contingent genres has restored a sense of oral spontaneity to electronic mediation of Pashto poetry, in elite and insurgent genres alike. And, it has preserved a sort of disembodied, contingent dialogism that long characterized Pashto poems. Even as the resurgent Taliban sought to control Pashtuns' access to mobile phones[50] (likely for tactical military reasons), streaming video on the internet continued to be rife not only with polished Taliban propaganda poetry, but with *a capella* songs in the field, obviously captured by participant *talibs* on phone cameras.[51]

Meanwhile, casually-recorded songs document a popular impact exerted on Taliban rhetoric through recirculation and public intervention on the village level; and they transnationalize that domain online. A 2009 clip of a blind singer in the south, Da'ud Haqyar, casually performing at a village *hujra* (men's house), admonished Pashtuns not to fight each other like jackals. Haqyar proclaimed that collective action, if realized, could rejuvenate history itself. The person who posted it on YouTube.com identified it as a Taliban hymn, or *nashid*, and certainly it praises the Taliban and condemns foreign intervention.[52] Such literature's popular appeal has not gone unnoticed by outside observers:

the Old Taliban, who smashed musical instruments, wireless sets, and televisions, have been replaced by a more media-savvy and culturally-sensitive group who produce what are said to be Afghanistan's most stirring contemporary poetry and catchy songs. Even opponents confess to buying their cassettes.[53]

Still, contemporary modes of circulation allow finer contextualization of performance than does sterile print, or even audio. The highly unequal power relationships captured in this *hujra* video, between patron landowners in Taliban territory and the destitute client entertainer Haqyar, allow us to read the praise, contextually, as both sincere and sarcastic in equal measure. The Taliban are praised for the egalitarian Pashtun unity that they promise, but have yet to deliver in practice—a failure that is especially striking in the direct context of the landowner/client relationship in this performance. It is hard to see that egalitarianism in this context, as Haqyar is certainly—probably painfully—aware.[54] Any potential view of such media as "propaganda" seems one-dimensional, given widespread grassroots skills in manipulating poetic ambiguity. Subject to direct surveillance and discipline both by localized paternalistic landlords and cross-district Taliban, Haqyar calibrates his message, verbally and nonverbally, skillfully enough to needle both hierarchies—and NATO—without liability.

Conclusions

In one way, Haqyar represents a full circle back to the marginal performers of the early to mid-twentieth century, composing songs that simultaneously praise and rebuke power while directly in the presence of powerful individuals. Much like the example in this chapter drawn from the Nangrahar Kanal ceremony, Haqyar's resistance is partially reactive: reminding the powerful of the obligations that they claim to take on and exploiting contradictions in the ideological edifices that others have set up. It is an exercise in "tactical" reuse of ideas, rather than the head-on "strategic" critique better exemplified by Malang Jan and his school. Still, the idiom in which Haqyar operates is rather more ambitious than in earlier periods. Rather than local youth uniting for the material prosperity of a locality as in 1965, Haqyar's imagination extends to cross-regional ethnic, national, and metaphysical scales that are unbounded by the mapped ideologies of administrative power:

> Don't call that Pashtun a Pashtun—Pick up a rifle; be honorable
> Don't fight in your own family—Pick up a sword
> Weep at the difficult task presented to [all] Afghans
> The point is, if God is present, then remake History anew![55]

This is an ambiguous realm. Literary activity in the public domain, as compared to "powerful" legal, bureaucratic, or military uses of language and communication, is not actually as harmless as it first appears. Nor are even the most powerless actors, among whom we must count Haqyar if we look only at economic or ordinary political agency. The triple mediation of these songs through *hujra* performance, Bluetooth cellphone sharing, and streaming internet video allows for a greater diffusion of marginal actors' speech now than at any point in modern history. And, by virtue of working in cross-class, cross-regional, and even cross-temporal awarenesses, arguing for greater integration of the rural poor, and framing audiences in particular categories such as "Pashtun" or "Afghan" (rather than local divisions), actors such as Haqyar create and recreate, in the awareness of their audiences, those categories that they treat as a given. That is, the idea of "Pashtun public opinion" itself, which spans regions and disregards borders and can be as flexible as activists construe it to be, is an inheritance of the oral and written literary activism of the twentieth century. It is an inheritance underappreciated in Pashtun modern social history writing—often structured around faction or tribe—yet one which has played a major part in nearly every Pashtun social movement in recent memory.

6

THE POETRY AND PROSE OF PAZHWAK

A CRITICAL LOOK AT TRADITIONAL AFGHANISTAN

Chaled Malekyar
(Translated from the German by Nushin Arbabzadah)

A Life at Home and Abroad

'Abd al-Rahman Pazhwak (1919–95) came from a Pashtun household that was attached to tradition but nonetheless lent Pazhwak enough freedom to allow him to develop into a "free spirit" as a young adult. He grew up to become not only a famous poet and writer but also a successful diplomat who was respected in the highest international circles.[1] Pazhwak's work and life must be viewed in close connection with his homeland of Afghanistan, because taken together they build something close to a coherent whole. A loyal citizen of Afghanistan, in his writings Pazhwak occasionally allowed readers authentic insight into important problems of his country in the twentieth century. However, so far only a fraction of Pazhwak's literary works have been published and for this reason an understanding of his literary work is quite limited.[2] Pazhwak was born on 7 March 1919 in the historical city of Ghazni, south of Kabul, where his father, Qazi 'Abdullah Khan, served as a provincial judge. He spent his childhood years in a traditional family environment, living partly in his ancestral village of Baghbani in Nangrahar province and partly in the capital city of Kabul. In accordance with his father's official appointments, the family moved from Ghazni to Kabul and from Kabul to the Khugiani district of Nangrahar province in eastern Afghanistan, near the family's ancestral village in Surkhrud district. Pazhwak's forefathers were descendants of a prominent Pashtun family of the Ma'ruf Khel clan, which traced its roots to the Ahmadzai tribes of the Ghilzai Confederation. He also grew up in a traditional region inhabited by Pashtuns, where generations of his family enjoyed renown as landowners, educators and public servants.

Pazhwak's father and his older brother, Hafizullah Khan (also a judge), were major contributors to the development of Pazhwak's character, upbringing and education. Under their guidance, he received home schooling, studying theology and literature. He studied the works of major Afghan writers and Sufi poets, and this training seems to have encouraged his philosophical and spiritual turn of mind. At the age of fourteen, Pazhwak had apparently already mastered Islamic *fiqh* (jurisprudence) and read most of the classics of Afghan literature. His father, 'Abdullah Khan, was serving as the Chief Justice of Afghanistan's Supreme Court in Kabul when the Tajik rebel Habibullah Kalakani and his followers took control of the capital city in 1929. Kalakani rejected any kind of modern innovation and forced the reformist King Amanullah (r. 1919–29) to abdicate, seizing the throne for himself. In response, 'Abdullah Khan joined the resistance against the usurper. Amidst the anarchy and chaos, Pazhwak's progressive older brother, Qazi Hafizullah, was murdered at the hands of Habibullah Kalakani's followers in Shomali, where he had been appointed as a judge.

At the end of Habibullah Kalakani's interregnum, Pazhwak attended the Habibiyya High School in Kabul, which was among the first modern schools in Afghanistan. In the course of the twentieth century, the school trained a whole section of the country's open-minded and educated elite. Among Pazhwak's teachers in Kabul were two prominent poet-scholars: Sufi 'Abd al-Haq Bitab (1887–1969), who taught at the Habibiyya High School itself, and Khalilullah Khalili (1909–85), who acted as Pazhwak's part-time private tutor. As a result, a lifelong friendship was forged between Pazhwak and his ten-years-senior teacher, Khalili. At this time, the poet laureate, Bitab, and the equally learned poet and diplomat, Khalili, were widely celebrated and highly valued for their Dari-Persian literary prose. This was a key reason why Pazhwak, whose first language was Pashto, was able to stand out as a Dari-Persian writer whose work was testimony to his sensitivity to the subtleties of the Persian language. However, at the Habibiyya High School, English was also taught as a foreign language and this in turn played a significant role in Pazhwak's subsequent career as a diplomat and literary translator. His knowledge of English already came in handy to him at a young age, enabling him to read and translate into Dari-Persian the works of English language authors. Scattered pieces of Pazhwak's first poems and essays appeared in the Afghan press in the first half of the 1930s when he was still completing his education. At the time, the young Afghan literatus used various pen-names: first Wafa, then Marlaw and then Armanjan. It was only towards the end of the 1930s that he settled permanently for the pen-name *Pazhwak*, which means "echo" in both Dari-Persian and Pashto.

After high school, Pazhwak was designated to study medicine at university but felt compelled to interrupt his studies due to a lack of interest in the field and the loss of his father, who was the family's bread-winner. As a result, he decided to join the workforce and started his career working as an English translator for the Kabul Literary Society (*Anjuman-e Adabi-ye Kabul*). Pazhwak subsequently made a career in Afghanistan's information and press sector, taking on the challenge of producing serious journalism of professional standards. Pazhwak and his colleagues coped with a series of intellectual restrictions triggered by state censorship. Nonetheless, the period was still one of excitement and impact for Pazhwak and his fellow wave-makers, many of whom subsequently became leading figures in the artistic, literary and intellectual life of Afghanistan. In the 1940s, Pazhwak and his colleagues were an active and integral part of the first phase in the development of a structured independent news and press sector in Afghanistan.

Pazhwak was particularly inspired by his superior, Salah al-Din Saljuqi (1895/7–1970). A scholar, philosopher and diplomat known for his active patronage of young talent, Saljuqi was the president of the Afghan Press and Information Office. He recognized and cherished Pazhwak's independent thinking and self-reliant and critical approach. In private correspondence dating from the mid-1950s, Saljuqi implored Pazhwak "not to put aside the fearless writing that is pouring out of your pen!"[3] Pazhwak was at the time the lead editor of the important newspaper, *Islah* ("Reform"), and subsequently worked as the director of the Afghan international news agency, *Bakhtar* ("Bactria"), before eventually occupying the post of the Director of the Pashto Academy (*Paxto Tolana*). In 1943, Pazhwak became director-general of publications and took charge of the entire operational side of the

Afghan press and information sector. Pazhwak resigned the post in the mid-1940s, possibly to express his opposition to the newly-issued press law that restricted press and intellectual freedom. Shortly afterwards, Pazhwak entered the world of diplomacy at the age of twenty-seven. His initial job was as a press attaché and this took him first to London and then Washington. But differences of opinion with the embassy's leadership, whose members all belonged to the ruling royal family, forced Pazhwak to find work outside of the Afghan government and he was able to find a position with the International Labor Organization in Montreal. However, the Afghan government soon approached Pazhwak to rejoin public service and to put his political and literary skills to work at the Foreign Ministry in Kabul.

In diplomatic terms, these were important times. On 19 November 1946, the Kingdom of Afghanistan joined the United Nations as a full member. Pazhwak attended the meetings of the UN General Assembly for the first time in 1947 and henceforth became a regular participant in its

Fig. 13: The Poet as Diplomat: Pazhwak at the United Nations.

meetings. Starting off as an ordinary member of the Afghan delegation, in 1958 Pazhwak rose up to become Afghanistan's ambassador to the United Nations. He occupied this position with success and acclaim until 1972. During his tenure at the United Nations, he contributed significantly to achieving the UN's organizational goals. Simultaneously, his hard work and passion left significant marks at the UN on various political and diplomatic levels. As a result, Pazhwak was elected president of the nineteenth United Nations Human Rights Commission in 1963 in Geneva. By 1966 he was elected president of the United Nations General Assembly in New York. In tandem, he headed several UN committees and was significantly involved in elevating the principle of the self-determination of nations and peoples to an internationally-binding right enshrined in the Universal Declaration of Human Rights. As leader of various United Nations-led fact-finding missions, he became familiar with important tasks and politically delicate investigations. Pazhwak felt that the United Nations served as a conduit for realizing the world's best hopes and sensed its significance in resolving conflict and injustice through political process on the world stage.[4] In 1968, Pazhwak was seen by some as a having a solid chance of occupying the position of UN Secretary General by replacing the hesitating Sithu U Thant, who spent a whole term dithering as to whether to run for another period. Pazhwak's constant advocacy of human rights granted him a lasting place in the history of this world organization. As he stated at the time, "only a world organisation can assume the responsibility of world guarantor of human rights and if the United Nations can be said to have an ideology, certainly that ideology, surpassing all others, must be human rights".[5]

In the 1950s and 60s, when the international political scene was marked by the dualism of western powers versus the Eastern Bloc, the Non-Aligned Movement emerged on the world stage as a third power. In 1961, Afghanistan became one of the founding members of this organization. As his country's sole representative, from the early phase of the movement's inception to its official founding to the period in which the movement became fully established, Pazhwak regularly attended it most important conferences. Known as a serious "advocate of non-alignment", Pazhwak is now counted among the Non-Aligned Movement's veterans.[6] It was also in the 1950s and 60s, when the author lived from time to time in such faraway places as the United States and Switzerland, that some of his most important works were published in Kabul. The key collection of stories, *Afsanaha-ye Mardum* ("Stories of the People"), appeared in 1957. Two poetry collections crafted in the neo-classical style, *Chand Shi'r az Pazhwak* ("Some Poems by Pazhwak") and *Gulha-ye Andisha* ("Thought Flowers"), were published several years later in 1963 and 1965 respectively. Other writings were printed only two decades later as part of a second wave of publications. We will turn more thoroughly to his writings below.

In the decade of relative democratization between 1963 and 1973, internal political changes took place in Kabul, including the nomination for the first time of a non-royal prime minister. The Afghan Constitution of 1964 revealed traits of a western-style parliamentary system by promising democratic freedoms that included free elections, a free parliament, freedom to set up political parties and freedom of opinion. Those who took advantage of this slowly-developing democratization were leftist groups, some of whom were supported by the Soviet Union. On the streets of Kabul, this attempt at democratization led to violent clashes, particularly between leftist students and the small group of Islamists who had their own student followers. The government tried to take serious action against both sides.

Politically responsible officials preferred not to see Pazhwak return to domestic politics, since he was known for his political independence and brilliance at the international scene. Remaining overseas engaged in important duties, he could only watch the turbulent years of democratization from a distance in New York. Some of the poems that he crafted at the time were in the "new style" (*sabk-e jadid*) and dealt with social and thereby critical themes.[7] It is possible that Pazhwak was simply waiting for the right time to engage in the politics of Afghanistan.[8] In that case, in his capacity as a government functionary, he would have been able to actively play a role in shaping internal political conditions. But it was never to come to that and his role instead was indirect. During the republican period of Muhammad Da'ud Khan (1973–78), Pazhwak's liberal and progressive mindset, his advocacy for freedom of opinion, his support for the political participation of the citizenry, and his championing of human rights fell on fertile grounds among Kabul's intelligentsia. Even so, it also became apparent that his views represented a threat to the ruling establishment. For example, while the new Afghan constitution was being prepared in 1963, Pazhwak (who was at the time president of the UN Human Rights Commission in Geneva) was asked by King Zahir Shah to return to Kabul and share his views regarding the constitution. However, Pazhwak later learned with disappointment that the written thoughts he had submitted for consideration had not even reached the committee set up to discuss the articles of the constitution. In

1973, after Muhammad Da'ud Khan came to power through a bloodless *coup d'état* which had considerable support among leftist and pro-Moscow elements in the Afghan army, he too relied on Pazhwak as an experienced diplomat to promote Afghanistan's national security interests abroad. Once again, Pazhwak was kept outside of the country, spending the 1970s far away from Afghanistan, taking charge of the Afghan embassies in Bonn, Delhi and London. Then, on 27 April 1978, another coup took place in Kabul, carried out by pro-Moscow military officers and members of the People's Democratic Party of Afghanistan (PDPA). The coup undermined Afghanistan's sovereignty and independence, allowing Kremlin to directly to exercise influence in Afghanistan. On learning of the nature of the coup, Pazhwak resigned his post as Afghanistan's ambassador to London and voluntarily returned home, where he was put under house arrest.[9]

Purging campaigns were launched by the new communist power-holders, Nur Muhammad Taraki and Hafizullah Amin, triggering waves of terror throughout the country. Numerous Afghans—many of whom had no relationship with the PDPA—lost their lives. Towards the end of 1979, Hafizullah Amin (who had already murdered his predecessor, Taraki), was deposed by the Soviet military which instead installed Babrak Karmal as ruler. Pazhwak expressed his thoughts about the Soviet invasion in a poem called *Qushun-e Surkh* ("Red Army"), in a part of which he wrote:

Resembling a flood, the Red Army crossed the Oxus River, Where can I seek refuge from this devastating hurricane?[10]

For Pazhwak it was evident that profound resentment was spreading among a broad spectrum of the population, triggered by the Afghan communists' violent dictatorship and the occupation of Afghanistan by the Soviet army, whose brutal war against a country that had so far been intact amounted to a mockery of national sovereignty. He witnessed with his own eyes the protests and demonstrations of Kabul's male and female high school students. Deeply moved by the violent death on 9 April 1980 of Nahid Sa'id, who was a student in her final year of high school, Pazhwak later crafted a volume of poetry dedicated to "the martyr Nahid Sa'id, her sisters, and all those Afghan women who have stood up against the Red Army, inside or outside of the homeland".[11]

Pazhwak's health deteriorated during these years. Nevertheless, he distanced himself from the communists and first joined the resistance secretly by writing *shabnama* ("night-letters"), the influential political pamphlets distributed at night. Later, in exile in Pakistan and then the United States, he launched an open resistance against the communist rulers and the Soviet army's occupation of Afghanistan, both of which were against the principles of nations' rights. The long years of exile were repeatedly affected by health-related setbacks. Far from his homeland, Pazhwak's thoughts and feelings were about the present conditions and future affairs of his imprisoned country and its inhabitants. He processed his pain and grief through literary activity. But even in his resistance Pazhwak did not join any political leader, party or ideology and knew well how to avoid being monopolized for propaganda purposes. He formulated his goal for Afghanistan in the following manner:

> For me the goal of this sacred *jihad* is total independence, freedom, human rights and the inviolability of Afghanistan from the ruling, or the threat of being ruled by, foreign aggressors; the removal of communism; the strengthening of Islam and social justice; and the establishment of Afghanistan's self-determination in line with the wishes of the country's Muslim population.[12]

Looking back with the benefit of hindsight at the *mujahidin*'s resistance, we must here dismantle the myth of their inhabiting a seemingly harmonious cosmos. On the one hand, the Afghan resistance against the Soviet invasion was hardy and brave. On the other hand, the resistance weakened itself through its political and military divisions, splitting into numerous smaller groups either because of real or perceived ideological, ethnic and theological differences, as well as because of the deadly animosity that some resistance leaders felt for one other. Such circumstances prevented the creation of an organized and stable political and military united front against the Soviet army. Pazhwak's far-sighted vision for Afghanistan, which he presented to the United Nations, provided for bringing together all the relevant Afghan factions, parties and leaders to make them walk a shared path by gathering together at the negotiation table. But against this idea stood the lack of unity among Afghans which was in part directed by outside forces and in part a result of pre-existing internal disunity. Foreign interference (in particular the dubious role of Pakistan in questions of Afghanistan) and the absence of representatives of the Afghan resistance during the Geneva Peace Talks of 1982 to 1988 were rightly criticized by Pazhwak as the decisive flaws in attempting to create lasting peace in his homeland.

The final years of exile which Pazhwak spent in Peshawar were particularly painful and disappointing. Following the withdrawal on 15 February 1989 of the last contingent of what was once over a hundred thousand

Soviet soldiers, the Afghan struggle for freedom turned into a civil war which in turn exacted a heavy blood price. Following the *mujahidin*'s conquest of Kabul in 1992, Afghanistan revealed itself as a deeply divided country, drifting apart and in conflict with itself. Violent power struggles between the rival *mujahidin* factions in government, external interference and the deliberate politicization of ethnic issues and theological differences provoked further fighting. At this time, Pazhwak's long-lasting illness turned out to be cancer. He died on the morning of 8 June 1995 in the Pakistani city of Peshawar, only a few months after the death of his wife. His body was taken back to his beloved homeland where, in burial, he found eternal peace in his ancestral village of Baghbani in the Surkhrud district of Nangrahar province.

Works of Literature: Poetry and Prose

Pazhwak's Poetry

Pazhwak's literary activity stretched over a period of more than six decades. A majority of his works were composed in Dari-Persian while another (by comparison smaller) number of his works were written in Pashto. In this manner, Pazhwak made use of both of the cultural and national languages of Afghanistan, his vocabulary and command of the rules of both languages being masterly in equal measure. Some of his other works, particularly non-literary writings, were crafted in English. Altogether, Pazhwak's oeuvre comprised poetry and prose, though the division into these categories only sums up in a limited manner the stylistic diversity and plurality of genres evidenced in his work, as will become clear in the following pages.

Pazhwak's poetic works are simultaneously testimony to his considerable literary flexibility and his masterly command of the rules of both classical and modern poetry. A large number of the poems penned by Pazhwak were crafted in the neo-classical style (*sabk-e klasik-e muabbar*), including the poems that appear in the aforementioned collections *Chand Shi'r az Pazhwak* ("Some Poems from Pazhwak", 1963), *Gulha-ye Andisha* ("Thought Flowers", 1965) and *Banu-ye Balkh* ("Lady of Balkh", 2001). Pazhwak was a qualified connoisseur of the classical literature of his cultural realm and in his neo-classical poetry drew on regularly-appearing poetic images and motifs, at times adding new ones to them. In Pazhwak's work, the reader encounters universal themes concerning humanity such as faith, grief, love, hope and joy. A majority of these poems carry traits of classical Persian poetry and in them Pazhwak made use of such formal schemata of classical Persian poetry as *ghazal, qasida, masnavi, rubai and du-bayti* forms. 'Abd al-Ghafur Rawan Farhadi, a connoisseur of Afghan poetry and of Pazhwak's poetry in particular, made the following comparison: "Pazhwak's *ghazals* bring to mind memories of Rudaki, Sa'di, the *divan* of Shams Tabrizi, Hafiz and Sa'ib and his *qasida* and *masnavi* resemble those of Farukhi, Mawlana Balkhi [Rumi] and [Muhammad] Iqbal Lahori".[13] These are, of course, the names of some of the most distinguished medieval poets of classical Persian poetry, with the Indian poet Iqbal being the only poet to have lived later, having died in 1938. Their works have functioned as an endless fountain of inspiration for generations of Afghan poets who emerged later. For example, Pazhwak wrote the following verse:

> Stand up inn keeper and fill the cup with wine,
> It is said that spring has arrived, how much longer will you remain asleep?[14]

In writing this verse, Pazhwak was making use of important ingredients of classical Islamic poetry, such as the imagery of wine (*badah/mai/sharab*), the inn keeper (*saqi*), love (*'ishq*) and the beloved (*dust/mahbub*), images which were already known since the time of Hafiz (d.1389). Do the above mentioned motifs in Pazhwak's poetry stand for the sweet joys of earthy life? Or is there a deeper mystical meaning behind the motifs? Should they be understood the way we interpret 'Umar Khayyam, who, for example, can be seen to have used the image of wine to depict independent thinking and free reasoning?[15] In Pazhwak's case, it does not make sense to interpret the motifs as the reflections of a libertine: they are rather the expressions of a joyful affirmation of existence and a delight in living. These poems belong to the first phase of Pazhwak's literature which the critic Puiya Fariyabi describes as "the phase of passionate love and friendship" (*dawra-ye shur-e 'ishq va nishat*).[16]

On the other hand, Pazhwak also followed his own distinct poetic path, as Rawan Farhadi also stressed: "the Dari poetry of Pazhwak is more than anything the result of his own, natural talent for poetry".[17] We can be more precise about this aspect: Pazhwak was himself creative in the content he chose for his poetry and acted freely by filling the known formats of classical poetry with new, contemporary and sometimes critical themes and content which drew on his Afghan homeland and culture. Crafted in the neo-classical style, in Pazhwak's poetry we encounter at the same time moments of classical adaptation (mainly in form) and moments of innovation (mainly in contemporary themes and content). For example, Pazhwak was an independent thinker, capable of critical reflection about his homeland and its internal political circumstances and this appears regularly in his literary work, albeit in a subtle and aestheticized manner. Most obviously, he used the politically-charged theme of freedom—in the sense of political freedom and the political rights of citizens—in relationship to the conditions in Afghanistan. Trenchantly and elegantly, he expressed his worries:

> Today I am reminded of that land,
> Where the people are prisoners but the country is free.[18]

The format in which these verses appeared was traditional, but the content by contrast was linked to the happenings of the time. The key characteristic was the antithesis of the second part of the half-verse where the adjectives "free" and "imprisoned" are juxtaposed. In this verse, Pazhwak wrote about the theme of political conditions inside Afghanistan and his declaration in the content can be paraphrased as follows: even though Afghanistan had been freed from foreign (i.e. British) rule by the Third Anglo-Afghan War of 1919, it is the lack of freedom of thought that keeps its people imprisoned.

At the time Pazhwak was writing such verses, writers in the West also took a vivid interest in the Afghan resistance against the Soviet occupation. For example, the American poet William Pitt Root (1941–) expressed his sympathy for the Afghan resistance in his poem, *The Unbroken Diamond: Nightletter to the Mujahideen.*[19] Pazhwak translated Pitt Root's English poem into Dari-Persian and crafted a poem in response entitled *Almas-e Nashekan* ("Unbroken Diamond"), which was published from exile in Virginia in 1996. Indeed, it was only during this later period, when Pazhwak was living in exile from the mid-1980s until his death in the mid-1990s, that new collections of his poetry were published. *Hadis-e Khun* ("Blood Reports", 1985), *Maihan-e Man* ("My Homeland", 1989), and such posthumous publications as *Nahid-Nama* ("Book of Nahid", 1995), *Almas-e Nashekan* ("Unbroken Diamond", 1996) and *Banu-ye Balkh* ("Lady of Balkh", 2001), were all examples of poetry collections he published abroad. These late works, in particular *Nahid-Nama* and *Almas-e Nashekan*, significantly differed from Pazhwak's earlier poetry in such 1960s anthologies as *Chand Shiʿr az Pazhwak* and *Gulha-ye Andisha*. The poet in exile had clearly distanced himself from literary traditionalism and taken a new direction in both content and form. Although Pazhwak had already written some poems in which he disregarded the conventions of classical Persian poetry (for example, in metric and rhyming rules), it was only in the early 1980s that he fully crossed the frontiers of the classical format and used the modern and progressive styles of *shi'r-e naw* ("new poetry") and *shi'r-e azad* ("free verse"). Such new poetry movements had been gradually developing across the whole of the Muslim world since the 1940s, but had eventually reached Afghanistan as a result of modern developments in the West and under considerable western influence.

The obvious change of literary paradigms in this later phase of Pazhwak's poetry was linked to historical events that were taking place in Afghanistan. *Nahid-Nama* and *Almas-e Nashekan* were responses to the events that took

Fig. 14: Official Outlets: Baihaqi Government Bookshop, Kabul.

place in Afghanistan after 1978: the theme of both collections was the occupation of Afghanistan by the Soviet army and the Afghan *jihad* against the occupiers. These works are interesting for their outward format and their content; in other words, for the way their themes have been processed in verse. While Pazhwak drew on a variety of themes in writing the events of 1978, his poetic output did not reflect this multifaceted approach. Instead, one theme in particular emerged strongly: the tragic fate of Afghanistan whose traumatic events were in part lived by the poet and in part belonged to the collective experience of the Afghan people. The theme of the brutal war waged by the occupying forces was not suitable to be tackled by the formats of classical poetry and so, in his free handling of the peculiarities of format and language, Pazhwak made use of modern poetry. *Almas-e Nashekan*, for example, was a poetic rendition of what was in reality a collection of facts in which the total brutality of events was depicted in a manner making minimal use of the classical style. For example, Pazhwak wrote in the poem about the chemical weapons used by the Soviet army and about soldiers of the communist regime opening fire on the young male and female students who marched in protest on the streets of Kabul.[20] By comparison to his earlier neo-classical poetry, his modern poems make up only a small part of his total work. But crafted in exile, these late poems nonetheless opened a new chapter in the history of contemporary Afghan poetry.

Pazhwak's Prose

Pazhwak's prose writing was equally diverse and can be divided into two main categories: factual writing (non-fiction texts) and aesthetic writing (fiction). Pazhwak's factual non-fiction works include a small series of general introductory works about Afghanistan and the political question of "Pashtunistan", such as *Afghanistan—Ancient Aryana* and *The Question of Pashtunistan*.[21] These booklets were published during the 1950s by the Afghan Information Bureau, the media wing of the Afghan embassy in London. As texts written in English, their purpose was to serve western readers as sources of information about important political themes. In addition, dating from the late 1930s and 1940s was an essay written by Pazhwak about *Paxtunwali*, the ancient code of conduct prevalent among Pashtuns until today, and some journalistic writings. Finally in terms of non-fiction prose, we need to mention Pazhwak's reflections on the political situation in Afghanistan under the Soviet occupation as contained in the memoir *Muzakerat-e Jenev* ("Geneva Talks"), which appeared in Peshawar at the end of the 1980s.

However, Pazhwak was also an important writer of prose fiction. Some of his prose narratives have been published, such as the stories included in the key volume of his prose work, *Afsanaha-ye Mardum* ("Stories of the People"), which was published in Kabul in 1958.[22] While other examples of his prose writings are still unpublished, a booklet containing Pazhwak's two short stories, *Avarah* ("Wanderer") and *Yak Zan* ("A Woman"), was published posthumously in Kabul in 2006, with the English translation of the stories printed in the same volume. Also included in Pazhwak's body of fiction writing are a few plays, but the majority of his prose writings belongs to the genre of storytelling, including short stories and novelettes. The plays, short stories (*dastan-e kutah*) and novelettes (*nawil*) stem from the influence of western literature, though nowadays these genres have become an established part of modern Afghan prose writing (*nasr-e adabi*). As we have seen in Nushin Arbabzadah's chapter in this volume, the introduction of these genres to Afghanistan can be traced back to the early twentieth century through the important journalistic and literary efforts of Mahmud Tarzi (1865–1933). Published in his influential newspaper *Siraj al-Akhbar*, Tarzi's regular discussions of western literature and its various genres and movements were not only read by Afghan literati, but also actively influenced their work. In such ways, new forms of prose writing gradually entered the literature of Afghanistan and Pazhwak's own turning away from traditional prose styles (for example, his relatively limited use of picturesque metaphorical prose and his turn to an increasingly realistic style of writing) were in tune with what Tarzi defined as the criteria for modern prose writing.

Pazhwak was one of the earlier Afghan literati to write drama, short stories and novelettes and in some of his stories attended to the protagonist's deep thoughts, placing the human being and his inner life at the centre of the narrative. In recognition of his standing and contribution, in his research on modern Dari-Persian literature in Afghanistan the critic Sayed Haschmatullah Hossaini described Pazhwak as a "pioneer of Afghan short story writing".[23] Many of Pazhwak's fictional prose writings drew on the rich repertoire of Afghan folklore, revealing Pazhwak's fondness for this oral genre. In Pazhwak's stories, the austere landscape of Afghanistan often served as the main backdrop, while regions of Iran and India/Pakistan also occasionally appeared as secondary backdrops. This aspect made sense, given that historically the borders between these countries have been shifting and fluid. In terms of length, Pazhwak's prose writing was almost entirely made up of fairly short pieces in which the plot (often triggered by an unusual incident) followed an increasingly steep line of development. It is typical of the stories that romantic features were often added to them, though his stories' overall repertoire of themes included historical, folkloric, socially critical and sometimes psychological and philosophical matters. However, a repeated sequence of motifs run through the stories, particularly the bravery of the Afghans, their love for their homeland, the pathos of the Pashtuns, and the love between two young people from different backgrounds. His prose was written mainly in Dari-Persian and in comparison to these works, his Pashto prose has remained mostly unpublished despite including half a dozen short stories and dramas.

Reflecting his early education and diplomatic experiences abroad, Pazhwak also translated foreign literature into Dari, including both factual texts and fiction. Some of these translations were published in Afghanistan, while others still remain unpublished. His wide range of translations included the Psalms of David (from Urdu), the works of the Lebanese-American poet Khalil Gibran; the Indian Nobel laureate Rabindranath Tagore; the English poets Lord Byron and John Keats and the orientalist Reynold Nicholson; the American poets Henry Wadsworth Longfellow and William Pitt Root; and the French author Jacques Prévert (directly from the French). In addition, Pazhwak translated selected poems and dramatic fragments from the works of Johann Wolfgang von Goethe, William Shakespeare, George Bernard Shaw and Victor Hugo. Among the translations that were actually published were *Pishva* ("The Prophet") by Khalil Gibran and *Baghban* ("The Gardener") by Rabindranath Tagore.[24]

Themes, Motifs and Strategies

As we have seen, Pazhwak spent more than half of his life abroad living far away from his homeland in Europe, America and Asia. In spite or perhaps because of this, his love for his country and his patriotic intellectual and emotional connectedness to Afghanistan always remained present in his work. Moreover, his poetry and prose affords insight into certain problem sets that afflict Afghan society. For Pazhwak's experience of western democracies was often directly processed through his literary creativity and he interpreted Afghanistan through literary works in which his interpretation was always based on a critical stance that outlined an implicit message. Even so, it was up to the reader to extract the message. The implicit criticism which Pazhwak expressed in his writings allowed him as a citizen without political power to contribute to the social, political and intellectual development of Afghan society.

Yet Afghan society is mostly conservative and steeped in traditional norms, structures, and ways of thinking. During Pazhwak's childhood, the futility of trying to introduce changes to traditions that would affect the fabric of society was revealed in the failure of King Amanullah's reforms in the 1920s. Amanullah had intended to reshape his country by introducing it to modernity through political and social changes that followed the example of Mustafa Kemal Atatürk's Republic of Turkey. Amanullah's modernization measures for Afghan society included the removal of the *hijab*, the introduction of western clothing styles and compulsory education for girls. The measures were met with fierce resistance by a great section of the conservative rural and urban clerical establishment. As for citizens' participation in government matters, by the time Pazhwak reached adulthood, this had been nearly impossible for decades. The Constitution of 1923 (and that of 1931) did have progressive traits that introduced Afghanistan to modern constitutionalism, but in real terms governance still remained authoritarian and the majority of what were stipulated as constitutional rights turned out to be mere theory. As a result, we can say that for most of the twentieth century Afghanistan was in fact an absolute rather than a constitutional monarchy. Even if the country was not a police state, the central operations of the government were run by a series of more or less authoritarian figures, including Prime Minister Muhammad Hashim Khan (1929–46), Shah Mahmud Khan (1946–53) and Muhammad Da'ud Khan (1953–63). With the exception of the years between 1963 and 1973, during which the prime minister was a common citizen, all of the aforementioned figures belonged to the royal family. They did make achievements in certain fields, for example by firmly sticking to Afghanistan's political neutrality during the Second World War and working on modernizing the country with the help of foreign development aid. But under the rule of such powerful prime ministers, the political participation of citizens was hardly possible and in spite of the existence of a bi-cameral parliament, the final decisions were always made by the aforementioned power-holders. Discontent with and criticism of the inadequacies that affected social and political life hardly featured in the official sources of the time. Instead, they only appeared and were published decades later in such sources as the personal memoirs of important political figures of Afghanistan. Similarly, the Afghan press (which was relatively diverse for a third world country) had to constantly struggle against mild to serious forms of censorship. In 1952, for example, the government banned all privately-owned newspapers.

Despite or perhaps because of such difficulties, Pazhwak wanted to play a role in developing Afghan society. He had to express his criticism in a manner that would allow him to efficiently communicate criticism but without triggering life-threatening problems for himself. The themes which he openly or subtly dealt with in his texts included social conditions, the citizen's right to freedom, the peaceful handling of outside threats to Afghanistan, the damage to traditional nomadic lifestyles through sedentarization, and the anachronistic aspects of the *Paxtunwali* code. Early on, his literary and critical preoccupation with some of these themes already crossed the threshold of the power-holders' tolerance. This explains why Pazhwak was keen in his writings to voice criticism in an implicit manner but in a style that would nonetheless not rob his texts of their sharpness. He achieved this goal through the specific textual strategy explained in the following examples.

In some of his texts, for example, Pazhwak used the strategy of contrast by juxtaposing two opposite poles. One pole would be occupied by an Afghan example and the other one by a positive non-Afghan example, which inevitably had the effect of making the opposite pole appear in a negative light. In using this strategy, there was no need for the author to explicitly identify the Afghan pole as the one that represents negativity. For example, the theme of one of his unpublished texts is freedom and rain.[25] In this text, the more Switzerland and Afghanistan resembled each other topographically, the more different they were in terms of their internal political conditions. Indeed, freedom and rain were both of crucial importance to Afghanistan. Pazhwak connected freedom and rain to Switzerland, both of which appear in the text as something he could only yearningly wish for in Afghanistan. Pazhwak implicitly conveyed this message to his readers in the following manner. The conditions in Switzerland were depicted as altogether positive, indeed with Switzerland resembling paradise, and the basis for this state of affairs was the blossoming of freedom through regular rainfall. With this exaggerated, idealistic portrayal of Switzerland and its citizens, Pazhwak implied that despite its purely superficial topographic communalities with Switzerland, Afghanistan was far from reaching such heavenly conditions. Remarkably, Pazhwak managed to clearly demand freedom for his country's people without resorting to either classical clichés or revolutionary vocabulary. Thus, he used the term "wish" instead of "demand". Even so, the message was made clear to his readers. The gentle imagery and juxtapositions that Pazhwak used in the text were almost pedagogic in the way they made readers aware of the implied message. To this end, Pazhwak made use of a poetic device in which the linking of freedom with rain was central. For the metaphor of rain referred not only to the purely physical aspect of the land, but also in a metaphorical sense to the blossoming of freedom and the spirit.

Named after a place, the unpublished text *Padshir* firstly evoked the well-known image of the Spin Ghar mountains in the east of Afghanistan, portraying the mountains as an idyllic landscape. In one part of the narrative, Pazhwak even used the term "paradise" for the scenery, but in another part the story was suddenly interrupted by a description of utter misery. Hence we read: "In this place, human life has just emerged from the distant past and there is no sign, not even a trace, of contemporary human beings. The people of Padshir sow corn between the rocks".[26] Again, Pazhwak made use of contrast as a literary device. After doing his utmost to evoke the image of a pleasant and magical landscape in his readers' minds, the readers suddenly found themselves woken to a different reality as if splashed with cold water. The realization of this literary manoeuvre took place over several sections of the text, which, just as in the work on Afghanistan and Switzerland, gained its sharpness only when the pleasant imagery was contrasted with stark descriptions of misery.

Another favourite strategy of Pazhwak's was the merciless dissection of crisis situations through which he evoked specific conditions in Afghanistan. Here, the author adopted the perspective of a cold emotionless eyewitness who unaffectedly reported and described a horrific situation complete with gruesome detail. Using this device alone, the author managed to invoke in readers a feeling of repugnance against the conditions that had triggered the situation described. Once again, Pazhwak did not need to openly appear as a critic. Similarly, in his socially critical novelette *Dhamir* ("Conscience"), through a ruthless portrayal of the story's protagonist, Pazhwak demonstrated that decadence and the lack of a sense of justice on the part of elites in the Afghan feudal system were both immoral and un-Islamic.[27] Here too, he did not specifically point the finger of accusation at the perpetrator or depict a caricature or inhuman picture of the protagonist. Instead, the protagonist came across as a pleasant and ordinary person. But manifested with increasing clarity, the protagonist's treatment of the socially vulnerable clearly came across as immoral and beyond religious justification. In the course of the unfolding narrative, the initial possibility of the reader's identification with the protagonist was reduced and ultimately disappeared through the gradual but relentless unmasking of the protagonist by his own deeds.

One conspicuous characteristic of Afghan society is the immediate emergence of strife whenever there is a threat from the outside and Pazhwak tackled this theme in his famous poem, *Mardan-e Parupamizad* ("Men of Parupamizad"), written in the early 1940s.[28] In the poem Pazhwak made use of the artful, poetic language of the classical *masnavi* form. The poem still feels fresh and accessible today, even though the conditions of its reception have changed. Superficially speaking, the poem is about Afghan patriotism, but through the poem Pazhwak sought to make readers realize the different consequences that unity—and its opposite, divisiveness—would have in the case of a foreign threat to Afghanistan. Since classical antiquity, the history of Afghanistan has been marked by many invasions by foreign armies and, judging by historical evidence, Afghan resistance has been fiercely and frequently successful. However, even in times of war, unity has always been fragile and a recent example of this is the resistance movement during the decade of the Soviet occupation. Clear parallels to this recent example can be found in Afghans' struggle against the invading army of Alexander the Great in the fourth century BC, for neither group of invaders had anticipated the scale of their losses and the amount of time they would spend in Afghanistan. In Pazhwak's view, both also failed to take into account the inhabitants' strong desire for freedom and independence. Thus, in his poem *Mardan-e Parupamizad*, there first appeared a description of the time that Alexander the Great spent in Ariana (the historical name of Afghanistan and parts of Iran) and the experiences he had with the people of the country. Used to victory, Alexander saw the occupation of Afghanistan as the necessary step for the conquest of India and so his prolonged stay and campaign in Afghanistan began to cause anxiety among his Greek followers and subordinates. Alexander's mother, Olympia, wrote him a letter, pleading with him to explain to her what had caused the delay for which even Aristotle had failed to offer an explanation. In response, Alexander sent Afghan tribal leaders to Greece in order to illustrate the kind of problems he faced in Afghanistan. Ordered by her son, Olympia received the Afghan princes with much respect. But Alexander had also requested that during the princes' audience with his mother, a small amount of soil from Afghanistan should be secretly placed under the carpet at the palace entrance. When the Afghan princes arrived and inhaled the smell of Afghan soil, they immediately began displaying behaviour that was typical for Afghans: disunity and strife appeared among them, leading to a passionate and bloody struggle. In this manner, Alexander showed his mother that as soon as they somehow found themselves in proximity of the soil of their country, patriotically-minded Afghans immediately displayed bravery and passion, but these characteristics were also often used against their own people so as to cause harm to Afghans themselves. Towards the end of the poem, Pazhwak pointed out that not only Alexander but many other rulers and people who came to Afghanistan had experienced Afghan's strengths and vulnerability. This conflicting nature of the Afghan mindset was portrayed as a challenge that illustrated the fierce patriotism of Afghans as well as the cause of their downfall. This patriotism is best illustrated in the imagery Pazhwak used in the following verse:

> Thousands of wine-filled barrels fail to intoxicate a patriot
> So much as a tiny particle of the homeland's dust.[29]

In this verse, Pazhwak created an original way of comparing intoxication (or perhaps madness) with something else—in this case a tiny dust particle that can fully intoxicate the patriot. "Thousands of barrels" are a huge amount; a "tiny particle" by contrast is very small indeed. The imagery of the dust particle that has the effect of clouding the mind, an effect that even a thousand barrels of wine cannot achieve in a wine-lover, left no option for readers but to recognize the extraordinary status of the homeland for patriotic Afghans. The lines quoted above are the poem's key verses and have been frequently cited elsewhere. Furthermore, the verse needs to be regarded in the context of the following lines, for in the second half verse we read:

> Blind are the eyes which look at the path of hope for the homeland.[30]

In this verse Pazhwak explicitly criticized the people of his homeland, warning them that blindness creates disunity, leading to hatred and the killing of one other. The poem as a whole can be described as an epic about heroism with a didactic backdrop. It is remarkable that Pazhwak did not communicate the message contained in the poem by using nationalist or chauvinist clichés. His intention in the poem was ultimately to convey the idea that if Afghans unite and do not allow themselves to become prisoners of their own patriotism, they can handle any foreign aggressor.

Conclusions

Even though the internal political circumstances and social structures in Afghanistan in the twentieth century hardly allowed for open criticism, Pazhwak nonetheless expressed criticism through his literary work while avoiding direct clashes with the government. His implicit criticism had three advantages. Firstly, it achieved its desired effect of reaching an Afghan readership, even though the target group his work addressed was composed of a limited number of people. Included in this target group were numerous friends and acquaintances who belonged to Afghanistan's small group of educated elite. Secondly, despite his years abroad, Pazhwak did not place himself outside of a collectively "Afghan" society. Never accepting social or ethnic barriers, he always saw himself as an Afghan and never drew barriers in his writings to distance himself from his fellow compatriots. Thirdly, he did not try to divide his country. While he did desire change in Afghanistan, he sought it without causing division and strife. He was never a radical and his approach was always diplomatic and skilled, appealing to his readers' reason and moral integrity. This ultimately ensured him a lasting impact that is revealed among other things in the fact that among many Afghan intellectuals his criticism is still considered not only valid but also the basis for political planning. In the previous pages, we have seen that Pazhwak's literary work represents a valuable compendium of Afghan history and culture, even if the study of his work has only just begun.

7

MASTERING THE EGO MONSTER

AZHDAHA-YE KHODI AS AN ALLEGORY OF HISTORY

Wali Ahmadi

Objectively one always speaks only to the matter at issue; subjectively one speaks of the subject and subjectivity—and then, what do you know, subjectivity is the matter at issue! It has constantly to be stressed that the subjective problem is nothing about the matter at issue, it is the subjectivity itself. For since the problem is the decision and all decision lies […] in subjectivity, the important thing is that objectively there be absolutely no remaining trace of a matter at issue, for at that very moment subjectivity wants to sneak its way out of some of the pain and crisis of decision, i.e., make the problem a little objective.[1]

A marginalized voice of dissent upon receiving the Prix Goncourt in 2008 for his novella, *Syngué sabour: Pierre de patience*, the Afghan writer and filmmaker Atiq Rahimi described the rather unexpected discovery in his youth in Kabul of a "strange book" in Persian with an "enigmatic title"—*Azhdaha-ye Khodi*. It was "a text that seemed at once classic and modern, inaccessible and incomprehensible, yet [possessing] a force of magnetism" that can be "obsessive".[2] Rahimi thus paid tribute to the author of the book—this "monument"—Sayyid Baha' al-Din Majruh, a figure who remains largely marginalized within the institutionally sanctioned Afghan literary circles. "This silence reflects not only the intellectual inertia of our people, but also their bad faith [*sa mauvaise foi*] in recognizing in him a great writer, [one] who lived beyond frontiers—all sorts of frontiers, whether political or ethnic, linguistic or philosophical".[3]

Who was Majruh? After the *coup d'état* of April 1978 (known as the Sawr Revolution), which paved the way for the subsequent, decade-long Soviet invasion of Afghanistan in the 1980s, the self-described communist regime in Kabul introduced a series of significant measures aimed at essentially transforming the composition of Afghan culture. In this respect, literature and other forms of creative production assumed a central and quite contentious role. In numerous cases, many of the literati defied the cultural policies of the new regime and, in numerous cases, paid dearly for their principled stance. One such dissenting figure was the author of *Azhdaha-ye Khodi*, the intellectual and scholar Sayyid Baha' al-Din Majruh, a professor of Western philosophy at Kabul University.

Majruh was born in 1928 into a renowned traditional family of Pashto-speaking *sayyids* in the province of Konar in eastern Afghanistan. He learned the fundamentals of Islamic doctrines in the madrasa of his birthplace and was introduced to the canonical works of Persian literature by his family. Upon moving to Kabul in 1939, where his father served as a government official, he was enrolled in Lycée Estéqlal, the French-medium high school in the capital. Majruh left for Europe in 1952 and earned his advanced degrees in philosophy and psychology in Paris (1955) and in Marburg and Munich (1957). The impact of his university studies in Europe proved significant to his intellectual growth and his development as a scholar. It formed the core of his life-long interest in the tradition of German Idealism, especially G.W.F. Hegel, a portion of whose seminal *The Phenomenology of Spirit* Majruh translated into Pashto and whose *Reason in History* he investigated in detail in his lectures. The period during which he studied in France coincided with the consolidation of Existentialism, especially through the charismatic presence of Jean-Paul Sartre, as a formidable school of philosophy in France. Majruh's later writings, that somehow deal with existentialist psychoanalysis, show that he was impressed by Sartre's work, above all his influential *Being and Nothingness*. But Majruh always kept his intellectual distance from existentialist thought in general.

Upon returning to Afghanistan in 1957, Majruh assumed a lectureship in Philosophy at the Faculty of Letters, Kabul University, where he taught the history of Western philosophy and social science methodology. With the inauguration of a new constitution in Afghanistan in 1963, when the power of the monarchy was curtailed and democratic reforms were introduced, Majruh—perhaps anticipating some sort of meaningful participatory role for intellectuals in the fast changing political landscape of the country—briefly served as the governor of the province of Kapisa in 1964. Disappointed that the transformation was not sufficiently inviting the active involvement of intellectuals, he withdrew from administrative work and left for Munich in 1965. In the meantime, he continued his studies and was awarded a doctorate, with distinction, in philosophy from the University of Montpellier in 1968. Majruh returned to Kabul University where between 1969 and 1972 he served as Dean of Humanities. He was serving as the president of the History Society (*Anjoman-e Tarikh*) of Afghanistan when the Afghan monarch, Muhammad Zahir Shah, was deposed in a coup in 1973 and the former authoritarian prime minister and cousin of the King, Muhammad Da'ud Khan, launched a presidential system of government. Majruh returned to Kabul University and taught there regularly until the Sawr (April) Revolution of 1978. Following the Revolution, like so many other intellectuals and literati, Majruh suffered a period of internment in the notorious Pol-e Charkhi prison in Kabul. While he had shown little interest in Marxism during his earlier intellectual preoccupation, he turned into a relentless critic of the historical-determinist and materialist aspects of Marxian thought, an ideological formation that provided the theoretical grounding for the new Afghan state's vicious acts of sheer terror.

Majruh fled Afghanistan in February 1980, soon after the Soviet invasion, and settled in exile in Peshawar, Pakistan. There he devoted himself with much diligence to directing an Afghan cultural centre and information agency. Peshawar at this period had emerged as the city wherein Afghans from all walks of life found themselves forced to take refuge. Not only many ordinary Afghans who fled the Soviet atrocities in the 1980s settled there. Many intellectuals, artists, writers and poets also chose to live there or to use it as a springboard to migrate to Europe and North America. Numerous Dari-Persian (as well as some Pashto) magazines, journals and books, mostly of political content but also of undeniable literary merit, appeared in Peshawar in the 1980s and the 1990s, when Afghanistan fast descended into civil strife after the Soviet withdrawal. The Pakistani city also emerged as the main headquarter for the several, often squabbling, anti-Soviet, US-supported and Saudi-financed Afghan *mujahidin* guerrilla organizations. All of these groups received, to various degrees, extensive political guidance and military training from the Pakistani intelligence establishment.

Fig. 15: The Philosopher-Poet in Pakistan: Majruh in Peshawar, *circa* 1987.

Majruh's presence in exile in Peshawar proved rewarding and through the force of his personality he attracted many admirers. There, he was able to publish his books and help found a Writers' Union of Free Afghanistan (WUFA), to rival the similar association created by the Soviet-installed regime in Kabul. The information agency he headed was soon recognized as a most reliable source of news on the anti-Soviet struggle, and offered an alternative view of the state of resistance that differed greatly from the presentation of the conflict by the dominant Islamists and their Pakistani supporters. Insisting on the independence of the agency and the accuracy of its news, Majruh made himself many enemies among the *mujahidin*. He was murdered in Peshawar on 11 February 1988, by assailants affiliated with one of the extremist *mujahidin* groups.[4]

What follows engages with Majruh's magnum opus, *Azhdaha-ye Khodi*, a four-part philosophical narrative in Persian written and published between 1971 and 1983. Parts One and Two of the book had appeared in one volume in Kabul in early 1973, just before the advent of the republican regime.[5] It was during his exile in Peshawar that, in 1983, Majruh published Part Four of *Azhdaha-ye Khodi*, along with an elaborate summary of Part Three. The latter part, as Majruh maintained afterwards, was misplaced under "mysterious circumstances" during the author's escape from Kabul.[6] In 1981, substantial segments of the work also appeared in translation in the journal *Les Temps Modernes*, edited by Jean-Paul Sartre and Simone de Beauvoir. The entire book was later published, in a French translation by Serge Sautreau, in two parts, as *Le voyageur de minuit* (Ego-Monstre I) and *Le rire des amants* (Ego-Monstre II).[7]

A Literary-Philosophical Take on Modernity and Selfhood in an Afghan Context

As the title of the book, *Azhdaha-ye Khodi* (the "Ego Monster" or the "Dragon of Selfhood") conveys, at the heart of Majruh's project lies the concept of selfhood—a concept which seems to be intrinsically connected with the philosophical, psychological, and aesthetic permutations within the discursive formation of modernity. The text, whose limits or borders as either literature or philosophy are hardly self-evident, points to the epistemological and metaphysical consequences of the reign of an ever violent, hegemonic self and insists on the necessity of restraining, and ultimately dismantling this self. Assuming that selfhood had increasingly acquired an over-assertive, domineering definition for the individual human person, the text draws attention to the extraordinarily dangerous development in the part of the modern subject that prescribes the self an all-encompassing capacity and unaccounted agency to extend and aggrandize its stature, expand its might, seek supremacy over others and, above all, dominate the human consciousness and systematically suppress the potentials of its own inner voice(s) of dissent. As the text evolves, however, to accentuate some concrete developments within the temporal-spatial landscape of the project, the reflective, epistemological, and phenomenological constitution of selfhood further acquires a socio-historical embodiment of significant magnitude, where ideological programmes operate deep inside belief systems and political structures.

Selfhood in *Azhdaha-ye Khodi* appears fundamentally as a problematic, a problematic that involves both being and the consciousness of being. In the narrative progression throughout the four parts of the book, the allusions and references made to the subject discern in essence not the possibility of self-actualizing, self-determining agency or apparent grandeur and cultivation of individuality but rather the deep and seemingly unavoidable deficiency and paralysis of selfhood in modernity, a peculiar historical era where being is continuously circumvented by the chimera of becoming, where ideas turn into far-fetched ideals, and where ideologies overtake all aspects of human thought and actions, leading the human individual to tragically succumb to the horrors of ego-monstrosity.

It is important to note that in conceptualizing the contours of selfhood, the presentation of the capacity of the ego to manifest monstrosity, and affirming the necessity of destabilizing and ultimately denying the reign of the Ego Monster, Majruh is drawing creatively and productively from various European as well as non-European trends of thought on the subject. As this chapter will elucidate further, Majruh is nonetheless critical of the modern Western views that define the self on the basis of its quest for infinite power, its tendency towards domination, and its blind submission to the rule of what Majruh terms "Raw Reason" (*kherad-e kham*). In the meantime, Majruh opposes the traditional view on the subject—associated distinctively with the Perso-Islamic perspectives—for its proclivity towards superstition, religious indoctrination, and dogmatism in the name of an ill-defined concept of subjectivity. Both outlooks, Majruh maintains, have the inherent capacity to result in intellectual lethargy and have a propensity to further the demands for self-grandeur and ego-centrism, and eventually lead to ego-monstrosity.

As the text of *Azhdaha-ye Khodi* and especially the author's notes and references therein clearly show, Majruh was well aware, though hardly uncritical, of the epochal contributions of European thinkers towards the theorization of a strong, unified, and purposeful sense of selfhood and subjectivity. He certainly valued the Cartesian conceptualization of the nature and identity of the self as well as its emphasis on the individual as the ground for all knowledge and experience, introspective reflection, and the importance of the first person standpoint. As certain passages from *Azhdaha-ye Khodi* (especially in Part One) suggest, Majruh was indebted to the Rousseauian tragic view of the fallen nature of humankind as well as the praise of the uniqueness and autonomy of human individual experience.[8] Similarly, he appreciated the Kantian equation between selfhood and consciousness, where subjectivity can have content through awareness of the world. He was well aware also of the contributions of modern phenomenology for introducing new models of consciousness (whether ordinary or non-ordinary and mystical) into the forefront of modern discussions of interiority and intentionality in defining subjectivity and selfhood. Majruh seemed keenly interested in Sartre's attempt in *The Emotions*, as well as elsewhere, to situate the import of emotions with regard to consciousness and to affirm that,

> The emotion signifies, in its own way, the whole of consciousness or, if we put ourselves on the existential level, of human reality. It is not an accident because human reality is not an accumulation of facts. It expresses from a definite point of view the human synthetic totality in its entirety.[9]

Not only does one detect in *Azhdaha-ye Khodi* the implications of this Sartrean pronouncement. One also sees there the influence of Sartre's "existentialist psychoanalysis" (in *Being and Nothingness*) in defining the composition of the modern self primarily in terms of the Other. It also seems that Majruh must have been aware of theories that insisted on either refusing or denying the presence of the Other or—in what may resemble a form of dialogic inter-subjectivity—acknowledging the Other's significance in the evolving constitution of the self.

Furthermore, it is noteworthy that almost precisely at the time when Majruh was tackling the delineation of a theory of human subjectivity and selfhood in *Azhdaha-ye Khodi*, the concept of self had began to run into a deep quandary through the intervention of post-structuralist theory in the French intellectual scene. There, the Enlightenment humanist view of the autonomous and unified individual was vigorously challenged and the subject was assumed to be a split, unstable, and fragmented construct in language and discourse.[10] As early as 1966 in *Les Mots and les choses*, Michel Foucault had already pronounced the demise of man and argued that "[a]s the archeology of our thought easily shows, man is an intervention of recent date. And one perhaps nearing its end". Foucault had further maintained that "[O]ne can certainly wager that man would be erased, like a face drawn in the sand at the edge of the sea".[11] Meanwhile, the critic Roland Barthes had questioned the sovereignty of the author in producing texts and had written powerfully about the displacing of what has historically been 'the reign of the Author', the authoritative position of the creative, productive subject.[12] Nevertheless, Majruh's take on the question of the self is radically different from the post-structuralist theory that was based largely on denying the subject authority and active agency. In developing his notion of selfhood, Majruh is less interested in dethroning the sovereignty of the subject than in identifying the conditions where the self assumes a monstrous identity and indefinite will, on the one hand, to dominate the totality of the individual human faculties, including the dissenting elements within the self, and, on the other hand, to subjugate the entirety of humanity. For this reason, then, defeating the monster of the ego, rather than displacing the self in its entirety, would translate, in effect, into the restoration of the sovereignty of a limited but genuine self against a deceitful, arrogant and domineering ego.

If Majruh wrote *Azhdaha-ye Khodi* in the context of the enduring European philosophical preoccupation with the notions of selfhood and subjectivity from the Enlightenment Cartesian thought to post-structuralist theories, in defining the essential aspects of subjectivity and the perils and predicaments associated with ego-centricity of the modern subject, he drew generously and inevitably from the Perso-Islamic mystical and philosophical tradition. Terms such as 'self' (*khod*), 'selfhood' (*khodi*), 'I-ness' (*mani*, *ana'iyat*), and 'being' or '(self-) existence' (*hasti*, *wojud*) with specific reference to concepts of human subjectivity, agency, and identity permeate classical Persian literature and Islamic thought. While any attempt to present this tradition in less than a detailed and extensive manner will likely give rise to confusion and misunderstanding, it should be mentioned nevertheless that in various trends within Sufi (mystical) poetry, while human intuition and consciousness constitute an essential part of the classical mystical writings, self-definition and affirmation are bound paradoxically to a perilous but necessary process of self-elimination and negation.[13]

The scholar Annemarie Schimmel characterizes Islamic mysticism as consciousness of one reality, or as "love of the Absolute", and points out how this can lead to views of the world as a "limited reality"—"which derives its conditioned existence from the Absolute Existence of the Divine". By extension, this includes the individual human self, and can result in the denial or negation of its value(s), a process that is often figured in such images as "the boundless ocean in which the individual self vanishes like a drop, or as the desert, which shows itself in ever new sand dunes that hide its depths, or as the water out of which the world is crystallized like ice".[14] This is also what the Sufis refer to as the stage of *fana'*, a seminal mystical term succinctly defined by Toshihiko Izutsu as "the total nullification of the ego-consciousness, when there remains only the absolute Unity of Reality in its purity as an absolute Awareness".[15] *Fana'* is the annihilation of disparate, fragmented human "selves" into the grand unity of the absorbent absolute "Self"—the embodiment of the grand Truth (the Divine).

That the human individual can achieve a true identity through *fana'* can hardly be said to delineate a historically grounded concept of subjectivity and agency. This was precisely the point of criticism made about the mystical notion of *fana'* by the renowned Muslim Urdu and Persian poet and philosopher of India, Muhammad Iqbal (1877–1938). The key defining feature of Iqbal's aesthetic of selfhood (*khodi*) was its political implication. As Javed Majeed has recently pointed out, "His [Iqbal's] concept of *khodi*, of creative individuated selfhood, is articulated against mystical notions of *fana'*, or the annihilation of the individual self in the presence of God. [...] Iqbal inverts and plays with the mystical images in order to articulate his sense of *khodi*".[16] For Iqbal, in contrast, there is "an un-erasable reality of the self" that makes it "central to the fabric of reality, and even the ground of reality", which obviously means that the mystic seeking an organic fusion with the Divine (i.e. *fana'*), in which there is a total identification of the human subject with its divine object, would result in the loss of all personal identity.[17] To a certain extent, Iqbal argued, one could trace the decline of Islam as a political power in recent history, and the weakening of the Muslims' capacity to be effective actors in the world, directly to the preponderance of mystical notions of selfhood. To counter these notions, selfhood needs to be radically reinvestigated as a category, as a substantial reality. Rather than the human selves losing their individuality in approaching God, they should become more individuated, more vigorously seeking to define and realize their *khodi*.[18] As Majeed points out, a crucial context of Iqbal's redefinition of *khodi* was political and anti-colonial, that is, providing a "counter agency" to the traumatized population of Indian Muslims to resist "the systematic negation" of their humanity—i.e. the negation of their selfhood and subjectivity—by European colonial domination.[19]

One may suspect that in *Azhdaha-ye Khodi*—especially in the parts that were written in the wake of and immediately after the Soviet invasion of Majruh's homeland—the author would revisit his notion of selfhood and, just as Iqbal provided an anti-colonial politico-historical context to *khodi*, would similarly accord an acute political role to the individual subject in the larger war of liberation and anti-Soviet resistance in Afghanistan. Majruh, however, refuses to subscribe to the Iqbalian position on *khodi*. Ever suspicious of grand ideological positions, he steadfastly refuses to accord the self, as it is, the capacity to liberate the homeland from the claws of the Other. This is only possible if one realizes or comes to the consciousness that disentanglement from the bondage of one's own Ego Monster should take place in earnest before any liberation from the power of a colonial order can be realized. As the discussion below will try to explicate, for Majruh the rule of the Other—that is, a foreign power—over the tangible collective homeland of the hitherto free people is precisely the macrocosmic extension of the supremacy of the Ego Monster over individual selves. These are the very selves that constitute the collectivity of a people. Collective ("national") liberation, then, will remain wholly illusory so long as individual self-emancipation has not occurred.

As the following synoptic analysis of *Azhdaha-ye Khodi* will show, Majruh remains especially sceptical, if not totally dismissive, of ideological constructs that justify their own *raison d'être* through their functional use of such grand constructs and discourses as religion, class, ethnicity, gender, etc. Thus, while in Muhammad Iqbal's theorization of the subject, Islam is seen as a powerful force in defining and assimilating the expansiveness of a collective *khodi*, for Majruh it runs the serious risk of turning itself into one more ideological instrument, albeit a potent one, in strengthening—not subduing—the monster that reigns supreme within the self. In Parts One and Two of *Azhdaha-ye Khodi*, a particular claim is put forward where the various conceptions of the "self" tend to produce a theoretically synthetic form of "individual" that assumes a psychoanalytical overtone with clear reference to the unconscious, subconscious, and conscious structures of the human psyche. In this early segment of the work, the author makes copious references to both Freudian and Jungian psychology and devotes the appended "Aftermath" to the psychoanalytical elucidation and explanation of the project.[20] Significantly, in Parts One and Two, the subject appears to be removed almost entirely from political and ethical concerns.

Nevertheless, as a self-transformative philosophical narrative, *Azhdaha-ye Khodi* progressively moves away from a primarily psychological examination of the nature and appearance of the ego (Parts One and Two) to a philosophical-metaphysical inquiry into the possibility of redeeming and recovering an ego-less "subject" (Part Three). It then moves to a profoundly ethico-political investigation aimed at delineating a complex theory of the self that would be bound to the radical negation of the ego-hood of the individual person as well as the affirmation of its historical agency and active subjectivity on a more collective basis (Part Four). The entire project, however, can be said to offer throughout a trenchant critique of institutional ideological prototypes (including established religious models) and political apparatuses that reinforce rather than overcome what Majruh terms "ego-idolatry" and "ego-monstrosity" and suspend the emergence of the person as a discerning individual subject who is also the conscious subject of history.

MASTERING THE EGO MONSTER

The following synopsis traces the arduous, and ultimately tragic, journey of the Midnight Traveller (*Rahgozar-e nima shab*), the main character and the principal narrator of each one of the four parts of *Azhdaha-ye Khodi*. His journey is from being a captive of the Ego Monster to his successful "conquest of the ego", to his witnessing the apparent "death of the [Ego] Monster", to the fateful "return of the [Ego] Monster", and to the catastrophic—inevitable?—resumption of the "reign of the Monster" through the revitalization of "Egocentric Reason". Despite its disjunctive episodic schemes, the intricacy of the journey both reflects and generates a concept of selfhood that, while presented in a novelistic literary form and personal narrative voice, is deeply informed both by profound philosophical meditation and ethical concerns and by historical relevance. As for the latter, it should be clarified, *Azhdaha-ye Khodi* is not necessarily a form of narrative that, by its very definition, deals only with history as the product of tropological operations or narrative forces, providing little knowledge of what it purports to relate. On the contrary, the historical specificity of the very production of the narrative underlines the engagement of the text with an array of historical incidents and developments of paramount importance in contemporary Afghanistan.

Part One: "The Death of the Monster"

In Part One of *Azhdaha-ye Khodi* (entitled "The Death of the Monster") the narrator—that is, the Midnight Traveller (*Rahgozar-e nima shab*)—starts a perilous journey. The journey demonstrates that since human beings find a sense of safety within the confines of their reflective consciousness, they fail to acknowledge that the apparently well-fortified realm of human consciousness will not withstand the onslaught of the pre-reflective forces of the subconscious and the deluge of the unconscious. After all, the expanse of the unconscious and the subconscious is boundless, while the domain of the conscious remains limited.[21] As the author's copious endnotes and references appended to this part of the book maintain, the two realms once constituted a utopian, idyllic arena of perfect tranquility, where natural instincts were freely present and the repression of libido had not yet occurred. The successful surfacing of the ego within the human psyche—represented through the metaphor of the ferocious Ego Monster or Dragon—resulted in the irreparable bifurcation of the planes of the conscious and the unconscious, leading to the creation of a vast, horrific and unbridgeable chasm between the two.[22]

While the City of the Silent Ones (*Shahr-e Khamushan*) seems calm and its inhabitants appear to be unperturbed, the Midnight Traveller discovers that, just across the dividing chasm, "the dreaded dragon of Ego rises up in the darkness of the night, traverses the deserts and plains of the unconscious, and fast approaches the gates of the City of Consciousness".[23] The deleterious effects of the arrival of the Ego Monster are significant. Above all else, the Monster is the carrier of three contagious and fatal illnesses: *distress* (which afflicts especially the children and the elderly); *fury* (which afflicts the youth and gives them a proclivity to fight and shed blood); and *fear* (which affects all). With the arrival of the Monster, the residents of the city no longer trust each other; fear and secrecy overwhelm them and recurrent nightmarish dreams continually perturb them.[24] The ferocious Monster is not immune from this calamity either: ever deeply caught in the complex "inferno of illusions" (*jahanam-e awham*), he finally realizes that, despite his unchallenged domination over a multitude of docile souls, his power rings hollow: he remains a master with no disciple, a sovereign with no willing subject, a ruler with no devotee.[25] This tortuous living, this perpetual limbo, where the ever evasive Self is alienated from the rest of human selves, where life, nature, love, and eros are abandoned, can be superseded only when the Ego Monster is openly attacked, subdued and, ultimately, is forced to retreat from the city.[26] Only with the exile, and eventual death, of the Monster, will the mastery of the Ego come to an end.

Part Two: "he Return of the Monster"

With the apparent demise of the Ego Monster, the *Rahgozar* begins to contemplate on how he had lived his life so far "in the dead-end alleys of [anxiety-ridden] rational thought [...] away from the idyllic spring of life".[27] He finally opts to "tear apart the dark shroud of the night [of Reason] and welcome the morning sun of intuitive reflection". He serenely overcomes his erstwhile "illusions" and, "Phoenix-like", flies off the ashes of his former Self towards illumination.[28] However, exactly when he assumes that the Monster is overpowered, he painfully witnesses in a far corner of the plains of the soul the rebirth of the Ego Monster in the form of the gradual metamorphosis of a small worm into a gigantic dragon. With a feeling of utter anxiety—of utter "nothingness"—the "Midnight Traveller" (*Rahgozar-e nima shab*) concludes that despite all reflective human endeavors, the dragon monsters of the ego still dominate human psyches.[29] The ultimately dreadful and utterly despairing truth of existence—"*serr-e asrar*" (the secret of [all] secrets)—therefore consists of the following: "The world is meaningless and more meaningless is the [rational] search for meaning".³⁰

When the Traveller rushes towards the City to warn its people of the impending threat, to his dismay he finds out that the vicious *Azhdaha* (the little worm now transformed into a dragon) has already conquered the city and is ruling over it with an iron fist. Significantly, the terrain that the Monster is penetrating includes not only the core of the self but also the heart of the polis. Thus, the realms of the personal and the political become undistinguishable: the citizens are not the hapless victims of a monster from without but rather "victims of the monster who resides in the rubbles of their own hearts". Precisely for this reason, the *Rahgozar* conveys to the people, "building fortresses around the city is useless [...]. No enemy will attack you from the outside. No danger lies beyond these fortified walls. The real danger lies *within* the city. The enemy is in your own midst".³¹ Since "the Monster is homegrown—for each one of you contains a monster, who, in turn, feeds the greater Monster—to destroy the latter, you would have to destroy your own inner monsters", the Midnight Traveller urges.³²

Apparently, in spite of the insistence of the author to present *Azhdah-ye Khodi* primarily as a contemplative, psychological and philosophical narrative, the reception of the two early parts of the project by Afghan readers as a deeply political allegory grounded in the historical realities of the time seemed unavoidable. The clear political overtone of the subsequent parts of the book—where one discerns a progression of the effects of the Ego Monster from the individual to the collective, from the metaphysical to the material, from the psychological to the sociological—makes it abundantly clear why this should have been the case. Furthermore, it demonstrates how cunningly the Ego Monster translates itself into a form of ideological framework that successfully engulfs both individual and collective identities.

Written in a highly politically charged atmosphere in the later part of the 1970s (Part Three) and early 1980s (Part Four), *Azhdaha-ye Khodi* reveals how the City of the Silent Ones (*Shahr-e Khamushan*) under the rule of the demonic dragon of the self proved itself analogous to the situation in the author's homeland, Afghanistan, under the brutal Soviet occupation. In these parts of the book, the hitherto abstract (and apparently ahistorical) rendering of the oppressive reign of the Ego Monster in the realm of individual consciousness assumes a concrete historical embodiment. This involved the elaborate depiction of the perils and predicaments of a whole nation forced into submission to a devastating foreign occupation and invasion. What follows intends to show that, in Parts Three and Four, the Midnight Traveller discovers tragically how the demonic conquest of the City by the *Azhdaha* is completed, not only within the domain of the human reflective consciousness but also in the tangible realm of the actual polis.

Part Three: "The City of Dawn-of-the-Self"

As Majruh maintains in his introductory notes to Part Four, the unpublished text of Part Three of *Azhdaha-ye Khodi* was lost when the author left his homeland for neighbouring Pakistan, although some of his close associates had read it in manuscript form. What is especially revealing in Majruh's account here is that Part Three was meant to deal primarily with the reign of Muhammad Da'ud Khan's republican regime, which came to power in 1973 with the assistance of the pro-Soviet "Communists", and put an end to the long reign of the monarchy. His regime was itself eventually destroyed by its erstwhile "Communist" allies when, "in April 1978, the Khalq-Parcham coup succeeded and the children born of the Monster started to devour their own mother, the republican regime".[33]

According to Majruh's synoptic rendering of Part Three in the introductory pages of Part Four, the Midnight Traveller mournfully leaves the "City of the Silent Ones", which is now suffering under the overbearing rule of the *Azhdaha*. In his journey forward, the Midnight Traveller narrates the story of a man of incredible strength—in what appears to be a reference to the "invincible", authoritarian President Muhammad Da'ud Khan—who, to the delight of his fellow citizens of the City of the Soul, decides to take on the menacing Monster—a clear reference to Da'ud's populist discourse of triumphant nationalism.[34] The result of the battle between the two is that the strong man secretly sells his soul to the Monster and then returns to the City: in appearance, deceptively of course, he seems victorious. In reality, however, he is in a secret covenant with the Monster. In short, the Monster has conquered his Ego, turning him, in fact, into an Ego Monster. The strong man—as the apparent hero—opens the gates of the city to his ferocious new collaborator. Since it is in the nature of the Monster to enter into covenants but never uphold them, as soon as it extends its demonic shadow over the City, it devours and consumes the very same hero he made a contract with.[35]

In response to the question of some citizens as to why the once gallant hero—whose physical strength was equal if not superior to that of the Monster—made a pact with the Monster, the Midnight Traveller offers the following revealing answer: "Before the gallant hero was devoured by the huge Monster, he was consumed by the little monster of his own ego". It is therefore highly recommended that mere utopian promises, false dawns, and deceptive "great leaders" should not be trusted. To achieve true freedom, it is imperative to cleanse one's heart—and not only one's head—from the "spider web of illusions".[36] Anything less than this will be tantamount to continuing bondage in the claws of the Monster. After all, no genuine freedom can ever be ensued from the conditions of *un*-freedom.

Part Four: 'The Homeland of Freedom'

The fourth (and final) part of the project of *Azhdaha-ye Khodi* is entitled "In Search of the Homeland of Freedom" (*Dar Jostoju-ye Sarmanzel-e Azadi*) and was written in the immediate aftermath of the Soviet invasion of Afghanistan. This was after Majruh left his ancestral homeland and became a refugee in neighbouring Pakistan. Within the trajectory of *Azhdaha-ye Khodi*, it is in this segment that a specific historically-grounded presentation of the subject is charted out. The self assumes its definition—and encounters its constraints—within systems of knowledge, power, and ideology. In the meantime, the subject who hitherto could only be consumed by the Ego Monster is now implicitly in possession of the potential to exert itself in a meaningful form of resistance to the Monster.[37] It even assumes a role where resisting, and overcoming, the reign of the monstrous dragon of the ego turns into the *sine qua non* of the identity of the subject. Above all, it is also in Part Four of *Azhdaha-ye Khodi* that the self is given the task of realizing genuine emancipation and freedom, a realization that eluded it in earlier parts of the book. And, it is also in this part that the narrative completes its cyclical structural composition with a warning that there will remain a tangible likelihood of the now transformed subject to fall back into the fateful, perilous path that will inevitably lead to the re-conquest of the soul by the ever-lasting, ever-cunning, ever-vigilant Ego Monster.

In the first section of Part Four, the narrator (Midnight Traveller) finds himself wandering among the wretched exiles (*avaragan*) who, upon the destruction of the once glorious City of the Soul (*shahr-e jan*), were forced to take refuge in the Desert of Antipathy (*biyaban-e bi-dardi*). By all accounts, the exiles are the compatriots of Majruh who, upon the invasion of their homeland by the Soviets, took refuge in the not-too-welcoming territory of Pakistan, described as the Desert of Antipathy.[38] Here, the erudite Traveller acknowledges the hardships of exile and destitution. His chief mission, however, is not to portray the people as passive victims of circumstances. It is to bring them to the consciousness or realization that their own actions have actually paved the way for their destruction, and that deliverance will be possible only through their own conscious agency.

The second and concluding section of Part Four of *Azhdaha-ye Khodi* (entitled "Sohbat dar mahfel-e avaragan") contains a lengthy and substantive discourse, witnessed and narrated by the Midnight Traveller, between an old sage and a group of young men who inquire about the potential of realizing the liberty of their homeland from the claws of the reigning Monster. Freedom is, the old sage advises the youth, when one comes to the consciousness of the idea of freedom.[39] Indeed, the land of liberty is thirsty for the blood of the Monster. But there is an irony involved here: "It is imperative to take the Monster to the wide desert in the outskirt of the City of the Soul", the Midnight Traveller insists. "It is there that you'll realize that the Monster is no more than a mirror in which each and every one of you will observe his own true picture. You must cleanse the mirror by slaying the Monster".[40] In other words, the Midnight Traveller warns, a victory over the alien monster will be vacuous without vanquishing the inner monster(s) of one's own. After all, "the Monster arrives not from unknown terrains but springs from the depth of your own hearts. Each one of you bears and rears a monster inside you, which you aggrandize and metamorphose into a humongous idol, and then you worship your own creature".[41] The reigning Monster who now controls the physical space of the homeland is, paradoxically, one and the same as the Monster who is ruling over the being—the very texture of the soul—of individuals who intend to dislodge it. In a manner whose Hegelian overtone can hardly go unnoticed, the old sage maintains that the individual's coming to consciousness of his/her own monster, his/her recognizing of the extent of the danger it poses, and his/her taking steps towards mastering the monster of his/her own ego, are the foremost requisites for genuine realization of freedom. The main point is that the individual has the capacity of recognizing this and gaining consciousness of it.

The inference that can be further drawn from the above is that, unless the inner monsters of the abject subjects of domination are utterly tamed, shamed, exposed, disgraced and eradicated, victory over the vicious Ego Monster will remain illusory and true emancipation short-lived. An emancipation that is derived from altering one form of domination for another one, where one ideology is privileged over and above a rival one, is hardly genuine. In other words, any attempt to oppose the monstrosity of the dominant structures of power (that is, the communist regime of the pro-Soviet People's Democratic Party) through the valorization of a rival "emancipatory" ideology (that is, adherence to the Islamic ideological predilection promulgated by the *mujahidin* groups) will be tantamount to privileging one unfulfillable utopia with another vacuous ideal, and hence in continual subjugation of human actors in the claws of the Ego Monster. It is in this context that the narrator, again in the person of the Midnight Traveller, offers a most trenchant critique of modern ideologies, including the ideologization of religious beliefs and, in a crucial way, questions the entire project of modernity that engenders and reinforces such ideologies.

It is important to explain that in the formulation of this ideology-critique lies a paradigmatic point that Majruh attempts to highlight throughout the entire project of *Azhdaha-ye Khodi*. Within the framework of a general historical anthropology, the text puts forward the theory that human existence started in the idyllic Valley of the Idols (*vadi-ye asnam*) where primitive forms of idol worship were practiced in a harmonious manner.[42] Each human being worshiped his/her own idol without criticizing or undermining the adherents of other idols. Their common language further helped them live in a state of perpetual tranquility. The Midnight Traveller, then, affirms that the so-called primitive humans, like humans in general, were capable of creating further dissimilar images, of generating distinctive meanings. However, since these new images and meanings were created without the conscious efforts of their creators, the hitherto existing idols thereafter were transformed into disjointed, lifeless stones, into mere statues. Their human creators, devoid of consciousness and especially self-consciousness, helplessly prayed at the feet of their creatures and feverishly worshipped these stones. The created objects, in turn, acquired a life of their own. Thus, it was incumbent that one single object—a grand idol—be privileged over and above all others.[43]

Understandably, dissonance and discord appeared when one single idol was carved and placed amidst much fanfare on a pedestal in the grand central temple.[44] Two further developments ensued from this unprecedented act. First, the predominance of a commonly understood language was challenged and, instead, many languages began to appear. Second, a new concept of time—time as the unfolding of chronological events in accordance to the law of perpetual progress—emerged. The combination of these two developments further undermined and undeniably shattered the harmony of primitive human associations in the once-peaceful Valley of the Idols. Implicitly, it is in this stage, with the destruction of a once-unified language and the appearance of linear progressive time that, in what resembles a curious process of anthropomorphosis, a grand Monster or Ego Monster surfaces and starts to devour its own creators, who are devoid of self-consciousness and easily fall victim to the whims of the Monster. As we shall see now, above all else the reign of the Monster affects the very foundation of emergent human Reason.

Witnessing the painful destruction of the Valley of the Idols, the Midnight Traveller enters into the realm of the City of the Souls (*shahr-e jan*), where he meets an old hermit. The hermit reveals that the City was once the home of the Goddess of Reason, a beautiful young woman who never abandoned her irrational impulses and was madly and passionately in liaison with ecstatic drunkards, charming rogues, and enchanted lovers.[45] Nevertheless, when from amongst the elders of the city a certain "dark-hearted savant" (*hakim-e del-siyah*)—who was overcame by the Monster that watchfully monitored the events from the edge of the City—proclaimed with much arrogance that "the realm of Reason must be eternally distinct from the land of Love" and that no synthesis of reason and love would be acceptable, an infinite war began between "drunkards" (lovers) and the "sober" (rational), which culminated in the lovers' exile from their homeland.[46]

With the departure of her charming lovers and admirers, the Goddess of Reason died a slow and painful death. The narrator here is intent on conveying that originally both Reason (*'aql*) and Un-reason (*junun*) were the true inhabitants of the City of the (Human) Soul and the architects of the House of Hearts. Dialectically correlated, they mutually strengthened the human soul, enabling it to resist the Ego Monster. Their severance from each other will be tantamount to "opening the gates of the city [of the soul] to the monster", for both Reason and Un-reason, in isolation from each other, have the potential to turn demonic and monstrous. While Reason theoretically affords the human being the capacity to realize its distinctive subjectivity, the Monster effectively thwarts the emergence of true Reason and per force transforms selfhood into ego-centricity and ego-monstrosity. Reason, so inherently subservient to the Ego Monster, continually destroys the human capacity to pursue genuine selfhood and true subjectivity.

In the historical trajectory of *Azhdaha-ye Khodi*, the death of the Goddess of Reason coincides with the ushering of that era of modernity where instrumental reason becomes supreme. The old hermit recounts that subsequent to the death of the Goddess of Reason, of all the lifeless, bloodless idols that slowly acquire a life of their own, it is "the idol of Raw Reason" (*bot-e kherad-e kham*)⁴⁷ that assumes supremacy and repeatedly gives birth to two other, smaller but equally fateful, idols: one deceptive (*farib-kar*) and one bloodthirsty (*khun-khvar*).⁴⁸ The deceptive one Majruh calls the idol of "progress" (*pishraft*) and the bloodthirsty one he names the idol of "revolution" (*enqelab*).⁴⁹ He then posits that those who believed in coalescing the two in order to achieve "progress" through "revolution", "end up in the huge temple of Monster worship. They neither advance nor regress an inch. They neither leave the state of self-ignorance nor put foot into the state of self-consciousness. They neither transcend inferiority nor achieve superiority". All the revolution means is the strangling of the "bird of meaning" (*morgh-e ma'ni*), whose wings are already broken by the self-proclaimed vanguards (*pish-ahangan*) of "progress". The task at hand in the era of modernity would therefore be to reject the ideologies that adhere to the conventional view of "progress" through "revolution".⁵⁰

The implications of the recommendations of the Fourth (and final) Part of *Azhdaha-ye Khodi* to the concrete historical situation of Soviet-occupied Afghanistan in the early 1980s are clear. In fact, the historical grounding of the entire project comes to its concrete fruition when the author introduces, on the one hand, his critique of a specific ideology (Marxism) in the name of which the so-called "Glorious Revolution" of April 1978 was promulgated and execute and, on the other hand, his suspicion of another ideological formation (political Islam) in the name of which, the war of liberation from Soviet occupation was fought as a *jihad*. Here, one may suggest that, convinced that the *Azhdaha-ye Khodi* cannot be just an examination of consciousness but must be at the same time an examination of the actual world, Majruh moves away from an analysis of the ego in its abstract form (as in Parts One and Two) towards a more concrete, tangible and actual form in the larger social and political context.

In Parts One and Two of *Azhdaha-ye Khodi*, Majruh showed little explicit or even implicit interest in dealing with Marxism, whether critically or favourably. In the latter two parts, however, he pinpoints the main fallacy of Marxism as its historicist and determinist nature. Marxism, he speculates, emphasizes the inevitability of historical teleology, the certainty of the course of human destiny, and views history essentially as temporal development along a linear scope of progress. However, against the Marxian view of history, Majruh contends that it would be misleading to assume a single conception of temporality for diverse purposes and circumstances. History has no predetermined course to be followed universally. It has no itineraries, no signposts. There are no laws to history and it does not tend to any established goal. History admits of many possible directions, the determination of which depends on a complex array of conscious individual choices and only in part on collective human motives and communal-social aspirations. In a move that is strikingly Hegelian in essence, Majruh maintains that fundamental historical change starts with individual consciousness (*agahi*) and ends with individual self-consciousness (*khod-agahi*).[51]

According to Majruh, the other fallacy of Marxism is that Marx attempted to turn the Hegelian dialectic on its head and claimed the ontological primacy of the tangible, material world. He thought he was helping the masses break away the chains of exploitation, but he actually imprisoned the conscience, as well as the consciousness, of the people in the illusory and the realm of a distorted, unfulfilled and unfulfillable utopia. To Majruh, theorizing the establishment of communism through violence and revolution as the final socio-economic system of universal applicability makes Marxism a non-historical or rather ahistorical doctrine. In short, Marxism is a mere ideology not much different from the other ideologies it purports to critique.[52] Marx was able to offer his hypothesis because, as a prisoner of the Ego Monster, he was deeply impressed by the idol of Raw Reason that dominated the crucial era of nineteenth-century European modernity. Thus, he carved a humongous new idol, which he named "revolution", to achieve historical "progress". When non-European "revolutionaries" attempt to imitate Marx's scheme of historical progress, the end result of their efforts can only lead to total destruction and the loss of what they traditionally possessed.

By valorizing tradition (or at least privileging certain aspects of tradition) in the realization and buttressing of human consciousness, Majruh is keenly aware that he opens up his main argument to the possibility of being perceived as regressive and reactionary. Therefore, he admits that history obviously involves change (*digarguni*) but insists that, while "every leap towards perfection is a change, not every change is a leap towards perfection". Thus he further maintains that "every progress is movement, but not every movement is progress". Moreover, "progress is only that movement towards perfection that stirs consciousness within the self and comes to an end within the self". But fundamental historical alterations take place not because of sudden outbursts of violence (in the name of some abstract ideal of "revolution"), but because of the gradual accumulation of small-scale and apparently insignificant changes. Such a process of change can guarantee the overcoming of the tyrannical rule of the Ego Monster. The cycle of tyranny cannot be disrupted by "revolution" but, above all, by smashing the spell of the demon of the ego, by freeing oneself from the bondage of one's own self. The person who cannot release oneself from the prison of the ego can hardly bring freedom to others. Thus, a re-valuation of all revolutions is needed for, in essence, self-consciousness is revolutionary and real revolution is no less than coming to genuine self-consciousness.[53]

In offering a trenchant critique of Marxism, Majruh painstakingly and copiously discovers illusory ideals, utopian doctrines, and idolatrous practices within the very fabric of each and every modern ideology and ideological tendency that draws its legitimacy through its origination from the linkage between the dual monsters of "progress" and "revolution". The so-called "Islamic" resistance that fought the Soviet occupiers turns out to be no exception. In fact, the historical topicality of *Azhdaha-ye Khodi* consists of the fact that it deconstructs the equally "idolatrous" motives of the progressive "Communist" revolution as well the motives of the opposition "resistance" groups who used to wage an "Islamic" revolution in Afghanistan. Will an "Islamic" response to the "Communist" slaughter of the people of the City of the Soul genuinely break the tyrannical rule of the monsters? Majruh's response to this question is hardly an affirmative one.

Majruh's attitude towards institutionalized forms of religion is profoundly complex. He despises the religious authorities who expel the admirable "Goddess of Love" from the homeland, and accuse her of indecency. He finds advocates of institutional and established forms of religions little more than close minded hypocrites, pompous and self-righteous individuals (*chand pishva-ye bi-basar*). What is also significant is that nowhere in *Azhdaha-ye Khodi* does Majruh imply that only what is presented as religion by the self-righteous upholders of faith and morality is false and that there is a true, genuine meaning to religion, a meaning that needs to be unveiled and shored up. Rather, in several instances, he mocks the very pretence of religion, which he considers a system of beliefs that is open to all sorts of manipulation; above all, political manipulation, resulting in extending the reign of un-freedom and monstrosity.

In the meantime, in direct reference to the leadership of the so-called anti-Soviet *mujahidin* resistance in the 1980s, the *Rahgozar*, or traveller, warns the shipwrecked refugees of the former City of the Soul to be aware of the machinations of *Azhdaha*. Are not the so-called "*Amir-e Jihad*", the self-proclaimed pious advocates and leaders of the cause to resist domination by the monster-from-without, continuously mesmerized and enthralled by their own little monsters-from-within? Are not these leaders, in the name of freedom, inviting the greater Monster to bring upon the City an unstoppable and far more dangerous deluge of un-freedom? Do they not preach resistance but they themselves so pathetically cling to life in the fortress of their own pitiful egos?

The unimpeded horrors that have gripped Afghanistan since the "Communist" take over of 1978 and the "Islamic" revolution that ensued afterwards show that, though published as early as 1983, *Azhdaha-ye Khodi* has proven quite prophetic in its predictions. The reign of un-freedom continues, with no end in sight.

8

LYRIC REALISM

POETIC REFLECTIONS OF REFUGEE LIFE IN IRAN[1]

Zuzanna Olszewska

In istgah-e sevvom o labriz-e adam ast
Dobareh shish shodeh amma kasi kam ast
Hol midahand 'alam-o-adam, dar in mian
Yek pirmard goft, Boro! Sandali kam ast.
In bar-e chandom ast ke u dir mikonad
Ya sobh-e zud rafteh va hala Moqaddam ast.
Hala savar-e yek otobus-e qorazeh-am
Bazar-e chashmha-ye tamasha faraham ast.
Yek sandali-ye kohneh mara dar khodash neshand
Yek sandali ke mesl-e khodam gong o mobham ast
Bar u neveshteh and be kharab o zesht
"Dar in zamaneh 'eshq, khoda, pownd o derham ast"
Sad sareban-e taraneh o labha-ye khoshk-e man…
Be ta'neh goft ke aqa, Moharram ast!

*

Khab o khiyal amad o dar man 'obur kard
Aqa boland sho! Tah-e donya, moqaddam ast.[2]

This is the third bus stop and it's overflowing with people,
it's six o'clock again but someone is [still] missing.

185

> There's a world of people pushing and shoving, and in the midst of this,
> an old man says, Get out! There aren't enough seats.
> How many times has he [have I] got here late,
> or gone early in the morning and reached Moqaddam by now?
> Now I'm sitting on a dilapidated bus,
> and the bazaar is full of spectacle for my eyes.
> A worn-out seat has embraced me,
> a seat that, like me, is mute and vague.
> On it, they've written in a broken, ugly handwriting:
> "In this era, Love [and] God are the pound and the dirham".
> A hundred caravan-leaders of song and my dry lips…
> A mullah sarcastically says, Mister, [don't you know] it's Moharram!
>
> *
>
> Sleep and dreams came and passed through me.
> Mister, get up! This is the end of the world, Moqaddam.

This poem, by Gholamreza Ebrahimi, a young Hazara poet living in Mashhad, is an example of a poetic style that I wish to explore in this chapter: a style that has become increasingly visible among Persian-speaking Afghan refugee poets in Iran in the past decade. All translations from the Persian are my own. In the transliterations, I adopt Iranian-Persian vowel sounds because they more accurately reflect the accent of second-generation Afghans in Iran. I reproduce the poems discussed in full, as they are not all readily available. The reader of the Persian original is immediately struck by the fact that this poem is in the *ghazal* form of classical poetry, yet it uses contemporary, conversational language, departing from the traditional conventions of the genre by incorporating narrative elements, and recounting with a documentary immediacy the daily journey to work of an Afghan labourer on a rickety old minibus. It is realistic in that it describes the narrator's journey through his external environment, the bus and the throng of passengers, as his senses perceive them in vivid detail. But it is also intimately lyrical,[3] as it evokes his inner state: "mute and vague", full of songs which he is unable to sing and dreams from which he is jolted by cold reality.

This poem, and others like it, reflects a disillusionment with ideology and grand narratives and a search for other, more immediate, sources of poetic inspiration. The first generation of Afghan refugee poets in the 1980s had been steeped in the experiences of war and resistance against the Soviets, and used epic poetic forms and language to support the struggle against the occupation and the communist government. But from the late 1990s onwards, as the political circumstances in both Iran and Afghanistan changed and a new generation came of age, different preoccupations came to the fore. One of the hallmarks of contemporary poetry in Iran is a great diversity of form and content.[4] But while many poems do still use the highly metaphorical and elevated language typical of classical and some twentieth-century poetry, the fusion of subjective emotion, simple language and a reportage-style realism that I describe here appears to be a true innovation in the history of Persian-language poetry.

In this chapter, I outline the situation of Afghan refugees in Iran, including the circumstances which have led many to turn to creative activities including poetry writing. Next, I explain what I mean by realism as a mode of writing and the tropes with which it is associated, followed by a discussion of the historical precursors of this mode in Persian poetry. Finally, I present a close reading of five poems, demonstrating the ways in which realism works with other modes, particularly lyricism, to achieve particular effects. As the focus of my research has been the ethnographic study of poets and poetry, in what follows I will situate the works discussed in their social context. My personal acquaintance with their authors and their biographical details will allow me to shed light on the creative process. Furthermore, alongside my interpretations of the texts, I also discuss the pragmatic aspects of these poems as communicative devices: the impressions that they "give off" about their authors in addition to the message that they are intended to "give", in Goffman's terms.[5]

Afghans in Iran

Most of the approximately three million Afghan refugees who came to Iran in the past three decades were able to self-settle in Iranian cities rather than being confined to refugee camps.[6] Those with legal residence (currently still almost one million people) had access to the labour market, education and many social benefits in Iran, although some of these have been restricted in recent years. Among the Shi'a and Dari-Persian-speaking ethnic groups (including Herati Tajiks and Hazaras), a group of socially and politically conscious intellectuals arose, who came from the same families and social strata as the stereotypical Afghan manual labourers, but benefited from education in Iranian secular and religious schools. They played an influential role both in refugee communities and in the civil wars in Afghanistan in the 1980s and 1990s.

Through education, the mass media, and other state institutions such as health and family planning programmes, refugees have been exposed to an Iranian and Islamic modernity which has encouraged rising literacy, falling fertility, new religious practices and institutions, and increasing demands for participation in the public sphere by women and youth. There is also—perhaps paradoxically—increasing disillusionment with the state-sponsored religious orthodoxy and a greater emphasis on reformed religious discourses or outright secularism, individual thought and reflection, leading to a greater subjectivism in art and literature. Indeed, literature, particularly poetry, has been the focus of most Afghan cultural organizing in Iran.

Over the past three decades there has been a ferment of grassroots cultural, social, religious and political activity in the refugee areas of Iranian cities, particularly Mashhad, the metropolis closest to the border with Afghanistan. This has included literary organizations, hole-in-the-wall English and computer schools, women's groups, religious gatherings and youth theatre or photography clubs. My research focused on one such group, the Dorr-e Dari ("Pearl of Dari") Cultural Institute in Mashhad, whose main activities were weekly poetry and short story writing circles and the publication of a quality cultural, literary and art journal. Dorr-e Dari, as the centre is usually called, receives limited support from Iranian state bodies, but it is mostly funded by its subscribers and supporters in the wider Afghan diaspora, particularly former members who subsequently resettled in western countries.[7]

The older generation of poets, who founded and run the centre, include several prominent figures who have become relatively well-known in Iran and Afghanistan. Meanwhile, their young protégés frequently enter local and national literary competitions in Iran, and these, along with the blogs they write and the journals they publish, help to sustain fertile contacts with their Iranian peers. These exchanges mean that the poetic output of the younger generation at least can be considered part of the current of post-revolutionary Iranian poetry in form and style, albeit often with specifically Afghan or exilic themes. Dorr-e Dari members also have extensive contacts with fellow literati in Afghanistan, and those who repatriate to Afghanistan are beginning to leave a notable mark on the literary scenes in major cities like Kabul, Herat and Mazar-e Sharif.

Despite the dynamic activity of such organizations, many of the Iranian Afghans' new aspirations have been thwarted by the Iranian state. Even among educated refugees, very few have been able to obtain Iranian citizen-

Fig. 16: Literary Exiles: Zahra Hosseinzadeh (second from left) and Hossein Heidarbeigi (first from right) Hold Meeting at Dorr-e Dari Office, Mashhad.

ship or practice their professions, due to restrictive labour laws. Nonetheless, amidst the vagaries of shifting Iranian policies on education and employment of Afghans, Dorr-e Dari and other centres like it have offered an informal but continuous forum for literary and intellectual engagement to a generation of Afghan refugees with few resources.

What is Realism?

I will return now to Ebrahimi's *ghazal* and discuss its most striking features in such a way as to outline the sense in which I am using the term realism. Ebrahimi's poem, written in 2003 and entitled *Tah-e Donya* ("The End of the World"), seems to describe a daily bus ride; the early hour suggests that the narrator is on his way to work. With a little inside knowledge, we learn that it describes the journey of Afghan labourers in Mashhad, who go at dawn by bus to Chaharrah-e Moqaddam, the Moqaddam Crossroads where many bus lines terminate,[8] to wait with their picks and shovels for employers to pick them up for a day's labour. This practice is known as *sar-e falakeh*, "[standing] at the roundabout". Ebrahimi vividly describes the crowding, the competition and the pessimistic graffiti on the bus seats that mirrors his own pessimism and his own nondescript self-perception. In the penultimate couplet, he tries to sing a song under his breath like a caravan-leader (*sareban*) of yore might have, but his enthusiasm is stifled by a cleric who reminds him that it is the mourning month of Moharram and singing is inappropriate.

The vivid description of the environment here thus sets the scene for the reader and gives the select few who are familiar with this world the pleasure of recognition. Defining the characteristics of realism with a focus on the European novel, Donald Fanger writes that "[t]he language of realism seeks to present the object with maximum clarity and a minimum of emotional or stylistic deformation. Its task, in Conrad's words, 'is to make you hear, to make you feel—it is, before all, to make you *see*. That—and no more, and it is everything'".[9] Realism seeks to allow the reader to accurately perceive the world of the narrative, as if she were herself sensually experiencing it. Any emotion or moral commentary is implicit, to be actively derived by the reader from the narrative, rather than imposed by the author's rhetorical flourishes. The beauty and success of realist literature is measured by the extent to which it is able to give insight into a world not through stylistic excess, but through representations of scenes, events or moods through plain words that make them as tangible and as close to ordinary life as possible.

This term should never be assumed to refer to some immediate correspondence of art to "reality"—it is an aesthetic convention like any other, and the qualities that may be deemed plausibly "realistic" vary across historical periods and cultures, leading to a diversity of qualifying adjectives, such as social realism, magic realism, or romantic realism. The term may be applied to a specific moment in literary history—for example, European nineteenth-century realism in fiction—or to a mode of writing that may be found, to a greater or lesser extent, in different literary traditions at different times.[10] I use it in the latter sense, rather than subscribing to a teleological vision of literary history that assumes that Afghan literature has or must necessarily reiterate a certain period that other literary traditions have already passed through. Indeed, this chapter seeks to show how realism has been incorporated into the Persian lyric poetic tradition to achieve a particular local iteration of modern literature with its own distinct, and plural, "genealogies of the modern".[11]

LYRIC REALISM

But aside from the "documentary" style, which often seeks to capture the "spirit" of a particular place contemporary to the time of writing, realism is usually associated with a number of tropes, including irony, brutality, the contrast of appearance and reality, and lost illusions.[12] In American fiction, for example, the unexpected "twist" at the end of many of O. Henry's (1862–1910) short stories is a typical example of these tropes. Similarly, Paul Fussell points to the rise of irony as a common trope in twentieth-century English and American literature, identifying World War I as a great moment of disenchantment with the beneficent possibilities of modern civilisation.[13]

As we have seen, the theme of reality baldly reasserting itself over imagination is ever-present in Ebrahimi's poem. According to the graffiti on the bus seat, the ideals of Love and God have been reduced to currencies that may be bought and sold. If one sings, one will be cut off by the guardians of public morality, and if one falls asleep, one will inevitably be awakened by a stranger to another day of hard labour at the "end of the world". This shattering of illusions fits neatly with Fanger's definition of realism. Indeed, it lies at the very heart of the poem, in the ironic confrontation between formal frame—the *ghazal*, a genre traditionally dealing with earthly or divine love—with its prosaic content, and the cynical assertion scrawled in an ugly hand that Love and God are dead.

We have identified, then, a few of the features of the realist mode that concern us here: a documentary, descriptive approach that allows the reader to 'see' what the author sees; a fixing in space and time that attempts to capture the 'spirit' of a particular era in a particular place; and an atmosphere of disappointment, cynicism and broken illusions. These features are most commonly associated with the novel, so we must ask ourselves what realism brings to lyric poetry, including the *ghazal*. Here, as we see in Ebrahimi's poem, the combination of an eye on the external world and the narrator's inner responses to it turns the lyric realist style into one which allows Afghan poets to document their everyday struggles and reflect on their disillusionment and their small moments of humiliation.

These moments may be, but are not always, based on a poet's actual experiences; even when they are not, however, they will give the illusion that they are. Without knowledge of the poet's biographical details, it is often difficult to know to what extent they are products of the imagination, but one can assume that the poet has encountered similar experiences in a milieu that he knows well. Charles Baudelaire (1821–67), one of the first modern poets of the urban crowd and disenchantment in the big city, wrote that "[t]he poet enjoys the incomparable privilege of being himself and someone else, as he sees fit. Like those roving souls in search of a body, he enters another person whenever he wishes".[14]

But in this poem, the intertwining of the narrator's internal and external worlds "gives off" some idea of how he would like us to see him in that world. He is not a passive passenger, but a keen observer who derives what pleasure he can from the "spectacle" of the bazaar. Yet his daydreaming and songs suggest a romantic sensibility, set apart from the rest of the passengers. I guessed that the author was representing himself, Gholamreza, the young poet, forced into manual work out of necessity but dreaming of bigger things. When I asked him about it, he agreed: "I have lived 95 per cent of my poems. That is, I definitely have a record of them in my mind. Some of them I even have in my mind with all of their images, both general and specific". Ebrahimi was an active member of Dorr-e Dari and other poetry circles and editor of an Afghan student journal, and eventually obtained a sociology degree in the face of great obstacles. The poem represents the contradictory life of the exiled intellectual, who rubs shoulders with his disadvantaged fellow refugees but perceives his own status as different: as a thinker and possibly an agent of change. Crucially, the contrast between the narrator's imaginings with his moment of disillusionment is necessary to demonstrate the dual qualities expected of the poet-intellectual: sensitivity, thoughtfulness and empathy, combined with the capacity for clear-eyed and non-ideological appraisal of social conditions.

This figure, that of the *roshanfekr* or "enlightened thinker", has its own history in Persian-speaking countries, and it is to this that I turn next. Its outline will also enable us to locate more precisely the historical trajectories of realism in Persian literature. Although modern Persian poetry has involved much literary borrowing, it is perhaps most useful to ask how pre-existing genres have "handled",[15] accommodated and modified this mode of writing, whose contemporary use was inspired by a particular idea of its use in Europe.

Persian Realism

In the late nineteenth and early twentieth centuries in Iran, a nascent group of intellectuals believed that a new, critical approach to culture and a revolution in literary styles were necessary to modernizing the country.[16] They championed the culture of ordinary people rather than that of the royal court, which had dominated in Iran for centuries.[17] They brought contemporary spoken language into poetry and drew on folk narrative traditions, oral poetry and other verbal genres in their work. In fact, the first Iranian folklorists were writers, including the famous fiction writer, Sadeq Hedayat, who used folkloric material and pre-Islamic legends to promote a kind of Romantic nationalism.

"The masses" became the category of people in whose name political ideas were championed for the first time in Iranian history. However, different groups of intellectuals defined "the masses" and their needs in different ways, often representing their daily lives in their literary work. Thus, leftist intellectuals in the mid-twentieth century, such as Simin Daneshvar, Sadeq Chubak and Mahmud Dawlatabadi, wrote social realist fiction focusing on poverty, injustice and religious obscurantism, while post-revolution Islamist writers drew on much of the same rhetoric of the people's struggle, but now cast religion as saviour rather than oppressor.[18]

In poetry, too, various modernist developments paved the way for lyric realism. Following Nima Yushij's (1896–1960) formal innovations in the 1920s and 30s, there developed a freer approach to prosody, including "free verse" (*she'r-e azad*) without rhyme or metre, or intermediate forms with varying line lengths and liberal use of rhyme. However, even in metric verse forms such as the *ghazal*, efforts were made to bring the language closer to that of ordinary speech. Simin Behbahani (b. 1927) is notable for creating new metric patterns for her *ghazals* out of the rhythms of everyday conversation, and has several poems entitled "From the Street" that might be considered realist representations of voices overheard and scenes witnessed, including one in which a woman gives birth in a queue for food rations.[19]

Later, Forugh Farrokhzad (1935–67) and Sohrab Sepehri (1928–80) were praised for offering poetic resonance to simple, everyday moments and mundane things, unlike the grander political and social concerns of, say, Ahmad Shamlu (1925–2000). Farrokhzad's confessional poetry of the 1950s and 60s expanded the bounds of the kinds of personal experiences that could be talked about in poetry, particularly female sexuality. She and Sepehri have been credited with defying "aesthetic objectification" to make poetry more directly representative of experience: "Their poetry is an active insurgency against that objectification in reaching for the immediate experience of the world before its mediated modulations".[20]

We should note here that frankness in self-expression is not the same thing as realism, which is frequently employed in fiction. Even so, in the context of lyric poetry we may expect there to be some overlap between the two in the form of descriptions of life as observed and experienced directly by the poet, drawing attention to things that would be considered trivial or vulgar in more rarefied poetic forms.

Commentators on the poetry of post-revolutionary Iran often mention that poetry is facing a crisis, losing its readership and struggling with anxiety over the relevance of old poetic forms to contemporary concerns. Contemporary poets are much less well known in Iran than their popular twentieth-century predecessors, and all but unknown outside Iran.[21] After the propagandistic and highly politicised poetry of the Islamic Revolution and the Iran-Iraq war, the 1990s heralded a time of questioning, stylistic proliferation and linguistic experimentation. The following characteristics may, however, be seen as a general trend, in line with the definition of realism outlined earlier: "[A] rejection of romantic, epic, and mystical language and expressions… A conscious effort to evade lofty language and search for a language that is surprisingly close to spoken language… Looking for new horizons and subjects which have been neglected in the past… Use of bitter and harsh satire".[22]

In the case of Afghan refugees, however, it must be remembered that many of them are only a generation removed from communities in which oral folk literature played an important role. Its hallmarks include the use of colloquial language and direct expression of emotions, particularly grief and loss. The singing of improvised verses, particularly the folk quatrains and lullabies of women, is often addressed to a named individual who may be a friend or a family member, not the beloved.[23] Finally, "sorrow, sadness and loss are important themes in Afghan expressive culture".[24] This presents us with the intriguing idea that the air of disillusionment that may be detected in much refugee poetry is an elaboration of an existing cultural tradition, rather than simply a direct importation of western irony and modern disenchantment.

The fact that contemporary Persian literary criticism, of which Dabashi's statement above is a typical example, places such great—often moral—value on more "direct" and unconstrained forms of expression as compared to the ostensibly straitened, ossified and conventionalised forms of the classical past, confirms that such "immediacy" is now a desirable trait in high art poetry also. Indeed, it is itself culturally mediated. For an audience to rec-

Fig. 17: A Slow Day at the Dorr-e Dari Office, with Poet Ali Jafari (Hossein Heidarbeigi in background).

ognise a poem simultaneously as frank, valuable and aesthetically pleasing, and to champion it at the expense of older forms of expression, an entire array of social, political, linguistic and aesthetic changes need to have occurred.[25] Indeed, such critiques should be seen in the context of heated debates about what literature is, what it should do, and what responsibilities the writer has.

For much of the twentieth century, the idea of the "committed" writer who accurately portrays and diagnoses social ills so that they might be addressed has been dominant in Iran (but also, increasingly, in Afghanistan). Dorr-e Dari and other refugee cultural organisations seek to sustain this tradition at the grassroots; even though the ideals intellectuals like them once espoused have worn rather thin in the face of failed political experiments. This was a complaint I heard regularly from the regulars at the centre, and it was readily apparent in their work. When I asked Ebrahimi why many young people were increasingly using realism in their poetry, he said he thought that "[s]ometimes imagination is a good way of escaping from reality. And sometimes reality's power is greater".

Four Afghan Poems

I will now take a closer look at four more poems by contemporary Afghan refugee poets. What features are characteristic of realism, and how does this mode work with others to achieve particular effects? What effect is produced by the combination of lyricism and realism?

The poem below, written by an Afghan living in Tehran, is similar to "The End of the World" in its sense of detached alienation, and also meets with a rude awakening in the denouement. It is a *ghazal* by Seyyed Zia' Qasemi, a poet, film director and former director of a cultural group called the House of Afghan Literature in Tehran, who eventually moved back to Afghanistan to work in Kabul. Once again, we see a narrator moving through an urban landscape weighed down by his troubles, only to be jolted out of his reverie by someone cursing him:

Khiaban, zohr, khalvat bud o u por-mowj o tufani
Qadam mizad khod-ash ra, gharq dar afkar-e tulani
Ze ru-ye rah sib-e gande ra ba pa be juy andakht
—Che bihude ast in donya-ye madfun dar faravani!
Pok digar be sigar-ash zad o chashman-e khod ra bast
—Jahan talkh ast, talkh-e talkh, por-e ashub o zolmani!
Jelotar yek pol-e 'aber,
az an yek bala,
ba'd
Negah-e su-ye bala ba do chashm-e ru-be virani
—Che aram o che sard ast asman—in marg-e dur az dast
Faqat yek lakke abr an gushe, mashghul-e parishani
Agar an abr ra ham bad mishod ba khod-ash… khandid
—Che miguyi to ke hatta gham-e khod ra nemidani?
Be ru-ye pol resid o andaki raft o tavaqqof, ba'd
Negah kard az an bala be ashbah-e khiabani

Be sigar akharin pok ra zad o an ra be zir andakht
Sepas dast keshid aram bar muh vo pishani

LYRIC REALISM

Do dast-ash ra gereft az narde gharq-e khiaban shod
Ze ashkal-e mozakhraf khaste, chashm-ash por ze heirani
Be zir-e lab sorud khand o ba u ham-seda khandand
Mian-e sine-ash sadha ruh-e zendani
Be ru-ye narde kham shod… ba'd chashman-e khod-ash ra bast
Az posht-e sar u ra seda zad: Ay Afghani![26]

The street was empty at noon, and he, stormy and full of waves,
was walking, drowning himself in long [rambling] thoughts.
From the path, he kicked a rotten apple into the gutter.
"How useless is this world, buried in abundance".
He took another puff of his cigarette and closed his eyes:
"The world is bitter, bitter, full of discord and darkness".
Ahead there was a pedestrian bridge,
steps leading up,
then,
he glanced up with eyes on the verge of ruin:
"How quiet and how cold the sky is, this inaccessible death,
just one stain of a cloud in a corner, busy with [its own] distress.
What if the wind took that cloud away with it, too…" He laughed.
"What are you saying, you who don't even understand your own sorrow?"
He reached the top of the bridge and, after starting and stopping a little,
he looked down from above on the phantoms of the street.

He took a last puff of his cigarette and threw it down,
then quietly drew a hand across his hair and forehead.
He put his two hands on the railing and was engulfed by the street,
exhausted by the absurd shapes, his eyes full of perplexity.
Under his breath, he hummed a song, and along with him hummed
the hundred thousand ghosts imprisoned in his chest.
He leaned over the railing, then closed his eyes.
Someone called him from behind: "Hey, Afghani!"

This poem veers between the tangible world with its small, trivial details—such as the rotten apple, the pedestrian bridge, the cigarette, the railing—and the stream of consciousness of the man who is feeling increasingly despondent and alienated from that world. Although it is not a first person narrative, it moves in and out of an internal monologue that gives it a lyrical aspect. It is never made clear if the man is about to commit suicide—we are left with a cliffhanger as he leans over the railing—but he seems to be contemplating it, seeing death in the cold, silent sky, and ghosts on the street below him. (It should be noted that pedestrian bridges are a well-known site for suicides in Iran.) Yet even in his hour of despair, he is brought back down to earth by someone taunting him with the pejorative epithet, "Afghani".

Once again, the poem oscillates between a realistic description and fantasy. In this case, however, instead of taking refuge in comforting dreams, the illusions are full of dread: the "phantoms of the street" and the "ghosts" in the man's chest. Here, the fantasy is not strictly internal but worked into the imagery of the poem, giving it a surrealist quality at times. Nonetheless, the yell in the denouement fulfills the same role as the awakening in Ebrahimi's poem: it shatters the illusion and reasserts the unforgiving reality of life as a despised refugee.

In a third poem describing an Afghan man moving through an urban space, the narrator confronts a different kind of interruption.

Mohemm nist
Khorshid az kodam su amadeh bashad
Mah be kodam su rafteh bashad
Dar kucheha-yat anduh
Dar kucheha-yat ziba'i
Dar kucheha-yat seda-ye mardan-e garichi
Ke tazegi ra faryad mikeshand
Qadamha-e ke az khab miparanad
Divarha-ye hamisheh gong ra
Va chashman-e ke be hazian mibarand
Nimeha-ye shab-e tarik-am ra
Dar kucheha-yat
Par-par-e bal-i-st ke az kuhestanha-ye dur amadeh bashad.

Az akharin divarha-yat aghaz mishavam
Ja-e ke hatta dustanam digar nemiayand
Ba kif-e kohneh-e bar dast
Chenan chupan-e ke tamam-e gusfandan-ash ra gorgha darideh bashand
Chenan sarhang-e ke hich nameh-e bara-yash post nemishavad.

Deltang-e badha-ye vahshi-ye Pamir
Avaz-e dobeiti dar kuh
Deltang-e mahiha-ye tazeh-ye Helmand
Va sarbazan-e ma'lul-e az jang
Az khiabanha-yat migozaram
Pir mardan dar kenareh-ye sayeh-ye tarik
Khatereh-ye yalha-ye aspan-eshan ra morur mikonand
Va juybarha-ye ke be sepidar o sib miraftand.

Kudakan-e khakestari labkhand mizanand
Tileha-ye bazi dar khak ra

LYRIC REALISM

Bi khial-e in hameh ghorbat
Bi khial-e naghmeh az dur
Na chenan baghha-ye sabz-e 'Baghchar'
Na gandomzarha-ye 'Sangtakht'
Ke sobh-ash khomar o sharab o shorb bud
To kuzeh-ye khali bar dush-am
Ke bayad bekeshanam
Ta abha-ye roshan-e Bamyan o shetah o masti-ye Jeyhun
Va khom khaneha az yad rafteh-ye Ghazni
Goluleh engar,
Ke shellig shodeh bashi bar zakhmha-ye narafteh az yad-am.

Deltangiha-yat ra be khaneh miavaram
Ba 'Ali qesmat mikonam
Ba Masih qesmat mikonam
Chun sib ke az mardan-e garichi gerefteh basham
Sabzi az zanan-e mazra'eh.
To barfkuch hasti ke nagehan fara gerefteh bashi-am.

It doesn't matter
from which side the sun came up,
on which side the moon went down.
In your alleys, sorrow
In your alleys, beauty
In your alleys, the sound of the handcart-men
who cry out the freshness [of their wares];
the footsteps that startle
the always-mute walls out of sleep;
the eyes that turn my dark midnights
into delirious muttering.
In your alleys
is a fluttering of wings that comes from distant mountains.

I begin from your farthest walls,
a place where even my friends don't come anymore,
with a tattered briefcase in my hand,
like a shepherd whose sheep have all been torn apart by wolves;
like a commander to whom no letter is posted.

Longing for the wild winds of the Pamirs,
the song of a *dobeiti* in the mountains;
longing for the fresh fish of Helmand
and soldiers invalided by war,
I pass through your streets.
Old men on the edge of the dark shadows
relive the memories of their horses' manes
and the water channels that ran to the white poplars and apple trees.

The dusty children smile
at the marbles they play with in the dust,
not caring about all this exile,
not caring about the melody from afar;
not the green orchards of Baghchar
nor the wheat fields of Sangtakht
whose mornings are drunkenness and wine and drink.
You are an empty water-jar on my shoulder
that I must carry
to the bright waters of Bamyan and the speed and intoxication of the Jeyhun
and the forgotten wine-taverns of Ghazni
as if you were a bullet
shot towards my unforgotten wounds.

I bring your longings home with me.
I share them with Ali
I share them with Masih,
like an apple that I got from the handcart-men,
or herbs from the women in the fields.
You are an avalanche that suddenly takes over me.[27]

This poem in free verse by Hossein Heidarbeigi is unusually addressed to a city or a part of a city. Indeed, it was commissioned in 2007 by Qasemi, the author of the previous poem, who was making a documentary film about Golshahr, a district of Mashhad primarily inhabited by Afghans and impoverished Iranian migrants from rural areas. The poem was read as a voice-over in the film. It vividly describes the streets and lanes of Golshahr, with their noisy handcart vendors, old men watching the world go by from the shadows, children playing marbles, and the nearby fields in which farmers cultivate herbs. Once again, the poet locates himself in the poem: he (a long-time student of philosophy and recent author of a magic realist novel set in the Hazarajat) is to be seen walking through Golshahr's streets with his tattered briefcase. To those who know Heidarbeigi, his own presence is even more explicit—the poet's sons are indeed named Ali and Masih. The briefcase, again, is a symbol of aspirations to a different social status, that of an intellectual or scholar in a working-class neighbourhood, as poignant a contradiction as the other figures who have been demoted in life: the shepherd and the military commander.

This poem owes its aesthetic effect to the constant rending of this observable canvas by lyrical interruptions in the narrator's mind: memories of former times in another place (Afghanistan), which are apt to arrive suddenly like an avalanche, an alighting bird, a melody from afar, a bullet, or footsteps that awaken one at night. These times and places coexist in the space of the poem, and in the memories of those who have experienced them: Golshahr—the real place of exile—and the painstakingly enumerated place names and historical eras that make up the imagined expanse of Afghanistan are addressed in the poem as "you". Reality here is interrupted by a keenly-felt and intoxicating nostalgia for the homeland.[28]

The fact that this visually rich poem was composed to accompany a documentary film is not a coincidence. In fact, the influence of film, television and other visual media, which occupy a prominent position in Iranian society today, on the emergence of this kind of realism in poetry should not be underestimated. Although many scholars have written of the "poetic" qualities of post-revolutionary Iranian art cinema,[29] the Afghan poets I knew also self-consciously spoke about using "cinematographic" techniques in their work.

In their movement through these urban spaces as observers, solitary and discriminating even when among the crowd, these narrators appear to be cousins of the flaneurs in European cities described by Walter Benjamin.[30] It is interesting to note that this portrayal in the poems is based on actual practices. Indeed, many young Afghan poets spoke of wandering around the city, usually in their own neighbourhoods, either when they needed some solitude and space to think, or with friends simply because they did not have anything else to do. Some would turn their weekly trip to the Dorr-e Dari office into an hour-long walk. Their employment was often irregular and they frequently complained of *allafi*, idleness. While they were often self-deprecating about this, they used this time to discuss politics and philosophy, or to spin plans and dreams to improve their lives, such as going to university, taking advantage of better job opportunities in Afghanistan, or finding a way to emigrate to a third country.

The next poem is by Amanullah Mirzai, one of the youngest regular members of Dorr-e Dari who went on to study public relations at university. This poem, written in free verse, takes us off the streets and into the home of a refugee family:

> *Seda-ye khamush-e charkh-e khayati*
> *Avazha-ye ghamgin-e madar-am bud*
> *Ke dar basat-e pedar*
> *Shalvar-e kordiha-yash*
> *Mitavanest mara be madraseh beferestad*
> *Javab-e sahebkhaneh ra bedahad*

AFGHANISTAN IN INK

Fig. 18: Amanollah Mirzai Walks through Back Alleys of Mashhad towards Dorr-e Dari Office (on right).

Va daru bekharad
Marzieh khaharam ke marizi-ash ra hichkas nemifahmad
Va hatta dar haram shafa-yash nemidahand
Mesle suzan-e charkh-e khayati
Yekriz sorfeh mikonad
Narmi-e ostokhanha-ye kuchak-ash
Shahvat-e khak ra bishtar karde ast
Madar nakh-e suzani ast
Ke ba sorfeha-ye Marzieh
Har dam band-e del-ash pareh mishavad
Pedar dar baran basat-ash ra jam' nemikonad
Va man dar ja-e ke kasi nabashad
Ba khod-am harf mizanam

LYRIC REALISM

Rowshanfekran dar ruznameha
Maqaleha-ye mara minevisand
Dar hali ke hamvatanan-am
Lezzat-e jashn-e gol-e sorkh ra faramush kardeh and
Madar, shabaneha payeha-ye charkh-e khayati ast
Milarzad
Pedar, chaharchub-e dar ast
Dar khod basteh
Yek quri chay-e talkh
Marzieh dar album-e 'aks aram mikhandad
Man be hameh chiz fekr mikonam.[31]

The sewing machine's quiet hum
was my mother's sad song.
At my father's stall
it was her workman's trousers
that could send me to school
answer the landlord
and buy medicine.
Marzieh, my sister, whose illness nobody understands,
and they cannot cure her even in the shrine,
coughs continuously
like the sewing machine's needle
and the softness of her little bones
only feeds the earth's lust.
Mother is the needle's thread
With Marzieh's every cough,
with every breath her heartstrings rend.
Father doesn't close his stall even in the rain
and I, in a place where there is nobody else,
talk to myself.
The intellectuals in the newspapers
write articles about me
while my countrymen
have forgotten the pleasures of the red poppy festival [of Mazar]
Mother is the sewing machine's foot by night,
she trembles;
Father is the doorframe
closed within himself.
A pot of bitter tea,
in the photo album Marzieh gently laughs
and I think about everything.

This poem provides insight into the life and livelihoods of a poor Afghan family: the father is a street vendor and the mother is a tailor who makes

"Kurdish" (loose traditional workman's) trousers. Their poverty is suggested by the fact that the mother is obliged to work through the night to make ends meet, while the father must man his stall even in bad weather. They are also stricken by the incurable illness of their daughter, who, the only named character in the poem, gives it particular poignancy. The family are also exiles who have forgotten even the simple pleasures of the red poppy festival (*jashn-e gol-e sorkh*) of their hometown, Mazar-e Sharif. The narrator, although possibly still a child, is already a disillusioned social observer who "think[s] about everything". He is critical both of the intellectuals who write articles about poor refugees in the newspapers but cannot change anything; neither can religious superstition, as even visits to the "shrine" (presumably the Holy Shrine of Imam Reza in Mashhad) have not been able to cure his sister. Even communication fails: the narrator talks to himself when no one else is around, while his father is closed up like a door in its frame.

Mirzai told me that his inspiration for this poem was not his own experience, but a poor refugee family he saw in Golshahr one night, trying to flag down a taxi to take a young child to hospital. Nonetheless, he and several other members of his family have worked as tailors, and they hail from Mazar-e Sharif, which is obliquely mentioned in the poem, although he himself has never been there. The poet, through his use of the first person, thus tries to identify with the narrator, and perhaps imagines him as a less fortunate version of himself.

The final poem I will consider here is written by Zahra Hosseinzadeh, an award-winning poet considered one of the most proficient at the use of the *ghazal* form in a flowing, natural way, yet dealing with contemporary topics. Zahra is one of the leading members of Dorr-e Dari and one of the increasing number of young women it attracts. She has studied philosophy and theology and has worked as a journalist and a teacher.[32]

>*Belit, noskhah o yak mosht pul-e parah begir*
>*Beist akhar-e saf, shambaha shomarah begir*
>*Dobarah Tayyebah hal-ash bad ast, zang bezan*
>*Morakhassi-e kh od-at ra az an edarah begir*
>*Be shekl-e part o pala, har che did, howsela kon*
>*Az astin-e khod-ash mah ya setarah begir*
>*Kharid chiz-e bad-e nist, rang-e delkhoshi-ash*
>*Lebas, kafsh, alangu o gushvarah begir*
>*Havas-etan naravad az pey-e parandah o sang*

LYRIC REALISM

Begu be Tayyebah az mardoman kenarah begir
Agar ke doktor-e 'asab baz vaqt nadasht
Do qors-e kuchak-e mashkuk ra dobarah begir
Na, sinama bebar-ash, ya bezan be kuh o kamar
Fesharha-ye jahan ra to hich karah begir
Az in ketab-e moghaddas bepors khahar-e man
Dobareh khub mishavad ya na, estekharah begir
Belit, noskhah yak mosht pul-e parah begir
Beist avval-e saf, shambha shomarah begir.

Take a ticket, the prescription, and a handful of torn money,
stand at the end of the queue on Saturdays, take a number.
Tayyebah's unwell again, make a phone call,
take a day off from that office.
In her haphazard way, whatever she sees, be patient;
take the moon or a star out of her sleeve.
Shopping isn't bad, the colours that make her happy—
buy her some clothes, shoes, bangles and earrings.
Don't lose sight of your chase of a bird or a stone;
tell Tayyebah to keep away from people.
If the nerve doctor [psychiatrist] has no time once again,
Take two small, suspicious pills again.
No, take her to the cinema, or head for the hills—
don't give in to the pressures of the world.
Ask this holy book if my sister
is going to get well again: do a divination.
Take a ticket, the prescription, and a handful of torn money,
stand at the front of the queue on Saturdays, take a number.

Here, the poet appears to be talking to herself, going through the steps she needs to take to care for her sister, who seems to be mentally ill. Caring for her, however, involves confronting a bureaucratised, clinical world: getting a day's leave from the office, taking a number and standing in a queue with a prescription, going to a doctor for mental disturbances (rather than blaming them on jinns and fairies, as was common in Afghanistan) and taking pills, no matter how suspicious. The poverty of the narrator is suggested by the "handful of torn money" and the ticket, which no doubt refers to a city bus ticket, the cheapest mode of transportation in Iran. The narrator appears to have tried everything to make her sister feel better when she has a bout of her illness, from medication to shopping to watching films or going on a daytrip away from society and its "pressures". Ultimately, however, as she grows increasingly desperate or weary, she turns to religion of the traditional kind and does a divination (*estekharah*) on the Quran. But the repetition of the first couplet at the end is the moment of disillusionment in this *ghazal*: things do not get better, and all the narrator can do is resolve to get to the queue earlier next time.

This poem has an autobiographical element, since the poet's sister Tayyebeh is a real person whom I had the opportunity to meet. When reciting the poem, too, Zahra adjusts the pronunciation of certain words to make them sound more "Afghan", for example saying "Tayyebah" rather than Tayyebeh. The location of the poem is nonetheless betrayed as Iran by a number of factors, including the vocabulary and the commonplace acceptance of a psychiatric discourse.

The poem suggests that these two young women have freedom of independent movement within and even outside the city, and that the female narrator bears a heavy responsibility for the support of her family. This was a situation that I observed at first-hand in many refugee families, in which young women pursued various personal activities throughout the city of Mashhad, studied and worked to support their families, and often used their superior knowledge of the Iranian dialect and institutions to take care of family affairs instead of their parents. Nevertheless, the women's movement through urban space appears to be much more purposeful than the flanerie of the men: idle loitering would not be considered proper for grown women. The image given off by this poem, perhaps unintentionally, is of an impoverished but capable working woman who shoulders a good deal of responsibility for the care of her family. This is in sharp contrast to the state of affairs in Afghanistan at present, male relatives are expected to take care of most of a woman's needs and fewer women work outside the home.

Conclusions

Although there are evident stylistic differences among the poems discussed here, and all of their authors also write other poems in very different styles, they represent an unmistakable current that combines the Persian lyric poetic tradition with realism. The poets use this combination in various ways to meditate on the position of Afghan refugees in Iranian society, describing the environment in which they live, their hard work, their physical and mental ailments and their small pleasures. While these works might still fall into the category of "poetry of exile", the exile is increasingly internal, reflecting the poverty and social marginalisation of refugees in their host country. With the notable exception of Heidarbeigi's poem, they do not dwell on nostalgia for the homeland.

The narrators also frequently set themselves apart from their surroundings, portraying themselves as day-dreaming poets who "think about everything". The poet-intellectual as represented in these poems must be empathetic and identify with the plight of his or her compatriots, yet be sober and dispassionately critical enough not to be swayed by the ideologies and dogmas which have caused so much harm in the region in recent decades. Perhaps paradoxically, however, adopting such a persona may be young Afghans' only chance to acquire a higher status position in Iranian society.

Twentieth-century Iranian novelists and poets often idealised "the masses" and the poor in their work, and the "dispossessed" were celebrated in post-revolutionary art and propaganda. An important factor that distinguishes refugee poets from their more famous middle-class predecessors, however, is that they themselves are members of the urban poor, marginalised not only by their poverty but also by their lack of citizenship. Thus, when they write poems in the lyrical realist mode, they are authoritatively portraying the everyday experiences of the urban poor as seen through their own eyes. Although the events described may be ideal-typical or fictional, their use of the present tense, first-person narration, and detailed descriptions of places, objects, people and activities allow them to be seen as remarkable reflections of the lives of Afghan refugees at a given historical moment. Indeed, they are representative of a literary culture which places increasing importance on such expression. Particularly when working in the *ghazal* form, their work may be seen not as a western transplant, but simply the latest iteration in a poetic current that has been continuous for over a thousand years.

9

AFGHANISTAN AND THE PERSIAN EPIC *SHAHNAMA*

HISTORICAL AGENCY AND THE EPIC IMAGINATION IN AFGHAN AND AFGHAN-AMERICAN LITERATURE

Shafiq Shamel

Introduction: Memory, Writing and Identity

The poem *Alaya Pasdar-e Kuy-e Wakhshuran* ("O the Watchman of the Region of Message-Bringers"), written by Wasef Bakhteri in 1976, adresses figures such as History, the Singer of History, the Royal Crown of History and the Guard of the Path of History.[1] The poem unfolds as a sequence of calls to these figures to do certain things: "Begin the song of sorrow, Singer of History" or "Stand up and cheer up, Guard of the Path of History". The poem operates in two temporal dimensions, the past and the future. Although it sets out with mourning the lost glory of the Afghan past, it does not unfold as a lament. On the contrary, it immediately announces a vision of the future that is filled with promise and hope, surpassing whatever has been before:

O Watchman of the Region of Message-Bringers
O Guard of the Path of History

Stand up: a new guest is on his way…
A proud, victorious, courageous wrestler from the noble lineage of history.

The poem concludes by referencing *darafsh-e Kavian* ("flag of Kava"), the legendary royal standard of the Persian Sassanid kings until their defeat by Arab Muslims in 641. This poem derives its value, for the purposes of this chapter, not so much from how it relates to any personal or political event in particular, but from its general historical and political context of mid-1970s Afghanistan. It exemplifies an intellectual tendency among the three Afghan writers this chapter discusses through an examination of the structural and intellectual functions of textual and epic memory in selected poems by Wasef Bakhteri, in the short novel *Earth and Ashes* by the Afghan-French writer, Atiq Rahimi, and in the novel *The Kite Runner* by the Afghan-American writer, Khaled Hosseini.[2] Before turning to these writers, it is useful to outline something of the Persian epic tradition which this chapter argues is so important to all three of them.

After the spread of Islam and the establishment of Arabic linguistic and cultural dominance in the Middle East between the seventh and the tenth centuries, the Persian language underwent substantial change. Apart from the adaptation of the Arabic alphabet, the Persian language absorbed a wide range of Arabic words. Modern forms of Persian, as spoken today in Afghanistan, Iran and Tajikistan, evolved as a result of this process. The linguistic and cultural dominance of Arabic was, however, balanced by the fact that at this early phase of Islamic civilization many scholars, philosophers, grammarians and influential thinkers on governance and administration were of Persian-Iranian origin. But it was the intellectual and literary tradition of Persian poetry that helped shape the Iranian intellectual and cultural identity in the modern era. As part of this cultural evolution process, poetry played an important role in preserving many aspects of the pre-Islamic culture of Persian speakers throughout the modern nation states of Afghanistan, Iran, Tajikistan, Turkmenistan and Uzbekistan. It is important, however, to note that this process began in the areas that were far away from Baghdad, the then centre of the Muslim rule under the 'Abbasid dynasty (750–1258). In this periphery of the Muslim world, the courts of various local rulers of Iranian descent, particularly those in the eastern part of the Islamic/Arabic sphere of influence in Central Asia, supported poetry in Persian rather than Arabic, the dominant language in the Islamic world of the time.[3] This trend has been considered by some historians to have marked a period of identity-formation for Persian-speakers after the Arab conquest.[4]

AFGHANISTAN AND THE PERSIAN EPIC *SHAHNAMA*

The *Shahnama*, the celebrated Persian heroic epic written by Abu'l-Qasim Ferdowsi (d.1020) at the end of the tenth and the beginning of the eleventh century, constituted the culmination of this process of literary-cultural formation.[5] In more than 60,000 verses, the *Shahnama* tells the story of the development of the Iranian civilization prior to the Arab conquest of Iran. Ferdowsi uses the term *Iran* to refer to a region that is considerably larger than the modern state of Iran and many of the events narrated in the poem take place in what is today known as Afghanistan. As such, the *Shahnama*'s significance is comparable to the way the *Iliad* and *Odyssey* came to be paradigmatic for literary and cultural developments in the West.[6] Yet the *Shahnama* derives its cultural-historical value primarily from the fact that it is both the record of a pre-Islamic Iranian worldview and culture (including ancient mythology and Zoroastrian ideas) and the formulation of an alternative cultural-historical identity based on dominant Arabic-Islamic paradigms.

More importantly for our purposes here, in both Afghanistan and Iran, the legacy of the *Shahnama* has been intertwined with memories and notions of heroism. The most important heroes in the *Shahnama* are Rostam and Sohrab, whose story is similar to the Greek story of Oedipus. However, the story of Oedipus is reversed in the *Shahnama* where it is the father who kills his son. In the *Shahnama*, the epic hero Rostam fights against a skilled warrior, a highly respected young man and leader of the anti-Iranian forces. This young man, Sohrab, is Rostam's own son but Rostam has never met him before and does not know him in person. In spite of Sohrab's attempts to meet his father Rostam, the encounter does not take place, even during a battle that stretches into days. Hence, when Rostam comes out victorious in his fight against this young man, his victory turns into mourning as soon as he finds out that the brilliant fighter he had just slain is none other than his own son. Even in modern times, the stories of Rostam and Sohrab have played a crucial role in shaping heroic ideas of courage, valour, dignity and perseverance in the face of hardship. In other words, the heroes of the *Shahnama* have been remembered time and again in poetry and prose as models to be emulated in order to overcome existential or socio-political difficulties and to restore the dignity of oneself, one's people or one's nation.

AFGHANISTAN IN INK

Epic Memory and Historical Agency

Muhammad Shah Wasef Bakhteri was born in 1950 in the northern Afghan city of Balkh and is one of the most influential and innovative Dari-Persian poets of recent decades.[7] He completed his BA in Dari-Persian language and literature in 1966 at Kabul University and for a period of time was a textbook editor for the Department of Education in Kabul. In 1975, he received an MA in education from Columbia University in New York. While living in Kabul between 1967 and 1997, he held positions as a member of the editorial board of the official Dar al-Ta'lif ("publishing house") established during the communist era to oversee literary as well as other print publications. Dar al-Ta'lif's members were, at best, tolerated by the government and its creation had mainly to do with integrating (and eventually silencing) opponents of the government. Between the late 1960s and 1990s, Bakhteri was also editor-in-chief of the magazine *Zhawandun* ("Life") and editor of its poetry section, as well as a professor of literature at Kabul University. He was forced to leave Afghanistan in 1996 when the Taliban took control of the country. Like Sayyid Baha al-Din Majruh, discussed by Wali Ahmadi in this volume, Bakhteri lived for some years in the Pakistani city of Peshawar, but while Majruh was murdered there Bakhteri was granted political asylum in the United States and now lives in Southern California. From both Kabul and Peshawar, Bakhteri has published seven volumes of poetry between 1982 and 2001: *Va Aftab Namimirad* ("And the Sun Won't Die"); *Az Ma'yad ta Hargiz* ("A Place for Meeting, Never"); *Az In Ayina-ye Beshkasta-ye Tarikh* ("Of the Broken Mirror of History"); *Ta Shahr-e Panjzal'a'i-e Azadi* ("Until the Pentagonal City of Liberty"); *Dibacha'i dar Farjam* ("A Prolegomenon in the End"); *Dar Ostva-ye Fasl-e Shekastan* ("Along the Season of Breaking"); and *Muwiya-ha-ye Asfandiyar-e Gomshoda* ("The Moaning of the Lost Asfandiar").[8]

Bakhteri's poetry emerged from experiences in the 1970s when events in Afghanistan were marked by crucial changes on both political and social levels. The decade saw the end of the constitutional monarchy in 1973 and the first republic with Muhammad Da'ud as the president; the 1978 *coup d'état* by the communist parties Khalq ("People") and Parcham ("Flag"); the Soviet invasion of Afghanistan in 1979; and the beginning of armed resistance to both the communist regime and the Soviet invasion since the late 1970s. Bakhteri's engagement with socio-political realities of his time is not only of a literary nature. For a period of time in the 1960s, he was actively involved in political affairs in Afghanistan: he joined one of the liberal-leftist parties at the time and became an active member of Kabul University's Student Union. As in many other places around the globe, 1960s Afghanistan was a time of political and cultural transformation. The first constitution was passed to establish constitutional monarchy in Afghanistan in 1964; political parties of diverse ideological orientation (left, right and moderate liberals) were formed; freedom of press led to the establishment of a wide range of socio-political newspapers and magazines; and socio-political reforms were gradually acted upon as representative democracy began to take root in the country.[9] While Bakhteri's poetry from the late 1960s was filled with idealism and hope for a better future, from the mid- to late 1970s onwards his poetry lost its earlier optimism.

Dating from 1976, the Bakhteri poem referred to in the beginning of this chapter is an example of a long tradition among Persian poets of evoking the epic heroes of the *Shahnama* as agents for social, political and cultural transformation. Afghan readers familiar with this discourse of cultural identity, particularly as it relates to the geography and cultural vision of the *Shahnama*, would know that "a proud, victorious, courageous wrestler from the noble lineage of history" cannot but refer to one of the epic heroes of the *Shahnama*, almost certainly Rostam. The evocation of the *darafsh-e Kavian* ("flag of Kava") is also an epic marker, ending the poem with a vision of the return of a glorious past. The end of the poem thus transforms historical time into the epic past, which is paradoxically envisioned temporally and literarily as the future. Hence, the future is envisioned as the return of a glorious—and victorious—past. In doing so, the poem absorbs a moment of historical transition in epic figuration. Time and historical process seem to come to a final, complete, and non-contradictory state in the figure of epic memory. The transition from one phase to another, expressed in epic figuration and historical fulfilment at once, is filled with hope and the promise of a glorious future. The poem holds an optimistic vision about history and does not seem to distinguish between historical and epic agency. In fact, the completion of history is envisioned to coincide with the fulfilment of epic memory.

This vision of history and epic memory is also articulated in two other poems in the collection, *Az Ma'yad ta Hargiz* ("A Place for Meeting, Never"). The poems *Basharat* ("Good News") and *Sohrab Zinda Ast* ("Sohrab is Alive") reiterate the same optimism, as the direction of action points in the spirit of the *Shahnama* in both poems to the fall of the evil force or the defeat of those threatening the authority and nobility of Iran in the figure of the king of Turan, Afrasiab, at the hands of the Iranian epic heroes Siavash and Bahman respectively. In other words, the poet remembers the past as it will manifest itself in the future.

As another contemporary Afghan poet, Latif Nazemi (b.1947), has emphasized, Bakhteri's poetry has two trajectories: literary intertextuality and socio-political consciousness.[10] Bakhteri's connection to the more than a millennium old tradition of Persian poetry is apparent in all of his writing. He not only uses traditional forms of Persian poetry such as the *ghazal* ("lyric"), but also textual and intellectual traces in his poems, recalling Persian poets from centuries ago. His deep roots in Persian poetry and poetics, however, have not made him a traditionalist without reflective memory and knowledge of poetic trends of his time. Bakhteri has been among the pioneers of a new movement in Persian poetry called "free verse" (*she'r-e azad*), primarily involving a departure from the principle of equivalence in rhyme and metre (such as in the form of couplets) that emerged in Iran with Nima Yushij (1896–1960) in the early twentieth century and from there spread to Afghanistan.[11] Yet regardless of following traditional or contemporary poetic forms, Bakhteri's poems are marked by time and are never disconnected from the socio-political reality from which they emerge.

As in the poems *Alaya Pasdar-e Kuy-e Vakhshuran* ("O the Watchman of the Region of Message-Bringers", 1976), *Basharat* ("Good News"), and *Sohrab Zinda Ast* ("Sohrab is Alive") from the collection of poems *Az Ma'yad ta Hargiz*, in his collection of poems, *Dibacha'i dar Farjam* ("A Prolegomenon in the End") published twenty-one years later in 1997, the sixth couplet of the poem *Kuhsar-e Ghamin* ("The Mourning Mountain") is a lyrical *ghazal*.[12] It too alludes to epic memory when contemplating the reality contemporaneous with the poem, that is, "History":

> *Empty is*: the seventh ordeal of history, forever –
> The passionate language of pride—to learn from whom?

History and epic memory are still envisioned here as identical or synonymous, as the literary topos of the "seventh ordeal of Rostam" (referring to the seven ordeals that the main epic hero of the *Shahnama* overcomes as a testimony to his heroism) is substituted for the "seventh ordeal of History". The logic of this relation of equivalence between an epic hero and history is based on the fact that both of these figures or forces—namely Rostam and History—are associated with actions that mark a turning point and even rupture in the continuity of cultural, political and social paradigms. The poem registers the shift as the quoted line mourns the disappearance and absence of the last or "the seventh ordeal", in which Rostam kills the white monster and subdues another adversary, confirming his status as the most celebrated and undefeated hero of the *Shahnama*. The absence of "the seventh ordeal", however, distinguishes this poem's vision of the relationship between history and epic from the poem *Alaya Pasdar-e Kuy-e Vakhshuran* ("O the Watchman of the Region of Message-Bringers"). While the latter envisions the future to hold the promise of victory and historical fulfilment, *Kuhsar-e Ghamin* ("The Mourning Mountain") announces the impossibility of epic fulfilment of time in history as it mourns both the lack and the absence of the force of epic agency.

More importantly, the poem projects both a cultural-intellectual and a poetic trajectory that constitutes a testimony to (the paradox of) poetic silence, namely: the impossibility of poetic practice in the language of poetry. In other words, *Kuhsar-e Ghamin* ("The Mourning Mountain") stages a crisis in poetic language that is contemporaneous with the loss of epic hope. *Kuhsar-e Ghamin* is a *ghazal* ("lyric"), so the phrase "empty is" not only has a semantic function, qualifying both physical destruction as well as the absence of epic fulfillment in history, but is also the *radif* ("rhyme") of the poem. "Empty is" acts as a poetic valance; it qualifies epic emptiness while occupying a position in the phonetic structure of the poem that is probably the most important structural position in a *ghazal*, namely, the aural and visual locus of the rhyming word. In other words, "empty is" is uttered exactly when the lines come to their formally defining position, namely in the rhyme. This fact in the poem acquires significance beyond prosodic rules as it constitutes a semantically reflective locus whereby it is at once the rhyme and a comment on the lyrical *ghazal* poem. It is not only the disappearance of rhymed poetry that the speaker in the poem mourns. As already mentioned, Bakhteri is among the pioneers of "new poetry" in Afghanistan, following poetic trends in Iran as well as Afghanistan since the 1930s. The poem therefore also mourns the recognition of the loss of the urgency and relevance of repeated patterns of sound, namely, song.

It is at this juncture that the poem asserts its relation to the socio-historical context from which it emerged. Yet "empty is" is a figure not so much of the absence of song, as of the realization of its impossibility. *Kuhsar-e Ghamin* ("The Mourning Mountain") thus stages the loss of song and simultaneously mourns it within the texture of the traditionally most celebrated form of lyric in Persian poetry, the *ghazal*. The staging of the realization of the impossibility of song is embedded in a dialectical structure: the lyrical *Kuhsar-e Ghamin* speaks of the absence of those objects, elements, visions, or experiences that define the form and content of the Persian *ghazal*: rhyme, love, wine and song. The tension and the dialectical relationship between both the intellectual orientation and structural quality of the *ghazal* and the historical time and place within which it speaks are at the heart of this *ghazal*. In other words, the poem is an enactment of this dialectical relationship—sounding almost like a dictum announcing the end of the *ghazal* as a poetic form.

However, the poem does not articulate that the form of the *ghazal* lost relevance as a means of mediating poetic vision, but that writing one in Afghanistan in the early 1990s was impossible. This was a time of civil war and complete lawlessness after the fall of the Najib government at the hand of the various *mujahidin* factions, including Hezb-e Islami ("Islamic Party"), Hezb-e Harakat ("Movement Party"), Jami'at-e Islami ("Islamic Association") and many other smaller groups. After the fall of the communist regime under Najib, the socio-political situation in Afghanistan deteriorated enormously. Different *mujahidin* factions laid claim to different parts of the country and it was only a short time before they began to fight each other. Kabul's inhabitants witnessed the worst: divided among the various groups, the city of Kabul was turned into a war zone, where members of the ruling factions in different sections of the city had free rein to do as they pleased. Rape, vandalism and arbitrary execution became daily routine. As members of rival factions fought each other along various neighbourhoods of Kabul, the city was transformed into a battlefield. Nothing could escape destruction: roads, houses, schools, government buildings, or any structure that could be used as a shield was either destroyed completely or rendered uninhabitable. It was only to get worse, albeit in different ways, under the subsequent rule of the Taliban between 1996 and 2001.

But considering the formation of the Afghan polity and the politics of national identity, particularly from the end of World War II until the reign of the Khalq and the Parcham communist parties in the 1980s, the remembrance and evocation of epic figures from the *Shahnama* gestures towards a cultural and intellectual lineage that crosses the political, geographical and intellectual boundaries of dominant nationalistic discourse in modern Afghanistan. Epic memory is thus the figuration of a double negativity in these poems by Bakhteri: loss of hope in the present historical-political situation (i.e. the era of the *mujahidin* and the rise of the Taliban) and a sense of helplessness about the reclamation of a cultural and intellectual identity that has been disrupted and denied. The irony of the situation is particularly evident as epic memory is absorbed into various poems in bits and pieces—the poems make only very brief allusions to epic figures and their legacy. In other words, instead of inspiring visions of the totalizing, glorious, and promising spirit of the epic tradition, epic memory remains a textual locus that marks both a non-identical and alienated relationship to the historical situation it witnesses and the impossibility of remembering fragments of a past cultural and intellectual identity.[13] Hence, the recurrence of epic memory in certain poems by Bakhteri reinforces the notion that the speaker in these poems has a non-identical relationship with the world and the historical reality of which he is part.

Not surprisingly, in the poem *Dar Sukut-e Shomathaha* ("On the Silence of Clock Bells"), in the same 1997 collection of poems, *Dibacha'i dar Farjam* ("A Prolegomenon in the End"), the agent of change is no longer envisioned as an epic hero but as "History".[14] As it was twenty years earlier in the poem *Alaya Pasdar-e Kuy-e Vakhshuran* ("O the Watchman of the Region of Message-Bringers"), the addressee of the poem is "History". However, "History"—which is also the word the poem begins with—is envisioned in the figure of one of the best-known storytellers in the history of literature around the world, namely, Shahrzad of the *Thousand and One Nights*: "O History, the white-haired Shahrzad of now". But the lines immediately following the first line qualify "History" in the following way:

> O History
> A jungle green in half and half in fall
> Enemy and the friend
> Conjoining all evil and goodness

Such an understanding of the paradox of history as a field of contradictory and opposing forces contrasts with Bakhteri's earlier poems.[15] Epic memory is radically challenged by the non-teleological direction of real political history. Although epic memory is activated in the twenty-sixth line when the speaker describes History as "Zal [the father of the *Shahnama*'s main hero, Rostam] and the story-teller", the shift from heroic certainty and epic fulfilment to the uncertainties of historical time resonates already in the title, "On the Silence of Clock Bells". For there are no clock bells, no announcements of temporal turning points, and no fulfilled endings of

Fig. 19: The Circulation of Texts: Booksellers in Kabul, 2011.

stories. Besides, the speaker in the poem speaks of the "virgin years" of "Zal, the story-teller", which cannot refer to Rostam's father in the *Shahnama*. Rather, the name Zal must be understood in terms of its lexical meaning, a very old man or woman, representing "History" in the figure of the old white-haired Shahrzad. The recognition of historical time as a force, however, does not result in loss of hope and ethical disavowal, antithetical to inherent features of the epic imagination. Twenty years earlier and shortly before the fall of President Muhammad Da'ud in 1978, the poem *Alaya Pasdar-e Kuy-e Vakhshuran* ("O the Watchman of the Region of Message-Bringers") was filled with optimism that a powerful, courageous wrestler (Zal in Persian, again referencing Rostam) "from the noble lineage in history" will arrive on the plane of history. The later poem *Dar Sukut-e Shomathaha* ("On the Silence of Clock Bells") is still concerned about the forces that control the direction of history. The ethical concern is particularly highlighted in the last strophe of the poem. The last two lines mark the shift from the earlier poem:

> Every leaf of these bushes is a listening ear
> Can you end the *lineage* of ax?[16]

Instead of a sense of certainty about the course of history, the speaker claims to be neither the source of knowledge about nor the agency of history. Unlike the earlier poem, *Dar Sukut-e Shomathaha* stages the helplessness of temporal entrapment. The poem does not say how the future may unfold and any reference to future is articulated in the form of a question. But the use of the word "lineage" in the instances above highlights the fact that history is not understood as a sequence of random events or as accident but as the presence of struggling contradictory ethical—or political—forces that have always been there. In the same strophe, another question is put to 'History':

> In place of the aged trees
> Will you be able to plant other ones?

It is this vision of renewal and both intellectual as well as historical recovery that drives the 'horseman' in a poem published months later in the collection *Ta Shahr-e Panjzal'a'i-e Azadi* ("Until the Pentagonal City of Liberty").[17] *Darigha Chanin Bud Farjam* ("Alas: This Was the End!") is a narrative poem written from the point of view of an observer.[18] Unlike the previous poems, in which the poetic "I" is identical with the subject of utterances, *Darigha Chanin Bud Farjam* is thus marked by the language of objectivity—the poem unfolds the story of a rescue operation from a distant, safe position. An "enraged and hasty horseman, who had passed across the horizon", determined "to liberate the bride of the silky region of the dawn of imagination", is disillusioned to find the captive princess "a very old, white-haired woman". Bakhteri also uses the adjective *zal* ("white-haired") to describe the appearance of the bride when the horseman begins to speak:

> You white-haired, nasty old, old woman—spit on you!
> That I had been imagining
> The light of youth would still be shining on your throne

To refer to the bride as *zal* ("white-haired") resonates strongly with how "History" is cast in *Dar Sukut-e Shomathaha* ("On the Silence of Clock Bells"). Yet the epic connotation of *zal* cannot be entirely cancelled out in this instance. This is also reinforced by the fact that the narrator describes 'the horseman's' assault on the castle, where "the bride" is held captive, as "his Bahman-like storming". Both the language and the notion of a "horseman" as the protagonist and agent in the narrative of the poem evoke epic heroism. But the poem unfolds a story of defeat—a disillusionment of epic proportion. Although the poem does not relate or contemplate "History" in any way, the symbolic function of the poplar tree concludes the horseman's lament-speech. This vision is lyric and epic at once—what had figured as a question in *Dar Sukut-e Shomathaha* now becomes an imagined possibility:

And, so that
This barren, unfertile desert that once was the silky region of the dawn of imagination
Once again
Be blessed with the splendor, beauty, magnificence, and grandeur of proud, honorable *poplar trees*

The symbolic gesture toward a better future is made through the invocation of "proud, honorable poplar trees". Yet as the horseman acknowledges, "a very old woman" is not in the possession of the kind of powers required to transform a "barren, non-fertile desert" into a place filled with trees or to be the agency of fertility. The apparent pessimism is, however, not just narrated. The rhetoric of lament is constructed in such a way that the last line of the horseman's speech, which is also the title of the poem, is not his utterance. The horseman's line before the poem's last strophe, telling of the apocalyptic return of the horseman into "the volcano of aurora", is a comment the narrator makes on what he has been witnessing so far, namely the poem *Darigha Chanin Bud Farjam*. This structural inconsistency marks, however, a textual locus that is employed as a structural schema to erase the distinction between the narrator of the poem and the character whose story he tells. The use of both *darigha* ("alas") and *farjam* ("end", originally a Middle Persian word absorbed into classical Persian poetic diction since Rudaki in the ninth century) indicate the narrator's identical and sympathetic relationship to the horseman's story. This textual locus, where the narrator reflects on his narration, marks an instance of compositional rapture and a sense of poetic and historical disillusionment at once.

AFGHANISTAN AND THE PERSIAN EPIC *SHAHNAMA*

War, Trauma and Narration

Atiq Rahimi's short novel, *Earth and Ashes* (2000), also engages with political realities in Afghanistan during the Soviet invasion. Written in Dari-Persian as *Khakistar u Khak* by an Afghan living in diaspora in France and first published under the French title of *Terre et Cendres*, the novel was Rahimi's first work. Note that unlike Bakhteri, both Atiq Rahimi and Khaled Hosseini began writing long after they left Afghanistan due to political instability after the communist *coup d'état* of 1978. Yet both in tone and intellectual orientation, Rahimi's novel is a narrative representation of the same tendency present in Bakhteri's poems *Kuhsar-e Ghamin* and *Darigha Chanin Bud Farjam*: a sense of disillusionment and fragmentation. A loss of vision for a better future is also a central constituent element of this short novel. It tells the story of two traumatized survivors of a bombing campaign, a grandfather and his grandson who turns deaf as a consequence of an air attack on their village in northern Afghanistan during the Soviet occupation. The text encompasses the span of almost one day as the old man sets out to find his only son (the boy's father), who works in a mine, to let him know what has happened. The grandfather's story is not only about violence and war. Conflating proper narration with dream, vision, memory, dialogue and interior monologue, it is also an enactment of the experiences of trauma. Narrative linearity is frequently disrupted by fragments of memory, visions or episodes of inner monologue. The choice of the second person singular narrator, whereby the narrator frequently addresses himself, stages the narrative space as a place of/for solitude. It is this space of thought, vision, and memory that has expanded and has turned into a force of disintegration, disrupting the narrator's perception of time and place since he witnessed and survived the air strike. The traumatized man is trapped in an almost never-ending cycle of the same memories. This simultaneous sense of fragmentation and stagnation of a witness and victim of war unfolds in *Earth and Ashes* as a non-linear narrative. The text stages experiences of war as the disintegration of agency and crisis in narrative representation. The lack of a fulfilled ending, for example, registers the impossibility of ethics and, in so doing, the text highlights the non-literariness of the political and historical context it originates from.

Atiq Rahimi was born in 1962 in Kabul and attended the city's French-run Lycée Istiqlal.[19] Through his father's—a graduate of the German-run school Lycée Nejat—educational and intellectual orientation, he was introduced early on to some of the classics of world literature and Persian poetry.

Following the Soviet invasion, Rahimi fled Afghanistan in 1984, taking refuge in Pakistan for a year and then relocating to France after receiving political asylum. After studying at the Sorbonne, he joined a Paris-based production company and made several documentaries for French television. *Earth and Ashes* was also made into a film, directed by the author himself, and won awards at several film festivals, including the Prix du Regard Vers l'Avenir at the Cannes Film Festival in 2004. In 2008, Rahimi won the Prix Goncourt, France's most prestigious literary prize, for *La Pierre de Patience* ("The Patience Stone"), his first novel written in French. *Pierre de Patience* tells the story of a woman whose husband has been wounded in battle in a country resembling Afghanistan and now lies as paralyzed as a stone.

To return to *Earth and Ashes*, in the novel the medieval epic *Shahnama* is referenced during a conversation between the shop keeper Mirza Qadir and the protagonist, Dastaguir. Mirza Qadir, who considers the dead more fortunate than the living at this time of war and destruction, mourns the fact that no one remembers Rostam anymore. In his eyes, these days it is the son Sohrab who kills his father, Rostam, and takes advantage of his mother. For him, contemporary reality resembles the time of the tyrant Zohak, one of the villains in the *Shahnama*: once again, Zohak's snakes "feed on the minds of the young".[20] The figure of Rostam is cast as a proper and respectable hero antithetical to the agency and actions of contemporary figures the speaker relates to, namely the period of communist rule and the Soviet occupation of Afghanistan during the 1980s. Although initially not without the support of diverse segments of the population, the communist rule in Afghanistan turned very soon into a regime of terror. The initial euphoria among some Afghans was not so much a sign of welcome to those assuming power as it was to feeling a sense of relief and liberation from the despotic rule of President Muhammad Da'ud, whose defeat at the hands of the communist parties Parcham and Khalq—parties that at various points of the political game of power in Afghanistan were also allies of President Da'ud Khan—marked the end of a dynasty ruling Afghanistan since 1929.[21] But as soon as the communist government's machinery of terror began to govern, tens of thousands of Afghans were jailed and executed. Millions more fled to neighbouring countries—Iran and Pakistan—and others sought refuge in countries around the world.[22]

It is this oppressive, suffocating, and brutal period in Afghan history that Mirza Qadir expresses in the language of epic memory. The current condition is identical to how it was under "the tyrant Zohak", the evil character in the *Shahnama*. Epic memory is activated precisely at a moment in the text when one of the characters comments on things as they are now. In other words, the textual memory of the heroic epic constitutes a moment that, in turning to the past and to a text from the past, is actually looking at and reflecting on the historical present. Epic memory thus provides Mirza Qadir a framework of reference for understanding the meaning of the determining forces of contemporary life. His suffering recalls the horseman's disillusionment in the poem "Alas: This Was the End!" by Bakhteri. But what later poems by Bakhteri and Rahimi's *Earth and Ashes* have in common is, above all, the absence of a vision of a future. The disintegration of agency—epic or otherwise—is thus directly connected to temporality in both instances. The lack of agency and a sense of disillusionment in the discussed poems by Bakhteri constitute the kind of conditions under which the speakers in these poems remain trapped in the present, lacking the ability to envision the future. While Bakhteri associates this temporal deficiency with the discourse of "History", to the characters in *Earth and Ashes* temporality is reduced merely to matters such as "I am hungry", "there is the truck", "he is sleeping" or "I have to go there today". These characters are defined by what they lack: historical agency. The reality of the historical present marked by war, death, and destruction manifests itself in both Bakhteri's later poems and *Earth and Ashes* as temporal fragmentation, that is, the loss of any kind of vision of a future.

This sense of temporal fragmentation is also enacted at the level of narrative structure. Temporal linearity in the story is constantly disrupted by fragments of memory, vision, or episodes of inner monologue. While the story has temporal progression from the beginning to the end of the book, the episodes are not narrated as a linear sequence of events. The narrator constantly moves from one register of experience to another: from reality perception to the memory of an actual event in the past and back to a vision of an imaginary scene. In other words, the narrator is trapped in a kind of mental and emotional whirlpool that he can't even escape when asleep. This blurring of distinction between different realms of experience recalls at times cinematographic techniques of montage in visual arts, including film.[23]

The story unfolds throughout the book as fragments of memory, vision, monologues and the narrative proper of a grandfather (Dastaguir) on his way to tell his son (Murad) that his wife was killed by a bombing attack on their village and that his son, Yassin, has lost speech and hearing. This sense of fragmentation at the narrative level also has its correlative at the level of the main character's psychology. The story is told from the perspective of the second person singular. A large segment of the story consists of the narrator addressing himself: "You look for your box of nasvar [snuff]" or "From somewhere, you're not sure where, the voice of Murad's mother rises".[24] The employment of second person singular narrator reinforces, above all, the narrator's solitude. The external disorder is thus reflected in the inner world—or mental process—of the narrator as he wanders between different realms of experience: the barren and war-torn landscape around him; traumatic memories of death, war and destruction; the inner monologues; the conversations he has with other characters; and the uncanny observations he makes about other characters in the book. Entrapped in the cycle of disorder, both internally and externally, Dastaguir embodies a state of mental, emotional, and intellectual stagnation that is void of any sense of orientation or willpower.

Narrative Ending and The Kite Runner

The paradoxically contemporaneous presence of epic vision/memory and the absence of a redemptive perspective in Bakhteri's later poems and in Rahimi's *Earth and Ashes* are overcome in Khaled Hosseini's *The Kite Runner*, first published in 2003. According to his own website, Khaled Hosseini was born in Kabul in 1965 and from 1976 to 1980 lived in Paris, where his father worked for the Afghan Foreign Ministry.[25] Due to the communist coup in 1978 in Afghanistan, in September 1980 Hosseini's family moved to the United States and after some time were granted political asylum. After earning a bachelor's degree in biology from Santa Clara University in San José, California, he studied medicine at the University of California, San Diego. When he began writing *The Kite Runner* in 2001, Hosseini was a practicing internist living in northern California. The parallels between the author's own journey from Kabul to northern California and the protagonist's journey in the book foregrounds the semi-autobiographical texture of the novel. In contrast to Rahimi's *Earth and Ashes*, it is this dimension of the fictive account that connects *The Kite Runner* with American novelistic writing and offers a transnational vision of one of the most tragic periods in Afghan history. While Bakhteri's poetry and Rahimi's *Earth and Ashes* were written in Dari-Persian with a homogeneous audience of mainly Afghans in mind, *The Kite Runner* was written in English, making it a book primarily for English-speaking audiences in the United States and elsewhere, rather than Persian-reading audiences in Afghanistan and Iran.

AFGHANISTAN AND THE PERSIAN EPIC *SHAHNAMA*

Reflecting the author's own global itinerary, *The Kite Runner* concludes with the arrival of an Afghan boy called Sohrab in the United States during the iron rule of the Taliban in Afghanistan. Sohrab is saved from the Taliban's cruelties through the intervention of his half-uncle, Amir, the protagonist and narrator who left Afghanistan during the Soviet occupation and has since been living in the San Francisco area. *The Kite Runner* is thus marked by a strong sense of agency that sets the stage for actions of epic proportion in the world today. Before the novel refers to the boy rescued from the horrific conditions of Afghan life under the Taliban, Sohrab (the name of one of the most important heroic figures in the *Shahnama*) is referenced in a passage about the protagonist's childhood in Kabul, Afghanistan. When he lived in Kabul, Amir used time and again to read his and Sohrab's father's "favorite story", the epic story of Rostam and Sohrab.[26] Most of the time, at Hassan's request, he would read the *Shahnama* to Hassan, who is Sohrab's father and the son of Amir's family's servant.[27] This textual reference to the *Shahnama*, and particularly to the story of Rostam and Sohrab, highlights the significance of the Persian heroic epic in bringing about a personal bond between the two main characters of the novel, Amir and Hassan, who not only belong to different social classes but also different ethnic, religious and linguistic groups, as a Pashtun and a Hazara respectively. However, when Amir reads the *Shahnama* to the children, their heterogeneity is not yet apparent, except in the fact that Amir can already read as a child while Hassan will only become literate later as an adult. The *Shahnama* is presented in the novel as the most read and appreciated book by the protagonist Amir and his childhood best friend, Hassan. Ferdowsi's epic vision has left its impression not only on Hassan's world view, as he gives his son the name Sohrab after one of the heroes of the *Shahnama*, Amir has also been deeply affected by the poem. Amir and Hassan are thus bound to each other through their shared experience of reading the epic *Shahnama*.

It is this bond between Amir and Hassan that underlies the major trajectory of the novel's plot, which, aside from being the main constituent element of the plot structure, also offers a different model of resolving the ethnic, religious and linguistic conflicts in Afghanistan. But it is this second dimension of the presence of the *Shahnama* in the novel that contradicts the contemporary world of the novel. The novel takes the possibility of a Pashtun to read the Persian epic as an unproblematic practice in Afghanistan. Such a starting point truly transforms historical reality and neglects the dynamics of cultural and national identity in Afghanistan since its creation in the last decades of the nineteenth century until the present. This utopian transformation of the historical world, however, becomes understandable when the following two factors, one political and one generic/textual, are taken into consideration. On the one hand, the redemptive vision and the possibility of a better future in *The Kite Runner* is directly linked to the safe and secure space and perspective of American exile, a place distant from and near to home at once. On the other hand, it is related to the novel's adaptation of the structural element of closure from fictional genres, such as romance or comedy.[28] *The Kite Runner*'s relationship to its historical and political context is thus mediated both through the experience of American exile and the narrative paradigms of fiction. Diaspora thus creates a narrative space that facilitates exposure to alternative existential and textual paradigms that may be used to construct imaginary solutions to real contradictions. In other words, the text's geography and political vision is reflected in its textuality as its 'happy' ending and its temporal horizon simultaneously resonates with both the American Dream and the generic demands of romance or comedy. While the later poems of Bakhteri and Rahimi's *Earth and Ashes* are marked by the lack of temporal fulfilment and optimistic vision of history in and for Afghanistan, Hosseini's American horizon in *The Kite Runner* creates an alternative imaginary space that gives rise to hope and optimism.

Nonetheless, the decision by Amir, the protagonist in *The Kite Runner*, to go back to Afghanistan during the reign of the Taliban and expose himself to life-threatening situations has its correlates in the textual and intellectual tradition of the Persian heroic epic. In fact, the projection of various elements of the heroic epic are manifest throughout *The Kite Runner*, for example: in Amir's life of glamour and comfort in Afghanistan; in the hardship he endures throughout his adventurous journey from Afghanistan to Pakistan in order to reach the United States; in his decision and moral conviction to go back to Afghanistan or to knowingly embark upon a very dangerous path; and in his ability to go through extraordinary hardship to complete his mission. Despite the fact that the novel's ending resonates with such moral and religious principles as atonement and salvation, the sense of a fulfilled closure also resonates with the completeness and totalizing force of epic tradition.[29] The novel's organization of ethical forces also follows for the binary paradigm of the heroic epic: good versus evil. Another of the characters in the book, Asef, and the Taliban are depicted as manifestations of evil in the world, whereas Hassan and the narrator, Amir, are depicted as the forces of goodness. *The Kite Runner* thus stages an ongoing battle between the forces of good and evil and concludes with the partial victory of goodness in the world. Here again, the novel's epic orientation mediates the contemporary setting of the novel and in so doing fails to sufficiently engage the complexity of Afghanistan's current historical and political situation.[30] Narrative progression constructs the story of a journey from a place under the rule of evil forces to a secure and safe destination. In doing so, it casts the story of modern Afghanistan as an epic struggle of good against evil.

Whereas in *The Kite Runner*, epic memory, as mediated through the *Shahnama*, remains intact as one of the major forces of ethic and fictional aspiration, Bakhteri's later poems and Rahimi's *Earth and Ashes* acknowledge the irrelevance of epic memory as an intellectual force for understanding and navigating the contemporary world. For them, the contemporary world is simultaneously the product and the process of history that no longer reflects the epic narrative of tradition.

10

GNOMICS

PROVERBS, APHORISMS, METAPHORS, KEY WORDS AND EPITHETS IN AFGHAN DISCOURSES OF WAR AND INSTABILITY

Margaret A. Mills

Introduction

As Afghan scholarship has demonstrated, proverbs and aphorisms are abundant in Afghan Persian speech and in Persian literature.[1] However, their abundance has not provoked much detailed analytic study, textual or contextual. Most published proverb studies offer compendia of collected expressions with little or no explanatory gloss and still less use-context information, despite the fact that proverbs and related short, pithy evaluative statements (here collectively called gnomics) are the most performance context-dependent of all verbal art forms. The mix of oral and literary proverbs, aphorisms and metaphorical coinages that this chapter examines in context is gleaned from two contexts rich in critical social commentary: Afghan contemporary oral interviews and literary memoirs respectively. The conditions of gross physical, economic, political and psychological uncertainty in which Afghans now function sadly turn out to be a rich context for rhetorical attempts at summary evaluation, contestable bids for meaning which, by nature of the circumstances, can only be less definitive than the verbal genre's rhetorics would plead.

The first sample of proverbs and other gnomic expressions in use is gleaned from a set of open-ended interviews in Kabul, Herat and Mazar-e Sharif conducted in April-June 2009 in Dari-Persian with a wide spectrum of individuals. My research colleague, Dr. Omar Sharifi, and I sought a range of Afghans' experiences and views about current and recent Afghan politics, governance, and military occupation. We were not specifically in search of proverbial speech, nor did we seek strategic insight for the US or NATO occupying forces.[2] Rather we sought to explore the varieties of indeterminacy that Afghan citizens confront, in light of which they then try to interpret the presence and intentions of the US and NATO and their own government. The second, literary sample of proverbs, aphorisms and other gnomic expressions in this chapter—some explicitly framed by the authors as "Afghan"—is gleaned from published memoirs in English by two Afghan women activists: Malalai Joya (an education and civil society activist, ejected from her position as an elected representative to the Afghan National Parliament from Farah province because of her outspoken denunciations of the presence of alleged war criminals in that body) and Nelufer Pazira (an Afghan-born and raised journalist and filmmaker, screenwriter and star of the film *Qandahar*, now based in Toronto).[3] Both these writers (like other Afghan memoirists) translate and apply oral proverbial and other current gnomic expressions to help create a written rhetoric of "authentic" witnessing appropriate to critical memoir.

Taken together, these two samples illustrate the free flow of expressions and subject matter back and forth between oral and literary registers in Dari-Persian as in Pashto, as also discussed by Wide and Caron in this volume. The interviewees deployed a mix of oral and literary-attributed proverbs to characterize and assess political conditions in 2009, speaking usually to just two interviewers, one male, Dari-Persian native speaker and one female, Dari-Persian semi-fluent American (this author). The memoirists incorporated oral proverbs, none with literary attribution, into a literary genre (memoirs in English for non-Afghan readers), to varying rhetorical effect.

Proverb interpretation anywhere is a highly context-dependent matter. Afghans have maintained a rich store of proverbs in various languages, in daily speech and in didactic literary genres (e.g. *pand* advice literature and Sufi poetry). That this analysis of interviews and memoirs concerns current situations with dire implications but focuses on a few verbal tropes, the "how" rather than the "what" of the oral and literary expressions these Afghans used to describe and evaluate those conditions, is not an academic vanity. Ordinary Afghans' critical observations of the present dysfunctions and incoherencies of the Afghan state and socio-political life in general, and the role of foreign players in them, can only be anecdotal. Sense-making by Afghans under these conditions is mediated through fragmentary and ambiguous information, narratives of personal experience or reported events. Proverbs, aphorisms and strategically placed jokes are bids for interpretive authority over situations and events external to the texts and are hence always narratively embedded, either explicitly or implicitly. For these reasons, considerable space is dedicated here to the perceived historical contexts.

In the case of the two memoirs in English (Joya's being co-authored, perhaps ghost-written by an English native-speaker from her dictation, and deploying some current English catch-phrases as well), proverbs are deployed both as critical evaluations of described circumstances and as markers of claimed Afghan cultural identity not shared by the non-Afghan expected audience. A critical ethnography of speaking or witnessing (as in written memoirs) focuses on patterns in the choice of tellable experiences that members of a group cite as indicators of general situations and social principles, as well as their evaluative statements around such narratives. Among their other functions, proverbs are a honed tool for such evaluations.[4]

The proverbs, aphorisms and other expressions under examination here include some new metaphorical coinages or epithets, even some joke punch lines, that seem to bid for proverbial force, all of which I collectively call "gnomics". They claim authority in part by evoking conventional wisdom and also in proverbs by the use of familiar ranges of metaphor or analogy. They may also employ newly improvised images, epithets, similes, analogies or metaphors to address current circumstances. In that sense, the proverbial/aphoristic tradition in Persian remains a generative one.

Current events thus constitute the key narrative substrate, stated or not, for proverbs and aphorisms. Additionally, many well-known proverbs travel with their own, mostly un-restated but traditional narrative substrates or back stories, which in part guide current application.[5] Besides their compactness, these discursive forms share elliptical, allusive qualities, lending degrees of interpretive indeterminacy in application to utterances which otherwise discursively lay claim to definitive authority. For a non-insider audience (e.g. readers of Afghans' English-language memoirs), the writer or speaker may describe the expression as "Afghan", "Pashtun", etc., claiming cultural identity as an "other" to the reader, as cultural authenticity markers and/or identity-claiming moves. She may provide additional framing or decoding to guide the audience's interpretation; some "exported" expressions are more self-explanatory than others.

Though proverbs and aphorisms are meant to sound prescriptive and authoritative, to understand possible multiplex implications of such expressions can require considerable background cultural knowledge. In particular, several interviewees used proverbs attributed to literary sources, including classical Persian poets Rumi, Sa'di and Bedil. As such, these quotations carry not just an asserted application of their surface subject matter to present performance context (as do proverbs without authorial attributions). They also carry an intratextual context application within their literary sources, where they are evaluative statements upon other narrative substrates. The authority claimed by quoting highly revered literary figures invokes this specific textual deixis, as well as distinctive interpersonal deixis, creating an "in-group" of those who recognize the ascribed literary source and its authority, and an "out-group" or "other" who cannot.[6] For present purposes, the accuracy of these attributions is not the main issue. What is important is that they are so ascribed by speakers and at least some "in-the-know" listeners. The literary and the oral are thus intertwined, when literary authority is performed and thus (re)constituted in acts of transmission in oral performance in Afghanistan.

Oral Culture in Dari-Persian-Speaking Afghanistan

Afghan scholarly publications on proverbs were relatively numerous in the latter half of the twentieth century, proverbs being regarded as an important genre of intangible cultural heritage.[7] But, as already mentioned, the usual practice in these works was to present lists of collected proverb texts, sometimes indexed according to lexical contents but generally without discussing interpretation or contexts of use.[8] Here I offer a short, schematic excursus on oral communications and traditional speech genres in contemporary Afghanistan, including the topics favoured by twentieth-century Afghan scholars of oral tradition.[9] Though detailed census data is lacking, various mutually comprehensible Persian dialects constitute the first or home language of perhaps 40 per cent of the Afghan population, and a lingua franca for many more.

"Dari" has been the term used in official contexts to designate the official and literary form of the language. Many speakers of Persian dialects in Afghanistan also refer to the current and classical literary language, shared with present-day Iran, as "Farsi". In daily interaction, Afghanistan remains a predominantly oral society in all languages and dialects. Some rural-origin refugees living outside Afghanistan during the anti-Soviet war years had improved access to formal education, and educational opportunities, especially for women, increased in Marxist-controlled urban areas during that time. Since the departure of the Soviets and the repatriation of many refugees, interest in education has been avid among the increasingly urbanized population, all the more since the end of Taliban exclusion of female teachers and students and with the rising availability of employment-related technical education in cities. Yet it is likely that the overall literacy rate for women over the age of fifteen remains in the single digits in many rural areas, and in the teens in cities. Literacy for men runs at something over twice the rate for women in their respective communities, such that the overall literacy rate for the country may have reached about 38 per cent by 2011.[10] Any such "guesstimate" is, however, conditioned by the lack of any firm definition of functional literacy or current, reliable census data. Meanwhile, formal and informal negotiations of daily life matters proceed orally, with struggles over such matters as post-conflict legal land tenure claims complicated both by uneven registration procedures and conflicting witness accounts.

This predominantly oral everyday culture has for centuries interacted with an established literary tradition in Persian, addressing religious and secular matters in both poetry and prose. Revered works of literature and simpler popular entertainment genres have been made available to a non-reading public through reading aloud or recitation in formal settings (mosque and court) and informal ones (homes and bazaars). Traditional formal education, always beginning with the Quran, stressed memorization and oral performance from memory, including quotations from the Quran and from the *hadith* or traditions of the Prophet, as essential to text mastery and intellectual authority. Highly respected literary figures re-entextualized oral-sourced materials (prose legends and anecdotes, proverbs, verse genres). Such popular literary genres as *dastan* (romantic, multiepisodic adventure tales, usually in prose or prosimetric forms) and *ruba'i* (quatrain) have had equally prominent oral co-traditions. The *ruba'i*'s ubiquitous, corresponding oral quatrain form, called *charbayti* or *chaharbayti* (as well as a number of local dialect genre names), is locally composed by known or unknown poets and performed as song in formal and informal settings from weddings to workplaces, streets, schoolyards and home visits, and circulated in recorded and broadcast media. *Charbayti* shares the literary quatrain's *aaxa* rhyme pattern but uses stress metre rather than the complex version of quantitative metre used in the literary genre. By the mid-twentieth century, the *Shahnama* epic had virtually ceased to be performed from Ferdowsi's text in Afghanistan, though some prose tales from or related to the literary epic cycle could still be heard. In the north-east, a few Tajik singers still performed the oral *Gorgholi* epic in the 1970s.[11] Prose narrative forms such as fictional folktales (*afsana*) and legend (*qissa* or *naql*) were abundantly performed in informal settings prior to and into the 1980s.[12]

While short verbal art forms—especially sung verse genres, sometimes set to crossover musical accompaniment, conversational anecdotes and jokes, as well as proverbs and aphorisms—survived the social upheavals of the last thirty years, other oral performance genres are more compromised. Elders who still remember and can perform folktales and longer *dastan* episodic romance narratives find themselves upstaged by television.[13] The chapbook versions of some dozen or more well-known *dastan* no longer are for sale in bazaar bookshops and curbside stands as they were prior to the 1980s. Comic and satirical folk plays performed by itinerant troupes in the Herat area into the 1970s had virtually disappeared by the 1990s, wiped out by rural and urban insecurity, the collapse of the traditional patronage system and physical displacement of traditional artists.[14] Children's traditional games were also feared to be a casualty of displacement and refugee camp life, though to my knowledge no new research has been done on their continuance. One type of extended oral performance, quoted in conversation and also circulating these days in recorded form from hand-to-hand and through commercial sales (in what literacy theory has dubbed a "post-literate" form) is the sermon (*khutba*). Television is now cited in conversations as an authoritative source for news, as well as rumours, legends and conspiracy theories concerning ongoing warfare and local insecurity issues.

The Interviews

Our research plan between April and May 2009 was simple and direct: through open-ended interviews and informal conversations, to elicit political expectations and evaluations from a wide range of Afghans. This discussion focuses on a few interviewees who had the most striking recourse to proverbial and aphoristic speech, though all the speakers used such expressions to a varying extent. Most of the formally arranged interviews with people outside my personal network were conducted jointly with one of three Afghan male colleagues.[15]

The opinions we heard in spring of 2009 were of that time. The overall pessimism of the respondents can only have been exacerbated by the 2009–11 deterioration of security in formerly quiet areas of the country and the widespread instances of corruption in the presidential and parliamentary election processes, which our respondents for the most part already anticipated.

By not recording the interviews, but only taking notes and reviewing interview points with each other soon after, we aimed to encourage the interviewees' candour in everyday political discussions. Nonetheless, the lack of recording limits the level of detail available for this analysis.[16] It also made it more likely that we would favour in recall certain key words and traditional expressions, as well as tellingly narrated events, sacrificing fewer marked details in the whole conversational flow. As the general state of research shows, proverbs have been hard to recover or examine in "natural use", so these interviews provided an opportunity of sorts for studying Dari-Persian proverbs in context.[17] The fact that the subject matter of the interviews was so vexed, with such indeterminacy of outcome, threw into high relief proverb use as interpretive and evaluative moralizing "bids", rather less definitive than their categorical phrasing might make them appear.

Across a broad spectrum of political opinions, from highly religious to secular-leftist, from pro- to anti-Karzai, from centralist to federalist, a good number of general assessments we heard in 2009 amounted to, "There can be no rapid pull-out. If you leave now, it will be a disaster, civil war. You would leave us to the opportunistic intervention of *komandan* ['warlords' in English, local and regional 'commanders' in Dari] and/or *hamsayah* ['neighbours', specifically Pakistan and Iran]".[18] We were interviewing in non-combat zones, amidst great Afghan uncertainty as to the position of the new Obama administration on the US war effort. This state of anxiety undergirded urgent critiques of the effects of international presence so far and of the moral responsibility of the US-led coalition to try to "get it right" in the near future. The relationship between the failures of the current government and those of the NATO (ISAF) coalition is a tangle that Afghan interviewees could not easily sort out.

AFGHANISTAN IN INK

Afghan Principles and Perceptions as Contexts of Proverb Performance

Inevitably, interviewees' descriptions of current conditions slid into evaluative statements and moralization. While I hoped to elicit specific advice for future action, what we heard was a long list of things needing to be fixed, especially concerning breakdown of trust among citizens and accountability of authorities, and thence debates over local versus centralized governance. Corruption was a major critical focus. Anecdotes of failures of answerability were abundant and detailed.[19] Positive strategies to take control and achieve answerability in governance were harder to come by, though there was some consensus among those who did offer strategies, demanding the replacement of centrally appointed executives with locally elected officials. Presently, everyone down to the level of assistants to the subprovincial district governors is appointed directly by the executive branch in Kabul.

As became apparent from our interview data, Afghans perceive coalition forces (military and civil) as unclear and uncoordinated in either strategies or objectives. This lack of clarity leads not just to allegations of incompetence, insincerity and lack of commitment, but also to some fairly intricate conspiracy theories—as I plan to discuss in more detail in forthcoming works. The US military and ISAF (NATO command) argue that different sectors of a counterinsurgent or post-counterinsurgent state will differ regarding stability, security, reconstruction, etc., and thus require varied activities on the ground. But in the more secure areas of Afghanistan where we interviewed, these variations are perceived by ordinary citizens and activists alike as uncoordinated, with the distribution of services, activities, and resources skewed toward less secure areas. Populations that have "bought in" to national governance and cooperation with occupying forces may thus feel neglected and discouraged from further supporting the central government. Sustainability in governance is not simply the product of physical security. A then-repatriated attorney from an elite Herat family, who was formerly active in the anti-communist *jihad* in western Afghanistan, but was later at odds with increasingly violent Islamists and received asylum in the US, said, "the Bonn process set out to create a government, not a nation. But government [*dawlat*] even if created, cannot function without a nation [*mellat*]".

Political parties are a debatable matter for Afghans. For some, the term *hezb* ("party") was introduced by the communists and implies violent repression of alternative views. For others opposed, it evokes the spectre of ethnic factionalism. Those who support the development of political parties, including some civil society activists we interviewed, argue that political parties, enabling debate and negotiation over diverse ideologies and programmes, are essential to the development of a national representative democracy, beyond ethnic and sectarian identity politics. While a Sunni madrasa teacher in Herat would plead against parties in the name of what he sees as an elusive but vitally necessary national unity (*mellat*), a Shi'a (minority) scholar and clergyman with similar responsibilities in Kabul says, "Afghanistan has never been one *mellat* [nation]". An army general who said, "I am not a political person [*siyasatmadar*]", opined that political parties are alright if they offer policies for development, but not as armed groups. They should not be about *qaum* (lineage group) or *fard* (individual), *mazhab* (religious sect) or *zaban* (language). At the same time, and somewhat contradictorily, he advocated retention of "useful" Afghan social values, such as respect for elders and leaders of *mazhab*, forms of respect that parties would need to maintain *alongside* international legal principles in support of national unity.

One of the major differences of opinion on the problem of national unity has a geographical basis. Even in border areas that are not combat zones, local populations tend to see the central government as extracting resources in the form of commandeered transit taxes or tolls, whereas in provinces lacking a national border (e.g. Hazarajat), the population fears that, without central government control and redistribution of such resources, nothing whatsoever would reach them. With the majority of government resources generated by external donors, the central government has had little or no motive to cooperate with local players. A former elected member of the Constitutional *Loya Jirga* residing in Mazar-e Sharif described how, in an interaction with the ministry of the interior, his group, petitioning for a desired project for Balkh province, was simply told, "We don't need you to advise us; we make the decisions from here".

Nor has centralization as envisioned in the post-Taliban constitution resulted in unitary lines of responsibility and authority, but rather in multiple competing lines, for example in land deed registration, urban planning, etc.[20] One senior member of an elite Pashtun family, formerly in exile and by 2009 trying to regain control of Kabul-area real estate confiscated in the communist period and then passed from hand to hand, described four years of indeterminate appeals processes involving three land deed registration offices as well as the courts. These were ultimately unsuccessful, despite a final court finding in his favour, because the land is presently occupied by the nephew of a very prominent Northern Alliance figure who is now high up in the government. A thirty-year-old taxi driver in Herat (non-land-owning and married with children), commented on such processes: "I'd vote for the *shoes* of the Taliban before I'd vote for this lot! If you took a matter to them [for adjudication], you'd have a decision in half an hour, good or bad. The way it is now, you can run around for years, spend endless amounts of money [on bribes], and still have no decision".[21]

Such varied fundamental attitudes, reflected in the use of key words and concepts, have influenced rhetorics, including proverb applications. However traditional proverbs may be, their application is not constrained by a single set of values; they are "goods to think (and argue) with". For instance, "democracy", considered a foreign term, is received with scepticism and some interpretive ambiguity. By contrast, the *shura* (Dari-Persian) or *loya jirga* (Pashto) is often represented to non-Afghans as an indigenous Afghan consultative democratic institution. Essentially it is an ad hoc council of elders (usually excluding women) or chiefs of lineage groups, convened to arbitrate a particular dispute or address a particular problem. (Since 9/11, the government has convened *loya jirgas* to organize the drawing up and ratification of a new Afghan constitution, or in November 2011, a "non-binding" *loya jirga* to debate the terms of US reduction of forces.) Decision-making traditionally is by consensus rather than by individual ballot vote, such that debate is enabled (within the dynamics of differential prestige and power among the attendees) but collectivity is ultimately reinforced. Pre-manufactured consensus was a feature of *jirgas* convened by the Marxist governments.[22] The Taliban rejected the institution as unIslamic. Consensus remains an ideal feature of Afghan grassroots governance: in a 2008 Asia Foundation Afghan national opinion survey, the majority of respondents opined that in democracy, group decisions and not individual opinions should prevail. Thus, Afghans observe differences between the *shura/loya jirga* model and that of western electoral democracy, some criticizing "democracy" (under that term) for overstressing selfish, individual interest-based choices over consensus decision-making in a corporate social group. One interviewee, asked about how his female cousin-in-law, an elected member of parliament, was doing in office, said, "She's just like all the rest; she goes to Kabul for her own benefit, not to represent anyone else".

GNOMICS

Group and Individual

Individualism in its western form may be deemed pathological at the same time that good or bad governance is described as a function of individual personalities, with recourse to proverbs. One proverbial couplet, quoted by a young male social activist and university student in Kabul, drew ruefully laughing agreement from his colleagues in a group interview:

> *Ba malek besaz, deh-ra betaz.*
> Make [a deal] with the headman, and [you can] plunder the village.

Effective leadership is likewise a matter of individual qualities. In commenting on police recruitment and training, a senior member of the Afghan National Police, who holds the rank of general, offered the maxim:

> *Siahi lashkar nayayad be kar,*
> *Yak mard-e jangi beh az sad hazar.*
> An army [numerous enough] to blacken [the earth] isn't useful/necessary,
> One warlike man is better than a hundred thousand.

Some similes improvised to describe the human predicament of Afghans have near-proverbial rhetorical compactness. Reflecting on current political and security conditions, a grandmother with little or no formal education said, "We Afghans are like sheep: who knows where we'll get a shepherd". This is not "sheep" in the English pejorative sense, but sheep as innocent, pure, sacrificial animals, for whom the shepherd is a strong and faithful protector against predators. The female head of an Afghan NGO in Herat similarly emphasized (though without metaphors) that the only solution to Afghan governance failures would be a leader who was strong and honest (*sadeq*, also "truthful"). The shepherd metaphor is not hard to find in Persian literature, though it is extremely unlikely that my housewife friend was aware of its literary development. A.K.S. Lambton discussed the early Shi'a scholar Abu Yusuf's representation in his *Kitab al-Kharaj* of the divinely appointed ruler as a shepherd answerable for the well-being of his flock.[23]

In many ways, the patrimonial system implied by these remarks is already juridically in place, though hardly delivering *sadeq* governance. As already mentioned, centralism in Kabul today includes the appointment by the president's office of all executives down to the rank of assistant to the district governor. Elected office holders at the provincial level, such as the provincial councils, have no executive or legislative power. Antonio Giustozzi and Dominique Orsini have analyzed the corrupting effect of centralized district-level appointments in Badakhshan.[24] They argue that President Karzai's appointment pattern supports the creation and maintenance of patrimonial, not institutional, power structures. Karzai further avoids appointing any available local aspirants, however, because they might seek to consolidate lasting local power relations through combinations of exploitation and patronage.

Local observers cite corollary effects in the outsider/insider debate. The then-governor of Herat, Dr. Yusuf Nurestani, was described by one Herati interviewee who is friendly to the Karzai regime as a man "without a *qaum* ['lineage group', 'co-ethnics'] in Herat".[25] This means he has no preordained constituency of clients, which might seem to lead to even-handedness, but the speaker's point was that he was so deracinated, with no group behind him, that he would be hard put to get anything done, however good his intentions. By contrast, two other interviewees, who are not otherwise admirers of the Taliban, opined that under the Taliban, civic governance in Herat worked fairly well in part because they appointed a Herati Talib as mayor. Thus individual social identity and character are deemed central to effectiveness, good or bad, in positions of governance. Individual identity is a matter of having a social network, of non-autonomy, within which character plays out. A man's network is, in a way, a map of his character and his likely behaviour. We pressed people to say where reforms could begin and whether local initiatives could or should be a starting point. Even though Herat and Mazar-e Sharif interviewees in general strongly supported reforms to achieve the local election of executively-empowered officials, most who articulated a position on how to address corruption said that reform has to come from the top down. This is further evidence of the apical power structures most Afghans believe in and expect, whether for good or ill.

Trust, Group and Network

Under the present conditions of massive demographic displacement—Kabul grew from 0.9 million people in 2001 to over 4.5 million by 2011—Beall and Esser identify an acutely felt demise of trust among urban dwellers that was vividly described by a number of our interviewees.[26] The concept of "neighbours" (*hamsayah*, literally, "those who share one's shade" in hot and dry Afghanistan) is an important one, implying consensual rather than congenital patterns of mutual trust and reciprocity. (Of course non-relative neighbours may become relatives through marriage as well.) Neighbours are both a source of support at need (e.g. for short-term loans of equipment or money and for contributions to wedding or funeral expenses) and also enforcers of group values and security through the everyday surveillance of the urban or village neighbourhood. The present impersonality of Kabul was experienced in radically different ways: as *anomie* by a fifty-year-old male career development worker and native of Herat ("When I go to Kabul, I feel like I'm in jail"), and as freedom by his unmarried, twenty-something daughter, a young attorney pursuing advanced training in Kabul ("When I leave the house in Herat, someone's always going to observe it and say something. When I'm in Kabul, I can go where I want, no one says a thing").

Some key words carry not so much metaphorical as extended analogical meanings that are of deep cultural importance. The idea of *hamsayah* ("neighbour") carries connotations of mutual responsibility and support but also of potential competition, or predation if one neighbour is strong and the other poor or weak. Neighbours can also be mischievous in their attention to private family business. A bad neighbour is a malicious gossip and/or a "user" who doesn't reciprocate concern, help and support. "Neighbours" becomes an even more loaded term, ethically and politically, at the national level in that neighbours, ideally collaborative, can be lethally interfering and predatory. Some Afghans we interviewed asserted, "We could take care of our problems were it not for the interference of our neighbours [here meaning Pakistan and/or Iran]". The Afghan army general we interviewed offered a proverb to evaluate the "neighbour" Pakistan's growing problem with Taliban activities at home, with a sense of retributive justice as well as an implied mutual dependency:

> The same flame [they lit] burns their beards.

Whether or not interviewees could offer a detailed analysis of the weight of neighbourly interference on Afghan social and political stability, many Afghans feel it acutely. There is in any case a rhetorical tendency in these unstable times to assert that pathologies are the result of polluting influences from outside.

Discourse Matters

Because Afghanistan is still fundamentally an oral society, not only face-to-face interaction but also spoken words themselves matter profoundly. An

Afghan aphorism states, "Stones wound temporarily, words permanently".[27] Our interviewees thus made use of proverbs and aphorisms (some quoted above) to epitomize their interpretations of present situations. Proverbs gain their power not simply by what they stipulate in relatively or thoroughly familiar form, but by their deployment, creating fresh applications to situations whose interpretation the speaker is trying (perhaps inconclusively) to control. Proverbs are not simply handy clichés of fixed meaning, but are somewhat multivalent bids for interpretive power; their relevance to (*seem* to) sum up an indeterminate situation critically is indirect. Because they rely on metaphor, their exact application to the situation is somewhat open. Proverbs' indirection may also provide a safe margin of deniability and deferred authority where the speaker's desire to criticize may outweigh his or her power or authority to do so.

A political joke heard in Herat suggests, however, that all is not well in the traditional Afghan world of consequential words:

The Communists and the Taliban told the people, "You can have basic security, food, and shelter, but you just have to *shut up!*" The present government says, "No security, no shelter, no food, but you can *say* anything you like!"

Freedom of speech is a dubious value where words have become inconsequential and appeals for life's basics are unmet. In this connection, an oath or promise (*qaul*) is supposed to be binding, but people have heard a lot of promises without delivery, a basic form of corruption in this oral world.

The conversational/topical context of the proverb is crucial. When a senior Herat police officer said, "The naked man is not afraid of water [*luch az ab namitarsad*]", he ruefully characterized the present situation of those Afghans who allow themselves to be recruited as modestly-paid fighters by the resistance because they have "nothing left to lose". But this is not, in his application, a devil-may-care or ascetic liberation. It is instead a dangerous state, the remedy for which, as he explained, lies firstly in jobs for economic survival and secondly in the Afghanization of security and reconstruction. Insecurity itself becomes less of a threat when the "naked" are again clothed, with something to lose. His interpretation of the proverb is enclosed in his sense of the problem and its solution.

New ideologies and their terminologies are mystifying (or mystified), perhaps to be decoded with a proverb or aphorism. A radio journalist and lifelong civil society activist in Mazar-e Sharif sums it up with a trenchant verse fragment:

GNOMICS

We've had thirty years of ideologies, all these "isms". People don't understand the grand terminologies. The Russians came with Communism and Internationalism [and] everyone thought it just meant "You have to deny God". Today the Taliban also say that democracy is godlessness. Now comes capitalism, the free market concept, which seems to mean, "*Dari, bokhor; nadari, bomor!*" ["If you've got, eat; if you don't, die!"] Nobody wants to die. Today if we have corruption, it's because some just try to survive, others try to have a [decent] life. We've had such a terrible experience of the "free market" with everything lost and wasted, first by NGOs, then by our government, then by the government and NGOs together.

Fig. 20: Literary Beginnings & Ends? Muhammad Ghulami's *Jangnama* ("Book of War").

This speaker, a lifelong campaigner for responsible government, finds "corruption" a qualified term during such extreme economic and social disorder.

An elderly, retired cook and shopkeeper from Herat describes a current (since deceased) local armed resistance leader, Siaushani, with a proverb: "He's a man on foot between two donkeys [and can't ride either of them]", the two donkeys being the government and the Taliban, with neither of which he can safely ally himself. This description, while not laudatory, is also not totally dismissive: the man is in a predicament. The speaker himself was in just such a predicament in the early 1980s when, as he tells it, he was caught between a communist functionary who was demanding his teenaged daughter in marriage (an unwelcome alliance) and a *mujahidin* commander who was demanding tribute. His response was to "walk" out from between the two donkeys to Iran with his family as refugees. Concerning donkeys as even more explicit political metaphors applied to leadership, we will see further examples below from Malalai Joya's written memoir.

The sense of confused leadership also finds form today in a materially apt rhymed-couplet proverb from a secular leftist party representative in Herat:

> *Khaneh az bombast, veyran ast,*
> *Ama khvaja dar fekr-e aivan ast.*
> The house is in ruins from bombardment,
> Yet the master is worrying about the verandah.[28]

The same speaker and a second very different individual, a devoutly religious ex-*mujahid* parliamentary representative from Badakhshan, both applied to the coalition the same proverbial verse assessment of wrongheadedness attributed to the classical poet Sa'di:

> *Tarsam naresi be Ka'ba, ay 'Arabi,*
> *Kin rah keh to miravi be Turkestan ast.*
> I fear you will never reach the Ka'ba, oh desert Arab,
> Because this road you have taken leads to Turkestan.

The reference to the foreign occupying forces in the metaphor of "desert Arab" in this implicitly narrative-based proverb is interestingly polyvalent: the classical poetic persona of the "desert Arab" is wild and uncivilized, as well as "foreign" from the Persian or Afghan point of view, but also naively sincere. The Badakhshani speaker continued later with a more daring verse attributed to Jalal al-Din Rumi:

Jan Baba, "iltaja'" avordehi,
Lik surakh-e dovom gom kardi!

Dear old soul, you're undertaking the genital ablution [literally the "seeking protection"],
But you've lost track of which hole!

The narrative context is that the speaking persona observes someone else doing his ablutions, but reciting the prayer for the nose while washing his privates. Thus, again the disastrously, even comically, wrong understanding of the internationals (this time with ritual incompetence as the trope) despite potentially righteous intentions.

The same speaker's third literary proverb, offered as the same short interview progressed, also criticizes the limits of the internationals' perception. But this proverb was not addressed to the likes of me as a representative outsider, but perhaps to Ruhullah, my then co-interviewer, who is known to the speaker as someone with serious theological, mystical and literary interests. The verse comes from Bedil (d.1720)—an Indo-Persian mystical poet beloved in Afghanistan—and is less generous:

> *Bedil, az shabpareh kayfiyat-e khorshid mapors,*
> *Haqq nehan nist vali kheyreh negahan kur and.*
> Bedil, don't ask the bat about the qualities of sunlight,
> The truth is not hidden, but those who go about with half-shut eyes [the supercilious gazers] are blind.

In this third example, the addressee "Bedil" (the poet himself) stands not for the clueless foreign Other but for the Afghan who must protect himself from that (now bad-intentioned) misperceiving Other. This proverb elaborates the contrast between the religiously rightly-guided and, now more culpably, the wilfully blind. "Bedil", the poet as speaker, admonishes himself (the putative listener) to avoid such.

Apart from the specific propositional content of these verses, the very selection of verses attributed to classical and mystical poets regarded as intellectual and spiritual giants to evaluate the confusions and intrusions of outsiders in the present situation establishes a powerful claim to interpretive authority for and with the most ethically prestigious Afghan literary tradition, the religious-poetic. Galit Hasan-Rokem makes a more precise, parallel argument concerning prestige and identity claims implicit in Iranian Jews' use of literary Persian proverbial verses after resettlement in Israel.[29] Both oral and literary proverbs have authoritative force as they refer to (and help to define) categories of common human experience. But expressions attributable to literary giants command more authority, as they partake of all four of Stefan Morawski's functions of quotation: the stimulative-applicative, which changes the overall structure and meaning in a new application; the authoritative, which grants the speech act and the speaker the credence belonging to the quoted source; the ornamental, aesthetic function, "adorning" the text in the new combination with the poetic qualities of the quoted source; and the erudite function, establishing the status of the speaker as a cultural expert.[30]

Some metaphors, such as the Herati grandmother's "Where will we find a shepherd?" query quoted above, stop short of crystallized proverb status, let alone claim literary authority. Certain metaphors were nonetheless productive of such proverbial coinages for a variety of speakers. Analogies of the Afghan state to a human body were frequently invoked. A revered senior civil society activist in Herat says of the prospect of premature international withdrawal, "If you start a course of 'vaccine' to eliminate a 'virus', and stop it before it's finished, the virus becomes more virulent". The analogy simultaneously invokes the power of the empirical and rational in scientific discourse, cushions the criticism by indirection and enriches its ethical implications, in this case with the idea that Afghanistan is a living body that requires healing and protection of its integrity *vis à vis* "doctors" of questionable competence. Other body metaphors of the state or nation:

You don't treat a cancer patient with aspirin, and tell him he has a headache!
(Journalist, Mazar-e Sharif)

Afghanistan is a newborn child right now.
(Army general, concerning the need for the military to protect civil institutions.)

Democracy in Afghanistan had a premature birth, it cannot survive.
(Madrasa teacher and democracy skeptic, Herat.)

The substrates for such metaphors, though implicitly narrative, may be very compact, what folklorist Susan Kalcik called "kernel stories", evoking in their brevity a cluster of implicit cultural ideas not readily apparent to the uninitiated.[31] In a country where child mortality is still twenty per cent by age five, in the two examples above intense anxieties about childbearing and reproduction of the family undergird the bodily metaphor. In one particularly pungent coined proverbialism (an extended metaphor), a male political activist described the current insecurity as the product of poverty, first of all, and secondly, of current leadership born in the "lap" (*daman*) and "nurtured at the fat breast of war" (*az postan-e charb-e jang taghziyah mishand*), an allusion to former commanders ("warlords" in English) now running the country.

GNOMICS

In such compact expressions, ambiguities and ironies of the situations to which they refer are made available for thought and not defined away. Ethics are mapped and in some measure defended, but their limits may be suggested as well: *Dari, bokhor; nadari, bomor!* ("If you've got, eat; if you don't, die!"). The compaction of discourse forms can open interpretations and not just close them, through productive ellipsis allowing for multiple (re)interpretations. Gnomic expressions—including proverbs, aphorisms, epithets, jokes or kernel narratives—are, in linguistic terms, restricted codes, in that they are not transparently referential, but rather a kind of shorthand requiring a good deal of ambient cultural knowledge shared by a group to be competently deciphered. When interviewees wish aloud that foreign soldiers could just refrain from "farting in public" (Herat police general) or "pissing while standing around in the road" (two different interviewees from Jalalabad), these are kernel narratives in which the briefest report of an iconic behaviour carries an implied but unstated subtext ("these are people who act like animals or infants and so we cannot be socially/ethically co-present with them"). One thing laid open by the unspoken implications of these two kernel narratives is the Afghan social imperative of personal interaction needing to be governed by *adab* ("manners, etiquette"), which encompasses a range of social values from mere politeness to the most profound social ethics.

It is the very packedness of such expressions—their rich, unspoken implications and associations with multiple possible connections to the immediate context—that make them socially powerful. Take, for instance, the post-9/11 epithet, *sagshu* ("dogwasher", a new coinage), applied by some stayed-on Afghans (who may have been refugees in Iran or Pakistan but have never migrated to non-Muslim locales) to Afghan professionals who return from exile in non-Muslim societies with claims to administrative or other expertise and large international salaries. Many return out of feelings of ethical responsibility or national loyalty, but still they may be called *sagshu* and resented on the assumption that they held menial jobs in Europe or America, iconically as dog-groomers who have only come back "home" to claim undeservedly high positions. The dog-washer label is particularly pejorative because dogs are considered ritually unclean by observant Muslims, who avoid touching them. These expatriate Afghans are thus considered so demeaned and culturally alienated that for money they would allow themselves to become more polluted than the dogs, the unclean pets of unbelievers, by washing them. "Washing a dog" is in any case a kind of pointless oxymoron, given the generically polluted nature of dogs. A returned *sagshu* has parlayed a menial work experience and skill set plus foreign language fluency into a position of specious authority and productivity (and ill-gotten prosperity) in his native country. Bilingual and often bi-national, his holding two passports is considered a tangible index of his lack of commitment to Afghanistan. When things get tough, the stayed-on predict, the bi-nationals will disappear.

Afghan understanding of cultural alienation may have shifted emphasis since the pre-war years. There was a pre-war joke, which I heard from Afghan language instructors working for the Peace Corps in the 1970s: "If you want to make an Afghan a Communist, send him to the US for study. If you want to make him a capitalist, send him to the Soviet Union". This dialectical joke inferentially defines the unalienated Afghan as neither of the above, but it also suggests that the danger of alienation lies not just in being "turned into" something else, but in being turned into something antithetical even to the intentions of the "alienators". The dialectics of alienation have become less elegantly clear now. Exposure to capitalism and democracy results not in any ideologically corrective boomerang effect, but in the aphorism, "*Dari, bokhor; nadari, bomor*" ("If you've got, eat; if you don't, die"). Paradoxically, the aphorism itself may validate an anti-ethic of unilateral acquisition and consumption as a matter of survival.

Proverbs for Outsiders: Paremiology in Afghan Women's Memoirs

Gnomics are key cultural text forms in Afghanistan and other chaotic environments where making an observed mess into a cognitively accessible enigma is intellectually and emotionally useful. But an essential part of their power is in a degree of non-transparency ("packedness"). In some proverbs and aphorisms, including ones quoted above, literary or oral poetic language (rhyme, metre) adds an aesthetic dimension to their power by way of memorability and perceived eloquence. But what of proverbs identified as "Afghan" but offered in English to outsiders not fluent in Afghan cultural values or language? Among recent Afghan women memoirists, Malalai Joya (born 1978) is a notoriously outspoken political activist who wields a particularly pungent and abundant gnomic repertoire, both traditional and newly-coined. Numerous proverbs and aphorisms of relatively universal force punctuate her 2009 English-language memoir, *A Woman among Warlords*. Furthermore, she repeatedly identifies proverbs and aphorisms with quite transparent, immediate referentiality as "Afghan", making a claim both for her own Afghanness and for Afghan common sense and common humanity:

In Afghanistan there is a saying: Every anguish passes except the anguish of hunger. [Discussing the history of ongoing economic hardship, under globalization, privatization and the vulnerability of the poorest].[32]

A river is made drop by drop. [Discussing political movements].[33]

Our enemies can cut down the flowers, but nothing can stop the coming of Spring. [Again naturalizing the revolutionary process].[34]

In Afghanistan, we have a saying: Ask the truth from a child. [Summing up her recollection of a very young adolescent girl who joined Joya's parliamentary campaign early on, in opposition to her own father, who backed a "fundamentalist candidate". This saying echoes a key moment in the literary Persian version of the famous biblical and Quranic story of Yusuf and Zulaykha, Joseph and Potiphar's wife, in which a little child points out that if Yusuf's shirt is torn from behind, the woman was the aggressor, not he].[35]

Those we cry with, we never forget, but those we laugh with, we forget too soon. [Recalling children met at an orphanage].[36]

Animal metaphors are particularly productive for Joya.[37] When she was criticized for "joining this corrupt warlord-ridden Parliament, [she said] 'How can you catch tiger cubs, without entering the tiger's den?'" Regarding an infamous interview which ultimately was the reason for the vote to expel her from parliament, she recalled a man-in-the-street interview aired on television in which the interviewee said parliament was like a "street bazaar because it was so chaotic ... many MPs complained about this comment ... [but] I said that if we continue to do nothing with this Parliament and not solve any of the people's real problems, today they may call it a bazaar but tomorrow they will call it a zoo. As usual the MPs started banging their desks in anger and the speaker cut off my microphone". She complained that Tolo TV, a major Kabul private television channel, edited this and similar remarks for broadcast to make it sound like she was accusing the entire parliament of being a zoo. In the memoir, she goes on, "a stable or zoo isn't even adequate because in a stable we have cows [for milk], a donkey [to carry burdens], a dog [proverbially the most loyal animal, though unclean]. But they are dragons".[38]

Joya shows the metaphor of the donkey as particularly productive for Afghans:

They had been hoping for better conditions following the civil war, but instead, as the Afghan saying goes, "When the earth tore apart, the donkeys came out". [The "donkeys" being the Taliban].[39]

Joya also reports a popular saying of the civil war period, when seven major *mujahidin* parties fought one another, "Take away these seven donkeys and give us back our 'Cow'!" *Gau* ("cow/ox") was the unflattering nickname of the burly Najibullah, the communist-turned-nationalist president and former head of the KHAD Afghan secret police who took refuge in the UN compound in Kabul during the civil war of the 1990s, only to be dragged out, castrated and hung in the street by the Taliban when they entered Kabul. Of warlords in the constitutional *Loya Jirga*, Joya says, "In Afghanistan, there is a saying: It's the same donkey but with a new saddle".[40]

In contrast to the proverbs and metaphors employed by our interviewees, Joya repeatedly labels her proverbs and metaphors as "Afghan wisdom" and, because the sayings she highlights are relatively culturally transparent, she thus presents Afghans to her non-Afghan audience as both interculturally wise and non-exotic. She also at times deploys idiomatic Americanisms, another distance-reducing technique: "The American President's clueless wife", or "During her drive-by visit to Kabul, Mrs. Bush ..."[41]

In her English-language memoir from 2005, Nelufer Pazira, a professional journalist who has native fluency in English, goes so far as to say in her conclusion (contrary to my observations) that, "In the new Afghanistan there isn't much time for metaphors".[42] While this statement has the quality of eulogy for cultural loss, Pazira herself nonetheless skilfully weaves some proverbs and a number of metaphorical coinages into her account. She sums up Marxist media propaganda and the jamming of other news sources during her young adult years in Kabul proverbially: "the louder the drum, the emptier it is".[43] Regarding a young woman she and her friends called "Miss Oppressed", who appeared in various public Marxist forums to complain of her pre-Marxist gender oppression and who was then publically claimed as a bride by one of the more sententious and tedious male Marxist propagandists, Pazira uses the proverb, "she got out of the rain to sit under the drain pipe".[44] She also describes a new coinage in Marxist Kabul: people who opportunistically pretended to share Marxist ideology were called "Bubble Gums" for trying to "stick onto" any new power elite for their own gain.[45] She also points out semantic shifts in key words: among progressives and others who had fled the Marxist regime to Pakistan during the unfolding civil war of the 1990s, *mujahid* ("holy warrior") became an insult. For the most part less sententiously than Joya, Pazira glosses such sayings to make them accessible to her non-Afghan audience, but without the 'this is Afghan' label deployed by Joya.

Pazira invokes one very well-known Persian/Afghan political proverb without seeming to know (or stopping to explain) its full provenance and back story. Of her father's dangerous political outspokenness, she says, "Though Habibullah had officially disentangled himself from politics, he had never lost his passion for change. He managed to conceal his sharp tongue—his 'red tongue', his friends used to call it—inside his mouth for years. But once in a while …"[46] This proverb was deployed and discussed by Herati Akhund Mulla Mahmad at a politically-charged storytelling session in 1975.[47] It cautions against politically injudicious speech as lethally dangerous, and is traditionally encapsulated in the catch phrase, "*Agar/magar*" ("If/but"). The basic metaphorical expression is, "The red tongue gambles away [or, in variant, 'casts to the wind'[48]] the green head".[49]

So What?

The range of metaphors, epithets, catch phrases and full-fledged proverbs and aphorisms deployed in these two types of text—for insider and outsider, oral and written—perform a range of rhetorical, social and political tasks that are only sampled in this chapter. The authority and prestige of classical literary attribution for proverbs add special weight to semantic forms (proverbs and aphorisms) already regarded as weighty through their legacy of traditionality and long use.[50] Different writers and speakers deploy such expressions variously to insider and outsider audiences, for purposes of identity-claiming in solidarity or distinction, of critique, admonition, or sometimes rueful commentary on the inevitable or tragic in human nature or historical events. Present but not overwhelming in these expressive registers is the still-fertile interchange between oral and written, text and performance. But no less noteworthy is the continuing and now global capacity of Afghans to generate and deploy new gnomic coinages within available speech and writing registers in order to purvey with freshness the intensity of new and highly disturbing events and experiences.

NOTES

PREFACE AND ACKNOWLEDGEMENTS

1. Nile Green, "Tribe, Diaspora and Sainthood in Afghan History", *Journal of Asian Studies* 67, 1 (2008) and *idem.*, "The Trans-Border Traffic of Afghan Modernism: Afghanistan and the Indian 'Urdusphere'", *Comparative Studies in Society and History* 53, 3 (2011).

1. INTRODUCTION: AFGHAN LITERATURE BETWEEN DIASPORA AND NATION

1. Vizārat-e Maʿārif (Ministry of Education), *Darī* (s.n., 1388s/2010), published in six parts for class seven (*senf-e haft*) through class twelve (*senf-e davāzdah*).
2. Fārūq Wardak, "Payām ['Message']", in *Darī* (s.n., 1388s/2010), all editions, page *dāl* ('d').
3. See Homi K. Bhabha (ed.), *Nation and Narration* (London: Routledge, 1990), Vincent Newey & Ann Thompson (eds), *Literature and Nationalism* (Liverpool: Liverpool University Press, 1991) and Yasir Suleiman & Ibrahim Muhawi (eds), *Literature and Nation in the Middle East* (Edinburgh: Edinburgh University Press, 2006).
4. On the foundation of the Afghan state, see Shah Mahmoud Hanifi, *Connecting Histories in Afghanistan: Market Relations and State Formation on a Colonial Frontier* (New York: Columbia University Press, 2008), M. Hassan Kakar, *A Political and Diplomatic History of Afghanistan, 1863–1901* (Leiden: Brill, 2006) and Leon B. Poullada, *Reform and Rebellion in Afghanistan, 1919–1929: King Amanullah's Failure to Modernize a Tribal Society* (Ithaca: Cornell University Press, 1973).
5. Cf. Paul Jay, *Global Matters: The Transnational Turn in Literary Studies* (Ithaca: Cornell University Press, 2010) and Christie McDonald & Susan Rubin Suleiman (eds.), *French Global: A New Approach to Literary History* (New York: Columbia University Press, 2010).

6. For surveys of Afghan literature, see: Wali Ahmadi, *Modern Literature of Afghanistan: Anomalous Visions of History and Form* (New York: Routledge, 2008); Hasan Anūsha, *Dānishnāma-ye Adab-e Fārsī*, vol. 3, *Adab-e Fārsī dar Afghānistān* (Tehran: Sāzmān-e Chāp va Intishārāt Vizārat-e Irshād-e Islāmī, 1378/1999); Alessandro Bausani, *Le Letterature del Pakistan e dell'Afghanistan* (Milan: Accademia, 1968); Hughes Jean de Dianous, "La littérature Afghane de langue persane", *Orient* 31 (1964); Mīr Ghulām Muhammad Ghubār, *Tārīkh-e Adabiyāt-e Afghānistān: Dawrah-ye Muhammad Zā'ī-hā* (Peshawar: Ārash, 1378/1999); 'Abd al-Hayy Habībī, *Da Paxhtū Adab Land Tārīkh: da Pohantūn da Drem aw Salūrm Tolagyo Lah Pārah* (Qandahar: 'Alāmah Rashād Khprandwiyah Tolana, 2008); Philip G. Kreyenbroek & Ulrich Marzolph (eds), *Oral Literature of Iranian Languages: Kurdish, Pashto, Balochi, Ossetic; Persian and Tajik*, Companion Volume 2 (London: I.B. Tauris, 2010); Arley Loewen & Josette McMichael (eds.), *Images of Afghanistan: Exploring Afghan Culture through Art and Literature* (Karachi: Oxford University Press, 2010); Muhammad Afzal Rizā, *Pashtō Lōg Adab* (Islamabad: Akādimī Adabiyāt-e Pākistān, 1989) (Urdu); Dunning Wilson, "Afghan Literature: A Perspective", in George Grassmuck & Ludwig W. Adamec (eds), *Afghanistan: Some New Approaches* (Ann Arbor: Center for Near Eastern and North African Studies, University of Michigan, 1969).
7. Cf. Kamran Talattof, *The Politics of Writing in Iran: A History of Modern Persian Literature* (Syracuse: Syracuse University Press, 2000).
8. On the diasporic history of Afghans, see Nile Green, "Tribe, Diaspora and Sainthood in Afghan History", *Journal of Asian Studies* 67, 1 (2008) and Robert Nichols, *A History of Pashtun Migration* (Karachi: Oxford University Press, 2008).
9. Benjamin Hopkins, *The Making of Modern Afghanistan* (London: Palgrave Macmillan, 2008).
10. Benjamin Hopkins, "The Bounds of Identity: The Goldsmid Mission and the Delineation of the Perso-Afghan Border in the 19th Century", *Journal of Global History* 2, 2 (2007).
11. On the earliest usages of the name, see Christine Noelle-Karimi, "Historiography XI: Afghanistan", in *Encyclopaedia Iranica* and *Shams al-Nahar*, year 1, vol. 1 (Muharram 1290/March 1872), p. 2.
12. Angela Parvanta, "Afghanistan—Land of the Afghans? On the Genesis of a Problematic State Denomination", in Christine Noelle-Karimi, Conrad Schetter & Reinhard Schlagintweit (eds), *Afghanistan: A Country without a State?* (Frankfurt am Main: IKO, 2002).
13. M. Hasan Kakar, *The Pacification of the Hazaras of Afghanistan* (New York: Afghanistan Council, Asia Society, 1973).
14. Ashraf Ghani, "Islam and State-Building in a Tribal Society: Afghanistan, 1880–1901", *Modern Asian Studies* 12, 2 (1978).

15. Vartan Gregorian, *The Emergence of Modern Afghanistan: Politics of Reform and Modernization, 1880–1946* (Stanford: Stanford University Press, 1969), Senzil K. Nawid, *Religious Response to Social Change in Afghanistan, 1919–29: King Aman-Allah and the Afghan Ulama* (Costa Mesa: Mazda Publishers, 1999) and Poullada (1973).
16. May Schinasi, *Afghanistan at the Beginning of the Twentieth Century: Nationalism and Journalism in Afghanistan: A Study of Seraj ul-Akhbar (1911–1918)* (Naples: Istituto Universitario Orientale, 1979), p. 55.
17. Milan L. Hauner, "Afghanistan between the Great Powers, 1938–1945", *International Journal of Middle East Studies* 14, 4 (1982) and Paul Robinson & Jay Dixon, "Soviet Development Theory and Economic and Technical Assistance to Afghanistan, 1954–1991", *The Historian* 73, 3 (2010).
18. David B. Edwards, *Before Taliban: Genealogies of the Afghan Jihad* (Berkeley: University of California Press, 2002).
19. Noelle-Karimi in *Encyclopaedia Iranica*.
20. Muhammad Alam Miran, "The Functions of National Languages in Afghanistan", Afghanistan Council Occasional Paper (New York: Asia Society, 1977) and Gabriele Rasuly-Paleczek, "Ethnic Identity Versus Nationalism: The Uzbeks of Northeastern Afghanistan and the Afghan State", in Touraj Atabaki & John O'Kane (eds), *Post-Soviet Central Asia* (London: Tauris Academic Studies, 1998).
21. Yaʻqūb Hasan Khān, "*Tārīkh-e Zabān-hā dar Afghānistān*", *Sālnāma-ye Kābul* 1313/1935, *qismat-e avval* (part 1), pp. 119–47.
22. Sir Percy Sykes, *A History of Afghanistan*, 2 vols (London: Macmillan, 1940), vol. 2, p. 229.
23. On the earlier trans-regional history of Persian, see Muzaffar Alam, "The Pursuit of Persian: Language in Mughal Politics", *Modern Asian Studies* 32, 2 (1998) and Francis Robinson, "Perso-Islamic Culture in India from the Seventeenth to the Early Twentieth Century", in *idem.*, *Islam and Muslim History in South Asia* (Delhi: Oxford University Press, 2000).
24. Ingeborg Baldauf, *Materialien zum Volkslied der Ozbeken Afghanistans*, 2 vols (Emsdetten: A. Gehling, 1989) and Gunnar Jarring, *Uzbek Texts from Afghan Turkestan* (Lund: C.W.K. Gleerup, 1938).
25. Afshin Marashi, *Nationalizing Iran: Culture, Power, and the State, 1870–1940* (Seattle: University of Washington Press, 2008), pp. 124–32 and *idem.*, "The Nation's Poet: Ferdowsi and the Iranian National Imagination", in Touraj Atabaki (ed.), *Narrating Modern Iran: Historiography and Political Culture in the Twentieth Century* (London: I.B. Tauris, 2009).
26. Green (2008).
27. "*Chand Kitāb-e Paxtō dar Maktaba-ye Islāmiyya Kālij, Peshāwar*", *Āryānā* no. 48, year 4, issue 12 (1325/1947), pp. 22–5.
28. Farīd Qāsimī, *Avvalīnhā-ye Matbūʻāt-e Īrān* (Tehran: Nashr-e Ābī, 1383/2004)

and C.A. Storey, "The Beginnings of Persian Printing in India", in J. D. Cursetji Pavry (ed.), *Oriental Studies in Honour of Cursetji Erachji Pavry* (London: Oxford University Press, 1933).

29. See the list of the earliest Afghan publications in 'Abd al-Rasūl Rahīn, "Āghāz-e Kitābnavīsī va Tab'-e Kitāb dar Afghānistān", *Āryānā-ye Birūn Marzī* 5, 3 (Skärholmen, Sweden: Afghanistan Cultural Association, 2003), pp. 3–16.

30. On the beginnings of Afghan printing, see 'Abd al-Rasūl Rahīn, "Talī'a-ye Matbū'āt dar Afghānistān", *Āryānā-ye Birūn Marzī* 1, 2 (1999), *idem*. (2003), *idem*., "Matbū'āt dar Dawra-ye Zamāmdārī-ye Muhammad Nādir Shāh", *Āryānā-ye Birūn Marzī* 6, 1 (2004–5) and Muhammad Haydar Zhobal, "Mahmūd Tarzī, Pedar-e Matbū'at", *'Irfān* (Kabul) 2 (1958).

31. For the poems on coal and newspapers, see *Sirāj al-Akhbār*, year 1, no. 17 (1291/1912), p. 15 and *Sirāj al-Akhbār*, year 2, no. 2 (1291/1912), p. 15. Thanks to Nushin Arbabzadah for these references. For studies of the newspaper's political role, see Vartan Gregorian, "Mahmud Tarzi and Saraj-ol-Akhbar: Ideology of Nationalism and Modernization in Afghanistan", *Middle East Journal* 21, 3 (1967) and Schinasi (1979).

32. Ahmadi (2008), p. 26.

33. Umbro Apollonio (ed.), *Futurist Manifestos* (London: Thames and Hudson, 1973).

34. Nile Green, "The Road to Kabul: Automobiles and Afghan Internationalism, 1900–1940", in Magnus Marsden & Benjamin Hopkins (eds), *Beyond Swat: History, Society and Economy along the Afghanistan-Pakistan Frontier* (New York: Columbia University Press, 2012) and Richard Humphreys, *Futurism* (Cambridge: Cambridge University Press, 1999).

35. On Tarzi as a literary and political figure, see Ashraf Ghani, "Literature as Politics: The Case of Mahmud Tarzi", *Afghanistan* 29, 3 (1976) and Muhammad 'Azam Sīstānī, *'Allāma Mahmūd Tarzī, Shāh Amānullāh va Rūhāniyat-e Mutanaffiz* (Peshawar: Kitābkhāna-e Dānesh, 2004).

36. Mehrdad Kia, "Persian Nationalism and the Campaign for Language Purification", *Middle Eastern Studies* 34, 2 (1998) and John R. Perry, "Language Reform in Turkey and Iran", *International Journal of Middle East Studies* 17, 3 (1985).

37. Mahmūd Tarzī, "Maqāla-ye Makhsūsa", *Sirāj al-Akhbār*, year 2, no. 10 (1291/1913), pp. 11–14.

38. Ghubār (repr. 1378/1999), Muhammad 'Alī Kohzād, "Āryānā yā Afghānistān Qabl az Islām", *Kābul* 9, 11 (1939), Muhammad Kāzim Kahdūyī (ed.), *Adabiyāt-e Afghānistān dar Advār-e Qadīma: bar Girifta az Jeld-e Sevvum-e Āryānā* (Tehran: Intishārāt-e Bayn al-Milalī al-Hudā, repr. 1384/2006), Muhammad Haydar Zhobal, *Tārīkh-e Adabiyāt-e Afghānistān* (Peshawar: Sabā Kitābkhāna, 1957).

39. See e.g. Muhammad Ali, "Ahmad Shāh Bābā, Father of the Nation", *Afghani-*

stan 18, 2 (1963) and Mīr Ghulām Muhammad Ghubār, *Ahmad Shāh Bābā-ye Afghān* (Kabul: Matbaʿa-ye ʿUmūmī, 1939).

40. Recent research suggests that Rumi/Balkhi was in fact born in the city of Vakhsh in what is now the Republic of Tajikistan. See Franklin D. Lewis, *Rumi: Past and Present, East and West* (Oxford: Oneworld, 2000), pp. 45–55.
41. For one case study, see Robert D. McChesney, "Architecture and Narrative: The Khwaja Abu Nasr Shrine", *Muqarnas* 18 (2001) & 19 (2002).
42. Observation of the French minister to Kabul, René Dollot, quoted in May Schinasi, *Kaboul 1773–1948: Naissance et croissance d'une capitale royale* (Naples: Università degli Studi Napoli "L'Orientale", 2008), p. 185.
43. Wali Ahmadi, "Kabul Literary Society", in *Encyclopaedia Iranica*.
44. Chaled Malekyar, *Das Bild Afghanistans im 20 Jahrhundert: Das Werk des Schriftstellers und Diplomaten Ostad Abdol Rahman Pazhwak (1919–1995)* (Berlin: Klaus Schwartz, 2008), p. 82.
45. Abd al-Hayy Habibi, "A Glance at Historiography and the Beginning of the Historical Society of Afghanistan", *Afghanistan* 21, 2 (1968).
46. "Fan-e Rumān Navīsī", *Āryānā* year 3, no. 32, issue 8 (1324/1946), 38–50.
47. Roland Wild, *Amanullah: Ex-King of Afghanistan* (London: Hurst & Blackett, 1932), p. 180–1.
48. *Ibid.*, p. 181.
49. Official university statistics cited in Najibullah Habib, *Stadtplanung, Architektur und Baupolitik in Afghanistan: eine Betrachtung traditioneller und fremdkultureller Einflüsse von 1880–1980* (Bochum: Studienverlag Brockmeyer, 1987), pp. 234–5.
50. Bibliographic details for the multiple titles of these Iqbal translations may be found in Shaista Wahab, *Arthur Paul Afghanistan Collection Bibliography*, vol. 1, *Pashto and Dari Titles* (Lincoln, NE: Dageforde Publishing, 1995), pp. 45–6.
51. Habib (1987), pp. 234–5.
52. Green (2008).
53. On Pashto "cheap print" editions, see Wilma W. Heston, "Pashto Chapbooks, Gendered Imagery and Cross-cultural Contact", in Cathy Lynn Preston & Michael J. Preston (eds), *The Other Print Tradition: Chapbooks, Broadsides, and Related Ephemera* (New York: Garland Publishing, 1995).
54. See e.g. *Sirāj al-Akhbār* year 4, no. 3 (1293/1914), 9; year 4, no. 6 (1293/1914), p. 4.
55. Sālih Muhammad, *Mawlavī Lumra Kitāb da Paxtō, yaʿnī Kitāb-e Avval-e Afghānī* (Kabul: Matbaʿ-ye Māshīnkhāna, 1335/1916) and *idem.*, *Hadiya-ye Huzūr-e ʿĀlī va Risāla-ye Pashtō Itāʿat Ūlū'l-Amr* (Kabul: Dār al-Saltana, 1334/1916).
56. Mahmūd Tarzī, "Zabān-e Afghānī Ajdād-e Zabān-hā-ast", *Sirāj al-Akhbār*, year 2, no. 9 (1291/1913), pp. 9–12.
57. *Sirāj al-Akhbār*, year 2, no. 21 (1292/1913), p. 6. Thanks to Nushin Arbabzadah for this reference.

58. Hafizullah Emadi, *The Dynamics of Political Development in Afghanistan: The British, Russian, and American Invasions* (New York: Palgrave Macmillan, 2010), pp. 45–6.
59. Muhammad Gul Muhmand, *Da Musavvide Pah Davul Lumray Pasxto Sind: Avvalīn Qāmūs-e Afghānī bih Tarīq Musavvidah*, 2 vols (Kabul: Vizārat-e Maʿārif, 1937).
60. Sālih Muhammad Khān, *Paxtū Zabā: Da Paxtū Tulanī Nasriyat* (Kabul: ʿUmūmī Matbaʿa, 1937). More generally, see D.N. MacKenzie, "The Development of the Pashto Script", in Shirin Akiner & Nicholas Sims-Williams (eds.), *Languages and Scripts of Central Asia* (London: School of Oriental and African Studies, 1997).
61. Kia (1998), p. 22.
62. John R. Perry, "Script and Scripture: The Three Alphabets of Tajik Persian, 1927–1997", *Journal of Central Asian Studies* 2, 1 (1997).
63. For the purported text, see Mohammed Hotak, *Pata Khazana (Trésor caché)* (Kabul: Paxto-Tolana, 1944), translated by Khushal Habibi as *The Hidden Treasure (Pata Khazana): A Biography of Pashtoon Poets* (Lanham: University Press of America, 1997). See also ʿAbd al-Hayy Habibi, "The Oldest Poems in Pashto", *Afghanistan* 1 (Kabul, 1946).
64. Emadi (2010), p. 50.
65. Muhammad Gul Nūrī, *Millī Hindāra* (Kabul: ʿUmūmī Matbaʿa, 1318/1939). See James Caron, "Reading the Power of Printed Orality in Afghanistan: Popular Pashto Literature as Historical Evidence and Public Intervention", *Journal of Social History* 45, 1 (2011), p. 178.
66. ʿAbdullāh Afghānī Navīs, *Afghān Qāmūs* (Kabul: Paxtō Tōlana, 1957–58).
67. ʿAbd al-Hayy Habībī, *Da Pashtō Adabiyyātō Tārīkh* (Kabul: Paxtō Tōlana, 1963). Also Caron (2011), pp. 177–8.
68. Emadi (2010), pp. 67–8.
69. Faridullah Bezhan, "Ideology/Politics and Literature in Afghanistan*:* Assadullah Habib and his Narrative Works", *Transcultural Studies* 2–3 (2006–2007) and Nancy Hatch Dupree, "The Conscription of Afghan Writers: An Aborted Experiment in Socialist Realism", *Central Asian Survey* 4, 4 (1985).
70. Henry S. Bradsher, *Afghan Communism and Soviet Intervention* (New York: Oxford University Press. 1999), p. 5.
71. Bradsher (1999), pp. 10–12.
72. Jiří Bečka, "Young Afghan Prose in Dari", *Afghanistan Journal* 5, 3 (1978).
73. Rolf Bindemann, "Hazara Research and Hazara Nationalism, 1978–89", in Noelle-Karimi et al (2002), p. 81.
74. Mir Hekmatullah Sadat, "The Afghan Experience Reflected in Modern Afghan Fiction (1900–1992)", *Comparative Studies of South Asia, Africa and the Middle East* 28, 2 (2008), p. 307.

75. On the Defoe translation, see Sadat (2008), 297. I have been unable to verify the publication in the list of early Afghan editions provided in Rahīn (2003), pp. 3–16.
76. See Nushin Arbabzadah's chapter in this volume and Senzil Nawid, "Political Advocacy in Early Twentieth Century Afghan Persian Poetry", *Afghanistan Studies Journal* 3 (1992).
77. Ahmadi (2008), p. 56.
78. See the booksellers' advertisements in the newspapers *Sirāj al-Akhbār* year 2, vol. 17 (1292/1913), 16 and *Anīs* vol. 5, no. 31 (1310/1931), 11. Thanks to Nushin Arbabzadah for this reference.
79. Sadat (2008), p. 296.
80. Faridullah Bezhan, "A Woman of Afghanistan: *A Warning Portrait*, Afghanistan's First Novel", *Critique: Critical Middle Eastern Studies* 15, 2 (2006).
81. Sirdar M.A.K. Effendi, *Royals and Royal Mendicants (A Tragedy of the Afghan History, 1791–1947)* (Lahore: Lion Press, n.d. 1948), p. 244.
82. Effendi (n.d.), pp. 242–340.
83. Effendi (n.d.), pp. 250–63.
84. Ralph Russell, "The Development of the Modern Novel in Urdu", in T.W. Clark (ed.), *The Novel in India: Its Birth and Development* (Berkeley: University of California Press, 1970), pp. 110–22.
85. Ahmadi (2008), pp. 57–8.
86. Sadat (2008), p. 297.
87. Nile Green, "The Trans-Border Traffic of Afghan Modernism: Afghanistan and the Indian 'Urdusphere'", *Comparative Studies in Society and History* 53, 3 (2011).
88. Alessandro Bausani, *Le letterature del Pakistan e dell'Afghanistan* (Milan: Edizioni Accademia, 1968), p. 271.
89. Mahmūd Tarzī, *Zhulidah: Ash'ār* (Istanbul: s.n., 1933).
90. Ahmed Ateş & Abdülvehhab Tarzi, *Farsca Grameri* (Istanbul: Bozkurt Matbaası, 1942–5).
91. Schinasi (1979), p. 57, note 31.
92. Ahmadi (2008), pp. 76–9.
93. David B. Edwards, "Summoning Muslims: Print, Politics, and Religious Ideology in Afghanistan", *Journal of Asian Studies* 53, 3 (1993) and *idem.*, "Words in the Balance: The Poetics of Political Dissent in Afghanistan", in Dale F. Eickelman (ed.), *Russia's Muslim Frontiers: New Directions in Cross-Cultural Analysis* (Bloomington: Indiana University Press, 1993).
94. Günter Hirt & Sascha Wonders (eds), *Präprintium: Moskauer Bücher aus dem Samizdat* (Bremen: Temmen, 1998).
95. Ahmadi (2008), p. 119, p. 125 and Malekyar (2008), p. 101.
96. Ahmadi (2008), pp. 134–9.

97. On currents of exile literature, see Wali Ahmadi, "Intertextual Influences and Intracultural Contacts: History and Memory in the Poetry of Akhavan-sales and Wasef Bakhtari", in Ahmad Karimi-Hakkak & Kamran Talattof (eds.), *Essays on Nima Yushij: Animating Modernism in Persian Poetry* (Leiden: Brill, 2004).
98. Angela Parvanta, "Bacha-ye Saqqa'—Afghan Robin Hood or Bandit? Khalil-Allah Khalili's Revision of the Events of 1929", in Charles Melville (ed.), *Proceedings of the Third European Conference of Iranian Studies*, Part 2 (Wiesbaden: Ludwig Reichert, 1999).
99. On the cultural and social position of these refugees, see Pierre Centlivres & Micheline Centlivres-Demont, "The Afghan Refugee in Pakistan: An Ambiguous Identity", *Journal of Refugee Studies* 1, 2 (1988) and Diane Tober, "'My Body is Broken Like my Country': Identity, Nation, and Repatriation among Afghan Refugees in Iran", *Iranian Studies* 40, 2 (2007).
100. Homayrā Qādirī, *Gūshvāra-ye Anīs: Majmūʻa-ye Dāstān* (Tehran: Nashr-e Rūzgār, 1387/2009).
101. See e.g. the poetry anthology ʻAbd al-Qayūm Malikzād (ed.), *Bahār dar Āyina-ye Kalām-e Nakhsūrān-e Muʻāsir-e Afghānistān*, *Rāh-e Nayistān* 3 (Bahār 1387 h.s/Spring 2008).
102. Mir Tamim Ansary, *West of Kabul, East of New York: An Afghan-American Story* (New York: Farrar, Straus and Giroux, 2002); Muhammad Hasan Sharq, *Karbāspūsh-hā-ye Barahna Pā: Rāz-hā-ye Nahufta, Jaryānāt-e Pusht-e Parda va Inkishāfāt-e Takān Dahanda, 1310–1370 H.Sh.* (Peshawar: Sabā Kitābkhāna, 1994); Mullā ʻAbd al-Salām Zaʻīf, *Da Gwāntānāmū Andzwar* (Peshawar: s.n., 2006).
103. Sediqa Massoud, Chékéba Hachemi & Marie-Françoise Colombani, *Pour l'Amour de Massoud* (Paris: XO Editions, 2005); translated by Afsar Afshārī as *Ahmad Shāh Masʻūd: Rawāyāt-e Sidīqa Masʻūd* (Tehran: Nashr-e Markaz, 2009).
104. Fariba Nawa, *Opium Nation: Child Brides, Drug Lords, and One Woman's Journey through Afghanistan* (New York: HarperCollins, 2011) and Shabibi Shah, *Where do I Belong?* (London: Longstone Books, 2001).
105. An Afghan edition of *The Kite Runner* has, however, been published as: *Gudīparānbāz*, trans. Zībā Ganjī & Parīsā Sulaymānzāda (Kabul: Shirkat-e Kitāb-e Shāh Muhammad, 1386/2007).

2. MODERNIZING, NATIONALIZING, INTERNATIONALIZING: HOW MAHMUD TARZI'S HYBRID IDENTITY TRANSFORMED AFGHAN LITERATURE

1. Vartan Gregorian, "Mahmud Tarzi and *Siraj al-Akhbar*: Ideology of Nationalism and Modernization in Afghanistan", *Middle East Journal* 12, 3 (1967) and May Schinasi, *Afghanistan at the Beginning of the Twentieth Century: National-*

ism and Journalism in Afghanistan: A Study of Seraj ul-Akhbar (1911–1918) (Naples: Istituto Universitario Orientale, 1979).
2. Muhammad Akbar Sanā Ghaznavī, *Tārīkh-e Adabiyāt-e Darī* (Kabul: Maiwand Publishing, 2006), p. 317.
3. Chaled Malekyar, *Das Bild Afghanistans im 20 Jahrhundert: Das Werk des Schriftstellers und Diplomaten Ostad Abdol Rahman Pazhwak (1919–1995)* (Berlin: Klaus Schwartz, 2008).
4. Ashraf Ghani, "Literature as Politics: The Case of Mahmud Tarzi", *Afghanistan* 29, 3 (1976).
5. Schinasi (1979) and Gul Ahmad Shīfta, "Shi'r-e Navīn", *Āryānā-ye Birūn Marzī* 5, 2 (2003), p. 63.
6. For Tarzi's account of the period, see Mahmud Tarzi, *Reminiscences: A Short History of an Era (1869–1881)*, trans. & ed. Wahid Tarzi (New York: Afghanistan Forum, 1998).
7. Mahmūd Tarzī, *Sīyāhat Dar Se Qat'a Rū-ye Zamīn Dar 29 Rūz: Āsyā, Urūpā, Afrīqā* (Travels through Three Parts of the World in 29 Days: Europe, Asia, Africa) (Kabul: 'Ināyat Press, 1308/1929), p. 248.
8. Ernst Johannes Kläy, "Endstation 'Islambol': Die Türkei als Asylland für muslimische Glaubensflüchtlings und Rückwanderer (*muhacir*) im 19. und 20. Jahrundert", in Micheline Centlivres-Demont (ed.), *Migrations en Asie* (Berne: Société Suisse d'Ethnologie, 1983) and Kemal H. Karpat, "Muslim Migration", in Kemal H. Karpat (ed.), *Studies on Ottoman Social and Political History: Selected Articles and Essays* (Leiden: Brill, 2002).
9. Tarzī (1308/1929), p. 211.
10. On being fluent in Arabic and Turkish and at ease in Alexandria, see respectively Tarzī (1308/1929), p. 249 and Tarzī (1308/1929), p. 320.
11. Tarzī (1308/1929), p. 653.
12. Tarzī (1308/1929), p. 310.
13. Tarzī (1308/1929), p. 334.
14. Matti Moosa, *The Origins of Modern Arabic Fiction* (Washington: Three Continents Press, 1983), p. 91.
15. Tarzi (1308/1929), p. 146.
16. 'Abd al-Rasūl Rahīn, "Talī'a-ye Matbū'āt dar Afghānistān", *Āryānā-ye Birūn Marzī* 1, 2 (1999/2000).
17. On 'Abd al-Ra'uf's education, see Ghaznavī (2006), p. 315.
18. *Sirāj al-Akhbār*, year 1, no. 1 (1290/1911), p. 12.
19. *Sirāj al-Akhbār*, year 1, no. 2 (1291/1912), p. 7.
20. *Sirāj al-Akhbār*, year 1, no. 2 (1291/1912), p. 8.
21. Tarzī (1308/1929), pp. 161–4, pp. 169–70.
22. Typographic print was also used for printing state decrees and official communications. See Mīr Ghulām Muhammad Ghubār, *Tārīkh-e Adabiyāt-e Afghānistān: Dawrah-ye Muhammad Zā'ī-hā* (Peshawar: Ārash, 1378/1999), p. 144.

23. *Sirāj al-Akhbār*, year 4, no. 20 (1294/1915), p. 8.
24. Benjamin C. Fortna, *Imperial Classroom: Islam, the State and Education in the Late Ottoman Empire* (Oxford: Oxford University Press, 2002).
25. *Sirāj al-Akhbār*, year 2, no. 7 (1291/1912), p. 11.
26. *Sirāj al-Akhbār*, year 2, no. 2 (1291/1912), p. 13.
27. *Sirāj al-Akhbār*, year 2, no. 7 (1291/1912), p. 13.
28. *Sirāj al-Akhbār*, year 5, no. 2 (1294/1915), p. 2.
29. *Sirāj al-Akhbār*, year 1, no. 1 (1290/1911), p. 12.
30. *Sirāj al-Akhbār*, year 1, no. 1 (1290/1911), p. 10.
31. *Sirāj al-Akhbār*, year 5, no. 2 (1294/1915), p. 2.
32. *Ibid.*
33. *Ibid.*
34. Mahmud Tarzī (1308/1929), p. 295.
35. *Sirāj al-Akhbār*, year 5, no. 2 (1294/1915), p. 2.
36. *Ibid.*
37. *Sirāj al-Akhbār*, year 2, no. 1 (1291/1912), p. 2.
38. *Ibid.*
39. Ghaznavī (2006), p. 331.
40. *Sirāj al-Akhbār*, year 1, no. 1 (1290/1911), p. 3.
41. *Ibid.*
42. *Sirāj al-Akhbār*, year 4, no. 20 (1294/1915), p. 17.
43. *Sirāj al-Akhbār*, year 4, no. 20 (1294/1915), p. 7.
44. *Sirāj al-Akhbār*, year 4, no. 20 (1294/1915), p. 8.
45. *Ibid.*
46. *Sirāj al-Akhbār*, year 2, no. 2 (1294/1915), p. 14.
47. Mīr Ghulām Muhammad Ghubār, *Tārīkh-e Adabiyāt-e Afghānistān: Dawrah-ye Muhammad Zā'ī-hā* (Peshawar: Ārash, 1378/1999).
48. *Sirāj al-Akhbār*, year 4, no. 3 (1293/1914), p. 9.
49. *Sirāj al-Akhbār*, year 1, no. 10 (1290/1911), 9 [Urdu poem]; *ibid.*, year 2, no. 8 (1291/1912), p. 12 (translated Bengali poem).
50. For details of Tarzi's circle of political poets, see Ghaznavī (2006), p. 298.
51. Wali Ahmadi, *Modern Literature of Afghanistan: Anomalous Visions of History and Form* (New York: Routledge, 2008), chapter 1.
52. *Sirāj al-Akhbār*, year 1, no. 13 (1291/1912), p. 6.
53. *Sirāj al-Akhbār*, year 1, no. 10 (1291/1912), p. 13.
54. *Sirāj al-Akhbār*, year 1, no. 17 (1291/1912), p. 14.
55. *Ibid.*
56. *Ibid.*
57. Mahmūd Tarzī, *Zhūlīdah: Ash'ār* (Istanbul: s.n., 1933).

3. THE AFGHAN AFTERLIFE OF PHILEAS FOGG: SPACE AND TIME IN THE LITERATURE OF AFGHAN TRAVEL

1. David Spurr, *The Rhetoric of Empire: Colonial Discourse in Journalism, Travel Writing, and Imperial Administration* (Durham: Duke University Press, 1993). For fuller discussion of external criticism of Afghanistan's modernization, see Nick Cullather, "Damming Afghanistan: Modernization in a Buffer State", *Journal of American History* 89, 2 (2002).
2. Lieut.-Col. Sir Alexander Burnes, *Cabool: A Personal Narrative of a Journey to, and Residence in that City, in the Years 1836, 7, and 8* (London: J. Murray, 1842), Charles Edward Yate, *Northern Afghanistan: or Letters from the Afghan Boundary Commission* (London: Blackwood, 1888), Eric Newby, *A Short Walk in the Hindu Kush* (London: Secker, 1958), Rory Stewart, *The Places in Between* (London: Picador, 2004).
3. Marcus Schadl, "The Man Outside: The Problem with the External Perception of Afghanistan in Historical Sources", *ASIEN* 104 (2007). On Afghanistan in European fiction, see Robert Nash, "Fictional views of Afghanistan" *Afghanistan Studies Journal* 5 (1997).
4. The newspaper articles have been collected in Annemarie Schwarzenbach, *Alle Wege sind offen: die Reise nach Afghanistan 1939/1940* (Basel: Lenos, 2000). Ella Maillart, *The Cruel Way* (London: W. Heinemann, 1947). Also Dominique Miermont, *Annemarie Schwarzenbach ou le mal d'Europe, Biographie* (Paris: Payout, 2004). On the centrality of travel to literary modernism, see Dennis Porter, "Modernism and the Dream of Travel", in Michael Hanne (ed.), *Literature and Travel* (Amsterdam: Rodopi, 1993).
5. Nicolas Bouvier, *L'Usage du monde* (Geneva: Droz, 1963).
6. Max Eiselin, *Wilder Hindukusch: Erlebnisse in Afghanistan und dem zweithöchsten Gebirge der Erde* (Zurich: Orell Füssli, 1963). Cf. Jean-Jacques Rousseau, *Les rêveries du promeneur solitaire*, ed. Marcel Raymond (Geneva: Librairie Droz, 1967).
7. Hans Queling, *Adler, Berge und Menschen: mit Flugzeug und Karawane in die unbekannte gewaltige Gebirgswelt Afghanistans* (Radebeul: Neumann, 1958).
8. Mary Louise Pratt, *Imperial Eyes: Travel Writing and Transculturation* (Abingdon: Routledge, 1992) and David Spurr (1993).
9. Patrick Holland & Graham Huggan, "Varieties of Nostalgia in Contemporary Travel Writing", in Glenn Hooper & Tim Youngs (eds), *Perspectives on Travel Writing* (Aldershot: Ashgate Publishing, Ltd., 2004).
10. J.-P. Ferrier, *Voyages en Perse, dans l'Afghanistan, le Bélouchistan et le Turkestan*, 2 vols. (Paris: E. Dentu, 1860) and Charles Masson, *Narrative of Various Journeys in Balochistan, Afghanistan, the Panjab, & Kalât, During a Residence in those Countries*, 4 vols. (London: Richard Bentley, 1844).

11. Annick Fenet, *Documents d'archéologie militante: La mission Foucher en Afghanistan (1922–1925)* (Paris: Academie des Inscriptions et Belles-Lettres, 2010).
12. See e.g. *Recherches archeologiques a ; Begram; chantier no. 2 (1937) par J. Hackin, avec la collaboration de madame J.R. Hackin* (Paris: Les Editions d'art et d'histoire, 1939) and J.-J. Barthoux, *Les fouilles de Hadda* (Paris: Les Editions d'art et d'histoire, 1930).
13. Robert Byron, *The Road to Oxiana* (London: Macmillan, 1937). See also Robert Byron, "The Shrine of Khvaja Abu Nasr Parsa at Balkh", *Bulletin of the American Institute for Persian Art and Archaeology* 4/1 (1935) and *idem*., "Islamic Architecture. K. Tīmūrid. (a) General Trends", in A.U. Pope & P. Ackerman (eds.), *A Survey of Persian Art from Prehistoric Times to the Present* (New York, 1939).
14. Arnold Toynbee, *Between Oxus and Jumna* (London: Oxford University Press, 1961), pp. 51–6.
15. Toynbee (1961), p. 52.
16. Peter Levi, *The Light Garden of the Angel King: Journeys in Afghanistan* (Harmondsworth: Penguin, 1984).
17. Tadao Umesao, *Mogōruzoku Tankenki* (Tokyo: Iwanami Shoten, 1956).
18. Among the many Michaud publications, see Roland & Sabrina Michaud, *Afghanistan* (London: Thames & Hudson, 1990) and *idem*., *The Orient in a Mirror* (New York: Abrams, 2004).
19. Casey Blanton, *Travel Writing: The Self and the World* (London: Routledge, 2002).
20. Raja Mahendrapratapa, *My Life Story of Fifty Five Years, December 1886 to December 1941* (Dehradun: World Federation, 1947), pp. 42–61 and 'Ubaydullāh Sindhī, *Kābul men Sāt Sāl, Aktūbar 1915–1922: Ek Tārīkhī Yāddāsht*, ed. Muhammad Sarvar (Lahore: Sindh Sāgar Akādmī, 1976).
21. Larisa Reišner, *Oktober: ausgewählte Schriften*, ed. Karl Radek (Berlin: Neuer Deutscher Verlag, 1930), pp. 309–440. Also Alla Zeide, "Larisa Reisner: Myth as Justification for Life", *Russian Review* 51, 2 (1992).
22. Nile Green, "The Trans-Border Traffic of Afghan Modernism: Afghanistan and the Indian 'Urdusphere'", *Comparative Studies in Society and History* 53, 3 (2011). Note that for the transliteration of names and other words from Urdu, the *vav* is rendered as w to reflect Urdu pronunciation.
23. Sayyid Sulaymān Nadwī, *Sayr-e Afghānistān* (Lahore: Sang-e Mīl, 2008), especially pp. 11–12 and pp. 38–41. A short version of the travelogue was first published in the Urdu journal, *Ma'ārif*, vol. 10 (December 1933).
24. *Payām-e Mashriq* and *Musāfir* are printed in Muhammad Iqbāl, *Maykada-ye Lāhūr: Kulliyāt-e Fārsī-ye 'Allāma Iqbāl*, ed. Muhammad Baqā'ī (Tehran: Iqbāl, 1382/2003), pp. 129–234 and pp. 489–504.
25. Nile Green, "The Road to Kabul: Automobiles and Afghan Internationalism,

1900–1940", in Magnus Marsden & Benjamin Hopkins (eds), *Beyond Swat: History, Society and Economy along the Afghanistan-Pakistan Frontier* (New York: Columbia University Press, 2012). Also Patrick Clawson, "Knitting Iran Together: The Land Transport Revolution, 1920–1940", *Iranian Studies* 26, 3–4 (1993) and E. Caspani & E. Cafnacci, *Afghanistan, crocevia dell'Asia* (Milano: A. Vallardi, 1951), pp. 211–14.
26. On this period, see Leon B. Poullada, *Reform and Rebellion in Afghanistan, 1919–1929: King Amanullah's Failure to Modernize a Tribal Society* (Ithaca: Cornell University Press, 1973) and May Schinasi, *Afghanistan at the Beginning of the Twentieth Century: Nationalism and Journalism in Afghanistan: A Study of Seraj ul-Akhbar (1911–1918)* (Naples: Istituto Universitario Orientale, 1979).
27. Nadwī (2008), p. 9.
28. A.C. Jewett, *An American Engineer in Afghanistan, From the Letters and Notes of A. C. Jewett*, ed. Marjorie Jewett Bell (Minneapolis: University of Minnesota Press, 1948).
29. Queling (1958).
30. Jason Elliot, *An Unexpected Light: Travels in Afghanistan* (London: Picador, 1999) and Stewart (2004).
31. Burhān al-Dīn Khān Kushkakī, *Rāhnamā-ye Qataghan va Badakhshān: ya'nī Mulakhkhas-e Safarnāma-ye Sana-ye 1301 H. Sh. Sipahsālār-e Ghāzī Sardār Muhammad Nādir Khān Vazīr-e Harbiya* (Kabul: Vizārat-e Harbiya, 1302/1923), translated by Marguerite Reut as Mawlavi Burhān al-Dīn Khān Kushkakī, *Qataghan et Badakhshân: Description du pays d'après l'inspection d'un ministre afghan en 1922* (Paris: Éditions du CNRS, 1979), 3 vols.
32. Jalāl al-Dīn Siddīqī, *Bā Sarzamīn-e Nūristān Āshnā Shavīd* (Kabul: Da Kitāb Chāpawulo Mu'assisah, n.d.) and Sūfī Pāyanda Muhammad Kūshān, *Bā Kābul-e Qadīm Āshnā Shavīd* (Peshawar: Markaz-e Nashrāt-e Sa'īd, 1384/2006).
33. 'Abd al-Akbar Khān Akbar, *Da Rūsī Turkistān aw Afghānistān Safarnāmah: da Mulk da Āzaday Pah Silsilah Kshe* (Peshawar: Akbar Buk Stāl, 1968) and Amīr Hamzah Shinwārī, *Da Hijāz Pah Lor* (Peshawar: Shāhen Barqī Pres, 1970).
34. Sidīqullāh Rixtīn, *Da Hind Safar* (Kabul: Paxtō Tōlāna, 1334/1955).
35. William Butcher, *Verne's Journey to the Centre of the Self: Space and Time in the Voyages Extraordinaires* (London: Macmillan, 1990).
36. Christoph Herzog & Raoul Motika, "Orientalism 'Alla Turca': Late 19th/Early 20th Century Ottoman Voyages into the Muslim 'Outback'", *Die Welt des Islams* 40, 2 (2000), pp. 156–7.
37. Jules Verne (trans. Mahmud Tarzi), *Siyāhat bar Dawr-e Kurrah-ye Zamīn bih-Hashtād Rūz* [*Le tour du monde en quatre-vingts jours*, 1873] (Kabul: Matba'a-ye 'Ināyat, 1330/1912); *ibid.*, *Siyāhat dar Javv-e Havā* [*Robur-le-Conquérant*, 1886] (Kabul: Matba'a-ye 'Ināyat, 1331/1913), *ibid.*, *Jazīrah-e Penhān* [*L'Île mystérieuse*, 1874] (Kabul: Matba'a-ye 'Ināyat, 1332/1914), *ibid.*, *Bīst Hazār*

Farsakh Siyāhat dar Zīr-e Bahr [*Vingt mille lieues sous les mers*, 1869]) (Kabul: Matbaʿa-ye ʿInāyat, 1332/1914).
38. Louis Dupree, *Afghanistan* (Princeton: Princeton University Press, 1973), p. 439.
39. "Yekdō Sukhan dar Bāb-e Tabʿ-e Ketāb", in Jules Verne (trans. Mahmud Tarzi) (1331/1913), pp. 2–5.
40. *Sirāj al-Akhbār* year 2, no. 20 (1292/1913), back cover and front cover. Thanks to Nushin Arbabzadah for this and all other references to *Sirāj al-Akhbār*.
41. *Sirāj al-Akhbār* year 1, no. 8 (1290/1911), p. 11.
42. Helena Heroldova, "Glass Submarines and Electric Balloons: Creating Scientific and Technical Vocabulary in Chinese Science Fiction", in Michael Lackner & Natascha Vittinghoff (eds), *Mapping Meanings: The Field of New Learning in Late Qing China* (Leiden: Brill, 2004).
43. Mahmūd Tarzī, *Sīyāhat Dar Se Qatʿa Rū-ye Zamīn Dar 29 Rūz: Āsyā, Urūpā, Afrīqā* [Travels through Three Parts of the World in 29 Days: Europe, Asia, Africa] 3 vols (Kabul: Matbaʿa-ye Mubāraka-ye ʿInāyat, 1333/1915).
44. Joseph Farrell, "The Age of Icarus: The Adventure of Flight in Gabriele D'Annunzio and Lauro de Bosis", in Hanne (1993).
45. Cf. Afshin Marashi, "Performing the Nation: The Official Visit of Reza Shah to Kemalist Turkey, June-July 1934", Stephanie Cronin (ed.), *Iran under Reza Shah* (London: Routledge, 2003).
46. On Habibullah Khan's knowledge of Urdu, see the 1911 letter of his engineer in Jewett (1948), p. 25.
47. Khāksār Nādir ʿAlī, *Al-Habīb, jis-mēn Aʿlā-Hazrat Hiz Majestī Amīr Habībullāh Khān kē Sayr ū Siyāhat-e Hindustān kē Wāqaʿāt* (Agra: Sādiq Husayn, n.d. [c.1908]) and Mawlānā Zāhid al-Qādirī, *Aʿlā-Hazrat Shāh Amānullāh Khān Ghāzī Tājdār-e Afghānistān kā Safarnāma*, 2 vols (Delhi: Qurēshī Buk Depō, 1928).
48. Khāksār Nādir ʿAlī, *Mirʾāt al-ʿArab* (Agra: Khwāja Sadīq Husayn, n.d.) and *idem.*, *Wāqaʿāt-e Hijāz* (Agra: Khwāja Sadīq Husayn, n.d.).
49. G.F. Abbott, *Through India with the Prince* (London: Edward Arnold, 1906).
50. Hājjī Muhammad Khān, *Zikr-e Shāh-e Islām* (Delhi: Matbaʿa-ye Nizāmī, n.d. 1907).
51. On the diplomatic background, see Ludwig W. Adamec, *Afghanistan's Foreign Affairs to the Mid-Twentieth Century; Relations with the USSR, Germany, and Britain* (Tucson: University of Arizona Press, 1974), chapter 1.
52. Khāksār Nādir ʿAlī (n.d.), pp. 43–52.
53. Khāksār Nādir ʿAlī (n.d.), p. 35.
54. E.g. Khāksār Nādir ʿAlī (n.d.), p. 35, p. 41, p. 43, p. 50, p. 56, p. 57, p. 62, p. 71, p. 77, p. 80.
55. Khāksār Nādir ʿAlī (n.d.), p. 68.
56. Khāksār Nādir ʿAlī (n.d.), p. 74.

57. Khāksār Nādir 'Alī (n.d.), p. 76.
58. Khāksār Nādir 'Alī (n.d.), p. 64, p. 70.
59. For more details, see Green (2012).
60. E. Alexander Powell, "A Modern Magic Carpet", *The Century Magazine* 104, 2 (1922), 204. On the gift of the cars, see Jewett (1948), p. 24 and p. 225.
61. E. Alexander Powell, *By Camel and Car to the Peacock Throne: Syria, Palestine, Transjordania, Arabia, Iraq, Persia* (New York: Century Co., 1923).
62. Jewett (1948), p. 219 (letter dated 1914).
63. Cf. Jeremy Prestholdt, *Domesticating the World: African Consumerism and the Genealogies of Globalization* (Berkeley: University of California Press, 2008).
64. Khāksār Nādir 'Alī (n.d.), pp. 66–7, p. 69, p. 75, p. 78.
65. Khāksār Nādir 'Alī (n.d.), pp. 64–5, pp. 67–8.
66. Khāksār Nādir 'Alī (n.d.), p. 59.
67. On the direct links between these projects and the tour of India, see Jewett (1948), p. 22, p. 24, p. 122, p. 170, pp. 218–26.
68. On the tour in its diplomatic and strategic context, see Adamec (1974), pp. 113–31.
69. Mawlānā Zāhid al-Qādirī (1928), 64–5. This and all subsequent references refer to volume 1, which contains the travelogue itself.
70. Mawlānā Zāhid al-Qādirī (1928), pp. 74–82.
71. Mawlānā Zāhid al-Qādirī (1928), p. 89.
72. Mawlānā Zāhid al-Qādirī (1928), p. 92.
73. Mawlānā Zāhid al-Qādirī (1928), pp. 101–2.
74. Mawlānā Zāhid al-Qādirī (1928), p. 113.
75. On the train naming, see Lutz Peter Koepnick, *Framing Attention: Windows on Modern German Culture* (Baltimore: Johns Hopkins University Press, 2007), p. 134.
76. On the short Dar al-Aman railway, see Paul E. Waters, *Afghanistan: A Railway History* (Bromley: P.E. Waters & Associates, 2002), pp. 27–33.
77. Mawlānā Zāhid al-Qādirī (1928), pp. 5–6.
78. Mawlānā Zāhid al-Qādirī (1928), p. 7, p. 47, p. 87, p. 112.
79. Byron (1937), Mawlānā Zāhid al-Qādirī (1928), 138.
80. Mawlānā Zāhid al-Qādirī (1928), pp. 16–17, pp. 61–2.
81. Mawlānā Zāhid al-Qādirī (1928), pp. 111–12.
82. Mawlānā Zāhid al-Qādirī (1928), pp. 95–6.
83. Mawlānā Zāhid al-Qādirī (1928), p. 109.
84. Mawlānā Zāhid al-Qādirī (1928), pp. 110–11.
85. Mawlānā Zāhid al-Qādirī (1928), pp. 16.
86. Mawlānā Zāhid al-Qādirī (1928), p. 2. Also p. 20, p. 93.
87. *Idem.*
88. Mawlānā Zāhid al-Qādirī (1928), p. 123.

4. DEMARCATING PASHTO: CROSS-BORDER PASHTO LITERATURE AND THE AFGHAN STATE, 1880–1930

1. See Nile Green, "Tribe, Diaspora and Sainthood in Afghan History", *Journal of Asian Studies* 67, 1 (2008) and Robert Nichols, *A History of Pashtun Migration* (Karachi: Oxford University Press, 2008).
2. Sergei Andreyev, "Pashto Literature: The Classical Period" in Philip G. Kreyenbroek & Ulrich Marzolph (eds.), *Oral Literature of Iranian Languages: Kurdish, Pashto, Balochi, Ossetic; Persian and Tajik*, Companion Volume 2 (London: I.B. Tauris, 2010), p. 90.
3. See D.N. Mackenzie "Pashto Verse", *BOAS* 31(1958), pp. 319–33.
4. Andreyev (2010), p. 92.
5. H.G. Raverty, *Selections from the Poetry of the Afghans* (London: Williams and Norgate, 1868), pp. 197–8.
6. I am indebted to Professor M. A. Ziyār for his insights on this issue.
7. Raverty (1868), pp. 226–7.
8. See Andreyev (2010) 104–07 for an account of one such "orthodox" Pashto writer, and bitter rival of Bāyezīd Ansāri, Ākhund Darvēza.
9. D.N. Mackenzie, *Poems from the Divan of Khushāl Khān Khattak* (London: Allen and Unwin, 1965), p. 13.
10. For a discussion of these folk traditions see Ghulām Jīlāni Jalāli, *Da Paxtō Zantanēy Adab aw Mūsīqi* (Kabul: Paxtō Tōlana, 1360/1981), pp. 41–50.
11. For the militarization of religious authority during the period, see Sana Haroon, *Frontier of Faith: Islam in the Indo-Afghan Borderland* (London: Hurst, 2007), ch. 3 esp., pp. 85–90.
12. Cf. Nasr Allāh Nāsir, *Da Xkārandū'ī Ghōri par Qasīdē Mushā'ira*, ed. Gul Pacha Ulfat (Kabul: Da Afghānistān da Ulūmō Akādēmī, 1383/2004), 5 for a discussion of the apprenticeship system, as well as one of the few histories of *musha'ira* poetry; on the long-distance travel of Pashto songs see Darmesteter (1887), 3 in which he describes the circulation of one Pashto song, "Zakhme", as far as Uttar Pradesh and Hyderabad.
13. *Ibid.*, p. 4.
15. Darmesteter (1888), pp. 30–1.
16. Darmesteter (1888), p. 38.
17. Darmesteter (1887), p. 16.
18. Benedicte Grima, "The Performance of Emotion among Paxtun Women", *Modern Middle East Series* 17 (Austin: University of Texas Press, 1992), p. 147.
19. Abubakar Siddique, "A Review of Pashto Language and Literature", *Middle East Studies Occasional Paper*, No. 2 (Quantico: Marine Corps University Press, forthcoming), p. 22.
20. Darmesteter (1888), pp. 64–7.
21. *Ibid.*, p. 36.

22. Darmesteter (1887), p. 22.
23. *Ibid.*
24. See Shah Mahmoud Hanifi, *Connecting Histories in Afghanistan: Market Relations and State Formation on a Colonial Frontier* (New York: Columbia University Press, 2008) for a discussion of the Afghan economy and its relation to British India during the period.
25. H.G. Raverty, *A Grammar of the Pukhto, Pushtu or the Language of the Afghans* (Calcutta: Baptist Mission Press 1855), p. 34.
26. Quoted in *ibid.*
27. V.V. Kushev, "The Dawn of Pashtun Linguistics: Early Grammatical and Lexicographical Works and Their Manuscripts", *Manuscripta Orientalia* 7, 2 (2001), p. 8.
28. For discussions of popular printing in nineteenth-century British India, see Frances. W. Pritchett, *Marvellous Encounters: Qissa Literature in Urdu and Hindi* (Maryland: the Riverdale Company, 1985). For Pashto chapbooks see Wilma W. Heston, "Pashto Chapbooks, Gendered Imagery and Cross-cultural Contact", in Cathy Lynn Preston & Michael J. Preston (eds.), *The Other Print Tradition: Chapbooks, Broadsides, and Related Ephemera* (New York: Garland Publishing, 1995).
29. Heston (1995), p. 151.
30. Niyāzī mentions that two books were published in Pashto during 'Abd al-Rahman's reign—a book of sermons by Ghulām Jān Afghānī and a version of Yūsuf and Zolaykhā. Cf. Shahsawār Sangarwāl Niyāzī, *Da Paxtō Adabiyātō Muʾāṣar Tārīkh* (Peshawar: Dānesh 1997), p. 317. There is, however, just one Pashto document extant from 'Abd al-Rahman's reign, and it is a copy of the minutes of a meeting he had with Lord Dufferin in 1885, also transcribed in Persian. Ghulām Jān Laqmānī, *Suʾāl wa Jawāb-e Dawlatī va Band va Bast Saltanatī Muʾallafahu da Mullā Ghulām Jān Lamqānī Paxtō Nivīs* (Kabul: Dār al-Saltanah, 1303/1886), accessible online at http://hdl.handle.net/2333.1/9s4mw6qk.
31. Mir Munshi Sultan Mahomed Khan (ed.), *The Life of Abdur Rahman: Amir of Afghanista*n (London: John Murray, 1900).
32. *Sirāj al-Akhbār*, year 3, no. 20, 11, 13.
33. For a discussion of one such prominent lineage, the Akhundzādas, see James Caron, "Cultural Histories of Pashtun Nationalism" (Ph.D. dissertation, University of Pennsylvania, 2009), p. 23.
34. For a detailed account of the return of such exiles, see Fayz Muhammad Katib, Siraj al-Tawarikh, Jilte Chaharom, (Kabul: Intisharat ex Amiri 2001), especially part 2.
35. *Ibid.*, pp. 23–48.
36. For biographical information on these men, I have relied on Zelmāī Hēwādmal, *Farhang-e Zabān va Adabiyāt-e Paxtō* (Kabul: Riyāsat-e Tāʾlīf va Tarjume-ye Vizārat-e Taʾlīm va Tarbīya, 1356//1976).

37. Quoted in M.A. Ziyār, "Pa Sirāj al-Akhbār ke da Paxtō Wanda", in Muhyī al-Dīn Afghān, *Da Ghulām Muhyī al-Dīn Afghān Afkār aw Āsār* (Kabul: Kabul University, 1360/1980), p. 3.
38. Niyāzī (1997), p. 278.
39. The term is Caron's (2009), p. 55.
40. Quoted in Ziyār (1980), p. 3.
41. *Sirāj al-Akhbār*, year 5, no. 2, p. 7.
42. Quoted in Ziyār (1980), pp. 5–6.
43. *Ibid.*, pp. 90–6.
44. *Sirāj al-Akhbār*, year 5, no. 4, pp. 7–8.
45. See ʿAbd al-Dāwī's poem in *Sirāj al-Akhbār*, year 5, no. 2, pp. 7–8.
46. *Ibid.*
47. *Sirāj al-Akhbār*, year 2, no. 9, pp. 9–12.
48. Quoted in Ziyār (1980), p. 8.
49. Sālih Muhammad Qandahārī, *Lumra Kitāb da Pashtō, Yaʿnī Kitāb-e Avval-e Afghānī* (Kabul: Matbaʿa-ye Māshīnkhāna, 1335/1916), accessible online at the Afghanistan Digital Library http://hdl.handle.net/2333.1/66t1g1.
50. Quoted in Ziyār (1980), p. 4.
51. *Ibid.*, 5.
52. On the key role of Mullas in disseminating this information, particularly by reading out newspapers at mosques, see Haroon (2007), pp. 72–3.
53. Caron (2009), p. 45.
54. For a discussion of the role of Pashto language textbooks in Pashto literary development, see A. Gerasimova & G. Girs, *Literatura Afganistana: Kratkiy ocherk* (Moscow: Izdatelstvo vostochnoy literatury, 1963), pp. 78–9.
55. This is mirrored in Amanullah's use of self-consciously "Pashtun" symbols, such as the calling of a *Loya Jirga* (the Pashto phrase for "Grand Assembly") to sanction his rule in 1921. As M. Jamil Hanifi has illustrated, this form of assembly in fact had little royal precedent, and was more an invention of a "tradition" designed at stressing Amanullah's Pashtun credentials. See M. Jamil Hanifi, "Editing the Past: Colonial Production of Hegemony through the 'Loya Jerga' in Afghanistan", *Iranian Studies* 37, 2 (2004).
56. For an example of the integration of Qandahari merchants with aristocratic lineages in Qandahar and Kabul, see the discussion of the career of Sālih Muhammad Qandahārī in Caron (2009), pp. 56–70.
57. For a discussion of the Paxtō Maraka and its "official" character, see Niyāzī (1997), pp. 324–6.
58. See the article "*Da Paxtō Fōlklōr Da Maʿrifi Lūmraney Risāla*", 2, in Jalāli (1981).
59. Mawlavī ʿAbd al-Wāsiʾ Kākar Qandahārī (1305/1926–27), first printed in ʿAbd al-Hayy Habībī (ed.), *Da Afghān Yād* (Kabul: Academy of Sciences, 1360/1981). The translation is by James Caron.

60. *Ibid.*
61. For a nuanced discussion of Amanullah's fluctuating relations with British India, see Haroon (2007), pp. 113–24.
62. *Ibid.*, p. 107.
63. Abdul Ghaffar Khan, *My Life and Struggle: Autobiography of Badshah Khan* (Delhi: Hind Pocket Books, 1969), p. 51.
64. Abdul Rauf, "Socio-Educational Reform Movements in NWFP—A Case Study of Anjuman-e-Islahul Afaghina", *Pakistan Journal of History & Culture* 27, 2, (2006), p. 39.
65. *Ibid.*, p. 49.
66. *Ibid.*
67. *Ibid.*, p. 51.
68. 'Abd al-Ghaffar Khan quoted in D.G. Tendulkar, *Abdul Ghaffar Khan: Faith is a Battle* (Bombay: Popular Prakashan, 1967), p. 50.
69. *Ibid.*
70. *Ibid.*
71. Quoted in Tendulkar (1967), pp. 52–3.
72. *Ibid.*, p. 52.
73. *Ibid.*, p. 55.

5. AMBIGUITIES OF ORALITY AND LITERACY, TERRITORY AND BORDER CROSSINGS: PUBLIC ACTIVISM AND PASHTO LITERATURE IN AFGHANISTAN, 1930–2010

1. Fazl-e Rahim Marwat, "The Impact of the *Wikh Zalmiyan* Movement on Afghan Politics", *Central Asia* 36, 2 (1995), p. 45.
2. Sayyid Qāssem Reshtiyā, *Khātirāt-e Siyāsī-ye Sayyid Qāsim Reshtiyā: 1311 tā 1371*, ed. Muhammad Qavī Kūshān (Virginia: Matba'a-ye Amerīkan-e Sapīdī, 1997), p. 263.
3. Here I find it useful to adopt the vocabulary of Michel de Certeau, *The Practice of Everyday Life*, trans. Steven Rendall (Berkeley: University of California Press, 1984).
4. M. Ma'sūm Hōtak, "Da Afghānistān pa Matbū'ātō kē da 'Hawād' aw 'Hēwād' par Kalamō Yawa Pakhwānai Khpara Shawē Munāqasha", *Khpalwākay* 2, 1 (1995), pp. 160–4.
5. Nasr Allāh Nāsir (ed.), *Gul Pāchā Ulfat: Da Xkārandūī par Qasīda Mushā'ira* (Kabul: Da Afghānistān da 'Ulūmō Akādēmī, 1983).
6. Nāsir, *Xkārandūī*, p. 8.
7. Nāsir, *Xkārandūī*, p. 10.
8. Habib Allāh Rafi', *Da Khalqō Sandarē* (Kabul: Da Afghānistān Akādēmī, 1349/1970), pp. 274–81 and Ajmal Khattak, *Qīssa Zmā da Adabī Zhwand* (Charsadda: Riyāzī Buk Ējansī, 2005), *passim*.

9. Khattak, *Qīssa*, pp. 31–4.
10. Wāris Khān, *Da Āzāday Tahrīk* (Rashakai, Pakistan: s.p., 1988) provides a good view of this in memoir.
11. Sana Haroon, *Frontier of Faith: Islam in the Indo-Afghan Borderland* (New York: Columbia University Press, 2007).
12. The *Ōsanī Līkwāl* series compiled by Benawa is particularly useful, in that many subjects supplied their own self-narratives to the editor.
13. Muhammad Mu'min Patwāl, *Osanī Shā'irān* (Kabul: Da Afghānistān da 'Ulūmō Akādemī, 1988) contains fine examples.
14. For a late 1940s anecdote, see 'Abd Allāh Bakhtānai, "Yawa Khātira", pp. 403–5, in Sedā Gul Gharībyār (ed.), *Star Paxtūn* (Peshawar: Da Dānish Khparandūī Tōlana, 1383/2004).
15. Nāsir, *Xkārandūī*, p. 12.
16. 'Abd Allāh Bakhtānī, *Ze, Malang Jān, aw Khwaǵē Naghmē* (Peshawar: Dānish, 2004) contains concrete description.
17. I thank Professor F. Marwat for sharing with me the original *jihad* announcement in his possession.
18. Muhammad Da'ūd Wafā, *Da Nangarhār Farhangī Bahīr ta Yawa Katəna* (Peshawar: Da Afghānistān da Mutāli'ātō Markaz, 1377/1998), p. 43.
19. Shah Mahmud Hanifi, "The British Colonial Policy of Pensioning Afghan Political Elites in India", paper presented at Association for Asian Studies meeting, March 2010. Cited with permission.
20. Amīr Hamza Shīnvārī, *Da Kābul Manzūma Safarnāma*, compiled by M. Shīnvārī and edited by D. K. Dā'ūd (Peshawar: Hamza Academy, 1998).
21. In an article series published the same year, the minister of national economy, 'Abd al-Majīd Zābulī, points to exactly these two shortages as emblematic of the government's role during the economic crisis. See 'Abd al-Majīd Zābulī, *Mushkilāt-e Iqtisādī-ye Mā va Mujādila bā Ān-hā* (Kabul: Mudīriyat-ye 'Umūmī-ye Intibātāt, 1328/1949).
22. Anonymous, *Da Paxtō Munāsira* (Kabul: Da Paxtō Tōlana, 1328/1949), p. 26.
23. James Caron, "Reading the Power of Printed Orality: Popular Pashto Literature as Historical Evidence and Public Intervention", *Journal of Social History* 45, 1 (2011).
24. 'Abd Allāh Bakhtānī, personal interview, Peshawar, 1 May 2007.
25. Malang Jān, *Da Malang Jān Khwaǵē Naghmē* (Oxford: Da 'Allāma Sayyid Jamāl al-Dīn Afghān Farhangī Tōlana, 1998), p. 104.
26. M. Hasan Kākar, "Da Malang Jān Shā'irī", pp. 13–18 in Rahmat Rabī Zīrakyār (ed.), *Malang Jān: da bē Darbāra Millī Zhabē Millī Shā'ir* (Santa Barbara, CA: All Afghan, 1995).
27. See 'Abd al-Wājid "Wājid", *Da Malang Jān pa Ash'āro kē da Āzādī aw Hēwād Pālənē Angāza* (Kabul: Da Afghānistān da 'Ulūmō Akādēmī, 2005) for details especially regarding the biographies of Malang Jan and his students.

28. Marwat, "Impact", pp. 66–7.
29. 'Abdullāh Bakhtānī, personal interview, Peshawar, 1 May 2007.
30. Mustafā Jihād, *Da Gulō Źōlay* (Kabul: Da Italā'ātō aw Kultūr Vizārat, 1368/1989), vol. 1, pp. 279.
31. Patwāl (1988) contains other examples.
32. Sayyid Bahā' al-Dīn Majrūh, *Da Źānźānī Xāmār* (Peshawar: Afghānistān Akādemī, 1985), Book One.
33. See http://www.youtube.com/watch?v=EwJsP8ESzgk (posted 28 November 2007 by 'Pokhton'; accessed 27 September 2010).
34. See Lā'iq's introduction to *Paxtō Landay* (Kabul: Da Afghānistān da 'Ulūmō Akādēmī, 1363/1984).
35. Zarīn Anźōr, *Da Ŝawr pa Trāzhedī kē Farhang, Adabiyāt aw Āzādī* (Peshawar: WUFA, 1372/1993).
36. Anźōr (1372/1993), p. 73.
37. *Ibid.*
38. Partaw Naderi, "Literature in the Course of Politics in Afghanistan": http://www.khorasanzameen.net/rws/pnaderi01e.html (accessed 30 September 2010).
39. Nasr Allāh Hāfiz, *Stā da Cham Gulūna* (Kabul: 1365/1986), pp. 119–20, quoted in Anźōr (1372/1993), p. 78.
40. Asad Allāh Sho'ūr, *Mufāhama-ye Shifāhī va Sayr-e Tārīkhī-ye Ān dar Afghānistān* (Kabul: Da Zhūrnālīstānō Ittihādiyya, 1367/1988).
41. David Edwards, "Words in the Balance: Poetics of Political Dissent in Afghanistan", in Dale F. Eickelman (ed.), *Russia's Muslim Frontiers* (Bloomington: Indiana University Press, 1993) and 'Awaz Siddīqī, *Da Paktiyā Walesī Shā'irān* (Peshawar: n.p., 1370/1992).
42. Anźōr (1372/1993), p. 87.
43. Kārwān, *Da Xāpēray Warghōway* (Peshawar: Da Dānish Khparandūī Tōlana, 1379/2000), pp. 34–6.
44. For an overview of Danish, see: http://www.tolafghan.com/societies/14-danish-publishing-association (accessed 30 September 2010).
45. Karwan (1379/2000), pp. 30–2. I was told by Asad Danish himself, in personal conversation at his shop in Peshawar in 2006, that this references a discussion he had with Karwan.
46. This cassette was supplied to me in 2003 by a Pashto instructor of mine, for which I am continuously grateful.
47. Anźōr (1372/1993), p. 90.
48. See http://www.youtube.com/watch?v=bdGL3w6lQDI (posted 14 March 2009, by Qandahar0093; accessed 1 October 2010).
49. Indira Lakshmanan, "Mobile Phones Combat Taliban's Afghan 'Information Wastelands'", *Bloomberg Business Week*, 22 March 2010; http://www.businessweek.com/news/2010-03-22/mobile-phones-combat-taliban-s-afghan-information-wastelands-.html.

50. Yaroslav Trofimov, "Cell Carriers Bow to Taliban Threat", *Wall Street Journal* (22 March 2010); http://online.wsj.com/article/SB10001424052748704117 304575137541465235972.html.
51. For example, see http://www.youtube.com/watch?v=ExyUnQM3fig&feature= related (posted 11 March 2009 by Pakhtoonhalek; accessed 19 December 2010).
52. http://www.youtube.com/watch?v=P_UfSewCFiQ&feature=related (posted 19 May 2009 by Haazco; accessed 1 October 2010).
53. Stephen Masty, "Review of Crews and Tarzi, *Taliban and the Crisis of Afghanistan*", *Asian Affairs* 41, 2 (2010), p. 268.
54. I thank Yaser Hussain for helping me develop this analysis.
55. http://www.youtube.com/watch?v=P_UfSewCFiQ&feature=related (posted 19 May 2009 by haazco; accessed 1 October 2010).

6. THE POETRY AND PROSE OF PAZHWAK: A CRITICAL LOOK AT TRADITIONAL AFGHANISTAN

1. H.J. De Dianious, "La Littérature Afghane de la Langue Persane", *Orient* 31 (1964), L.N. Dorofeeva, "Abd al-Rahman Pazhwak—Novellist", *Kurze Mitteilungen des Instituts der Orientalistk* 37 (Moscow: Akademie der Wissenschaften der UdSSR, 1960), and A. Gerasimova, "Zeitgenössische Literatur", in Alevtina Sergeevna Gerasimova & Georgij FedorovicGirs (eds.), *Die Literatur Afghanistans: Kurzer Abriß* (Moscow: Akademie der Wissenschaften der UdSSR, 1963).
2. This chapter draws on the following writings of 'Abd al-Rahmān Pazhwāk: *Khāterāt: Ya'nī Sarguzasht-e Yak Afghān-e Muhājir* (unpublished memoirs); *Afsānahā-ye Mardum: Āsār-e Pazhwāk* (Kabul: 1957); *Almās-e Nāshekan: Sh'ir-e Shā'ir-e Inglīs W. Pitt Root bih Mujāhidīn-e Afghānistān va Javāb-e Pazhwāk* (Virginia: 1996); *Bānū-ye Balkh: Majmū'a-ye Ash'ār-e 'Abd al-Rahmān Pazhwāk* (Peshawar(?): n.p., 2000); *Chand Sh'ir az Pazhwāk* (Kabul: 1963); *Gulhā-ye Andīsha az 'A. R. Pazhwāk* (Kabul: 1965); *Hadīs-e Khūn az Ash'ār-e Ustād Pazhwāk*, ed. H. Rafi'(Peshawar: 1985); *Mayhan-e Man: Az Ashā'r-e Ustād Pazhwāk* (Peshawar: 1989); *Muzākirāt-e Jenev: Majmū'a-ye Maqālāt-e Ustād 'Abd al-Rahmān Pazhwāk* (Peshawar: 1987); *Nāhīd-Nāma: Āsār-e Ustād 'Abd al-Rahmān Pazhwāk* (Toronto: 1995); *Pakhtunistan Day—Ninth of Sunbola, 1328/1949* (Hove:1950); "*Tamulat-e Huqūqiya va Jazāya-e Mellī*", in *Sālnāma-e Kābul, 1318* (Kabul: 1940), and *Afghanistan (Ancient Aryana): Brief Review of the Political and Cultural History and the Modern Development of the Country* (Hove: 1950s).
3. A copy of this correspondence is in the possession of the author.
4. "Man in The News—Diplomatist Who Sees U.N. as World's Best Hope", in *Kabul Times* (21 September 1966), p. 6.
5. Pazhwak in "Pacts to Safeguard Human Rights", *Kabul Times* (10 December 1966), 2. Later, UN Secretary General Kofi Annan directly quoted Pazhwāk's words.

6. "Fact-Finder in Vietnam: Abdul Rahman Pazhwak", *New York Times* (28 October 1963), p. 12.
7. Sayed Qassem Reshtiā, ed. Muhammad Qavi Kushan, *Khātirāt-e Siyāsī-ye Sayyid Qāsim Reshtiā: 1311 tā 1371* (Virginia: Matbaʻa-ye Amerīkan-e Sapīdī, 1997)
8. *Ibid.*
9. Pazhwāk told his grandson, Farhād Pazhwāk: "My boy, even though I have resigned from my post, I have not retreated from being an Afghan". See ʻAbd al-Rahmān Pazhwāk, *Khātirāt: Yaʻnī Sarguzasht-e Yak Afghān-e Muhājir* (unpublished memoir).
10. *Qushūn-e Surkh*, in ʻAbd al-Rahmān Pazhwāk, *Mayhan-e Man: Az Ashāʻir-e Ustād Pazhwāk* (Peshawar: n.p., 1989), p. 31.
11. ʻAbd al-Rahmān Pazhwāk, *Nāhid-nāma: Āsār-e Ustād ʻAbd al-Rahmān Pazhwāk* (Toronto: n.p., 1374 *hs*/1996), p. 118.
12. ʻAbd al-Rahmān Pazhwāk, *Muzākirāt-e Jenev: Majmūʻa-ye Maqālāt-e Ustād ʻAbd al-Rahmān Pazhwāk* (Peshawar: n.p., 1366 *hs*/1988), p. 41.
13. ʻAbd al-Ghafūr Rawān Farhādī in *Gulhā-ye Andīsha* (Kabul: n.p., 1344 *hs*/1966), p. 2.
14. From "Yak khanda va khāmushi", in *Gulhā-ye Andīsha* (1344 *hs*/1966), p. 63.
15. Friedrich Rosen, *Die Sinnsprüche Omars des Zeltmachers* (Leipzig: Insel-Verlag, 1922), p. 61, note 59.
16. Puiyā Fariyābī, "Rind-e Surkhrūd: Bih Munāsibāt-e Darguzasht-e Pazhwāk", *Naw Bahār* 12–13 (1375 *hs*/1997), p. 19.
17. ʻAbd al-Ghafūr Rawān Farhādī in *Gulhā-ye Andīsha* (1344 *hs*/1966), p. 2.
18. Quoted by ʻAbd-al Hakīm Tabībī, "Marg-e Ustād Pazhwāk: Yak Dhaiyah-ye Buzurg-e Adabī va Ijtimāʼī", *Omīd* 165 (19 June 1995).
19. William Pitt Root, *The Unbroken Diamond: Nightletter To The Mujahadeen* (n.p.: Pipedream Press, 1983).
20. *Nāhid-Nāma*, p. 15.
21. A. Rahman Pazhwak (Afghan Bureau of Information in London), *Afghanistan—Ancient Aryana: Brief Review of the Political and Cultural History and the Modern Development of the Country* (Hove: Key Press, 1955).
22. The slim volume *Afsanaha-ye Mardum* was later translated into French and published as Abdurrahman Pazwak, *Contes d'Afghanistan*, trans. Jaqueline Verdeaux & Omar Sherdil (Paris: Stock & Plus, 1981).
23. Sayed Haschmatullah Hossaini, *Die Erzählprosa der Dari-Literatur in Afghanistan 1900–1978* (Hamburg: Verlag Dr. Kovac, 2010).
24. ʻAbd al-Rahmān Pazhwāk (trans.), *Pīshwā, Nawīsanda: Jibrān Khalīl* (Kabul: 1334 *h sh*).
25. ʻAbd al-Rahmān Pazhwāk, "Excerpt from Correspondence with a Friend" (working title of translation by Chaled Malekyar).
26. Chaled Malekyar, *Das Bild Afghanistans im 20. Jahrhundert: Das Werk des Schrift-*

stellers und Diplomaten Ostad Abdol Rahman Pazhwak (1919–1995) (Berlin: Klaus Schwartz, 2008), p. 184.
27. *Dhamir* is one of seven texts from the collection of stories in 'Abd al-Rahmān Pazhwāk, *Afsāna-hā-ye Mardum*: *Āsār-e Pazhwāk* (Kabul: 1336*h sh*).
28. Pazhwak's famous poem was published in several collections as for example in *Gulhā-ye Andīsha* (1344 *h sh*), pp. 151–7.
29. *Gulhā-ye Andīsha* (1344 *hs*/1966), p. 157.
30. Ibid.

7. MASTERING THE EGO MONSTER: *AZHDAHA-YE KHODI* AS AN ALLEGORY OF HISTORY

1. Søren Kierkegaard, *Concluding Unscientific Postscript to the Philosophical Crumbs*, edited and trans. Alastair Hannay (Cambridge: Cambridge University Press, 2009), p. 107.
2. Atiq Rahimi, *Syngué sabour: Pierre de patience* (Paris: P.O.L, 2008); English trans. *The Patience Stone*, trans. Polly McLean (New York: Other Press, 2009).
3. Atiq Rahimi, "Majrouh, voie magnétique", *Magazine Littéraire*, no. 481 (2008). http//www.magazine-litteraire/content/recherché/article?id=12106.
4. For biographical information on Majruh, see Siddīq Rāhpō-Tarzī, "Zendagīnāma-ye Sayyid Bahā' al-Dīn Majrūh", in www.afghanasamai.com (accessed on 7 December 2011). See also Tāj al-Dīn Nūshābādī, "Majrūh" entry in *Dāneshnāma-ye Adab-e Fārsī*, (ed.) Hasan Anūshāh, vol. 3 (Tehran: Vizārat-e Farhang va Irshād, 1378/1999), pp. 876–7.
5. Sayyid Bahā' al-Dīn Majrūh, *Azhdahā-ye Khōdī*, Parts One and Two (Kabul: Matbaʿa-ye Dawlatī, 1352/1973).
6. Sayyid Bahā' al-Dīn Majrūh, *Azhdahā-ye Khōdī*, Part Four (Peshawar: Anjuman-e Navīsandagān-e Mujāhid-e Afghānistān, 1983).
7. Published in Paris by Phébus in 1989 and 1991 respectively. Other works of Majruh that are translated into French include: *Chants de l'errance*, trans. Serge Sautreau (Paris: La Différence, 1989); *Rire avec Dieu* (aphorisms and Sufi tales), trans. Serge Sautreau (Paris: Albin Michel, 1994); and *Le suicide et le chant* (popular songs of Pashtun women), in collaboration with André Velter (Paris: Gallimard, 1994). This latter text also appears in English. See *Songs of Love and War: Afghan Women's Poetry*, translated from the French by Marjolijn de Jager (New York: Other Press, 2003).
8. Sayyid Bahā' al-Dīn Majrūh, *Azhdahā-ye Khōdī*, Parts One and Two (Kabul: Matbaʿa-ye Dawlatī, 1352/1973). Chapter 2, "Qahramān-e Siyāh-Pōsh", pp. 35–44.
9. Jean-Paul Sartre, *The Emotions: Outline of a Theory*, trans. Bernard Frechtman (New York: Philosophical Library, 1948), p. 17.

10. On this topic of great importance see, among others, Peter Dews, *Logics of Disintegration: Post-structuralist Thought and the Claims of Critical Theory* (London: Verso, 1987).
11. Michel Foucault, *The Order of Things: An Archeology of the Human Sciences* (New York: Vintage, 1973), p. 387.
12. Roland Barthes, "The Death of the Author", in *Image, Music, Text*, trans. Stephen Heath (New York: Hill and Wang, 1977), pp. 142–8.
13. In this respect, the few extant epistles of Junayd of Baghdad (d. 910) well elucidate the paradoxical nature of the notion of the self in Islamic mysticism. See Baldick's discussion of the notions of *fana'* and *baqa'* (with a reference to the celebrated Hegelian idea of "negation of the negation") in Julian Baldick, *Mystical Islam: An Introduction to Sufism* (New York: New York University Press, 1989), p. 45.
14. Annemarie Schimmel, *Mystical Dimensions of Islam* (Chapel Hill: University of North Carolina Press, 1975), p. 5.
15. Toshihiko Izutsu, "The Basic Structure of Metaphysical Thinking in Islam", in *Collected Paper on Islamic Philosophy and Mysticism*, eds. Mehdi Mohaghegh & Hermann Landot (Tehran: n.p., 1971), 39f. Quoted in Schimmel (1975), p. 143.
16. Javed Majeed, *Muhammad Iqbal: Islam, Aesthetics and Postcolonialism* (London and New Delhi: Routledge, 2009), p. 21.
17. *Ibid.*, pp. 20–1.
18. See, in particular, Iqbal's two valuable *masnavis* in Persian, *Asrar-e Khodi* and *Romuz-e Bikhodi*, in Muhammad Iqbāl, *Kulliyat-ye Ash 'ār-e Fārsī*, ed. Ahmad Surūsh (Tehran: Kitābkhānah-ye Sanā'ī, 1343/1964), pp. 2–104.
19. Majeed (2009), p. 23.
20. *Azhdaha-ye Khodi*, Parts One and Two, "Pasgoftar", pp. 127–52.
21. *Ibid.*, p. 32.
22. *Ibid.*, p. 36.
23. *Ibid.*, pp. 32–3.
24. *Ibid.*, pp. 43–4.
25. *Ibid.*, pp. 58–9, pp. 64–5.
26. *Ibid.*, p. 74.
27. *Ibid.*, p. 89.
28. *Ibid.*, p. 91.
29. *Ibid.*, p. 98.
30. *Ibid.*, p. 99.
31. *Ibid.*, p. 116.
32. *Ibid.*, p. 119.
33. Sayyid Bahā' al-Dīn Majrūh, *Azhdahā-e Khōdī*, Part Four (Peshawar: Anjuman-

e Navīsandagān-e Mujāhid-e Afghānistān, 1983), p. 11. In a crucial note he wrote to a later edition of the book (*ibid.*, 10), Majrūh maintained that "When in July 1973, [the former authoritarian prime minister] Muhammad Da'ud brought the monarchy to an end through a military coup, some readers regarded Part Two of the book—"The Return of the Monster"—as a curious prediction of this ominous turn of [political] events".

34. *Ibid.*, pp. 14–18.
35. *Ibid.*, pp. 20–1.
36. *Ibid.*, p. 22.
37. *Ibid.*, p. 195.
38. *Ibid.*, pp. 27–38.
39. *Ibid.*, pp. 149–50.
40. *Ibid.*, p. 151.
41. *Ibid.*, p. 153.
42. *Ibid.*, p. 178.
43. *Ibid.*, pp. 177–8.
44. *Ibid.*, p. 179.
45. *Ibid.*, p. 184
46. *Ibid.*, p. 185.
47. *Ibid.*, pp. 180–5.
48. *Ibid.*, pp. 186–97.
49. *Ibid*, p.190.
50. *Ibid.*, p. 195.
51. *Ibid.*, p. 198.
52. *Ibid.*, p. 201–3.
53. *Ibid.*, p. 197.

8. LYRIC REALISM: POETIC REFLECTIONS OF REFUGEE LIFE IN IRAN

1. This chapter is based on ongoing research, begun in 2004, with Afghan refugee poets in Iran, focusing on the work of an Afghan cultural organization based in Mashhad, the Dorr-e Dari Cultural Institute (*Mo'assese-ye Farhangī-ye Dorr-e Darī*).
2. Fātemeh Sajjādī (ed.), *Gisuān-e Gij: Daftar-e az She'r-hā-ye Nasl-e Javān-e Mohājer* [*Tangled Locks: A Book of Poems from the Young Generation of Refugees*] (Mashhad: Nedā-ye Sokhan, 1384/2005), pp. 27–8.
3. Lyric (adj.): (of poetry) expressing the writer's emotions, usually briefly and in stanzas or recognized forms (*Oxford English Dictionary*).
4. "The 1990s is probably a unique period in which all trends of Persian poetry in a wide range of spectrum [*sic*] from traditional classical to post-modernist poetry are actively engaged in literary production", Alireza Anushiravani and Kavoos

Hassanli, "Trends in Contemporary Persian Poetry", in Mehdi Semati (ed.), *Media, Culture and Society in Iran: Living with Globalization and the Islamic State* (London: Routledge, 2007), p. 164. For an overview of literary currents and institutions among Afghan refugees in Iran, see Zuzanna Olszewska, "'A Desolate Voice': Poetry and Identity Among Young Afghan Refugees in Iran", *Iranian Studies*, 40, 2 (2007).

5. Erving Goffman, *The Presentation of Self in Everyday Life* (Edinburgh: University of Edinburgh, 1956), pp. 14–17.
6. For more information, see Zuzanna Olszewska, "Afghan Refugees in Iran", *Encyclopedia Iranica Online, http://www.iranica.com/articles/afghanistan-xiv-afghan-refugees-in-iran-2*, December 2008.
7. Subsequent to my primary fieldwork in 2005–6, Dorr-e Dari has expanded to include branches in South Australia and Kabul, following some of its founding members who relocated there.
8. Now officially named the *Meidān-e Shahid-e Gomnām* ("The Unknown Martyr's Square"). This is a popular place for the police to arrest Afghans without (sometimes even with) Iranian residence permits. One of the minibuses was nicknamed *Tābut*, the "Coffin", by the Afghans who rode it everyday: they could not be sure if they would return home in the evening or be detained and deported.
9. Donald Fanger, *Dostoevsky and Romantic Realism: A Study of Dostoevsky in Relation to Balzac, Dickens and Gogol* (Cambridge, MA: Harvard University Press, 1965), p. 6.
10. Ibid., p. 3.
11. This useful concept is elucidated by Jessica Winegar in *Creative Reckonings: The Politics of Art and Culture in Contemporary Egypt* (Stanford: Stanford University Press, 2006).
12. These, argues Fanger, point to realism's origins in the comic genre, according to the classical Greek distinctions, because it deals with the vulgar aspects of human life rather than the elevated acts of men and gods appropriate to tragedy or epic (Fanger, 3).
13. Paul Fussell, *The Great War and Modern Memory* (New York: Oxford University Press, 1975).
14. Charles Baudelaire, *Oeuvres*, vol. 1, *Le Spleen de Paris*, "Les Foules", pp. 420–1.
15. In this, I echo Mohamed-Salah Omri's take on the Arabic novel: "Instead of asking how the novel as such has created room for itself in Arab culture, I will focus attention on the ways in which local narrative forms handled the novel". See Mohamed-Salah Omri, "Local Narrative Form and Constructions of the Arabic Novel", *Novel: A Forum on Fiction* 41, 2–3 (2008), p. 246.
16. Although similar developments were taking place on a smaller scale in Afghanistan, I focus here on the Iranian literary-historical context because that has

been most influential for the refugee poets I worked with, most of whom received much of their education in Iran. See Wali Ahmadi, *Modern Persian Literature in Afghanistan: Anomalous Visions of History and Form* (London: Routledge, 2008).

17. The extent to which this was a new development is moot, however: all we know of the literature of the past is what has been passed down by the powerful. One point which I have not seen considered in the literature is that contemporary trends in poetry may have antecedents in the urban poetry of the *bazari* classes in the *shahr-ashub* tradition which dates back at least to the fifteenth century, and even then was very different in tone and content to the didactic abstractions of mystical and court poetry. See Jiří Bečka, "Tajik Literature from the 16th Century to the Present", in Jan Rypka (ed.), *History of Iranian Literature*, Dordrecht, D. Reidel, 1968), p. 508.
18. Kamran Talatoff, *The Politics of Writing in Iran: A History of Modern Persian Literature* (Syracuse, Syracuse University Press, 2000).
19. Simin Behbahani, *A Cup of Sin: Selected Poems*, trans. and ed. by Farzaneh Milani & Kaveh Safa (Syracuse: Syracuse University Press, 1999), p. 52. On Behbahani's metric innovations, see *ibid.*, xxiii.
20. Hamid Dabashi, *Close Up: Iranian Cinema, Past, Present, and Future* (London: Verso, 2001), 44. See also *idem.*, "The Poetics of Politics: Commitment in Modern Persian Literature", *Iranian Studies* 18, pp. 2–4 (1985).
21. Anushiravani & Hassanli, "Trends in Contemporary Persian Poetry", p. 164.
22. *Ibid.* pp. 160–1.
23. Veronica Doubleday, "Gendered Voices and Creative Expression in the Singing of *Chaharbeiti* Poetry in Afghanistan", *Ethnomusicology Forum*, vol. 20, no. 1, April 2011.
24. *Ibid.* p. 6.
25. For one of the most nuanced studies to consider Persian literary change as a long-term process in its broader contexts, see Ahmad Karimi-Hakkak, *Recasting Persian Poetry: Scenarios of Poetic Modernity in Iran* (Salt Lake City: University of Utah Press, 1995).
26. Seyyed Zia' Qasemi, untitled poem in *Bāghhā-ye Mo 'Allaq-e Angur* [Suspended Vineyards] (Tehran: Sureh-ye Mehr, 1386/2007), pp. 16–17. The unusual format of the text is reproduced from this published version.
27. The Pamirs are a mountain chain in north-west Afghanistan; Helmand is the name of a river and province in the south. A *dobeiti* is a folk quatrain often sung by Hazara shepherds. The town of Bamyan is the economic and cultural centre of the Hazarajat, while Ghazni is a city at its eastern edge. Baghchar and Sangtakht are villages in the Hazarajat. The Jeyhun or Amu Darya, known as the Oxus by the Greeks, is the river that demarcates the border between Afghanistan and Tajikistan in the north.

28. Intoxication (*masti*) is a major trope in Persian poetry, both classical and modern, as a metaphor for the altered spiritual state caused by love for an earthly or divine Beloved; or indeed by the recitation of poetry or indulgence in other art forms. The multiple references to wine, taverns, intoxication and drunkenness in the penultimate stanza, therefore, turn it into a love poem for the homeland—a common feature of modern Persian poetry.
29. See e.g. Khatereh Sheibani, "Kiarostami and the Aesthetics of Modern Persian Poetry", *Iranian Studies* 39, 4, (2006), pp. 509–37; Shohini Chaudhuri and Howard Finn, "The Open Image: Poetic Realism and the New Iranian Cinema", *Screen* 44, 1 (2003), pp. 38–57.
30. Benjamin's influential discussion of this figure has already been applied fruitfully to non-European contexts, see e.g. Craig Jeffrey, "Timepass: Youth, Class, and Time among Unemployed Young Men in India", *American Ethnologist* 37, 3 (2010), p. 475, on the "loitering" habits of educated lower-middle-class young men in a provincial town in India; and on Iranian youth in Tehran who stroll around western-style shopping malls in a practice of voyeuristic consumerism, see Shahram Khosravi, *Young and Defiant in Tehran* (Philadelphia: University of Pennsylvania Press, 2009).
31. Amanullah Mirzai, untitled poem in *Khatt-e Sevvom* 12 & 13 (1387/2008), 106. A modified version of my translation appears in *Words without Borders*, "Writing from Afghanistan", May 2011, http://wordswithoutborders.org/article/the-sewing-machine.
32. The original and my more literary translation of this poem were published in *Words without Borders*, "Writing from Afghanistan", May 2011, http://wordswithoutborders.org/article/bilingual/take-a-number-on-saturdays.

9. AFGHANISTAN AND THE PERSIAN EPIC *SHAHNAMA*: HISTORICAL AGENCY AND THE EPIC IMAGINATION IN AFGHAN AND AFGHAN-AMERICAN LITERATURE

1. The poem was published in the collection, Wāsef Bākhtarī, *Az Ma'yād tā Hargiz* (Kabul: Nashr-e Anjuman-e Navīsandagān-e Afghānistān, 1985), p. 41. All translations and emphases of Bākhtarī's poems discussed in this chapter are by Shafiq Shamel. Note that in the main text, the poet's name is given according to his preferred spelling in English (Bakhteri), in references to printed texts in the footnotes the spelling is given according to its transliterated form (Bākhtarī).
2. Khaled Hosseini, *The Kite Runner* (New York: Riverhead Books, 2003) and Atiq Rahimi, *Earth and Ashes*, trans. Erdağ Gökner (New York: Harcourt Inc., 2002).
3. See Edward G. Brown, *A Literary History of Persia* (Cambridge: Cambridge University Press, 1964 repr.); Jan Rypka, *History of Iranian Literature* (Dodrecht: D. Reidel Publishing Company, 1968); and Zabīullāh Safā, *Tārīkh-e Adabiyat dar Īrān* (Tehran: Kitābfurūshī-e Ibn Sīnā, 1335/1956), 8 vols.

4. See, for example, Michael Axworthy, *Empire of the Mind: A History of Iran* (London: Hurst & Co., 2007).
5. For a recent English translation, see Dick Davis, *Shahnameh: The Persian Book of Kings* (New York: Penguin Books, 2007).
6. For more see *ibid.* and Dick Davis, *Rostam: Tales of Love and War from Persia's Book of Kings* (Washington, D.C.: Mage Publishers, 2007).
7. The biographical data as well as general considerations on Bakhteri's poetry included in this chapter are based on an article written by Latif Nazemi, another contemporary Afghan poet now living in Germany. The article is available on the Afghan literary-cultural website: www.afghanasamai.com.
8. Wāsif Bākhtarī, *Va Āftāb Namīmīrad* (Kabul: Nashr-e Anjuman-e Navīsandagān-e Afghānistān [Union of Afghan Writers of Afghanistan Press], 1982); *Az Ma'yād tā Hargiz* (Kabul: Nashr-e Anjuman-e Navīsandagān-e Afghānistān, 1985); *Az īn Āyina-ye Beshkasta-ye Tārīkh* (Kabul: n.p., 1990); *Dībācha'i dar Farjam* (Peshawar: n.p., 1997); *Tā Shahr-e Panjzal'a'i-e Āzādī* (Peshawar: n.p., 1997); *Dar Ostwā-ye Fasl-e Shekastan* (Peshawar: Maiwand Publishing Center, 1999); *Muwiya-hā-ye Asfandiyār-e Gomshoda* (Peshawar: Parnyan Publishing Foundation, 2001).
9. On the political history of Afghanistan, see Amin Saikal, *Modern Afghanistan: A History of Struggle and Survival* (London: I.B. Tauris, 2004).
10. www.afghanasamai.com.
11. For more information on the development of Persian poetry in the twentieth century in Iran and Afghanistan (in English) see Ahmad Karimi-Hakkak, *Recasting Persian Poetry: Scenarios of Poetic Modernity* (Salt Lake City: University of Utah Press, 1995) and Wali Ahmadi, *Modern Persian Literature in Afghanistan: Anomalous Visions of History and Form* (London: Routledge, 2008).
12. Bākhtarī, in *Dībācha'i dar Farjam* (1997), p. 15.
13. Whether or not a non-identical relation to historical reality could be attributed to the intellectual orientation resulting from the textual memory of epic tradition is an issue of significance that will need further analysis. Examples of this kind of scholarship include Dennis Walder, *Postcolonial Nostalgias: Writing, Representation, and Memory* (New York: Routledge, 2011); Igor Maver (ed.), *Diasporic Subjectivity and Cultural Brokering in Contemporary Post-Colonial Literatures* (Lanham: Lexington Books, 2009); and Bart Moore-Gilbert, *Postcolonial Life-Writing: Culture, Politics and Self-Representation* (New York: Routledge, 2009).
14. Bākhtarī, in *Dībācha'i dar Farjam* (1997), pp. 39–40.
15. Wali Ahmadi also registers this gradual shift in the figuration of history in Bakhteri's later poems. See Wali Ahmadi, "Intertextual Influences and Intracultural Contacts: History and Memory in the Poetry of Akhavan-Sales and Wasef Bakhteri", in Ahmad Karimi-Hakkak & Kamran Talattof (eds), *Essays on Nima Yushij: Animating Modernism in Persian Poetry* (Leiden: Brill, 2004).

16. Author's emphasis.
17. Wāsif Bākhtarī, *Tā Shahr-e Panjzal'a'i-e Āzādī* (Peshawar: n.p., 1997).
18. *Ibid.*, pp. 40–1.
19. For biographical data see: http://mantlethought.org/content/interview-atiq-rahimi.
20. Rahimi (2002), p. 33.
21. For more information see Saikal (2004).
22. The author left Afghanistan in 1983 after his father—a well-known political activist and intellectual supporting constitutional monarchy and representational democracy in the 1950s—was arrested and executed by the communist regime in 1979.
23. There are numerous passages in *Earth and Ashes* that can illustrate this dimension of the narrative structure. See, for example, Rahimi (2002), pp. 10–12.
24. *Ibid.*
25. http://www.khaledhosseini.com.
26. Hosseini (2003), p. 29.
27. *Ibid.*
28. See Fredric Jameson, *The Political Unconscious: Narrative as a Socially Symbolic Act* (Ithaca: Cornell University Press, 1982), chapter 2, "Magical Narratives: On the Dialectical Use of Genre Criticism". Jameson's discussion of Frye's theory of romance is particularly relevant in this context, since it analyzes the notion of salvation in relation to narrative structure.
29. Hosseini (2003), 1, p. 226.
30. See also Timothy Aubry, "Afghanistan Meets the Amazon: Reading *The Kite Runner* in America", *PMLA* 124, 1 (2009). Aubry discusses the representation of evil in the novel in the section, "Victims and Monsters", and considers the morality of the novel primarily an American projection rather than an account or representation of Afghanistan.

10. GNOMICS: PROVERBS, APHORISMS, METAPHORS, KEY WORDS AND EPITHETS IN AFGHAN DISCOURSES OF WAR AND INSTABILITY

1. E.g. 'Ināyatullāh Shahrānī, *Zarb al-Masal-hā-ye Darī-ye Afghānistān* (Union City, CA: n.p., 1999), which lists by the author's count about 40,000 proverbs.
2. The US military shows intensified interest in local cultural knowledge as strategic information, while opining that military intervention cannot suffice in counterinsurgency campaigns such as that in Afghanistan. See David H. Petraeus, James F. Amos, John A. Nagl & Sarah Sewell, *The US Army/Marine Corps Counterinsurgency Field Manual* (Chicago: University of Chicago Press, 2007). Nonetheless, the Manual's general concept of cultural information to be gleaned and applied in negotiations with adversaries and noncombatant populations is unre-

lentingly positivist, hardly adequate to instruct in the interpretation of indirect, metaphorical or otherwise coded cultural messages.

3. Respectively, the works are Malalai Joya (with Derrick O'Keefe), *A Woman among Warlords: The Extraordinary Story of an Afghan Who Dared to Raise Her Voice* (New York: Scribner, 2009) and Nelufer Pazira, *A Bed of Red Flowers: In Search of My Afghanistan* (New York: Free Press, 2005). These two are chosen for their relatively abundant use of proverbs; my work on them is part of a larger study of a total (so far) of ten women's memoirs published in the West.

4. For a condensed but detailed overview of proverbs' formal features and paradoxical array of social-pragmatic functions, see Outi Lauhakangas, "Proverbs in Social Interaction: Questions Aroused by the Multi-Functionality of Proverbial Speech", *Proverbium, Yearbook of International Proverb Scholarship* 24 (2007). Wolfgang Mieder, *Proverbs: A Handbook* (Westport, CT: Greenwood Press, 2004), supplies an overview of genre definitions and modes of analysis. I distinguish proverbs, as metaphorical "wise sayings", evaluative or prescriptive expressions, from aphorisms as non-metaphorical. This metaphorical stipulation parallels the standard Dari-Persian term for "proverb", *zarb al-masal*, literally "a blow/coinage by example/parable". Comparative paremiologists differ about this distinction, and on proverb definitions in general. Mieder's working, popular-consensus-based definition of proverb is as follows: "a short, generally known sentence of the folk which contains wisdom, truth, morals, and traditional views in a metaphorical, fixed and memorizable form ... handed down from generation to generation ... [But] certainly these short and general definitions do not pay proper attention to numerous fascinating aspects of proverbs as formulaic and metaphorical texts and as regards their use, function and meaning in varied contexts". Mieder (2004), p. 3, p. 4.

5. Amīrqolī Amīnī, *Dāstān-hā-ye Imsāl* (Isfahan: n.p., 1324/1945, 3rd ed. 1351/1972), is the key source on proverbs in Persian with traditional back stories.

6. I am indebted to Erik Aasland who applies concepts of deictic projection developed by Peter Stockwell (*Cognitive Poetics: An Introduction*, Routledge, 2002, Ch. 4: "Cognitive Deixis") to proverbs on the basis of Kazakh data. Briefly, Aasland summarizes deixis as "the means by which intersubjectivity is anchored" and thus the basic mechanism of communication. Furthermore, "Deictic construction is emergent, unique to each individual and situation".

7. For references, see Margaret A. Mills, "Oral and Popular Literature in Dari-Persian of Afghanistan", in Philip Kreyenbroek & Ulrich Marzolph (eds.), *Oral Literature of Iranian Languages: Kurdish, Pashto, Balochi, Ossetic, Persian and Tajik*, Volume XVIII = Companion Volume II to *A History of Persian Literature* (London: I.B. Tauris, 2010) and Margaret A. Mills & Abdul Ali Ahrary, "Folklore Studies II: Of Afghanistan", *Encyclopedia Iranica* (Ehsan Yarshater, general editor) (New York: Bibliotheca Persica/Eisenbrauns, Vol X, Fasc. 1, 1999), pp. 75–8.

8. There is nothing by Afghan scholars comparable to Amīrqolī Amīnī's invaluable compendium of proverbs and their traditional narrative substrates, though the substantial overlap of proverb repertoires between Iranian Persian and Afghan (Dari) Persian language communities makes that work highly relevant to Afghan proverb usage. See Amīnī (1324/1945).
9. For a lengthier review of Afghan oral literature and its study, see Mills (2010) or Mills & Ahrary (1999).
10. Estimates drawn from United States Central Intelligence Agency, *Factbook: Afghanistan*, updated as of 14 November 2011, accessed 20 November 2011 at: https://www.cia.gov/library/publications/the-world-actbook/geos/af.html.
11. H. Lorraine Sakata, *Music in the Mind*, 2nd ed. (Washington DC: Smithsonian Press, 2002), p. 28, pp. 57–8, pp. 97–8, p. 165, pp. 168–78.
12. Margaret A. Mills, *Oral Narrative in Afghanistan: The Individual in Tradition* (New York: Garland, 1990) and *idem.*, *Rhetorics and Politics in Afghan Traditional Storytelling* (Philadelphia: University of Pennsylvania Press, 1991) are case studies of oral prose storytelling (female and male respectively), the latter study including literary-source materials. Rawshān Rahmānī, *Afsāna-hā-ye Darī* (Tehran: Sorūsh, 1374/1995) is a collection of transcribed oral tale texts from the 1980s, some in dialect, with biographical profiles of individual tellers.
13. Various personal communications to Mills, 1994–5 and 2003–9.
14. Translated play transcripts and analyses are presented in Hafizullah Baghban, *The Context and Concept of Humor in Magadi Folk Theater*, 4 vols (Ann Arbor: UMI, 1978/Indiana University Dissertation, 1977).
15. I wish to thank profoundly Dr. Omar Sharifi, Director of the American Institute for Afghanistan Studies, Kabul, who was a full partner in this research, both locating and collaboratively interviewing respondents; Mr. Rohullah Amin, Assistant to the Director, AIAS, who assisted with interviews of Shi'a religious leaders and others in Kabul; and Mr. Aminullah Azhar, Business Manager, UNICEF/Herat, who assisted with some interviews in Herat and introduced other respondents. All showed remarkable patience and insight in collaboratively conducting and analyzing these interviews. Additionally, Abdul Jabar Sapand, Director, Open Media Forum for Afghanistan, conducted and summarized half-a-dozen interviews for us in Jalalabad, where we were not able to travel. The full list of about sixty interviewees included the then-governor of Herat province (still serving as of summer 2010); the city mayor of Herat (since removed from office under accusations of corruption); National Assembly members soon to be standing for re-election; senior officers in the Afghan National Army and Afghan National Police; the regional director of a national bank; an assortment of elected provincial *shura* (council) representatives, then facing an election; academics and Shi'a and Sunni religious leaders; representatives of civil society organizations and political parties; employees of international organizations

and Afghan NGOs; journalists and school teachers; local entrepreneurs and contractors, shopkeepers, salaried workers and housewives (these latter categories including some people I have known for more than thirty years, whose family oral history is also a subject of my ongoing research). The level of education ranged from a PhD or two through BA or post-BA-equivalent academic degrees and officer training down to a nominal few (one to three) years of mosque schooling, in the case of two of the women interviewed.

16. Since not all interviewees wished to be quoted by name, and all were interviewed candidly, without recording, most are described here only generically by locale, profession or general social position in ways that preserve the privacy of those who did not wish to be quoted by name.
17. Lauhakangas (2007).
18. I should stipulate that this population included no individuals openly self-identifying with the Taliban or other resistance or so-called IAGs, "illegal armed groups", though a few opined that the Taliban were less corrupt and more administratively effective than the current government. See further discussion below.
19. On the inherently anecdotal nature of the corruption experience, see Shiv Visvanathan & Harsh Sethi, (eds.), *Foul Play: Chronicles of Corruption* (Delhi: Banyan Books/Seminar Business India Publications, 1998), pp. 3–4.
20. Jo Beall & Daniel Esser, *Shaping Urban Futures: Challenges to Governing and Managing Afghan Cities*, Issues Paper Series (Kabul: Afghanistan Research and Evaluation Unit, 2005).
21. This notwithstanding the fact that he was arrested in a sweep operation on his wedding night by Taliban security forces responding to the report of a theft in his neighbourhood, and not released until two weeks later, after the theft victims petitioned for the release of their wrongly incarcerated neighbours.
22. Ahmed Rashid, *Descent into Chaos* (New York: Viking, 2008), p. 138.
23. A.K.S. Lambton, *Theory and Practice in Medieval Persian Government* (London: Variorum Reprints, 1980).
24. Antonio Giustozzi & Dominique Orsini, "Centre-Periphery Relations in Afghanistan: Badakhshan between Patrimonialism and Institution-Building", *Central Asian Survey* 28, 1 (2009), pp. 1–16.
25. The interviewee is American-educated and (in the interests of full disclosure) a friendly if distant acquaintance of mine since the 1980s in Peshawar.
26. *Ibid.*, p. 1.
27. This is exactly the inverse of the English saying, "Sticks and stones may break my bones but words will never hurt me".
28. Baha al-Din Majruh's more meditative discussion quoted by James Caron on p. 130 above seems to derive from and expand upon this same proverb.
29. Galit Hasan-Rokem, "Proverbs as Cultural Capital: A Structural and Functional

Analysis with Special Reference to Judeo-Persian and Georgian Jewish Examples", in Shaul Shaked & Julia Rubanovich, *Orality and Textuality in the Iranian World* (Leiden: Brill, forthcoming).

30. Hasan-Rokem quotes Stefan Morawski, "The Basic Functions of Quotation", in Algiras Greimas et al (eds), *Sign, Language and Culture* (The Hague: Mouton, 1970), pp. 690–705.
31. Susan Kalcik, "'… Like Ann's Gynecologist or the Time I was Almost Raped': Personal Narratives in Women's Rap Groups", in Claire R. Farrer (ed.), *Women and Folklore* (Austin, TX: University of Texas Press, 1975), pp. 3–11.
32. Malalai Joya, *A Woman among Warlords* (New York: Scribner, 2009), p. 192.
33. *Ibid.*, p. 228.
34. *Ibid.*
35. *Ibid.*, p. 117.
36. *Ibid.*, p. 118.
37. On the very pervasive use of maps of nature in proverb imagery, see Arvo Krikman, "The Great Chain Metaphor: An Open Sesame for Proverb Semantics?", *Proverb Semantics*, *Proverbium Supplementary Series* (ed. Wolfgang Mieder), vol. 29 (Burlington, Vt.: University of Vermont, 2009).
38. Joya (2009), p. 143. Note that dragons in Afghan folktale tradition are rapacious predators who often stop up water sources and demand virgins in sacrifice, not the romantic monsters of twentieth-century Euro-American fantasy fiction. In Sufi literature, the dragon (*azhdaha[r]*) is a metaphor for the unbridled ego, as in Baha al-Din Majruh's treatise, *Azhdaha-ye Khudi*, discussed in detail in James Caron and Wali Ahmadi's chapters in this volume.
39. Joya (2009), p. 39.
40. *Ibid.*, p. 69.
41. *Ibid.*, p. 178, p. 179. Having heard Joya lecture on one occasion, in articulate, grammatical, but not native-fluent English, I would guess this rhetorical strategy to have been a contribution of her co-author, Derrick O'Keefe.
42. Nelufer Pazira, *A Bed of Red Flowers: In Search of My Afghanistan* (New York: Free Press, 2005), p. 340.
43. *Ibid.*, p. 122.
44. *Ibid.*, p. 81.
45. *Ibid.*, p. 146. Another such coinage is reported by Deborah Ellis, *Women of the Afghan War* (Westport CT: Preger, 2000), 228. Here a young RAWA activist visiting Peshawar from hard-pressed Kabul in 1998 says, "People in Afghanistan call their guests 'rockets', because when a guest comes, of course it will not destroy the house, but because they are very poor, they cannot afford for themselves, and it is difficult to afford a guest. Both the rocket and the guest can ruin a family".
46. Joya (2009), p. 77.

47. Entextualized with its back story from the Akhund's oral performance and analyzed in performance context in Mills (1991), chapter 12, pp. 275–88.
48. The variant is cited in Yūsuf Jamshīdipūr, *Farhang-e Imsāl-e Fārsī* (Tehran: Forūghī, 1980), p. 146.
49. "Green" here connotes "thriving, flourishing, healthy" and not "naïve" as in English.
50. See Nile Green & Mary Searle-Chatterjee, "Religion, Language and Power: An Introductory Essay", in *idem.* (eds), *Religion, Language and Power* (London: Routledge, 2008), for a far more detailed and nuanced discussion of the differential authority provided by written language over the spoken because, as they argue, it sheds or transcends its context of origin or composition. While this is true, it should be added that attribution to a known and revered author re-establishes a context of origin which is a major part of the statement's authority claim. In the context of oral quotation of oral ("traditional") texts such as non-literary proverbs, attribution to tradition is another layer of extracontextual authority.

INDEX

'Abbasid dynasty (750–1258): 210
Abbott, G.F: *Through India with the Prince*, 80
Abdali, Ahmad Shah: 13; *Baba-ye Afgahnistan*, 13: biographies, 13; empire of, 7; establishment of Afghan sultanate, 50
Académie française: model of, 14
Academy of Sciences of Afghanistan: formation of (1979), 21
Adabiyat-e Afgahni ('Afghan Literature'): 103
Afghan, Muhyi al-Din: head of Kabul teacher training college, 105; member of Constitutional Movement, 102; poetry of, 103–4
Afghan High Council of Education: 52
Afghan Historical Society (Anjuman-e Tarikh-e Afghanistan): founding of, 15; incorporation into Academy of Sciences of Afghanistan (1979), 21; magazine of (*Aryana*), 10, 15
Afghan Information Bureau: *Afghanistan—Ancient Aryana*, 153; *The Question of Pashtunistan*, 153
Afghan National Parliament: 230

Afghan Press and Information Office: personnel of, 143
Afghan Tourist Organization: 27
Afghan Writers Union: 20, 28; collapse of (1992), 21; founding of (1980), 21;
Afghan Qamus ('Afghan Dictionary'): publication, 19
Afghans: as distinct term, 104
Afghanistan: 141, 152, 156–7, 173, 187, 195, 200–1, 205, 210, 214, 216, 224–6, 232; Badakhshan, 74, 102, 103, 240, 244; Balkh, 13, 212, 237; Civil War (1992–6): 21, 134, 136, 149, 187, 250; constitution of (1923), 156; constitution of (1931), 156; constitution of (1964), 146, 164–5; constitution of (2004), 8; Farah, 230; Foreign Ministry, 144, 224; founding member of Non-Aligned Movement, 145; Ghazni, 141–2; Hadda, 120; Hazarajat, 4: Herat, 102, 103, 188, 230, 236–8, 240–2, 246–7; Jalalabad, 97, 117–18, 123, 129, 247; Kabul, 4, 12, 14–15, 17–19,

289

INDEX

22–3, 25, 28, 32–3, 42, 46–7, 70–1, 73–4, 77, 80, 83, 85, 88, 90, 97–8, 101–2, 109, 114, 117–18, 120, 123–4, 141–2, 144–6, 153–4, 164, 188, 196, 212, 216, 221, 224, 230, 236–9, 241, 250; Kafiristan, 4: Kapisa, 165; Khyber Pass, 71, 81; Mazar e-Sharif, 102–3, 188, 204, 230, 237, 240, 242; membership of UN, 144–5; military of, 147, 241; Ministry of Education: 1; Nangrahar, 121, 123–4, 127, 129, 142, 149; National Assembly, 124; Paktia, 134; Qandahar, 3–4, 17, 85, 101–3, 107, 117–18, 123, 124, 137; Qataghan, 74; Spin Ghar mountains, 158

Afghanistan Cultural Association: *Ariana-ye Birun* Marzi, 28; foundation, 28

afsana (fairy-tales): 41, 56

Afshar, Nadir Shah: empire of, 3

Ahmad, Nazir: *Mir'at al-'Arus* ('Bride's Mirror'), 25

Ahmadi, Wali: 11

Akbar, 'Abd al-Akbar Khan: *Drai Yatiman* ('Three Orphans'): 110

Alexander the Great: family of, 159–60; invasion of Afghanistan (*c.* 400BC), 159

'Ali, Khaksar Nadir: *al-Habib*, 79–84; *Mir'at al-Arab* ('The Arab Mirror'), 79; *Vaqa'at-e Hijaz* ('Happenings in the Hijaz'), 79

'Ali, Shir: 11; reign of, 22

al-Azhar seminary: 6

al-Qaida: 7

al-Qadiri, Mawlana Zahid: Amunullah Khan travelogue, 79, 84, 86, 88

al-Rassaq, Munshi 'Abd: master printer, 11

al-Ra'uf, Mawlavi 'Abd: 62; background, 41; definition of *adabiyat*, 42, 49

al-Vahhab, 'Abd: 26; director of Afghan Tourist Organization, 27

Aman-e Afghan: founding of, 64

Ambela Campaign (1863): 95

Amin, Hafizullah: 147; education of, 6; role in murder of Nur Muhammad Taraki, 147

Amin, Rasul: founding of Writers' Union of Free Afghanistan (1985), 28

Angar ('Ember'): 124

Anis: 54

Anis, Muhyi al-Din: *Nada-ye Talaba-ye Ma'arif ya Huquq-e Millat* ('Voice of the Knowledge-Seekers, or the Rights of the Nation'): 25

Anjuman-e Islah al-Afaghina (Society for the Reformation of Afghans): 111–12; Annual meetings, 109; Founding by Ghaffar Khan, 109

Ansari, Bayazid: *Khair al-Bayan*, 93

Ansary, Mir Tamim: *West of Kabul, East of New York*, 29

Anti-colonialism: 122; in *Siraj al-Akhbar*, 52; Pashtun, 97

Anzor, Zarin: 135; *Da Sawr pa Trazhedi ke Farhang, Adabiyat aw Azadi* ('The Impact of the April Tragedy on Culture, Literature, and Democracy'), 132

Arabian Nights: 57

Arabic language: 13, 29, 32, 36, 41, 50–1, 94, 103; terminology of, 48

Aryana: 10, 15

Atan dancing: 94, 135

Atatürk, Mustafa Kemal: 156

Australia: 28; Sydney, 28

Azad Afghanistan: founding of (1951), 27

Azad High School: 110

INDEX

Baba, 'Abd al-Rahman: writings of, 16
Babarzai, Shafi'ullah: 136
Babur: founder of Mughal Empire, 72
Bactrian Greeks: 14; settlements, 70
Bactrian language: 9
Bakhtani, 'Abdullah: member of Wex Zalmiyan, 127
Bakhtar ('Bactria'): personnel of, 143
Bakhteri, Wasef: 214, 216–17, 223, 226; *Alaya Pasdar-e Kuy-e Wakhshuran* ('O the Watchmen of the Region of Message-Bringers') (1976), 209–10, 214–15, 217–19; *Az In Ayina-ye Beshkasta-ye Tarikh* ('Of the Broken Mirror of History'), 212; *Az Ma'yad ta Hargiz* ('A Place for Meeting, Never'), 212–13; background of, 212; *Basharat* ('Good News'), 213; *Dar Ostva-ye Fasl-e Shekastan* ('Along the Season of Breaking'), 212; *Dar Sukut-e Shomathaha* ('On the Silence of Clock Bells'), 217, 219–20; *Darigha Chanin Bud Farjam* ('Alas: This Was the End!'), 219–21; *Dibacha'i dar Farjam* ('A Prolegomenon in the End'), 212, 214, 217; editor-in-chief of *Zhawandun*, 212; *Kuhsar-e Ghamin* ('The Mourning Mountain'), 214–16, 221; member of editorial board of Dar al-Ta'lif, 212; *Muwiya-ha-ye Asfandiyar-e Gomshoda* ('The Moaning of the Lost Asfandiar'), 212; *Sohrab Zinda Ast* ('Sohrab is Alive'), 213–14; *Ta Shahr-e Panjzal'a'i-e Azadi* ('Until the Pentagonal City of Liberty'), 212, 219; *Va Aftab Namimirad* ('And the Sun Won't Die'), 212
Baluchi language: official language of Afghanistan, 21
Barakzai sadars: 95

Barelvi, Sayyid Ahmad: war with Sikhs, 95
Barthoux, Jules: member of Délégation Archéologique Française en Afghanistan, 69
Baudelaire, Charles: 191–2
Bayhaqi: official publisher of Ministry of Education, 21
Baz, Hazrat: writings of, 129
de Beauvoir, Simone: editor of *Les Temps Modernes*, 167
Bedil: 2, 13, 104, 232; poetry of, 245; studies of (*Bedil-shinasi*), 13
Behbahani: 193
Belgium: 84; Brussels, 85
Benawa. 'Abd al-Ra'uf: 20, 123
Benjamin, Walter: 201
Bible: New Testament in Pashto, 98; Psalms, 155
Bitab, Sufi 'Abd al-Haqq: poetry of, 15; teaching career of, 142
Bonaparte, Napoleon: 44
Bonn Agreement (2001): 236
Bouvier, Nicolas: *L'Usage du Monde*, 68
British East India Company: annexation of North West Frontier Province (1849), 98
British Empire: 71, 95, 98
British India: 8, 16, 24, 40, 48, 74, 80, 84, 88, 92, 99, 112, 122–3; attempt to ban *Siraj al-Akhbar*, 52; borders of, 98; government of, 52; Indian Muslim population of, 109; introduction of printing press, 98; Karachi, 36; military of, 5; North West Frontier Province, 111; Pashtun population of, 4, 18, 105–6, 108, 110–11, 119; relations with Afghanistan, 40, 80; subsidies to Afghanistan, 52; trade with Afghanistan, 107

291

INDEX

Buner, Battle of (1863): 95
Burnes, Sir Alexander 'Bokhara': travel writings of, 68
Burroughs, Edgar Rice: *The Land that Time Forgot*, 75, 90
Bush, George W.: family of, 250
Byron, Lord George Gordon: 155; translation of writings into Dari-Persian, 15
Byron, Robert: 73; *The Road to Oxiana*, 70, 86

Canada: Montreal, 144
Cavagnari, Louis: British representative in Kabul, 96
Chapbook poetry: 99
Charbayta poetry: 92, 94, 97, 127, 233; structure of, 99, 234
China: 77
Chubak, Sadeq: 193
Cold War: 6
colonialism: British, 97, 123, 133
Columbia University: 6
communism: 2, 7, 71, 131; Afghan, 6
Constitutional Movement: 106; members of, 102

D'Annunzio, Gabriele: 77
Da Khudai Khidmatgar ('Servants of God'): 119
Da Naranj da Gulo Mela ('Tangerine Blossom Festival'): 129
Daneshvar, Simin: 193
Danish Publishing Society: formation of (1987–8), 135
Dar al-Saltana Press: founding of, 11
Dar al-Ta'lif: editorial board of, 212; members of, 212
Dari: 142–3, 149–50; as official language of Afghanistan, 20, 230; Dari-Persian, 12–13, 15, 18–20, 29, 92, 99, 111–12, 116, 124, 131–2, 221, 224, 229, 235

Darmesteter, James: research trip to Peshawar, 94–5
dastan: 233–4
Dawlatabadi, Mahmud: 193
Dawi, 'Abd al-Hadi: 55, 101, 106; member of Constitutional Movement, 102; writings of, 55, 103
Defoe, Daniel: *Robinson Crusoe*, 22–3
Délégation Archéologique Française en Afghanistan: 69; excavation reports, 70
Directorate of Publications: promotion of Pashto, 114
Dorr-e Dari Cultural Institute: 189, 195; members of, 188, 192, 201, 204; office of, 201
Dums (poets): 95, 97, 99
Durand Line: 18, 117; drawing of (1893), 4, 98
Durrani, Ahmed Shah: 3
Durrani Empire: fragmentation of, 95

Ebrahimi, Gholamreza: 185–6, 196; member of Dorr-e Dari Cultural Institute, 192; *Tah-e Donya* ('The End of the World') (2003), 189–91, 196
Edwards, David: study of *jihadi* cassette songs, 134
Effendi, Muhammad 'Abr al-Qadir: 24–5; *Tasvir-e 'Ibrat ya Bibi Khor Jan* ('The Warning Picture or Bibi Khor Jan'), 24
Egypt: 6, 25, 42, 84–5; Alexandria, 36; Cairo, 33, 84
Eiselin, Max: travel writings of, 68
Elliot, Jason: *An Unexpected Light*, 74
English language: 9, 24–5, 33, 68, 149, 153; loanwords, 22, 50, 61, 84, 89
Enlightenment: 115
Etefaq-e Islam: 54

INDEX

Fanger, Donald: 190
Farhad, Ghulam Muhammad: inauguration of Kabul Municipal Theatre, 15
Farhadi, 'Abd al-Ghafur Rawan: 150
Farrokhzad, Forugh: poetry of, 193
Federal Republic of Germany (West Germany): Bonn, 147
Ferdowsi, Abu'l Qasim: 10, 76; *Shahnama*, 10, 211
Ferrier, Joseph Pierre: writings of, 69
de la Fontaine, Jean: fables of, 2
First Anglo-Afghan War (1839–42): 5
First World War (1914–18): 53, 105–6; political impact of, 191
Foucault, Michel: *Les Mots and les choses* (1966), 169
Foucher, Alfred: member of Délégation Archéologique Française en Afghanistan, 69
France: 14, 55, 76, 84; Afghan diaspora of, 221; Paris, 28, 85, 103, 222; Revolution (1789–99), 55; Sorbonne, 222
French language: 51, 131; loanwords, 22, 50, 61
Fu'ad I, King of Egypt: 84
Fussell, Paul: 191
Futurism: 11–12, 73; technological, 78

Gandhi, Mahatma: 68
Ganesh Flour Mills: 83
Geneva Peace Talks (1982–8): criticisms of, 148
Germany: 77, 84; Berlin, 85, 87; Hamburg, 28;
Ghalcha language: 9
Gharay poetry: 94
Gharjistan: foundation (1987), 21
Ghazal poetry: 33, 60, 92, 97, 186, 207, 216; examples of, 190–1, 196, 204, 215; in Pashto, 92

Ghaznavi, Mahmud: 72
Ghilzai Confederation: 142
Ghubar, Mir Ghulam Muhammad: founder of Vatan Party, 13; histories of, 13
Gibran, Khalil: 155; *Pishva* ('The Prophet'), 155; translation of writings into Dari-Persian, 15
Gnomics: concept of, 248
Goethe, Johann Wolfgang von: 65; translations of works of, 155
Great Western Railway: 85
Greece: 159; ancient mythology of, 211; archaeological legacy of, 70

Habib, Asadullah: 20; *Khashm-e Khalq* ('The People's Wrath'), 20; president of Writers' Union of Afghanistan, 20; *Sepidandam* ('The White Figure'), 20; vice-chancellor of Kabul University, 20
Habibi, 'Abd al-Hayy: 19, 20, 22; dean of Kabul University's Faculty of Letters, 15; discovery of *Pata Khazana*, 19; founding of Afghan Historical Society, 15; founding of *Azad* Afghanistan (1951), 27; member of Wex Zalmiyan, 19; poetry of, 118; president of Pashto Academy, 19
Habibiyya High School: curriculum of, 142–3; faculty of, 142; students of, 142
Hackin, Joseph: member of Délégation Archéologique Française en Afghanistan, 69
Hafiz: 42, 150
hajj: 79
Hanifi, Shah Mahmoud: 122
Haqyar, Da'ud: 138–9
Haroon, Sana: writings of, 120
Hazara: 186–7; ethnic community,

INDEX

21; presence in Afghani refugee population in Iran, 187
Hazaragi dialect: 21, 28, 59
Hedayat, Sadeq: writings of, 193
Hedin, Sven: travel writings of, 69
Hegel, Georg Wilhelm Friedrich: 182; *The Phenomenology of Spirit*, 164
Heidarbeigi, Hossein: poetry of, 200, 207
Hezb-e Harakat ('Movement Party'), 216
Hezb-e Islami ('Islamic Party'): 27, 216
Hijrat Movement (*c*.1920–1): 109
Hindko language: 115
Hindu Biscuit Company: 83
History Society of Afghanistan (*Anjoman-e Tarikh*): members of, 165
Homer: *Iliad*, 211; *Odyssey*, 211
Hosseini, Khaled: 28, 30, 37, 221; background of, 224; *The Kite Runner*, 28, 210, 224–7
Hosseinzadeh, Zahra: member of Dorr-e Dari Cultural Institute, 204; poetry of, 204–5
House of Afghan Literature: members of, 196
Hugo, Victor: translations of works of, 155

'Inayat Press: founding of, 11, 38, 39, 56; translation of French novels, 46, 56
India: 154; Agra, 80; Ajmer, 80; Bombay, 8, 80–1, 83, 86–7; Calcutta, 16, 80–1, 83; Delhi, 16, 28, 80, 120, 147; Gwalior, 80; Jabalpur, 80; Jalandhar, 24; Kanpur, 80; Madras, 24; Panipat, 80; Poona, 80; Serampore, 98; Sirhind, 80; travel infrastructure of, 88
Indian School (*sabk-e hindi*): poetry of, 13

Indonesia: printing in, 2
Informed Writers' Circle: founding of, 28; *Gah-nama* (journal), 28
International Labor Organization: personnel of, 144
International Security Assistance Force (ISAF): members of, 235–6
Iqbal, Sir Muhammad: 25; definition of *khodi*, 171; *Musafir* ('The Traveller'), 72; *Payam-e Mashriq* ('The Message of the East'), 72; writings of, 16, 26, 72
Iran: 6, 12–13, 28, 30, 45, 50, 72, 82, 84, 86, 131, 187, 192–3, 195, 206, 211, 214, 216, 222, 224, 235, 241, 244; Afghan refugee population of, 187–9, 200, 206–7, 247; Arab conquest of, 211; art cinema of, 201; Fars, 20; government of, 10; Islamic Revolution (1979), 194, 201; Jewish population of, 245; Mashhad, 3, 8, 10, 186, 188–9, 200, 204, 206; publishing economy of, 23; Shiraz, 13; suicides in, 197; Tehran, 28, 196; territory of, 4, 154; travel infrastructure of, 88
Iran-Iraq War (1980–8): 194
Iranian Academy: 18
Iraq: Baghdad, 24, 210
Islah ('Reform'): editorial staff of, 143
Islam: 1, 21, 41, 46, 72, 96, 97, 119, 121, 126, 150, 172; as unifying force, 95; critics, of, 40; *hadith*, 233; *hajj*, 79; modernist, 55; political, 6, 181; Shi'a, 187; spread of, 210; Sunni, 237; symbols of, 95
Islamic reformism: 121
Islamism: 7, 28–9, 55, 72; Afghan, 27; internationalist, 2; literature, 27, 193; transnationalist, 6
Islamiyya College, Peshawar: 10
Italy: 5, 84; Rome, 86

INDEX

Ittihad-e Mashriqi ('Eastern Unity'): 123; anti-British sentiment, 109, 122; founding (1919), 107, 122; support for monarchy, 122
Izutsu, Toshihiko: definition of *fana*, 170

Jahani, 'Abd al-Bari: 'Blue Sky', 137; *Wraka Mena* ('A Missing Homeland') (1989), 137
Jalali, Ghulam Jilani: endorsement by state, 106
Jami: 10
Jami'at-e Islami ('Islamic Association'): 216
Jami'at-e Ulama: standardization of religious curriculum, 121
Jan, Malang: 128, 139; poetry of, 123, 127–8
Jewett, A.C: writings of, 74, 82
jihad: 6, 8, 28; anti-Soviet, 181, 236; poetry: 27, 132–6
Journalists' Union: 133
Joya, Malalai: 230–1, 248; *Woman among Warlords*, 244
Jumna Cotton Mills: 83

Kabrit, 'Abd al-Rahman: languages spoken, 33
Kabul Literary Society (Anjuman-e Adabi-ye Kabul): 17; aims, 15; establishment of, 14; journal (*Kabul*) 15; library of, 14; members of, 143; merge with Da Paxo Maraka, 117
Kabul Municipal Theatre: inauguration, 15
Kabul Teachers' College: 20, 105
Kabul University: 16, 20, 28, 164; Faculty of Letters, 15, 19, 164; Student Union, 213; students of, 2
Kalakani, Habibullah: seizure of power (1929), 28, 115, 142

Kalcik, Susan: concept of 'kernel stories', 246
Karwan, Pir Muhammad: *Lag ra tam sha larawiya* ('Wait up for me a little, Traveller'), 134–6
Karzai, Hamid: opposition to, 235; President of Afghanistan, 240
Keats, John: translations of works of, 155
Kitchener, Lord Horatio Herbert: meeting with Habibdullah Khan, 80
Khadim, Qiyam al-Din: 123, 125–7; editor of *Ittihad-e Mashriqi*, 122; founding of Wex Zalmiyan, 127; member of Da Paxto Tolana, 121
Khalifat Movement (1919–24): 105
Khalili, Khalilullah: 2, 28; *'Ayyari az Khurasan* ('The Bandit Hero of Khurasan'), 28
Khalili, Mas'ud: founder of *Rah-e Nayestan* ('Road to the Reedbed'), 29
Khan, 'Abd al-Ghaffar: founder of Khudai Khidmatgar, 109; founder of *Paxtun* (1928): 110; meeting with Amunullah Khan, 109; Pashtun nationalism, 111
Khan, 'Abd al-Rahman ('Iron Amir'): 4, 38, 97–8, 107; autobiography (*Pandnama-ye Dunya va Din*), 8, 22, 99; centralization of state, 98, 100; death (1901), 80, 101; exile of Ghulam Muhammad Tarzi, 32, 35, 37; languages spoken, 99; reintroduction of printing to Afghanistan, 11
Khan, Amanullah: 5, 15, 64, 72, 77; accession to throne (1919), 32, 64, 106; Amanullah-Wagen, 85; establishment of National Museum of Afghanistan, 14; founder of

INDEX

Aman-e Afghan, 64; influence from *Siraj al-Akhbar*, 106; journey to Europe (1927–8), 78, 83–8, 90; languages spoken, 9, 109; marriage to Soraya Tarzi, 32; meeting with Ghaffar Khan, 109; modernization programme, 73, 100, 107
Khan, Dost Muhammad: 32, 35
Khan, Khavvas: Malik of the Afridis, 96
Khan, Khushhal: poetry of, 118
Khan, Ghani: poetry of, 110
Khan, Habibullah: 5, 76–7, 101; death of (1919), 83, 106; development of printing, 11; education drive, 49; journey to India (1907), 78, 80, 82–3; languages spoken, 9, 78, 106; modernization programme, 24, 53, 73, 82, 84; support for *Siraj al-Akhbar*, 32, 53
Khan, 'Inayatullah: 32, marriage to Khayira Tarzi, 32; founding of 'Inayat Press, 38, 56, 64
Khan, Muhammad Ayub: 24
Khan, Muhammad Da'ud: 156; overthrow of (1978), 130, 147, 218; Prime Minister of Afghanistan (1953–63): 124, 128, 129; President of Afghanistan (1973–8), 130, 146, 176
Khan, Muhammad Hashim: Prime Minister of Afghanistan (1929–46), 113, 124
Khan, Muhammad Na'im: minister of education, 17
Khan, Nadir (Nadir Shah): 5, 74, 115; consolidation of ideological apparatus, 121; establishment of Kabul Literary Society, 14; murder of, 72; Pashtunization of Afghanistan, 100
Khan, Qazi 'Abdullah: Chief Justice of Supreme Court of Afghanistan, 142; family of, 141
Khan, Ya'qub Hasan: 9, 136; flight to India, 97
Khattak, Ajmal: 119
Khattak, Kushhal Khan: 104; writings of, 16, 93
Khudai Khidmatgar ('Servants of God'): founding by Ghaffar Khan, 109
Khurasan: earlier name for Afghanistan, 4
Khusrow, Amir: 2
Khyber Pass Railway: 73
Kushkaki, Burhan al-Din Khan: writings of, 74

La'iq, Sulayman: 20; folklore studies of, 132; minister of television and radio, 20; poetry of, 131
Lambton, A.K.S.: *Kitab al-Kharaj*, 239
Landay poetry: 94, 97, 119, 132
Le Figaro: 12
Les Viveurs de Paris: 55; serialization of in *Siraj al-Akhbar*, 33
Lenin, Vladimir Ilyich: 71; tomb of, 88
Levi, Peter: writings of, 70
Liberalism: 121, 124, 128–9
Lodin, 'Abd al-Rahman: member of Constitutional Movement, 102
Longfellow, Henry Wadsworth: translations of works of, 155
Loya Jirga: 238; members of, 237, 250; Taliban rejection of, 238

Ma'rif-e Ma'arif: serialization of *Jihad e-Akhbar*, 23
Mahendraptarapa, Raja: writings of, 71
Mahmud Khan, Shah: 156; Prime

Minister of Afghanistan (1946–53), 114, 124
Maillart, Ella: memoirs, 68
Maiwand, Battle of (1879): 97
Majruh, Sayyid Baha' al-Din: 163–4; acting president of History Society of Afghanistan, 165; *Azhdha-ye Khodi* ('Ego Monster), 130, 132, 163, 166–81, 183–4; background of, 164; concept of *kherad-e kham* ('Raw Reason'), 168, 182; critique of Marxism, 181–3; exile of, 131, 166, 177; founding member of WUGFA, 166; murder of (1988), 134, 166; translation efforts of, 164
Malalai: poetry of, 97
Marinetti, Filippo Tommaso: manifesto of, 12
Marxism: 6, 88, 132; critiques of, 181–3
masnavi (poetic form): language of, 159
Masson, Charles: writings of, 69
Mas'ud, Ahmed Shah: 29
Mas'ud, Sir Ross: writings of, 72
Mas'ud, Sidiqa: memoirs, 29
Matal poetry: 94, 104
Medievalism: of Afghanistan, 69
Michaud, Roland: photography of, 70
Michaud, Sabrina: photography of, 70
Milli Hindara ('Mirror of the Nation'): 19, 119
Minto, Lord: meeting with Habibdullah Khan, 80
de Mirabeau, Comte: 44
Mir'at al-Arab ('The Arab Mirror'): 79
Mirzai, Amanullah: member of Dorr-e Dari Cultural Institute, 201; poetry of, 201–4
Misra' poetry: 95
Mohmand, Muhammad Gul: dictionary of Pashto, 17; founder of Pashto Literary Society, 17

Montagu, William, 9th Duke of Manchester: 81
de Montépin, Xavier: 12, 23, 55; *Les Filles de Platre* ('Platre's Daughters'), 55; *Les Viveurs de Paris*, 33, 55; imprisonment, 55
Morawski, Stefan: functions of quotations, 245–6
Mostaghni, 'Abd al-'Ali Khan: poetry, 59, 61–2
Mughal Empire: 16, 91, 93; expansion of, 92; language of, 92
Muhammad, Prophet: 233
Muhammad, Salih: 18; standardization of Pashto, 107; translation of Persian guide to Qur'an, 16
Muhammad, Sultan: secretary of 'Abd al-Rahman Khan, 8
Muhammadzai, Murtaza Ahmed: *Jashn-e Istiqlal dar Boliviya* ('Independence Celebrations in Bolivia'): 25
Mujaddidi, Sibghatullah: 6
mujahidin: 6–7, 131, 244; conquest of Kabul (1992), 149; dramatic depictions of, 134, 183–4; factions of, 149, 216; Saudi financing of, 165; US support for, 165
Murray, John: publisher of 'Abd al-Rahman Khan autobiography, 99
Mushar'ira poetry contests: 109, 118–19, 120–1, 123, 128–9, 133; anti-British sentiment, 110; Urdu, 18
Mustaghni, 'Abd al-Ali': poetry of, 103
Muslim Brotherhood: 6
Muquari, 'Abdullah: 136

Nada-ye Khalq ('Voice of the People'): 124
Nadwi, Sayyid Sulayman: *Sayr-e Afghanistan* ('Afghan Journey'): 71

INDEX

Najibullah, Mohammad: 250; regime of, 216
Nagina: poetry of, 110
Nangrahar Kanal project: 129, 138–9
Nasir, Nasrullah: notes on Pashto poetry, 118
National Museum of Afghanistan: founding of, 14
Nationalism: 1, 7, 16, 24; Afghan, 5, 9, 12, 13, 15, 18, 48–9, 51, 103, 106, 111–12, 117, 122; Iranian, 10, 18; Pashtun, 19, 20, 94, 102, 104, 109, 111–12, 119, 121–4; poetry, 28; Romantic, 193
Nawa, Fariba: *Opium Nation*, 29
Nazemi, Latif: poetry of, 214
Newby, Eric: *Short Walk in the Hindu Kush*, 68
Nicholson, Reynold: translations of works of, 155
Nizami: 76
Non-Aligned Movement: emergence of, 145; members of, 145
North Atlantic Treaty Organization (NATO): 138, 235–6; presence in Afghanistan, 230
Northern Alliance: members of, 238
Nurestani, Dr Yusuf: Governor of Herat, 240
Nuri, Muhammad Gul: editor of *Milli Hindara*, 19, 119
Nuristani language: official language of Afghanistan, 21

Obama, Barack: administration of, 235
Ottoman Empire: 5, 8, 12, 32, 38, 40, 44, 46–7, 52, 63, 65, 105–6, 109; Afghan diaspora, 22; Baghdad, 24; Damascus, 76; Istanbul, 36; territory of, 37, 51

Pakistan: 132, 148, 154, 177–8, 222, 226, 235, 241, 250; Afghan refugee population of, 247; Jamrud, 80, 81; Karachi, 26, 36, 80, 87; Lahore, 79, 80–3, 96; Multan, 3; North West Frontier Province, 96, 98, 105, 109, 111; Nowshera, 80; Pashtun population of, 126; Peshawar, 16, 18, 79–80, 94, 134, 149, 154, 165–6, 212; Quetta, 86, 136
Palmerstone, Viscount Lord: 44
Panjshiri, Ghulam Dastagir: literary teacher at Kabul Teachers' College, 20
Pan-Islamism: 46, 72
Pari-ye Surkh ('The Crimson Fairy'): 57
Pashai language: 8; official language of Afghanistan, 21
Pashto Academy (Da Paxto Tolana): 18, 126; founding of (1937), 17, 117, 121; incorporation into Academy of Sciences of Afghanistan (1979), 21; members of, 121, 143
Pashto Academy (Peshawar): 18
Pashto Committee (Da Paxto Maraka): establishment of Pashto Literary Society, 107, 117; founding (1922), 107; merge with Kabul Literary Society, 117
Pashto language: 9–10, 16–19, 29, 50, 51, 99, 102–3, 106, 114–15, 119, 124, 137, 142, 230, 238; alphabet, 18; literature, 91, 94, 96, 98, 107, 109, 112–16, 132; official language of Afghanistan, 20, 92; poetry, 91, 94, 97, 120, 135–6; printing, 117–18, 124; societies, 107; standardization, 105, 107; travelogues, 74; typography, 60; use in British India, 18, 98, 109
Pashto Literary Society (Da Paxto Adabi Anjuman): establishment

of (1932), 17, 107; journal (*Da Mu'alim Paxto*), 17; journal (*Paxto*), 17
Pashtunistan movement: 124–6, 129
Pashtunization: 100, 111
Pashtuns: 4, 92, 93, 98, 102–3, 108, 110, 114, 118, 120, 136, 139, 225, 232, 237; in America, 110; Ma'ruf Khel clan, 142; migration from British India, 109; nationalism, 19–20, 94, 102, 104, 109, 111–12, 119, 121–4; *Paxtunwali* code, 153, 157; population of British India, 4, 18, 105–6, 108, 110–11, 119; population of Pakistan, 126; ruling dynasty, 50, 51, 107, 112
Pata Khazana: 125; discovery of, 19; origins, 19
Paxtun: 111; founding (1928), 110; *Paxtun Jagh*: 111
Pazhwak, 'Abd al-Rahman: 27–8, 35, 144, 150–1, 155–6, 161; Afghan Ambassador to UN, 145; *Afsanaha-ye Mardum* ('Stories of the People') (1957), 145, 154; *Almas-e Nashekan* ('Unbroken Diamond) (1996), 151–3; *Avarah* ('Wanderer'), 154; background of, 141–2; *Banu-ye Balkh* ('Lady of Balkh) (2001), 149, 151; *Chand Shi'r az Pazhwak* ('Some Poems by Pazhwak') (1963), 146, 149, 151; criticism of Geneva Peace Talks (1982–8), 148; death of (1995), 149, 151; *Dhamir* ('Conscience'), 158; director of *Bakhtar*, 143; director of Pashto Academy (Da Paxto Tolana), 143; editor of *Islah*, 143; exile of, 148; family of, 141; *Gulha-ye Andisha* ('Thought Flowers') (1965), 146, 149, 151; *Hadis-e Khun* ('Blood Reports') (1985), 151; *Maihan-e Man* ('My Homeland') (1989), 151; *Mardan-e Parumpamizad* ('Men of Parupamizad), 159–61; *Muzakerat-e Jenev* ('Geneva Talks'), 154; *Nahid-Nama* ('Book of Nahid') (1995), 151–2; president of UN Human Rights Commission, 145; *Qushun-e Surkh* ('Red Army'), 147; *Padshir*, 158; translator for Kabul Literary Society, 143; works translated by, 155; writings of, 143; *Yak Zan* ('A Woman'), 154
Pazira, Nelufer: 230, 251; memoir of, 250
Peace Corps: 248
People's Democratic Party of Afghanistan (PDPA): 6, 20, 116, 131, 179; Khalq ('The Masses'), 6, 20, 131; members of, 147; Parcham ('The Flag'), 6, 20, 131; writings of, 131
Persian language: 8–10, 16, 30, 50–1, 103, 114–15, 218, 220; Afghan Persian ('Dari'), 12–13, 15, 18–20, 29, 92, 99, 111–12, 116, 124, 131–2, 221, 224, 229, 235, 238; Dari as official language of Afghanistan, 20, 233; Iranian Persian ('Farsi'), 12–13, 15, 18, 20, 103; *lingua franca*, 51, 92; Middle Persian, 220; Tajik Persian, 18
Poland: 84
Powell, Edward Alexander: travel writings of, 82
Prévert, Jacques: translations of works of, 155
Publications Directorate: 126
Punjabi, Mawlavi Muhammad Husayn: 25; background, 24; *Jihad e-Akhbar* ('The Greatest Jihad'): 23, 24

Qa'ani: 104

Qadir, Khan Khattak: poetry of, 118
Qadir, Mirza: 222–3
Qadiri, Homayra: *Gushvara-ye Anis* ('Anis's Earring'): 28
Qandahari, Mawlavi 'abd al-Ra'uf: member of Constitutional Movement, 102
Qandahari, Mawlavi 'abd al-Wasi': founding of Pashto Committee, 107; member of Constitutional Movement, 102; poetry, 107–8; position in government of Amanullah Khan, 106
Qandahari, Salih Muhammad: 118; deputy-director of elementary education, 105; endorsement by state, 106; founder of *Tulu'-e Afghan*, 107; member of Constitutional Movement, 102; poetry of, 99, 102, 103, 105
Qari, 'Abdullah: 15
Qasemi, Seyyed Zia: director of House of Afghan Literature, 196; poetry of, 196–200
Qasida poetry: 92
Qissa-ye Chahar Darvish ('Tale of Four Dervishes'): 76
Queling, Hans: travel writings of, 68, 74, 86
Qur'an: 16, 233; divination on, 206; language of, 41; memorization of, 233; verses of, 88
Qutb, Sayyid: ideology of, 6

Rabbani, Burhan al-Din: education of, 6
Rah-e Nayestan ('Road to the Reedbed'): foundation of, 29
Rahimi, 'Atiq: 30, 37; background of, 221; *Khakestar va Khak* ('Earth and Ashes') (2000), 29, 210, 221–4, 227; recipient of Prix Goncourt (2008), 163; *La Pierre de Patience* ('The Patience Stone'), 29, 222
Reišner, Larisa: news reports of, 71
Rixtin, Sidiqullah: 123; *Da Hind Safar* ('Indian Journey'), 74–5; member of Da Paxto Tolana, 121
Root, William Pitt: *The Unbroken Diamond: Nightletter to the Mujahideen*, 151; translations of works of, 155
Rousseau, Jean-Jacques: writings of, 68
Rowshaniyya Movement: 93
Royal Asiatic Society of Great Britain: 79
Ruba'i poetry: 92, 233
Rumi, Jalal al-Din (Balkhi): 10, 232, 244–5; name, 13
Russian Empire: 52, 105; attempt to ban *Shiraj al-Akhbar*, 52; expansion of, 4
Russian Federation: 16, 71, 84; Moscow, 88
Russian language: 9, 27

sabk-e jaded ('new style'): examples of, 146
sabk-e klasik-e muabbar ('neo-classical'): examples of, 149
Sa'di: 42, 150, 232, 244
Sa'id, Nahid: death of (1980), 147
Saljuqi, Salah al-Din: influence of, 143; president of Afghan Press and Information Office, 143
Samandar, Samandar Khan: translation of Muhammad Iqbal into Pashto, 26
Sana'i, Hakim: 10, 72
Sarshar, Ratan Nath: *Fasana-e Azad* ('Tale of Azad'), 25
Sartre, Jean-Paul: *Being and Nothingness*, 164, 169; editor of *Les Temps Modernes*, 167; *The Emotions*, 169

INDEX

Sassanids: *darafsh-e Kavian* ('flag of Kava'), 210, 213
Saudi Arabia: 6, 8, 74; financing of *mujahidin*, 165; Mecca, 79
Saur Revolution (1978): 21, 165, 181, 183, 212, 218, 224; political impact of, 164, 221
Sautreau, Serge: translator of *Ego Monster* ('*Azhdaha-ye Khudi*'/'Ego monstre'), 167
Schimmel, Annemarie: concept of Islamic mysticism, 170
Schwarzenbach, Annemarie: travel writings of, 68, 73
Science fiction: 38, 58, 77; in China, 77; as means of explaining technology, 45–6, 55; translations of, 39
Second Anglo-Afghan War (1878–80): 5, 96–7
Second World War (1939–45): 124, 126, 216; political neutrality of Afghanistan during, 156
Sepehri, Sohrab: 193
Shadi poetry: 94
Shah, King Zahir: 72, 146; consolidation of ideological apparatus, 121; deposed (1973), 165, 212
Shah, Shabibi: *Where do I Belong?*, 29
Shah, Reza: 5
Shah, Timur: 3
Shakespeare, William: translations of works of, 155
Shamlu, Ahmad: 193
Shams al-Nahar: 4; cessation of publication (1877), 11; founding of (1873), 11
Sharq, Muhammad Hasan: *Karbaspush-ha-yeBerahna Pa* ('The Wool-Wearing Bare-Foots'): 29
Shaw, George Bernard: translations of works of, 155
Shinwari, Amir Hamza: 18, 123; travelogue, 123

shi'r-e azad ('free verse'): use of, 152
shi'r-e naw ('new poetry'): use of, 152
Sho'ur, Asadullah: monograph, 133
shu'ara ye-mutajaddid ('innovative poets'): 34, 59
Siddiki, 'Awaz: poetry of, 134
Sikhs: 95–7
Sindhi, 'Ubaydullah: writings of, 71
Siraj al-Akhbar Afghaniya ('Torch of Afghan News'): 11, 17, 22, 76, 105; animosity towards, 53; anti-colonialism, 52; closure (1918), 32; contacts, 12; first issue, 43–4; founding of (1911), 11, 32; literature section (*adabiyat*), 33, 34, 43; Pashto content, 16, 99, 102, 104;
Siraj al-Atfal: 49
Soghdian language: 9
Soviet Union (USSR): 5, 9, 74, 133, 248; Invasion of Afghanistan (1979–89), 6, 27, 147–8, 153–4, 159, 165, 171, 177–8, 181, 183, 186, 212, 221–2, 225, 233, 236; Kremlin, 147; military of, 147; models of literature, 20; Moscow, 147; support for Afghan leftist groups, 146; support for government of Democratic Republic of Afghanistan, 6; territory of, 18, 71
Sri Lanka: Jaffna, 36
SS *Manila*: 86–7
SS *RajputanaI*: 86
Stein, Sir Aurel: travel writings of, 69
Sufism: 93, 130, 142; *fana'*, 170–1; mystical poetry, 170, 230
Sweden: Skärholmen, 28; Stockholm, 28
Switzerland: 68, 84, 145, 156–7; Geneva, 145–6; Swiss language, 68, 77
Syria: Damascus, 32, 36, 38, 47, 76

Tabrizi, Shams: 150

301

INDEX

Tadao, Umesao: ethnography, 70
Tagore, Rabindranath: 68, 155; *Baghban* ('The Gardener'), 155; translation of writings into Dari-Persian, 15
Tajik: 234; Herati, 187
Tajikistan: 210
Taliban: 6, 8, 134, 225–6, 237–8, 244, 250; production of Pashto poetry, 21, 137; propaganda, 137–8; rejection of *Loya Jirga*, 238; rule of (1996–2001), 216–17; supporters of, 240
Tappa poetry: 94, 119
Taraki, Nur Muhammad: 20, 147; leader of Khalq party, 132; murder of, 147; President of Afghanistan, 20
Tarikh-e Sultani: 4
Tarzi, Ghulam Muhammad (Ghular Muhammad Sardar): father of Mahmud Tarzi, 32, 35; exile of, 35; poetry, 38, 46, 59
Tarzi, Khayira: marriage to 'Inayatullah Khan, 32
Tarzi, Mahmud: 6, 22, 31, 104, 154; background, 32, 36; death (1933), 65; editor-in-chief of *Siraj al-Akhbar*, 33; editor of *Siraj al-Atfal*, 49; exile of, 5, 12, 22, 26, 33, 65, 76; foreign minister, 32, 106; founding of *Siraj al-Akhbar* (1911), 11, 32; ideology, 12; influence in court of Habibi Khan, 32; languages spoken, 9, 33; legacy of, 35, 64, 65; member of Constitutional Movement, 102; name of, 38, 47; poetry, 47, 59, 61, 62, 88; reframing of Pashto, 17, 51, 104; return from exile, 38; translation of works of Jules Verne, 22, 38, 58, 76, 81, 86, 89; travel diary, 37, 40, 47, 77, 89; writings of, 34, 37, 65; views on literature, 39
Tarzi, Soraya: marriage to Amanullah Khan, 32; Queen of Afghanistan, 83
Tazkira: 20, 115, 120, 134
Tendulkar, D.G: author of Ghaffar Khan biography, 111
Thant, U: UN Secretary General, 145
Theatre of Learning (Pulhani Nandari): founding of (1942), 19
Third Anglo-Afghan War (1919): 77, 84, 108, 122; political impact of, 151
Timurid architecture: 70
Tokgöz, Ahmad Sahan: translations of, 12, 76, 77
Toynbee, Arnold: 70
Transnationalism: 2, 8, 88, 134–6; Afghan, 8; Islamist, 6; Soviet, 6
Travel writing: 67–71, 74, 77, 82, 88–9
Tulu'-e Afghan ('Afghan Rising'): 107, 117–19
Turkmenistan: 210
Turkey: 12, 77, 84, 156; Ankara, 29; Istanbul, 2, 26, 33, 36–7, 44, 47, 65; publishing economy of, 23
Turkish language: 9, 18, 23, 32–3, 51–2, 55
Turkish Linguistic Society: 18

Ulfat, 'Aziz al-Rahman: assassination (1988), 134
Ulfat, Gul Pacha: 123; editor of *Ittihad-e Mashriqi*, 122; deputy of National Assembly, 124; member of Da Paxto Tolana, 121
United Kingdom (UK): 84; Bournemouth, 86; London, 8, 28, 85, 86, 103, 144, 153; Southampton, 86; Swindon, 85

INDEX

United Nations (UN): 145, 148; General Assembly, 144; Human Rights Commission, 145–6; members of, 144; Universal Declaration of Human Rights, 2, 145

United States of America (USA): 5, 6, 28, 145, 148, 224–6; 9/11 attacks, 238, 247; military of, 236; New York, 6, 145–6, 212; San Francisco, 28; support for *mujahidin*, 165; Washington DC, 144

Urdu language: 5, 9, 18, 23, 25, 33, 52, 61, 71–2, 82, 84–5, 89, 109, 115, 155, 171; print publics, 119; use of in Afghanistan, 78–9

Uzbek language: 8; official language of Afghanistan, 21

Uzbekistan: 210

Vatan ('Homeland'): 124
Vatan ('Homeland') Party: 13
Verne, Jules: 12, 22–3, 75–6, 86, 89; Dari translations of *Around the World in Eighty Days*, 56, 76, 80, 87; *The Mysterious Island*, 77; *Robur the Conqueror*, 76–7; *Twenty Thousand Leagues Under the Sea*, 77–8; reputation of, 76

Wex Zalmiyan ('Enlightened Youth'): arrests of, 129; 128; founding of (1947), 19, 127; membership, 127
Wild, Roland: correspondent for *Daily Mail*, 15
Writers' Union of Free Afghanistan (WUFA): formation of, 135, 166

Yate, C.E.: travel writings of, 68
Yemen: 84; Aden, 86
Young Afghans: 11, 12
YouTube: 138
Yushij, Nima: 193; poetry of, 214
Yusuf, Abu: depiction in *Kitab al-Kharaj*, 239

Za'if, Mullah 'Abd al-Salam: *Da Gwantanamu Andzwar* ('Picture of Guantanamo'), 29
Zabuli, 'Abd al-Majid: funding of *Wex Zalmiyan*, 127; minister of national economy, 124
Zhawandun ('life'): editorial staff of, 212
Zhulida ('Dishevelled'): 65
Zikr-e Shah-e Islam ('Commemoration of the King of Islam'): 80
Zmariyalai, Aminullah: 125
Zoroastrianism: 211